Romantic Critical Essays

Cambridge English Prose Texts consists of volumes devoted to selections from non-fictional English prose of the late sixteenth to the mid nineteenth centuries. The series provides students, primarily though not exclusively those of English literature, with the opportunity of reading significant prose writers who, for a variety of reasons (not least their generally being unavailable in suitable editions), are rarely studied, but whose influence on their times was very considerable.

This volume offers selections of English criticism from Wordsworth to Shelley, including pieces by Charles Lamb, William Hazlitt, Leigh Hunt, Thomas De Quincey, and Thomas Love Peacock. These writers were public critics, forming a tradition distinct from that represented by aesthetic theorists like Alison and Coleridge. Their miscellaneous writings for journals, though much admired in recent years, are now mostly out of print. In reviewing the work of such critics, the present anthology permits both an appreciative estimate of their thinking and an historically accurate view of their importance. Among the interests that recur in these essays are a new conception of genius; an effort to trace a history of language against a background of social circumstances; and a questioning of the relationship between knowledge and the realities of imagination. Of the twenty-one essays printed here – beginning with Wordsworth's "Essay, Supplementary to the Preface" and ending with Shelley's "A Defence of Poetry" – sixteen appear complete, without cuts.

David Bromwich has provided the texts with full annotations. Allusions to persons and events are glossed, and once-familiar tags, catch-phrases, and passages of special difficulty are explained in footnotes or endnotes. In addition, a biographical and critical headnote precedes the selections from each author. Bromwich's substantial introduction relates the critical essays of the period to the ideas of reading and interpretation which they helped to invent. There is a bibliographical guide for those who wish to pursue their study of the subject.

Romantic Critical Essays will be a valuable book for students of romanticism as well as for readers interested in the theory and practice of criticism in English.

CAMBRIDGE ENGLISH PROSE TEXTS

General editor: GRAHAM STOREY

Romantic Critical Essays

Edited by
DAVID BROMWICH

Professor of English
Princeton University

The right of the
University of Cambridge
to print and sell
all manner of books
was granted by
Henry VIII in 1534.
The University has printed
and published continuously
since 1584.

CAMBRIDGE UNIVERSITY PRESS

Cambridge
New York   New Rochelle   Melbourne   Sydney

Published by the Press Syndicate of the University of Cambridge
The Pitt Building, Trumpington Street, Cambridge CB2 1RP
32 East 57th Street, New York, NY 10022, USA
10 Stamford Road, Oakleigh, Melbourne 3166, Australia

First published 1987

Printed in Great Britain at the
University Press, Cambridge

British Library cataloguing in publication data

Romantic critical essays. – (Cambridge English prose texts).
1. English literature – Early modern (to 1700) – History and criticism
2. English literature – 18th century – History and criticism
3. English literature – 19th century – History and criticism
I. Bromwich, David
820'.9   PR83

Library of Congress Cataloguing in publication data

Romantic critical essays.
(Cambridge English prose texts).
Bibliography.
1. English prose literature – 19th century.
2. Romanticism – England. 3. Criticism – Great Britain.
4. English literature – History and criticism.
I. Bromwich, David, 1951–   . II. Series.
PR1302.R66   1987   809   87–9400

ISBN 0 521 24411 0 hard covers
ISBN 0 521 28672 7 paperback

CE

Contents

Contents

Acknowledgements

I gratefully acknowledge the assistance of the Princeton University Committee on Research in the Humanities, for a summer grant which helped me at an early stage of work on the present volume. Marc Wortman read the essays and suggested some places where the reader would want to see explanations in the footnotes or endnotes. Ross Borden, John Hollander, and William Keach made pertinent comments on a draft of the introductory essay. Andrew Brown, of the Cambridge University Press, added a great many suggestions of his own, so that the annotation is now much fuller than it would have been without him. Yopie Prins checked my translations and is blameless for any errors that persist. Much of the work was done in the British Library, to the staff of which I am indebted for their efficiency.

D. B.

Princeton University

Editorial note

This volume has in some degree the character of an anthology. The selections were made to represent a few authors vividly, and not to survey a kind of writing to which many lesser figures contributed. Different, and briefer, specimens would be required, in a book that attempted to recount a literary history by exhibiting a sequence of documents. Nevertheless it is hoped that the printing of some well-known essays, together with others now difficult to obtain, will give a fair impression of the variety of romantic criticism. Quotations are so integral to the thinking of all of the writers included here that it has seemed best to identify them in footnotes. They have been rendered in a regular format throughout, with double quotation marks to begin and end quoted passages. Otherwise, the texts appear exactly as in the sources listed in headnotes. Pertinent facts and commentary are in the endnotes, as are notes by the authors when these seem helpful. In choosing a version of each essay, the editor has been guided by an interest in coherence of statement rather than chronological priority. The place of publication for the bibliographical references is London unless otherwise stated.

Introductory Essay

The reader, looking at a collection such as the present one, may doubt at times whether specimens as diversely emphatic and variously intelligent as those printed here could ever have been supposed to represent a single tendency called romantic criticism. Similar questions have occurred to the editor as well, and a short anthology cannot pretend to answer them. At most, it can show that there are certain traits to justify the name of a movement and a period, together with a family resemblance that amounts to more than the sum of the traits. This function *Romantic Critical Essays* aims to serve by providing the reader with documents which seem responsive to each other. The essays that follow, however, suggest that the customary views of "romanticism" cannot be trusted far. To be a defensible convenience, the word itself needs to be less ideally and therefore less psychologically defined than it has been by every post-romantic age including ours. As a start at seeing what may be retained of both the word and the category, let us sort out some of the definitions that will have to be discarded.

Romanticism was not a program for the unification of man through an acknowledgement of his identity with nature. About nature, the testimony of romantic authors is equivocal: it sometimes does betray the heart that loved it, because its outward forms are indistinguishable from the effects of the mind's inward moods. Romanticism, again, does not imply a faith in the purposeless and spontaneous power of the creative imagination. Mention of *modifications*, and *conditions*, and *traces*, in the language of the period, always means to recall the fact that the imagination lives at a time and in a place, and that it addresses persons who are conscious of both. But, finally, romanticism cannot be reduced to the settled ideology of a single class in its striving to achieve a self-image. An important quality of romantic writing is the confidence with which it points to human truths it cannot yet represent. To see what was new in the judgements of the writers selected here, and to understand how they cooperated with an original spirit in politics and the arts, we have to read them against the background of judgements from an earlier age.

I

Introductory essay

In the late eighteenth century, even for the most flexible practitioners of criticism, success in literature implied success within a given kind. At the level of reviewing, this meant that a knowledge of the gradations between discrete genres would give a decided turn to a critic's opinion of a work. But a similar tendency may be remarked in more general and reflective essays as well. Goldsmith, for example, attacking "a new species of dramatic composition" called the "*sentimental* comedy, in which the Virtues of Private Life are exhibited, rather than the Vices exposed," deplores the crossing of tragic sympathies with comic indulgences, and concludes that the innovation is a "species of Bastard Tragedy." Johnson, a more pertinaciously moral critic, holds that the authors of pastorals rely on a meretricious charm. They follow conventions so esoteric as to detach books from the ideas of common life; but they forestall a discovery of the cheat by their flattering picture of a golden age. Accordingly, writes Johnson, we find that their productions are filled "with mythological allusions, with incredible fictions, and with sentiments which neither passion nor reason could have dictated, since the change which religion has made in the whole system of the world."[1] A change in the moral practices of men and women, such as the transition from pagan to Christian belief, ought to bring some conventions into credit, and others into discredit. Thus critical judgement is subordinate to "the whole system of the world," and, as Goldsmith's idea of an illegitimate kind also shows, probability within a genre is judged as part of a larger conformity between books and the sentiments of readers.

A later and smaller transition in the language of belief, from the "natural law" we read engraved on our hearts to the "human nature" we know by our relations with others, affected the thinking of every important critic from Wordsworth's generation on. Lamb, Hazlitt, Hunt, and De Quincey admit the force of the eighteenth-century distinction between enduring sentiments and ephemeral manners. But they see a fallacy in the lesson criticism had deduced from it. A sentiment, they concede, may have a longer life than a custom or habit, and yet it comes to be felt only through the striking details of an occasion. No sentiment, therefore, begins as a general possession: when we reflect on our experience, we recognize that the occasion embodies, it does not merely clothe, the sentiment. A new conception of style followed from this way of thinking. An author's idiosyncratic traits were now seen as belonging to the invention by which a work created and retained its interest. They could not be cherished, or despised, as special and separable exuberances. The link between feelings and their occasions had still broader consequences for the romantic understanding of the genres. Ode and pastoral as much as tragedy and epic were now open to revision, at the command of recognitions to which they themselves must respond.

When, to cite a famous instance, Wordsworth classified his poems under such headings as "poems founded on the affections," "poems on the naming of places," and "poems of the fancy," he was announcing his indifference to the usual genres of poetry.[2] The view that every lasting sentiment begins in a momentary feeling appears also to have weakened the claim of some traditional effects of decorum: the balance of wit, and the authority of classical *sententiae*. Two decades into the new century, deference to these will have become sufficient to establish an author's ironic relation to his contemporaries. An *ad hoc* classicist by elective affinity, Byron asserts an urbanity he has not yet earned when he presents himself as Pope's successor. Already in his day, this move has the air of a conversion to Anglo-Catholicism for the sake of its dogmas alone.

For it was now becoming possible to defend Pope's kind of poetry on altogether different grounds. Accordingly, Hazlitt, whose favorite "old books" include Rousseau and Richardson, can wonder why Byron and his antagonists dispute whether Pope was a great poet, since he was clearly a great writer of some sort. For Hazlitt, one idiom of writing does not exclude another, any more than success in one kind of painting limits appreciation to the kind: "We speak and think of Rembrandt as Rembrandt, of Raphael as Raphael, not of the one as a portrait, of the other as a history painter."[3] Hazlitt's generosity here was uncommon, but, among the original minds of his generation, his is the typical and Byron's the exceptional case. With a classicism deeper than either of theirs, Peacock nevertheless offers an appreciation on the pattern of Hazlitt's when he defends the narrative propriety of "Christabel." That poem's alternations of emphasis, between a scrupulous particularity in some passages and an omission of all detail in others, are entirely in keeping with the procedure of the old ballads: "always that of circumstantial evidence, never of complete and positive testimony." So the irregularities of a late original, as of its prototype, look naive only to the sentimental reader, whose assurance Peacock means to dispel.

It would be credulous to say of such an estimate that it makes a truth of prejudice give way to a truth of feeling: instead of "feeling" the less exalted word "context" will do. Still, moments of justification like these in Peacock and Hazlitt do seem to answer to a concern of the romantic critics in general. They attend to the mind's powers in the act of reading. This is, of course, a declared theme of some essays –

as of Lamb's "On the Tragedies of Shakspeare," which honors the plays above all as texts for the mind. But a respect for reading as a way of thinking may be discerned more subtly in occasional tactics of style. Seeking a context for Keats's first poems, but unhappy with the reviewer's duty to praise and blame, Hunt decides to give his verdict by means of an allusion which only the elect will overhear. He imagines a stricture others might enforce, in the shape of a line from Pope: "One glaring chaos and wild heap of wit." But the line itself appears nowhere in his review. Rather it is echoed for the reader by a sympathetic quotation from an earlier and greater poet. In these poems by Keats, says Hunt, one will find "a little luxuriant heap of 'Such thoughts as youthful poets dream / On summer eves by haunted stream.'" The encouragement from Milton tacitly outweighs the rebuke from Pope.

How did such criticism come to be written? Partly, under the influence of a single radical document of literary revisionism, Wordsworth's 1802 Preface to *Lyrical Ballads*. There, for the first time, appeared the definition of a poet as "a man speaking to men" – a man, therefore, who addresses an audience of equals rather than a consensus of taste. A suggestion almost as provocative, that "all good poetry is the spontaneous overflow of powerful feelings," is offered nearby in the essay; and it will be paraphrased, together with much else from the same source, in Shelley's "Defence of Poetry." A great poem, Shelley writes, is "a fountain for ever oveflowing with the waters of wisdom and delight; and after one person and one age has exhausted all its divine effluence which their peculiar relations enable them to share, another and yet another succeeds, and new relations are ever developed." The possibility Shelley saw, in the course of modifying Wordsworth's figure, was that texts owe their interest to relations which develop throughout the history of their reception. The author's conscious design of a work is not so much a secondary as an impertinent consideration. Nothing that is said about it will be false, because everything that is said about it will return to the critic's sense of the relations by which alone he judges the work.

This remains perhaps a distant implication of Wordsworth's argument in the Preface. Wordsworth, however, does maintain explicitly that poetry is valued for its ideas of power, and that these belong to the poem rather than their author. Indeed, of the author himself the Preface offers a somewhat guarded, though exalting, description. He differs from other men, in degree. He has, it is true, "a disposition to be affected more than other men by absent things as if they were present." But the latter faculty can be known only by reading the poet's words and not by observing his character. A widely distrusted commonplace, respecting the nineteenth-century faith in the poet as priest, is still alive enough to obscure the plainness of Wordsworth's levelling politics in these matters. Another commonplace, more narrowly concerned with the Preface itself, asserts that its leading doctrine was to establish the value of the concrete against the abstract, and of the particular against the general. From the important clause on the poet's disposition to be affected by remote objects, it appears that the Preface was in fact propounding a less familiar doctrine. Vividness, and accuracy of description, Wordsworth always ranked high among the poetic strengths. Yet in writing as he did about absence and presence, he was defending a kind of vividness that is associated with the power of abstraction. The poet, Wordsworth argues, can detach himself from the perspective commonly associated with his situation. He can see his subject as if from a distance, or across a reach of time that alters the very shapes of things. In this way the work of abstraction is consistent with an aim that Wordsworth affirms elsewhere in the Preface: "I have at all times endeavoured to look steadily at my subject."

Wordsworth and his followers, including Hazlitt and even Shelley, may be read as empiricists, if one construes that word rather broadly. They believe in the mutually responsive influence of experience and ideas. Poetry, however, as empirical reasoners understood its claims, had never been a credible rival of philosophy. It offered a smaller discipline of humanity, and its deficiencies were traceable, in particular, to a neglect of absent things in favor of present ones. Bacon may serve as a representative witness since he was admitted as a predecessor by Hazlitt and Shelley alike. In *The Advancement of Learning*, following his comparison of the mind of man to "an enchanted glass, full of superstition and imposture," he mentions a tendency in the mind for "the affirmative or active to affect more than the negative or privative. So that a few times hitting or presence, countervails oft-times failing or absence."[4] Bacon's example comes from painting but it might as well have come from poetry. He alludes to the pictures in Neptune's temple of those who had escaped drowning in a shipwreck, with the evident moral that Neptune answers the prayers of the faithful; and yet, he professes agreement with a comment on those pictures by Diagoras, who asked: "Where are they painted that are drowned?" A deep motive for Wordsworth's revised idea of the imagination is suggested by this contrast. If, as the Preface declares, poetry can abstract us from the immediate scene of its portrayals, then it may adequately represent human action or suffering, so that it does what Bacon would not trust it to do.

Together with republican sentiments concerning the character of a poet, the 1802 Preface offered a negative definition of the language of poetry. The notion that a special language was appropriate to verse seemed to Wordsworth as mistaken as the notion of a sublime style. Both ascribed to a regular diction the more striking effects of imagination; and both proceeded from a wrong understanding of what happens in reading. Wordsworth in this essay was the first to say, with an emphasis that could not be dropped ever after, that "there neither is, nor can be, any *essential* difference between the language of prose and metrical composition." In the ballads themselves, he reduced the argument to a practice, with a minute attentiveness to humble details; as when the speaker of "The Thorn" is made to say of a certain pond:

> I've measured it from side to side:
> 'Tis three feet long, and two feet wide.

But it is just as characteristic for Wordsworth to write of his attempt to recover "the hiding-places of man's power," or of the mind's "obstinate questionings" in search of a clue to its origin and fate. His poetry does not, that is, seek to establish the priority of sensations to thoughts. It regards them as always inseparable, in any given pulse of experience: so much so that for Wordsworth, poetry seems to be the place of their conversion into each other. The foregoing summary may be helpful as a conspectus of proposals that reappear later, not only in Wordsworth's 1815 "Essay, Supplementary to the Preface," but in the occasional criticism of Hazlitt, Hunt, and De Quincey. They were not yet part of the familiar stock when Wordsworth began to write, and a readiness to see them tested became a mark of the new movement in literature.

In this light Coleridge's discussion of Wordsworth in the *Biographia Literaria* looks like something of a rearguard action. It regretted certain artistic offenses by his collaborator in the *Lyrical Ballads* – for example, the lines quoted above from "The Thorn," which jarred all habitual canons of narrative pertinence. At the same time, it deplored Wordsworth's indifference to the shared sanction of poetic norms and social arrangements. Coleridge's objections were founded on what he took to be an Aristotelian conception of poetry as ideal, representative, and common. But the language of his chapter-gloss in the *Biographia* admits a prejudice about the character of Wordsworth's subjects: "*Rustic life (above all,* low *and rustic life) especially unfavorable to the formation of a human diction.*" So, fifteen years after the Preface, Coleridge sorts out the enduring from the eccentric features of Wordsworth's legacy, and this distinction turns on the acceptance in some poems, and rejection in others, of the educated diction that the Preface had set at defiance. An obvious effect of Coleridge's appreciation was to bring Wordsworth, though not the Wordsworth of the ballads, into harmony with the conventional taste of his day. It was not only quasi-academic reviewers like Francis Jeffrey, but earnest disciples too, like the young William Whewell, who had somehow felt drawn to Wordsworth's moralizing eloquence, but repelled by the anomalous sympathies which his poems seemed to urge, with an Idiot Boy, a Female Vagrant, a Waggoner, or a Pedlar.[5] Coleridge's statement of retraction confirmed their suspicions and asserted again the control of a "human diction" by literate persons of worldly means.

Still, long before De Quincey's summing up in 1845, one can point to unregenerate statements of loyalty to Wordsworth, from contemporaries who persisted in regarding the poet as a man speaking to men. Hazlitt represented the suffrage of younger readers like Keats, as well as that of his friends Lamb and Hunt, when he wrote in his review of the *Biographia*:

With chap. IV begins the formidable ascent of that mountainous and barren ridge of clouds piled on precipices and precipices on clouds, from the top of which the author deludes us with a view of the Promised Land that divides the regions of Fancy from those of the Imagination, and extends through 200 pages with various inequalities and declensions to the end of the volume. The object of this long-winding metaphysical march, which resembles a patriarchal journey, is to point out and settle the true grounds of Mr. Wordsworth's claim to originality as a poet; which, if we rightly understand … turns out to be, that there is nothing peculiar about him; and that his poetry, in so far as it is good for any thing at all, is just like any other good poetry. The learned author, indeed, judiciously observes, that Mr. Wordsworth would never have been "idly and absurdly" considered as "the founder of a school in poetry," if he had not, by some strange mistake, announced the fact himself in his preface to the Lyrical Ballads. This, it must be owned, looks as if Mr. Wordsworth thought more of his *peculiar* pretentions than Mr. Coleridge appears to do, and really furnishes some excuse for those who took the poet at his word.[6]

Terms of art such as fancy and imagination may serve, Hazlitt implies, chiefly as a hindrance in the reading of Wordsworth's poetry. Their appeal is metaphysical in the sense that it refers poetic invention to the authority of timeless attributes. Hazlitt for his part shifts the emphasis to Wordsworth's "peculiarity," and it is noteworthy that he uses the word with the intent to praise.

7

It is, in fact, another word for originality. And their interchangeable characters suggest that "originality" has come to be known as an
effect of regarding nature from a special point of view. Indeed, in the
first and second decades of the century allusions to nature as such, or
to the natural graces of writing, are growing less directly legible than
they had been throughout the preceding age of criticism. On the one
hand, nature cannot now mean the virtue good poetry exhibits when
it resembles all other good poetry. On the other hand, fidelity to a
familiar texture of life, as in the more elaborate backgrounds of Scott's
novels, is beginning to imply a secondary merit in the artist. The
paradox this leaves for criticism – memorable to English readers in
Blake's use of "imagination" as the antithesis of "nature" – received
perhaps its most distinct formulation from the anonymous Parisian
author of *A Blow Against the Salon of 1779*: "If the painter devotes his
time merely to the study of nature, he will produce nothing but
frivolous bagatelles. The answer to this is profound thought, which
will guide the artist's brush and furnish the spectator with enough
ideas and feelings to last a lifetime."[7] Thus nature, if applied as a rule
for art, is apt to weaken everything that stamps a work with its
peculiarity. Returning a last time to the *Biographia*, one may view its
distinction between fancy and imagination as an attempt, rather late
for much hope of success, to capture the ideas of shallow and deep
propriety as inhering in the associations of objects. In this it was the
successor of attempts to confine such ideas to the nature of the objects
themselves. By contrast, other critics of the time were so persuaded by
Wordsworth's arguments that they could forgo even the analytic
convenience of Coleridge's terminology. That is why they will often
be found to use the words fancy and imagination as near synonyms.

As for such related dichotomies as that between the natural and the
picturesque, or between the natural and the ideal, Hazlitt shows how
they may be disposed of in his essay "On the Picturesque and Ideal."
He there defines the picturesque as "something like an excrescence on
the face of nature," including as illustrations "a rough terrier-dog,
with the hair bristled and matted together," and, in a wider survey,
"an old stump of a tree with rugged bark, and one or two straggling
branches, a little stunted hedge-row line, marking the boundary of
the horizon, a stubble-field, a winding path, a rock seen against the
sky." When Hazlitt comes to oppose all these to the ideal, he still
keeps the latter within nature: the ideal is only "the height of the
pleasing, that which satisfies and accords with the inmost longing of
the soul." He can therefore add that "a morning mist drawing a
slender veil over all objects is at once picturesque and *ideal*," because it

excites a wish for a not yet completed pleasure to go on. It may be noted in passing that the picturesque landscape owed much of its earlier vogue to the improved estates of the nobility and the newly rich. Hazlitt was always conscious of this fact, and he knew Johnson's definition of the ideal as "mental; intellectual; not perceived by the senses." A calculated effect of this discussion of the natural, pictur-esque, and ideal along a single continuum (with the last rated highest), was evidently to reverse the aristocratic bias of our thinking about beauty. The picturesque may be enclosed for the pleasure of a few. The ideal is a conception without boundaries, an inalienable estate for all in common.

The refinement of distinctions like these belonged to a line of work that nobody yet would describe as a calling. Nor had it yet been placed on the regular footing of a profession. "The newspaper of the day," writes Peacock in his "Essay on Fashionable Literature," "the favorite magazine of the month, the review of the quarter" easily take precedence over the novel or the poem; and this has the further effect of teaching people to read novels and poems the way they would read reviews or magazines or newspapers: "The spring tide of metropoli-tan favor floats these intellectual *deliciae* into every minor town and village in the kingdom, where they circle through their little day in the eddies of reading societies." The languid tone which suggests Pea-cock's detachment from the scene, is of course largely a pretense, as the rest of his essay shows. And it conceals an uneasy truth about the role of the critic. Even when he used the language of ambassadorial politics, his *ipse dixits* might betray the equipment of the village functionary.

Indeed, the unattached critic at this time – who wrote neither to pay off enemies of the government, nor to arrange a reception for his friends – lived in daily intimacy with a mood of self-irony which Hazlitt caught in a phrase: "'We are nothing if not critical.' Be it so: but then let us be critical, or we shall be nothing." The tactics provoked by that mood now seem restless and speculative, in a style one has come to associate with criticism of a much later period. They often combine moral with figural analysis. But in doing so, they exhibit a freedom of wit without didactic sanction, for which it would be hard to find either a precedent or an analogy. Consider as a local instance a remark by Hazlitt, on the lines from *Paradise Lost*: "Leviathan, which God of all his works / Created hugest that swim the ocean-stream." In context, the metaphor has to do with the dissimulations that Satan may attempt against man, just as, more innocently, a whale's back may trick a mariner in his craft into

9

mooring beside it. "What a force of imagination," Hazlitt comments, "is there in this last expression! What an idea it conveys of that hugest of created beings, as if it shrunk up the ocean to a stream, and took up the sea in its nostrils as a very little thing!" The passage, in short, interests him for the way it shows objects through their relations, the Leviathan taking its size by comparison with the shrinking of the ocean itself. Yet he values the trope not chiefly as a piece of ingenuity (though exaggerated, it is not far-fetched) but because it affords a tremendous idea of the author's energy. Only conceptions as great as Milton's could trust a passing metaphor like this to loft rather than sink the fable of his poem.

As Hazlitt interprets the motives of genius, they are never high or low. If their results belong to moral judgement, their beginnings are closer to instinct. In reflecting on the power of Edmund Kean's performance as Iago, he speculates that we are drawn to works of art by "a natural tendency in the mind to strong excitement, a desire to have its faculties roused" to the utmost pitch. Writing on the knocking at the gate in *Macbeth*, De Quincey takes for granted a similar tendency: he notices, as equally natural to the mind, the inertia by which it restores a degree of calm, in the after-tremors of a catastrophe of whatever magnitude. The knocking at the gate is remarkable only in that it typifies other such intervals, which, to adapt De Quincey's figure, resemble the ordinary indicative sentence, following an exclamation and a dreadful parenthesis. But if one takes the reference to *Macbeth* as essential, the figure itself points to a curious moral. The arbitrariness of a verbal convention is here compared with the arbitrariness of a still-to-be-legitimated power. This sort of thought has become almost a commonplace by the 1820s. It reminds us that the interpretation of a moment in a poem looks like the interpretation of a contested action in a state. The critic addressing his readers asks them to realize, by extension, what the order of a poem may have in common with the order of a state. Both are made by human design, for the sake of a good they may exhibit but cannot judge. The acknowledgement of this fact limits an estimate of the motives of reading as well as writing.

At times, that limit may seem to be widened by an appeal to sympathy. Shelley, for example, writes of the joining of persons in a manner that would serve as appropriately for the joining of parts of a metaphor: "The great secret of morals is love; or a going out of our nature, and an identification of ourselves with the beautiful which exists in thought, action, or person, not our own." Yet, even in this formulation, thought and action are as likely objects of sympathy as persons. As for the power of writing, though Shelley here regards it as ameliorative, it remains inscrutable to itself. We come to know it only as a result of an error, an identification or taking for our own of something that is not ours. If, to return to an aphorism of Hazlitt's, *knowledge is conscious power*, then a main difference between learning and genius follows from the unstated corollary: imagination is unconscious power. In the medium of language, the work of imagination is so absolute that Hazlitt speaks of it as "right-royal." Shelley may sound more scrupulous in merely asserting that it is "arbitrarily produced." Yet in the reign of George III, as in the Regency years, political writers like these when they use the word "arbitrary" intend at least a distant political implication. It is important therefore to see where their usage deepens a related sense of the word that has become familiar in modern semiotics. For Shelley, the arbitrary character of language would primarily have implied not "indeterminancy," or the "unmotivatedness of the sign," but rather an authority beyond challenge or retraction, which obliged every reader to attend to verbal relations that come before the author. These are relations that he alters but still bequeaths with equal authority to his own successors. In consequence, no appeal can be made from language to the author's life and beliefs, as if the latter could naturalize the strangeness of his inventions.

In the curriculum of interpretation that has just been sketched, three distinct phases are visible. The power that the critic finds in great writing is displaced, first, from an author to a mind and, next, from a mind to its traces in language. Not the thoughts that inspired a poem, or the person in whom they "voluntary move / Harmonious numbers," but the words alone survive to bear the emphasis of great writing. This means that a poem is no longer justified by the advantages it may be supposed to yield to the readers who came to it first. Rather, it is justified as an object of always uncertain and always possible utility. It looks forward to human ends it will be found to have served later on, by a future whose interests are as unpredictable as its readings. A historical, rather than an ideal, sense may thus be given to the allusions both Hazlitt and Shelley make to "the spirit of the age." To bring out the originality of Shelley's conception in the "Defence," it will be helpful to compare that essay with a German work of similar scope, Schiller's *Letters on the Aesthetic Education of Man*. Shelley adopts poetry as a general name for the prophecy of change. His wide application will, he believes, be admitted as proper; for, when the first signs of a change appear among the customs of men and women, we see in retrospect that they were already alive in words or forms that had to be interpreted to be known at all: legislation, religious teachings, inventive systems of education, and public cere- monies of several kinds (ruling out such things as human sacrifice, but including such things as the theatrical competitions of ancient Greece), all on this view qualify as poetry. To make his argument, the only premise Shelley needs is that the great mutations which persist all move humanity in the direction of enlightenment.

With this premise Schiller of course agrees. And yet, in guarding poetry against the charge of immorality – or rather, of insufficiently predictable consequences for morals – Schiller chose a very different ground of defense. We must, he writes in his twenty-first letter,

acknowledge those people to be entirely right who declare the Beautiful, and the mood into which it transports our spirit, to be wholly indifferent and sterile in relation to *knowledge* and *mental outlook*. They are entirely right; for Beauty gives no individual result whatever, either for the intellect or for the will; it realizes no individual purpose, either intellectual or moral; it discovers no individual truth, helps us to perform no individual duty, and is, in a word, equally incapable of establishing the character and clearing the mind.[8]

Schiller here assigns poetry to a separate realm from that of the pure reason (intellect) and that of the practical reason (will). He enforces the distinction in keeping with a principle which he states explicitly in his twenty-seventh letter: in "the sphere of cultivated society" where "the aesthetic state" may be found, man need appear to man "only as shape," confront him only in free play. "*To grant freedom by means of freedom* is the fundamental law of this kingdom."[9] The ideal that is pictured in this summary aphorism requires two codes of conscience, one for aesthetic representation and another for ethical action.

Now whether they knew Schiller's book or not, the English critics of the next generation wrote without much regard to the sort of distinction he proposed. They look upon action and representation as infinitely permeable by each other. And they are able to do so because they do not believe that reflection occurs apart from reading. Once again, to exhibit the skepticism implicit in such a view, we have to take reading in the widest possible sense. As a mental activity it is like reflection in that it strengthens certain habits, unlike reflection in that it aims at no result. By contrast, the granting of "freedom by means of freedom" aims to realize a new form of self-recognition. Instead of a reader absorbed in the words on the page, it asks us to imagine a thinker occupied with a conception of the mind's freedom. This image of an aesthetic state, as liberal, contemplative, and established by unvaried means, is missing from the essays of Lamb and Hunt. The omission looks more deliberate in Hazlitt, whose essay on

Coriolanus may be read as a counter-statement to Schiller. But with the "Defence of Poetry" comes the first, and still the most cogent, attempt to argue a thesis original with Shelley: that poetry will serve the ends of freedom without having been constructed in principle to serve those ends. Poetry's greatness on this view lies in its power to merge insensibly with the facts, opinions, and persons of life. What distinguishes taste from other uses of judgement is only the intensity of its stimulus. No special faculty of the mind is involved in its arbitrations.

As a practical critic, Lamb closely anticipates Shelley's argument. He sees that a defense of poetry requires a defense of reading, and that the act of reading itself is threatened, not by the interpretative habits of common life, but by the conventions necessary to the performance of a written text. Lamb cites as an example the difficulty of rightly interpreting Hamlet's insults to Polonius and Ophelia. These are "parts of his character, which to reconcile with our admiration of Hamlet, the most patient consideration of his situation is no more than necessary." By an effort of abstraction, that is, which coincides with the pauses of reading, we feel his asperities as traits of self-command. The rival sense of Hamlet which an actor may project only weakens our imagination of the character; for

such is the actor's necessity of giving strong blows to the audience, that I have never seen a player in this character, who did not exaggerate and strain to the utmost these ambiguous features – these temporary deformities in the character. They make him express a vulgar scorn at Polonius which utterly degrades his gentility, and which no explanation can render palatable; they make him shew contempt, and curl up the nose at Ophelia's father, – contempt in its very grossest and most hateful form; but they get applause by it: it is natural, people say; that is, the words are scornful, and the actor expresses scorn, and that they can judge of: but why so much scorn, and of that sort, they never think of asking.

Lamb in this passage speaks on behalf of nature and truth. And yet, as he shows by removing the play from the aggregate judgements of a theatrical audience, nature and truth are ideas which the mind of each reader forms in a manner peculiar to itself.

The imagined characters of a play are thus exemplary fictions for the mind. But, since only the words on the page compose the reader's full idea of a character, only they carry an influence that touches all the mind's activities. To return briefly to a comparison with eighteenth-century styles: it is remarkable that in the general encomiums of Shakespeare which culminated in Johnson's great *Preface*, there is hardly a single attempt at dramatic analysis that explores motives as

Lamb's does. Given the idea of a nature freed from extrinsic or adventitious details, the omission was as inevitable as it was involuntary. Accordingly, Johnson can assert that "Shakespeare has no heroes; his scenes are occupied only by men, who act and speak as the reader thinks that he should himself have spoken or acted on the same occasion."[10] The main effect of such judgements is to conciliate esteem for the middle station of life: that station, above misery and below opulence, which was suited to the class of persons whom education had helped to prosper. But Johnson's praise of Shakespeare was also meant to harmonize with claims of the sort Reynolds would make for "middle forms," without exuberances or marked idiosyncrasies. Of course, the very idea of character may be inseparable from a feeling of sympathy with a moral agent: thus far at any rate Lamb seems in agreement with Johnson. For what I make of a character relates to my thought of how I should have spoken or acted in his situation. Lamb, however, goes on to observe that the idea cannot be either general or universal, since characters are sometimes found to have altered from one reading to the next. "The truth is, the Characters of Shakespeare are so much the objects of meditation rather than of interest or curiosity as to their actions, that while we are reading any of his great criminal characters, – Macbeth, Richard, even Iago, – we think not so much of the crimes which they commit, as of the ambition, the aspiring spirit, the intellectual activity, which prompts them to overleap those moral fences." Such promptings, if Johnson ever came to emphasize them, would render a work merely vicious to his judgement. For Lamb, they have joined the meditation that books are expected to yield.

Two features of this comment by Lamb are exceptionally interesting. First, in a curious phrase that stretches words beyond their common usage, he speaks of *reading the characters* that Shakespeare wrote. Second, the consequences in the mind of the reader appear to resemble those that Hazlitt traced in his account of Iago. As we read, our absorption in fictional characters somehow detaches us from an interest in moral judgements; and this is so, not because we respond aesthetically instead, but because we have ceased to judge at all. Rather, we read for a sense of the "intellectual activity" of the characters. This testifies to an interest in the powers of an individual mind – ours, and by implication the author's – so that we recognize the unique position of each: "the reading of a tragedy is a fine abstraction." By comparison, the stage presents a scene of embarrassing facsimiles, the weighing upon eye and ear of so much "acting, scenery, dress, the most contemptible things" which merely "call upon us to judge of their naturalness." Here then is a clear instance in which the exigencies of natural rendering work against the demands of imaginative truth. Lamb could write in this vein, without leaving an impression of overstrained paradox, because he understood both art and nature under the aspect of interpretation.

The other critics reprinted in these pages so far conform to a similar view that it is worth recalling a justification they took for granted. Two decades before Lamb's essay, F. W. Schlegel published some aphorisms which help to explain the difference between reading and acting. "Words," Schlegel wrote, "often understand themselves better than do those who use them."[11] The remark suggests a definition of romantic irony, for it supposes that words have a certain knowledge of themselves, and that this knowledge differs in kind from the author's or reader's. It is possible to follow Schlegel's remark into a non-didactic theory of allegory.[12] But his own design may have been more flatly skeptical. When we put words to their ordinary uses, we feel that we have given them a necessary sense; whereas, Schlegel observes, words themselves are under no such illusion. Words are nothing but the sum (never realizable) of all uses and the readings they serve. In this way the difference between the self-understanding of words and the understanding of those who employ them runs parallel to the difference between reading a play oneself and seeing it performed in the theatre.

Romantic poems, novels, and essays alike teach that the deeper assertions of the self come with a falling away of our usual interests or accustomed consciousness. But comments like Lamb's and Schlegel's recall how often the drama of self-recognition is played out explicitly as a drama of reading. Peter Bell, in Wordsworth's poem of that title, stares into a pool to see what may be his own face reflected, or may be the submerged face of a murdered man; and, as Wordsworth narrates the moment,

> He looks, he cannot choose but look;
> Like someone reading in a book –
> A book that is enchanted.

Hazlitt's memoir, "My First Acquaintance with Poets," returns to the same sort of figure in describing Wordsworth himself, with a phrase borrowed from another poet: "Wordsworth read us the story of Peter Bell in the open air; and the comment made upon it by his face and voice was very different from that of some later critics! Whatever might be thought of the poem, 'his face was as a book where men might read strange matters,' and he announced the fate of his hero in prophetic tones."[13] Both of these passages show that the imagination which occurs in reading is not reconciliatory, as Coleridge wanted it to be. Nor for that matter is it privative, as his critics have sometimes said in reply. Its single reliable property is to change.

"In order to write well about something," concluded Schlegel, "one shouldn't be interested in it any longer. To express an idea with due circumspection, one must have relegated it wholly to one's past; one must be no longer preoccupied with it."[14] The partial character, therefore, of reading as of comprehension, follows from an author's having relegated his work to the past in the very process of writing it. Interpretations are conditioned not by the presence of an author's interests but rather by the absence of them. We have no reason to suppose that the paths of interpreters, any more than those of authors, will converge, or somehow tend to converge, upon a single view of their object. It would be facile, however, to regard the partial character of reading as only a consequence, and not equally a cause, of the elusiveness of our idea of the author. For the author too is a reader with respect to his experience and to the books, anecdotes, and commonplaces that have shaped his understanding of experience. Indeed, Schlegel's most celebrated aphorism, "A classical text must never be entirely comprehensible," is not to be taken as holding in reserve a secret for interpretation. His point was that there is no such thing as a method of reading – a method to be preserved and transmitted. There are only readers.

Yet a classical text is by definition a canonical text. It requires a standard reading, if only as a stimulus to fresh revisions of the canon. How, then, are romantic critics entitled to speak of such texts at all? A short answer is that they write of them as personal monuments. This means that the greatest works are always on the brink of a permanence they cannot be allowed to attain. If Shakespeare has become unchallengeable, almost to the point of being identified with nature itself, the choice among his plays remains open; so that one may remark, for example, an unexpected partiality for the Roman plays: in Wordsworth, for *Julius Caesar*; in Hazlitt, for *Coriolanus*; and even in Coleridge, for *Antony and Cleopatra*. Spenser is not yet a secure classic: the tone of advocacy where his poems are concerned, especially in the writings of Hunt and Hazlitt, shows that he still wanted advocates. As for an out-of-the-way taste – Hazlitt's for Thomas Amory or Lamb's for Jeremy Taylor – it can be declared with as much gravity or delicacy as the occasion warrants. Yet some enthusiasms appear more generally within the period and milieu of this criticism. When Hazlitt in his sixth lecture on the English poets quotes in full Collins's "Ode to Evening," and adds a note of praise for his "Ode on the Poetical Character," he is following the lead of a generation of poets. Appreciations like these often convey the sense of a shared discovery. A less genial tone of eccentric confession is reserved for the rare dismissal of an old book, as when Hazlitt admits that, just as Burke could not love a French republic, so he cannot love the Countess of Pembroke's *Arcadia*. Wordsworth's and Coleridge's demotion of Pope is really an unrelated phenomenon: a fortification, raised by a still-militant avant-garde, against a normative style of elegance. From one age to the next, this sort of criticism has to occur, and its burden remains the same: "You can't say it that way any more."[15] Very characteristically, De Quincey mistook the Wordsworth–Coleridge polemic as the verdict of a mature ortho-doxy, and expanded it into a full-scale demolition of Pope, the more inventive sections of which have been printed below.

The conscious or institutional making of a canon was on the whole foreign to the interests of these critics. So, too, was an iconoclastic distrust of culture – the word culture is itself an anachronism. They simply assume that one may retain, without the support of doctrine, a lifelong passion for certain books and certain things. One can form a clear enough picture anyway of the conception of great writing against which they ventured their judgements of contemporaries. Hunt's predilections are the most impressive of the group in antici-pating a poetry that still lay mostly in the future. He admires above all Spenser, Milton (favoring his early poems), Marlowe, Swift (whose middle style was the pattern for Hunt's own prose), Chaucer, and Pope, on the last of whom his comments make an excellent foil to De Quincey's. "Perhaps, after all," he concedes, "nothing better than such a honey and such a sting as this exquisite writer developed, could have been got out of his little delicate pungent nature; and we have every reason to be grateful for what they have done for us. Hundreds of greater pretensions in poetry have not attained to half his fame, nor did they deserve it; for they did not take half his pains."[16] Near the top of his list Hunt adds the names of Keats and Shelley. Within poetry, Hazlitt for all his principled tolerance is a much more exclusive appreciator: Milton (the Milton of *Paradise Lost*) he holds to be unrivalled at the centre of a living tradition; but in the drama after Shakespeare, comedy alone has attained perfection, in the plays of Congreve and Wycherley; and nothing of their class survives in the present. Of contemporaries Hazlitt admires chiefly Wordsworth and Scott. The latter, he regrets to announce, is indifferent to *half* of life, the part that may connect the present with the future.

With Peacock, both of these critics share a pretty thorough immunity to the vogue of Byron. In looking at other writings of the period too, one comes to feel that this reservation is the mark of a critical, as distinct from a fashionable, taste. Whether by his surface classicism, or the traits that made him seem a continental poet by adoption, Byron piques their natural suspicion to the length of consistent rebuke. His politics go for little in the scale, and the critics incline to take him, with his manners and his mannerism, as a finished specimen of the *ancien régime* in letters. Wordsworth, on the other hand, is understood to be a revolutionary in spite of his politics. On this point we have an important piece of testimony from Hazlitt. When the *Lyrical Ballads* first appeared, he recalls,

the change in the belles-lettres was as complete, and to many persons as startling, as the change in politics, with which it went hand in hand. There was a mighty ferment in the heads of statesmen and poets, kings and people. According to the prevailing notions, all was to be natural and new. Nothing that was established was to be tolerated. All the common-place figures of poetry, tropes, allegories, personifications, with the whole heathen mythology, were instantly discarded; a classical allusion was considered as a piece of antiquated foppery; capital letters were no more allowed in print, than letters-patent of nobility were permitted in real life; kings and queens were dethroned from their rank and station in legitimate tragedy or epic poetry, as they were decapitated elsewhere; rhyme was looked upon as a relic of the feudal system, and regular metre was abolished along with regular government.[17]

Disinterested, as well as egotistical, motives are allowed their part in this change of literary manners. The theorists of Jacobinism in letters, Hazlitt continues, "founded the new school on a principle of sheer humanity." Yet they saw its effect would be to translate their own writings from marginal gestures into the distinctive expressions of the age.

When Hazlitt himself writes to reform the criteria of theatrical performance, in order to show the worth of Edmund Kean's acting, he appears as a convert to the same principle of sheer humanity. So, in their lesser degrees, are Hunt and Lamb; and, with self-conscious reservations, De Quincey. Reduced to the power of an individual, the best name for the principle is genius: with their varied shadings of tone and style, all of them doubtless would have consented to be known as defenders of genius. At the same time, they recognize that contemporary success dictates the terms in which the history of an art is narrated at a given moment. A common result follows from the effort to hold this principle and this perception together in a single thought. In reviews throughout the first three decades of the nineteenth century, critics often begin by telling a story about the recent past. They do this more openly than ever before; and from a motive they confess as openly: to supply a context agreeable to a new work, however uncertain its kind. The strategy presumes that before a poem or play or novel can give pleasure, its readers must sympathize with the larger movement to which it belongs by affinity. An instance in the present anthology is Hunt's claim for Keats as a direct successor to the school that includes preeminently Wordsworth, Southey, and Coleridge. Since other early articles on Keats had elected to deride his poetry, as the work of a primitive feigning the style of his literary betters, Hunt's was a subtle tactical choice. He was suggesting that to pillory Keats effectively, his critics would have to lengthen their strictures to cover poets with irreproachable Tory credentials. This mode of advocacy may have more to tell us about the age than, for example, the assured intimacy of De Quincey's essay on Wordsworth, which achieves a gravity that is almost posthumous.

To read the work of a contemporary as Hunt does, for the way it fits a personal idea of the classic; and to read a classic as Hazlitt does, for the way it disturbs the trust that a new intelligence will prevail: these complementary emphases imply a view of the poem, or play, or novel, as the expression of a purpose that cannot be fixed forever. They also point to a difference, of degree, between poetic and discursive argument. A critic writes to persuade readers who already share an interest in the work that is being discussed. A poet writes for readers who share something more elusive: an attitude of attention. The celebrated passages of Kant's *Critique of Judgment*, which distinguish poetry above all by its purposiveness-without-purpose, may exaggerate, and certainly have obscured for many readers, this difference between the rhetoric of poetry and the rhetoric of criticism. Here again, Schiller is closer to the thinking of the English romantic critics, when he proposes a conception of art as an always evolving purpose. Schiller affirms (more optatively than any English critic would have done): "give the world on which you are acting the *direction* towards the good, and the quiet rhythm of time will bring about its development."[18] This already sounds like Shelley's argument that poetry itself is exempt from the faults which the characters of poets disclose: "Their errors have been weighed and found to have been dust in the balance; if their sins were as scarlet, they are now white as snow: they have been washed in the blood of the mediator and the redeemer, Time." The effects of poetry evidently require a defense as sweeping as this, because they are felt as much in what people do as in what they think.

If romantic criticism may in part be understood as an effort to recall literature from ideas to practices, its means of doing so register the force of a particular audience. Critics no longer address themselves to lords, with the direct hope of patronage, or to a common reader unencumbered by peculiar traits. They write instead for the solitary man or woman, whose responses make for the value of public opinion. This is the reader whom Wordsworth and Hazlitt will occasionally speak of as another self. Critics therefore, with poets, compose a "fourth estate in society," and their calling is to show the things poetry says, or knows and cannot say. What freedom they have is owing chiefly to their association with genius, from the authority of which there is no appeal since it derives from no special class of persons. But the task of summoning a new audience to the texture of its practices implies the further aim of contributing to the march of intellect.

A strict historicism would oblige us here to admit that self-consciousness and intellectual advance form a natural alliance only for a middle-class reader. An even stricter historicism could reply that the term "middle-class" itself is anachronistic for the early 1800s.[19] Confining ourselves to a modest hope of provisional accuracy, let us observe that however parochial the connection of these two things may now appear, or however uncertain the identity of the class by whom they were parochially understood, the critics who wrote the following essays were among the first to assert their importance together. In consequence, one may feel that one has a tacit acquaintance with the readers of the essays. They are persons for whom writing can be a sort of ideal property. As such, it is related to the other ideal and material objects with which they furnish their lives. But it has the power to manifest, as nothing else can do, the relationship of mutual subjection between the speakers of a language, as between distant neighbors in a single community. For readers like these the essay in criticism, partly theoretical and partly practical, but in any case inquisitive and speculative, carried an interest apart from that of the wholly responsible praising and blaming review.

Some reasons for the preference may be surmised from Hunt's essay "On the Realities of Imagination." A reader's imaginings according to Hunt are not confined to an occasion. They begin equally in books and in the things that cross his mind – with perceptions that matter because they too have been interpreted. Thus, the ideas of experience and literature are always mingled. As for the character of the reader, this essay pictures him as a city stroller freshly concerned with life. It is true that Hunt's own impressions turn bookish as he proceeds; and yet his emphasis has nothing to do with the display of sensibility: it serves rather to illustrate our bias in favor of the things we care for (books, for Hunt, ranking high among these). The advantage such impressions have for others is that of exciting a fancy which Hunt declines to name without the help of a phrase from Davenant, "The assembled souls of all that men hold wise." But the realities that Hunt speaks of are more nearly those of another poet, Keats, in an early poem like "To One Who Has Been Long in City Pent." Keats himself also comes to an abstract idea of freedom by regarding the city's life from one of its suburbs. There he settles "into some pleasant lair / Of wavy grass, and reads a debonair / And gentle tale of love"; all for the sake of later regretting the passage of a day, which "so soon has glided by: / E'en like the passage of an angel's tear / That falls through the clear air silently." The note of light self-mockery, after the idleness of reading, occurs in a conspicuously readerly passage, linking as it does two moments of *Paradise Lost*: "tears such as angels weep" and "from morn / To noon he fell, from noon to dewy eve, / A summer's day." In such moments of poetry as well as prose, one feels it is the reader, and not solely the author, who makes good the promise of "health," in the special sense Hunt gives to that word.

A final remark seems to be in order concerning the relation between reading, interpretation, and the history of literature. Shelley, of all the romantic critics, gave the most sustained thought to these matters, yet his conclusions have so compressed a form that they still need some elaboration. He says in the "Defence of Poetry" that poets are the common interpreters – "unacknowledged legislators" – whose readings affect our lives beyond the possibility of acknowledgement. Further, this fact about poets is indissociable from the moral power which their works may have in spite of their lives. In choosing to defend poetry rather than the poet, Shelley was in fact repeating Sir Philip Sidney's declaration, in the "Apology for Poetry," that he spoke "of the art, and not of the artificer." But Shelley unlike Sidney does not assign to poetry the function of giving delight through fable, or assure the truth of the fable by the inward virtue of philosophical precept. Sidney had written to guard poets against the Platonic suspicion that they inculcated vicious mores. "The poets," he replied, "did not induce such opinions, but did imitate those opinions already induced."[20] Shelley's aim on the contrary is to show that the knowledge of poetry is such that it enables us to detect the falseness of the very opinions it imitates. It points the way, by irony or antithesis, or by suggesting a train of thought others can pursue, to a truth it does not articulate and an enlightenment it does not see. In the nature of poetry as Shelley reads it, this is a function it will always retain, no matter what happens to the opinions it wrongly elects to imitate.

But another charge against poetry complicates the argument of Shelley's defense. It is, that the sympathies awakened by poetry may strengthen a sense of reflex justice close to the spirit of revenge. This is the same difficulty that perplexed Shelley in his Preface to *Prometheus Unbound*, where he spoke of the process by which a reader was liable to vindicate Milton's Satan: the character "engenders in the mind a pernicious casuistry which leads us to weigh his faults with his wrongs, and to excuse the former because the latter exceed all measure."[21] By the time he came to write the "Defence," however, Shelley seems to have grown more confident of the eventually liberating effects of even such negative readings as this. "Milton's Devil," he now revises his comments to say,

as a moral being is as far superior to his God, as One who perseveres in some purpose which he has conceived to be excellent in spite of adversity and torture, is to One who in the cold security of undoubted triumph inflicts the most horrible revenge upon his enemy, not from any mistaken notion of inducing him to repent of a perseverance in enmity, but with the alleged design of exasperating him to deserve new torments.

If every age deifies its peculiar errors, future ages still discern the accuracy with which poetry has shown the work of deification. Our sympathy with the character of Satan, though at first it may rest on a narrow interest in justice as revenge, will evolve to the point where we recognize that justice resides in the act of sympathy alone. This, in turn, will help to expose a strange inversion of human good and evil, to which the poet's theology bound him but could not bind his poem. Finally then, the errors of poetry come to light through a development in morals which itself is a consequence of poetry.

So far, Shelley's sense of history may appear to have advanced beyond Wordsworth's in the "Essay, Supplementary" only by widening the definition of the central term, "poetry." Yet the place Shelley gives to two moments of creation – inscription (not meaning) and recognition (not deciphering) – makes his argument radically different from Wordsworth's. In the "Essay, Supplementary" the history of poetry was intelligible as a series of effusions linked with each other by accident. *Nature* there designated the choice of a series to call one's own. In the "Defence" the history of poetry is intelligible as an artifice of human survival, formed gradually and reformed for all by each individual act of the poetic will. Nothing takes the place of Wordsworth's nature, and nothing seems to be needed. Rather, we are asked to consider language as the best possible story to explain the continuity of human life. Poetry is "as it were the interpenetration of a diviner nature through our own; but its footsteps are like those of a wind over a sea, which the coming calm erases, and whose traces remain only, as on the wrinkled sand which paves it." It leaves a text as vivid and as contingent as that of existence itself, which Shelley elsewhere called "the web of human things." Within the argument of the essay, this, and not an idea of poetic *gnosis* or divination, is likely to have been the design of such otherwise mysterious turns as the allusion to individual poems as "episodes to that great poem, which all poets, like the co-operating thoughts of one great mind, have built up since the beginning of the world." Or again, the speculation that "Every original language near to its source is in itself the chaos of a cyclic poem." All poets require some such belief when they write their poems; often, their poems may induce readers to share it as well. But Shelley's belief differs only incidentally from a sentiment that the creation as we know it is the chaos of scattered but cooperating forces which science exists to realize. It suggests that every truth is historical, without adding that between any two finite perspectives we have no reason for choosing one. The good of recalling "the happiest and best moments of the best and happiest minds" is that they help us to choose.

All of these essays belong to the periodical culture of the early 1800s. Even the few which were written to appear separately, like Wordsworth's "Essay, Supplementary" and Shelley's "Defence," are conscious of the practical demands of a milieu they try to ignore. Of the critics proper, De Quincey is the most versatile performer in the mixed medium, half educational, half sensational, which the quarter-lies and magazines combined to offer. By contrast, Lamb, Hunt, and Hazlitt invented, by resistant adaptation to the same pressures, a style of writing which would remain a possible model to the end of the century. Against Hazlitt it was sometimes objected that he used too many quotations; yet when these are once read closely the objection loses its force. Hunt perhaps supports too cosy a family of pet words ("frank," "lovely," "luxuriant," "exquisite" are some of them) but as a rule he affixes precise meanings to each. Both Hazlitt and Hunt were criticized in their time as *low* writers, and the editor of the *Quarterly Review*, William Gifford, even nicknamed Hazlitt "the slang-whanger." The English language has forgotten Gifford, and most of what he thought slumming in the radical Hazlitt, or underbred in the cockney Hunt, has since been honored as part of what the language was destined to be. Criticism too, we may be reminded, shares in the prophecies of change by which Shelley recognized poetry. And appropriately it is now Shelley's "Defence of Poetry" most of all that impresses us with the mastery of an eloquent middle style. Hazlitt was thinking of Wordsworth's correct prose and Coleridge's florid prose when he wrote, "I have but an indifferent opinion of the prose style of poets." But the style of Shelley's posthumous essay would have pleased him as much as its tendency of thought. It has the enduring virtues of momentum and elasticity, for which he always kept an unreluctant praise.

William Wordsworth

(1770–1850)

Of the first generation of romantic poets, Wordsworth registered most deeply the effect of the French Revolution on the beliefs and feelings of an individual mind. Having grown up in the Lake District and attended St. John's College, Cambridge from 1787 to 1791, he went on a walking tour of the Alps and remained in France for some time after, from November 1791 to December 1792. These three kinds of place – the sites of a native community, of an education by books, and of an attempt to reduce to practice a theory of human nature – came to play distinct parts in Wordsworth's understanding of his life. As he recounts in his long autobiographical poem, *The Prelude*, his hope of modifying the limits of existence turned him back again and again to a reverence for the conditions of existence. Wordsworth uses a single word, "imagination," to imply both the adventurous power that leads him to think of such changes, and the admonitory power that restrains him. The object of his reverence he calls "nature": sometimes in the sense of local or picturesque surroundings, but always with a larger implication of habits, memories, observances, and the attachments that form so steady an accompaniment to life that they cannot be questioned. The poet's constant temptation, as Wordsworth describes it, is to detach himself from nature, either through the agency of ideas or of action. The French Revolution seemed to him to prove the danger of the temptation and the necessity of its disappointment.

But in Wordsworth's own life it was his understanding of France that changed rather than the shape of his ideals. In the early 1790s, when he adopted the revolutionary manner even in his spelling and personal dress, Wordsworth saw the enforcement of "the rights of man" as a heroic experiment in the regeneration of society. By the early 1800s, he saw the whole revolution, in the aftermath of the Terror, as a movement that radically threatened the survival of human solidarity, which from the first had been part of what he meant by nature. Wordsworth's motives remained the same throughout his career, and he does not typify the intellectual progress from idealism to disenchantment. What may be observed in his later writings is a wish to protect – where, earlier, it had been enough to represent – the natural sentiments of men and women. Between the composition of *The Prelude* in 1805 and the publication of his second long poem, *The Excursion*, in 1814, Wordsworth moved from a style of assertion to a style of defense. He had gradually ceased to feel that nature was an inevitable inheritance, and had begun to regard it as a vulnerable legacy, under attack from every modern tendency of social life. Even as a prophet of the past, however, Wordsworth kept up his protest against the system of misery that the new political economy was helping to create. Accordingly his works of every period have the eloquence of the solitary thinker for himself.

It could not have been clear to Wordsworth that he would be a revolutionary *poet*, until he met Coleridge in 1795. Indeed, something was brought to life by the meeting of the two men, which neither seems to have contained in himself. Till then Coleridge had been an eccentric avatar of the "poetical character," a disciple of Collins and Chatterton with a perfect delicacy in translation, imitation, and pastiche. Wordsworth had written some loco-descriptive poems and some shorter, drab, realistic studies of a kind that many readers would have associated with George Crabbe. When, in 1797 and 1798, he began to write ballads and meditations in a sparer diction than ever before, Coleridge encouraged his efforts immediately, and found in them a revival of the genius of English poetry. Nothing would have stopped Wordsworth from writing as he did in any case. But it was Coleridge who persuaded him that his poems were not, for all practical purposes, an anomaly, and that they gave proof of the advance of the language itself from the inspiration of Spenser and Milton. If, Coleridge reasoned, Milton had aimed to "justify the ways of God to men," his successors must aim to justify what was godlike in men. Coleridge and Wordsworth allude to this subject in various phrases, the most resonant of which is Wordsworth's "the mind of man." Yet a revised view of the poet's vocation seems to demand a revised history of poetry. Comedy, satire, most didactic and descriptive verse, everything to do with the mere costume or pursuits as distinct from the mind of man, Coleridge and Wordsworth condemned in principle. The kind of masterpiece from which the English Augustans derived their highest pleasure was now set at defiance, as proceeding from a wrong idea of poetry; the kind of energy in which Pope excelled all his contemporaries was now depreciated, beyond the possibility of a sane author's ever wishing again to emulate it. On the other hand, rebels against the dominant Augustan idiom, or those whom its leading critics had somehow defined as marginal, were cultivated as the presages of a better time to come: Gray for a few faultless lines, Thomson for exuberant fancy and Cowper for the general chastity of his diction. Like all original inventions, the poems of Coleridge and Wordsworth required not only a perception of their interest but an argument to prove their legitimacy.

Wordsworth did much of the work in the expanded version of his Preface to *Lyrical Ballads* (1802). In the disputes that followed, the usual ground of contention was Wordsworth's claim to have faithfully represented the real language of men, with the implication that this was what great poetry did. Coleridge disclaimed any attachment to such a view, and objections very similar to his may be found below on pp. 149–72, in De Quincey's essay "On Wordsworth's Poetry." But this was in fact a minor point of Wordsworth's argument – though perhaps one that he made too much of. More important was his claim that all genuine poetry was impassioned utterance, something that might be said by "men in a state of vivid sensation"; that the poet was nothing but "a man speaking to men," differing from others only in degree; that the eloquence he gained from looking steadily at his subject made him "the rock of defence for human nature"; and finally, that poetry appealed to "the grand elementary principle of pleasure" in man, "by which he knows, and feels, and lives, and moves." This last point is especially important in that it distinguishes pleasure from the state of being pleased. When Wordsworth says that "we have no sympathy but what is propagated by pleasure," it is plain that he intends the word to carry a new sense. For him, its value is at once aesthetic and moral.

One consequence of the definition is Wordsworth's almost inquisitorial concern with the sorts of pleasure his readers may properly take from reading poetry. He presumes the truth of Coleridge's dictum that "poetry which excites us to artificial feelings makes us callous to real ones"; and he seems to have supposed that a chief function of criticism is to anatomize the false modes of pleasure. The 1802 Preface gives a remarkable demonstration of his tact in such matters, by printing all of Gray's sonnet on the death of Richard West, and italicizing the five lines that have no disfiguring mannerism or counterfeit token of real emotion. His attack on the stereotyped verbal habits known as "poetic diction" – a second pair of inverted commas has to be imagined around "poetic" – was only the most conspicuous tactic in Wordsworth's labor of conquering the taste of his readers. By 1815, when the "Essay, Supplementary to the Preface" was published, he felt that the contest ought to have been won: the Preface to which it forms a companion is largely occupied with a discussion of fancy and imagination, and it is careful to illustrate both terms with substantial quotations from Wordsworth himself. But these extraordinary measures betray impatience rather than self-confidence. For his position at this time, unassailable within a small circle, was as doubtful as ever with the public at large. *Lyrical Ballads* had been accorded a modest but gratifying success, with four editions between 1798 and 1805. But the poor sales and uncomprehending criticisms of his 1807 *Poems*, and of his Burkean defence of Spanish national independence, *The Convention of Cintra*, dismayed Wordsworth sufficiently for him to withhold publication of *The White Doe of Rylstone*. His great hopes for *The Excursion* were likewise nullified by its poor reception, and the "Essay, Supplementary" must be read partly in the light of these several disappointments.

With its discourse of poetic genres and imaginative psychology, the 1815 Preface itself was evidently addressed to an audience of the converted. By contrast the "Essay, Supplementary" was written for readers who might admire certain of Wordsworth's poems, but who had not given up the customary reservations about his oddness. This may account for the occasionally ponderous didacticism of the essay, and its undercurrent of reprehension directed at unnamed critics – the chief of whom was certainly Francis Jeffrey, editor of the *Edinburgh Review*, whose dismissive article on *The Excursion* had begun, "This will never do." Wordsworth is at pains to disabuse his readers of the opinion that poetry is an exercise of wit, or a "fine art" in the practice of which the artist accommodates himself to people who know what will do. He chooses to compare it, not to the other arts, or to games or amusements, but rather to religion, since men and women are drawn to both by the sense of "something far more deeply interfused," a sense that the depth of the feeling which these callings touch in ourselves gives some promise of immortality. A confusion of the two vocations is therefore common, and may lead to the writing of devotional poetry, which in Wordsworth's view can adequately serve neither poetry nor religion.

Wordsworth's short history of English poetry, which takes up much of the essay, is offered as evidence for the assertion that no great poet can expect to be popular in his own time. Rather extravagantly he informs his readers that Spenser's reputation has fallen. Shakespeare himself, he adds, with still slenderer justification, often felt overshadowed by his contemporary rivals: had they competed for a prize, Shakespeare would of course have lost. A haphazard case is also made out for the neglect of Milton's early work, and the rightness of his decision to seek "fit audience though few." Thus Wordsworth shapes the facts to suit his thesis. Reflecting on Pope's undoubted success in his own time, he has to satisfy himself with a derisive allusion to the low arts by which he "contrived to procure" his reputation. Again, the immediate success of Thomson's *Seasons* is put down to the caprice of the audience's ignorant "wonder" having mimicked the effects of "legitimate admiration." But Thomson is an exception anyway, for, as Wordsworth remarks in an aside, "the poetry of the period intervening between the publication of the Paradise Lost and the Seasons does not contain a single new image of external nature." By a new image he means an image that is distinct (the subject having been looked at steadily), as well as one that is not yet included in the mind's habitual stock (the subject having been refreshed by juxtaposition or comparison).

After Thomson, in Wordsworth's list of heroes, come Collins in the high style, and Percy's *Reliques* in a humbler style. These are modest eminences, and they leave the way open for another great original, whose name is not given but whose lineaments are Wordsworth's own. Both the personal tone of the criticism and the concluding appeal to imagination show how far the "Essay, Supplementary" is intended as a story of the progress of poetry. Stories of this sort, concerning the successive stopping places of a spirit loftier than any individual whom it inhabits, were commonly told in verse by eighteenth-century writers, and it may be felt that Wordsworth was prudent to translate them into prose. Yet his appeal to the poet to *create* the taste by which he is to be relished – a thought he attributes to his "philosophical Friend" Coleridge – introduces something quite different from an idea of progress. It implies instead a history of catastrophic changes: a history in which, from any moment of apparent stability in an art, only personal and discontinuous reference can be made to earlier moments. In Wordsworth's account the poet himself has tremendous power in the shaping of his inheritance. The things of the past that he recognizes as great will be modified in keeping with the demands of his genius, and this is a way of saying that a new taste is created by every original, its character fixed but its limits not determined by his achievement. It follows that the sum total of such tastes is what we call the tradition, or rather the traditions, of poetry. By separating imaginative power from the imperatives of a unified history, Wordsworth urges a historicism founded wholly on individual acts of displacement or usurpation. What the poet teaches from age to age, the public must learn, for there is no equality of understanding between them. In the "Essay, Supplementary" then, as in later avant-garde manifestoes, the poet asserts the reality of a past that supports his imagination of the present. The cost of doing so is a permanent separation of his work from the familiar esteem of its readers.

1. *"Essay, Supplementary to the Preface"* [of 1815]

first published in *Poems* (1815); text of 1849–50, from *Prose Works*, ed. W. J. B. Owen and J. W. Smyser (Oxford English Texts edn, © Oxford University Press, 1974), vol. 3, pp. 62–84

WITH the young of both sexes, Poetry is, like love, a passion; but, for much the greater part of those who have been proud of its power over their minds, a necessity soon arises of breaking the pleasing bondage; or it relaxes of itself; – the thoughts being occupied in domestic cares, or the time engrossed by business. Poetry then becomes only an occasional recreation; while to those whose existence passes away in a course of fashionable pleasure, it is a species of luxurious amusement. In middle and declining age, a scattered number of serious persons resort to poetry, as to religion, for a protection against the pressure of trivial employments, and as a consolation for the afflictions of life. And, lastly, there are many, who, having been enamoured of this art in their youth, have found leisure, after youth was spent, to cultivate general literature; in which poetry has continued to be comprehended *as a study*.

Into the above classes the Readers of poetry may be divided; Critics abound in them all; but from the last only can opinions be collected of absolute value, and worthy to be depended upon, as prophetic of the destiny of a new work. The young, who in nothing can escape delusion, are especially subject to it in their intercourse with Poetry. The cause, not so obvious as the fact is unquestionable, is the same as that from which erroneous judgments in this art, in the minds of men of all ages, chiefly proceed; but upon Youth it operates with peculiar force. The appropriate business of poetry, (which, nevertheless, if genuine, is as permanent as pure science,) her appropriate employment, her privilege and her *duty*, is to treat of things not as they *are*, but as they *appear*; not as they exist in themselves, but as they *seem* to exist to the *senses*, and to the *passions*. What a world of delusion does this acknowledged obligation prepare for the inexperienced! what temptations to go astray are here held forth for them whose thoughts have been little disciplined by the understanding, and whose feelings revolt from the sway of reason! – When a juvenile Reader is in the height of his rapture with some vicious passage, should experience throw in doubts, or common-sense suggest suspicions, a lurking consciousness that the realities of the Muse are but shows, and that her liveliest excitements are raised by transient shocks of conflicting feeling and successive assemblages of contradictory thoughts – is ever at hand to justify extravagance, and to sanction absurdity. But, it may be asked, as these illusions are unavoidable, and, no doubt, eminently useful to the mind as a process, what good can be gained by making observations, the tendency of which is to diminish the confidence of youth in its feelings, and thus to abridge its innocent and even profitable pleasures? The reproach implied in the question could not be warded off, if Youth were incapable of being delighted with what is truly excellent; or, if these errors always terminated of themselves in due season. But, with the majority, though their force be abated, they continue through life. Moreover, the fire of youth is too vivacious an element to be extinguished or damped by a philosophical remark; and, while there is no danger that what has been said will be injurious or painful to the ardent and the confident, it may prove beneficial to those who, being enthusiastic, are, at the same time, modest and ingenuous. The intimation may unite with their own misgivings to regulate their sensibility, and to bring in, sooner than it would otherwise have arrived, a more discreet and sound judgment.

If it should excite wonder that men of ability, in later life, whose understandings have been rendered acute by practice in affairs, should be so easily and so far imposed upon when they happen to take up a new work in verse, this appears to be the cause; – that, having discontinued their attention to poetry, whatever progress may have been made in other departments of knowledge, they have not, as to this art, advanced in true discernment beyond the age of youth. If, then, a new poem fall in their way, whose attractions are of that kind which would have enraptured them during the heat of youth, the judgment not being improved to a degree that they shall be disgusted, they are dazzled; and prize and cherish the faults for having had power to make the present time vanish before them, and to throw the mind back, as by enchantment, into the happiest season of life. As they read, powers seem to be revived, passions are regenerated, and pleasures restored. The Book was probably taken up after an escape from the burden of business, and with a wish to forget the world, and all its vexations and anxieties. Having obtained this wish, and so much more, it is natural that they should make report as they have felt.

If Men of mature age, through want of practice, be thus easily beguiled into admiration of absurdities, extravagances, and misplaced ornaments, thinking it proper that their understandings should enjoy a holiday, while they are unbending their minds with verse, it may be expected that such Readers will resemble their former selves also in strength of prejudice, and an inaptitude to be moved by the unostentatious beauties of a pure style. In the higher poetry, an enlightened Critic chiefly looks for a reflection of the wisdom of the heart and the grandeur of the imagination. Wherever these appear, simplicity accompanies them; Magnificence herself, when legitimate, depending upon a simplicity of her own, to regulate her ornaments. But it is a well-known property of human nature, that our estimates are ever governed by comparisons, of which we are conscious with various degrees of distinctness. Is it not, then, inevitable (confining these observations to the effects of style merely) that an eye, accustomed to the glaring hues of diction by which such Readers are caught and excited, will for the most part be rather repelled than attracted by an original Work, the colouring of which is disposed according to a pure and refined scheme of harmony? It is in the fine arts as in the affairs of life, no man can *serve* (i.e. obey with zeal and fidelity) two Masters.

As Poetry is most just to its own divine origin when it administers the comforts and breathes the spirit of religion, they who have learned to perceive this truth, and who betake themselves to reading verse for sacred purposes, must be preserved from numerous illusions to which the two Classes of Readers, whom we have been considering, are liable. But, as the mind grows serious from the weight of life, the range of its passions is contracted accordingly; and its sympathies become so exclusive, that many species of high excellence wholly escape, or but languidly excite, its notice. Besides, men who read from religious or moral inclinations, even when the subject is of that kind which they approve, are beset with misconceptions and mistakes peculiar to themselves. Attaching so much importance to the truths which interest them, they are prone to over-rate the Authors by whom those truths are expressed and enforced. They come prepared to impart so much passion to the Poet's language, that they remain unconscious how little, in fact, they receive from it. And, on the other hand, religious faith is to him who holds it so momentous a thing, and error appears to be attended with such tremendous consequences, that, if opinions touching upon religion occur which the Reader condemns, he not only cannot sympathise with them, however animated the expression, but there is, for the most part, an end put to all satisfaction and enjoyment. Love, if it before existed, is converted into dislike; and the heart of the Reader is set against the Author and his book. – To these excesses, they, who from their professions ought to be the most guarded against them, are perhaps the most liable; I mean those sects whose religion, being from the calculating understanding, is cold and formal. For when Christianity, the religion of humility, is founded upon the proudest faculty of our nature, what can be expected but contradictions? Accordingly, believers of this cast are at one time contemptuous; at another, being troubled, as they are and must be, with inward misgivings, they are jealous and suspicious; – and at all seasons, they are under temptation to supply by the heat with which they defend their tenets, the animation which is wanting to the constitution of the religion itself.

Faith was given to man that his affections, detached from the treasures of time, might be inclined to settle upon those of eternity; – the elevation of his nature, which this habit produces on earth, being to him a presumptive evidence of a future state of existence; and giving him a title to partake of its holiness. The religious man values what he sees chiefly as an "imperfect shadowing forth" of what he is incapable of seeing. The concerns of religion refer to indefinite objects, and are too weighty for the mind to support them without relieving itself by resting a great part of the burthen upon words and symbols. The commerce between Man and his Maker cannot be carried on but by a process where much is represented in little, and the Infinite Being accommodates himself to a finite capacity. In all this may be perceived the affinity between religion and poetry; between religion – making up the deficiencies of reason by faith; and poetry – passionate for the instruction of reason; between religion – whose element is infinitude, and whose ultimate trust is the supreme of things, submitting herself to circumscription, and reconciled to substitutions; and poetry – ethereal and transcendent, yet incapable to sustain her existence without sensuous incarnation. In this community of nature may be perceived also the lurking incitements of kindred error; – so that we shall find that no poetry has been more subject to distortion, than that species, the argument and scope of which is religious; and no lovers of the art have gone farther astray than the pious and the devout.[1]

Whither then shall we turn for that union of qualifications which must necessarily exist before the decisions of a critic can be of absolute value? For a mind at once poetical and philosophical; for a critic whose affections are as free and kindly as the spirit of society, and whose understanding is severe as that of dispassionate government? Where are we to look for that initiatory composure of mind which no selfishness can disturb? For a natural sensibility that has been tutored into correctness without losing anything of its quickness; and for active faculties, capable of answering the demands which an Author of original imagination shall make upon them, associated with a judgment that cannot be duped into admiration by aught that is unworthy of it? – among those and those only, who, never having suffered their youthful love of poetry to remit much of its force, have applied to the consideration of the laws of this art the best power of their understandings. At the same time it must be observed – that, as this Class comprehends the only judgments which are trust-worthy, so does it include the most erroneous and perverse. For to be mistaught is worse than to be untaught; and no perverseness equals that which is supported by system, no errors are so difficult to root out as those which the understanding has pledged its credit to uphold. In this Class are contained censors, who, if they be pleased with what is good, are pleased with it only by imperfect glimpses, and upon false principles; who, should they generalise rightly, to a certain point, are sure to suffer for it in the end; who, if they stumble upon a sound rule, are fettered by misapplying it, or by straining it too far; being incapable of perceiving when it ought to yield to one of higher order. In it are found critics too petulant to be passive to a genuine poet, and too feeble to grapple with him; men, who take upon them to report of the course which *he* holds whom they are utterly unable to accompany, – confounded if he turn quick upon the wing, dismayed if he soar steadily "into the region;" – men of palsied imaginations and indurated hearts; in whose minds all healthy action is languid, who therefore feed as the many direct them, or, with the many, are greedy after vicious provocatives; – judges, whose censure is auspicious, and whose praise ominous! In this class meet together the two extremes of best and worst.

The observations presented in the foregoing series are of too ungracious a nature to have been made without reluctance; and, were it only on this account, I would invite the reader to try them by the test of comprehensive experience. If the number of judges who can be confidently relied upon be in reality so small, it ought to follow that partial notice only, or neglect, perhaps long continued, or attention wholly inadequate to their merits – must have been the fate of most works in the higher departments of poetry; and that, on the other hand, numerous productions have blazed into popularity, and have passed away, leaving scarcely a trace behind them: it will be further found, that when Authors shall have at length raised themselves into general admiration and maintained their ground, errors and prejudices have prevailed concerning their genius and their works, which the few who are conscious of those errors and prejudices would deplore; if they were not recompensed by perceiving that there are select Spirits for whom it is ordained that their fame shall be in the world an existence like that of Virtue, which owes its being to the struggles it makes, and its vigour to the enemies whom it provokes; – a vivacious quality, ever doomed to meet with opposition, and still triumphing over it; and, from the nature of its dominion, incapable of being brought to the sad conclusion of Alexander, when he wept that there were no more worlds for him to conquer.

Let us take a hasty retrospect of the poetical literature of this Country for the greater part of the last two centuries, and see if the facts support these inferences.

Who is there that now reads the "Creation" of Dubartas? Yet all Europe once resounded with his praise; he was caressed by kings; and, when his Poem was translated into our language, the Faery Queen faded before it. The name of Spenser, whose genius is of a higher order than even that of Ariosto, is at this day scarcely known beyond the limits of the British Isles.[2] And if the value of his works is to be estimated from the attention now paid to them by his countrymen, compared with that which they bestow on those of some other writers, it must be pronounced small indeed.

> "The laurel, meed of mighty conquerors
> And poets *sage*" – [a]

are his own words; but his wisdom has, in this particular, been his worst enemy: while its opposite, whether in the shape of folly or madness, has been *their* best friend. But he was a great power, and bears a high name: the laurel has been awarded to him.

A dramatic Author, if he write for the stage, must adapt himself to the taste of the audience, or they will not endure him; accordingly the mighty genius of Shakspeare was listened to. The people were delighted: but I am not sufficiently versed in stage antiquities to determine whether they did not flock as eagerly to the representation of many pieces of contemporary Authors, wholly undeserving to appear upon the same boards. Had there been a formal contest for superiority among dramatic writers, that Shakspeare, like his pre-

---

[a] *Faerie Queene*, Book I canto i st. 9

decessors Sophocles and Euripides, would have often been subject to the mortification of seeing the prize adjudged to sorry competitors, becomes too probable, when we reflect that the admirers of Settle and Shadwell[3] were, in a later age, as numerous, and reckoned as respectable in point of talent, as those of Dryden. At all events, that Shakspeare stooped to accommodate himself to the People, is sufficiently apparent; and one of the most striking proofs of his almost omnipotent genius, is, that he could turn to such glorious purpose those materials which the prepossessions of the age compelled him to make use of. Yet even this marvellous skill appears not to have been enough to prevent his rivals from having some advantage over him in public estimation; else how can we account for passages and scenes that exist in his works, unless upon a supposition that some of the grossest of them, a fact which in my own mind I have no doubt of, were foisted in by the Players, for the gratification of the many?

But that his Works, whatever might be their reception upon the stage, made but little impression upon the ruling Intellects of the time, may be inferred from the fact that Lord Bacon, in his multifarious writings, nowhere either quotes or alludes to him. His dramatic excellence enabled him to resume possession of the stage after the Restoration; but Dryden tells us that in his time two of the plays of Beaumont and Fletcher were acted for one of Shakspeare's. And so faint and limited was the perception of the poetic beauties of his dramas in the time of Pope, that, in his Edition of the Plays, with a view to rendering to the general reader a necessary service, he printed between inverted commas those passages which he thought most worthy of notice.

At this day, the French Critics have abated nothing of their aversion to this darling of our Nation: "the English, with their bouffon de Shakspeare," is as familiar an expression among them as in the time of Voltaire.[4] Baron Grimm is the only French writer who seems to have perceived his infinite superiority to the first names of the French Theatre; an advantage which the Parisian Critic owed to his German blood and German education.[5] The most enlightened Italians, though well acquainted with our language, are wholly incompetent to measure the proportions of Shakspeare. The Germans only, of foreign nations, are approaching towards a knowledge and feeling of what he is. In some respects they have acquired a superiority over the fellow-countrymen of the Poet: for among us it is a current, I might say, an established opinion, that Shakspeare is justly praised when he is pronounced to be "a wild irregular genius, in whom great faults are compensated by great beauties."[a] How long may it be before this misconception passes away, and it becomes universally acknowledged that the judgment of Shakspeare in the selection of his materials, and in the manner in which he has made them, heterogeneous as they often are, constitute a unity of their own, and contribute all to one great end, is not less admirable than his imagination, his invention, and his intuitive knowledge of human Nature?

There is extant a small Volume of miscellaneous poems, in which Shakspeare expresses his own feelings in his own person. It is not difficult to conceive that the Editor, George Steevens, should have been insensible to the beauties of one portion of that Volume, the Sonnets:[6] though in no part of the writings of this Poet is found, in an equal compass, a greater number of exquisite feelings felicitously expressed. But, from regard to the Critic's own credit, he would not have ventured to talk of an act of parliament not being strong enough to compel the perusal of those little pieces, if he had not known that the people of England were ignorant of the treasures contained in them: and if he had not, moreover, shared the too common propensity of human nature to exult over a supposed fall into the mire of a genius whom he had been compelled to regard with admiration, as an inmate of the celestial regions – "there sitting where he durst not soar."[b]

Nine years before the death of Shakspeare, Milton was born; and early in life he published several small poems, which, though on their first appearance they were praised by a few of the judicious, were afterwards neglected to that degree, that Pope in his youth could borrow from them without risk of its being known. Whether these poems are at this day justly appreciated, I will not undertake to decide: nor would it imply a severe reflection upon the mass of readers to suppose the contrary; seeing that a man of the acknowledged genius of Voss, the German poet, could suffer their spirit to evaporate; and could change their characters, as is done in the translation made by him of the most popular of those pieces.[7] At all events, it is certain that these Poems of Milton are now much read, and loudly praised; yet were they little heard of till more than 150 years after their publication; and of the Sonnets, Dr. Johnson, as appears from Boswell's Life of him, was in the habit of thinking and speaking as contemptuously as Steevens wrote upon those of Shakspeare.

About the time when the Pindaric odes of Cowley and his imitators, and the productions of that class of curious thinkers whom

[a] a standard neoclassical estimate of Shakespeare, deliberately stereotyped by Wordsworth
[b] *Paradise Lost*, IV. 829

Dr. Johnson has strangely styled metaphysical Poets, were beginning to lose something of that extravagant admiration which they had excited, the Paradise Lost made its appearance. "Fit audience find though few," was the petition addressed by the Poet to his inspiring Muse. I have said elsewhere that he gained more than he asked:[8] this I believe to be true; but Dr. Johnson has fallen into a gross mistake when he attempts to prove, by the sale of the work, that Milton's Countrymen were *"just* to it" upon its first appearance. Thirteen hundred Copies were sold in two years; an uncommon example, he asserts, of the prevalence of genius in opposition to so much recent enmity as Milton's public conduct had excited. But, be it remembered that, if Milton's political and religious opinions, and the manner in which he announced them, had raised him many enemies, they had procured him numerous friends; who, as all personal danger was passed away at the time of publication, would be eager to procure the master-work of a man whom they revered, and whom they would be proud of praising. Take, from the number of purchasers, persons of this class, and also those who wished to possess the Poem as a religious work, and but few I fear would be left who sought for it on account of its poetical merits. The demand did not immediately increase; "for," says Dr. Johnson, "many more readers" (he means persons in the habit of reading poetry) "than were supplied at first the Nation did not afford." How careless must a writer be who can make this assertion in the face of so many existing title-pages to belie it! Turning to my own shelves, I find the folio of Cowley, seventh edition, 1681. A book near it is Flatman's Poems, fourth edition, 1686; Waller, fifth edition, same date. The Poems of Norris of Bemerton not long after went, I believe, through nine editions. What further demand there might be for these works I do not know; but I well remember, that, twenty-five years ago, the booksellers' stalls in London swarmed with the folios of Cowley. This is not mentioned in disparagement of that able writer and amiable man; but merely to show – that, if Milton's work were not more read, it was not because readers did not exist at the time. The early editions of the Paradise Lost were printed in a shape which allowed them to be sold at a low price, yet only three thousand copies of the Work were sold in eleven years; and the Nation, says Dr. Johnson, had been satisfied from 1623 to 1664, that is, forty-one years, with only two editions of the Works of Shakspeare; which probably did not together make one-thousand Copies; facts adduced by the critic to prove the "paucity of Readers." – There were readers in multitudes; but their money went for other purposes, as their admiration was fixed elsewhere. We are authorised, then, to affirm, that the reception of the Paradise Lost, and the slow progress of its fame, are proofs as striking as can be desired that the positions which I am attempting to establish are not erroneous. – How amusing to shape to one's self such a critique as a Wit of Charles's days, or a Lord of the Miscellanies or trading Journalist of King William's time, would have brought forth, if he had set his faculties industriously to work upon this Poem, everywhere impregnated with *original* excellence.

So strange indeed are the obliquities of admiration, that they whose opinions are much influenced by authority will often be tempted to think that there are no fixed principles in human nature for this art to rest upon.[9] I have been honoured by being permitted to peruse in MS. a tract composed between the period of the Revolution and the close of that century. It is the Work of an English peer of high accomplishments, its object to form the character and direct the studies of his son. Perhaps nowhere does a more beautiful treatise of the kind exist. The good sense and wisdom of the thoughts, the delicacy of the feelings, and the charm of the style, are, throughout, equally conspicuous. Yet the Author, selecting among the Poets of his own country those whom he deems most worthy of his son's perusal, particularises only Lord Rochester, Sir John Denham, and Cowley. Writing about the same time, Shaftesbury, an author at present unjustly depreciated, describes the English Muses as only yet lisping in their cradles.[10]

The arts by which Pope, soon afterwards, contrived to procure to himself a more general and a higher reputation than perhaps any English Poet ever attained during his life-time, are known to the judicious. And as well known is it to them, that the undue exertion of those arts is the cause why Pope has for some time held a rank in literature, to which, if he had not been seduced by an over-love of immediate popularity, and had confided more in his native genius, he never could have descended. He bewitched the nation by his melody, and dazzled it by his polished style, and was himself blinded by his own success. Having wandered from humanity in his Eclogues with boyish inexperience, the praise, which these compositions obtained, tempted him into a belief that Nature was not to be trusted, at least in pastoral Poetry. To prove this by example, he put his friend Gay upon writing those Eclogues which their author intended to be burlesque. The instigator of the work, and his admirers, could perceive in them nothing but what was ridiculous. Nevertheless, though these Poems contain some detestable passages, the effect, as Dr. Johnson well observes, "of reality and truth became conspicuous even when the intention was to show them grovelling and degraded." The Pastorals, ludicrous to such as prided themselves upon their refinement, in spite of those disgusting passages, "became popular, and were read with delight, as just representations of rural manners and occupations."

Something less than sixty years after the publication of the Paradise Lost appeared Thomson's Winter; which was speedily followed by his other Seasons. It is a work of inspiration; much of it is written from himself, and nobly from himself. How was it received? "It was no sooner read," says one of his contemporary biographers, "than universally admired: those only excepted who had not been used to feel, or to look for anything in poetry, beyond a *point* of satirical or epigrammatic wit, a smart *antithesis* richly trimmed with rhyme, or the softness of an *elegiac* complaint. To such his manly classical spirit could not readily commend itself; till, after a more attentive perusal, they had got the better of their prejudices, and either acquired or affected a truer taste. A few others stood aloof, merely because they had long before fixed the articles of their poetical creed, and resigned themselves to an absolute despair of ever seeing any thing new and original. These were somewhat mortified to find their notions disturbed by the appearance of a poet, who seemed to owe nothing but to nature and his own genius. But, in a short time, the applause became unanimous; every one wondering how so many pictures, and pictures so familiar, should have moved them but faintly to what they felt in his descriptions. His digressions too, the overflowings of a tender benevolent heart, charmed the reader no less; leaving him in doubt, whether he should more admire the Poet or love the Man."[11]

This case appears to bear strongly against us: − but we must distinguish between wonder and legitimate admiration. The subject of the work is the changes produced in the appearances of nature by the revolution of the year: and, by undertaking to write in verse, Thomson pledged himself to treat his subject as became a Poet. Now it is remarkable that, excepting the nocturnal Reverie of Lady Winchilsea, and a passage or two in the Windsor Forest of Pope, the poetry of the period intervening between the publication of the Paradise Lost and the Seasons does not contain a single new image of external nature; and scarcely presents a familiar one from which it can be inferred that the eye of the Poet had been steadily fixed upon his object, much less that his feelings had urged him to work upon it in the spirit of genuine imagination. To what a low state knowledge of the most obvious and important phenomena had sunk, is evident from the style in which Dryden has executed a description of Night in one of his Tragedies and Pope his translation of the celebrated moonlight scene in the Iliad.[a] A blind man, in the habit of attending accurately to descriptions casually dropped from the lips of those around him, might easily depict these appearances with more truth. Dryden's lines are vague, bombastic, and senseless;[12] those of Pope, though he had Homer to guide him, are throughout false and contradictory. The verses of Dryden, once highly celebrated, are forgotten; those of Pope still retain their hold upon public estimation, – nay, there is not a passage of descriptive poetry, which at this day finds so many and such ardent admirers. Strange to think of an enthusiast, as may have been the case with thousands, reciting those verses under the cope of a moonlight sky, without having his raptures in the least disturbed by a suspicion of their absurdity! – If these two distinguished writers could habitually think that the visible universe was of so little consequence to a poet, that it was scarcely necessary for him to cast his eyes upon it, we may be assured that those passages of the elder poets which faithfully and poetically describe the phenomena of nature, were not at that time holden in much estimation, and that there was little accurate attention paid to those appearances.[13]

Wonder is the natural product of Ignorance; and as the soil was *in such good condition* at the time of the publication of the Seasons, the crop was doubtless abundant. Neither individuals nor nations become corrupt all at once, nor are they enlightened in a moment. Thomson was an inspired poet, but he could not work miracles; in cases where the art of seeing had in some degree been learned, the teacher would further the proficiency of his pupils, but he could do little *more*; though so far does vanity assist men in acts of self-deception, that many would often fancy they recognised a likeness when they knew nothing of the original. Having shown that much of what his biographer deemed genuine admiration must in fact have been blind wonderment – how is the rest to be accounted for? – Thomson was fortunate in the very title of his poem, which seemed to bring it home to the prepared sympathies of every one: in the next place, notwithstanding his high powers, he writes a vicious style; and his false ornaments are exactly of that kind which would be most likely to strike the undiscerning. He likewise abounds with sentimental common-places, that, from the manner in which they were brought forward, bore an imposing air of novelty. In any well-used copy of the Seasons the book generally opens of itself with the rhapsody on love, or with one of the stories (perhaps Damon and Musidora); these also are prominent in our collections of Extracts,

[a] *Iliad* (Pope's translation), VIII. 687–92

and are the parts of his Work, which, after all, were probably most efficient in first recommending the author to general notice. Pope, repaying praises which he had received, and wishing to extol him to the highest, only styles him "an elegant and philosophical Poet;" nor are we able to collect any unquestionable proofs that the true characteristics of Thomson's genius as an imaginative poet were perceived, till the elder Warton,[14] almost forty years after the publication of the Seasons, pointed them out by a note in his Essay on the Life and Writings of Pope. In the Castle of Indolence (of which Gray speaks so coldly) these characteristics were almost as conspicuously displayed, and in verse more harmonious, and diction more pure. Yet that fine poem was neglected on its appearance, and is at this day the delight only of a few!

When Thomson died, Collins breathed forth his regrets in an Elegiac Poem, in which he pronounces a poetical curse upon *him* who should regard with insensibility the place where the Poet's remains were deposited.[15] The Poems of the mourner himself have now passed through innumerable editions, and are universally known; but if, when Collins died, the same kind of imprecation had been pronounced by a surviving admirer, small is the number whom it would not have comprehended. The notice which his poems attained during his life-time was so small, and of course the sale so insignificant, that not long before his death he deemed it right to repay to the bookseller the sum which he had advanced for them, and threw the edition into the fire.

Next in importance to the Seasons of Thomson, though at considerable distance from that work in order of time, come the Reliques of Ancient English Poetry; collected, new-modelled, and in many instances (if such a contradiction in terms may be used) composed by the Editor, Dr. Percy.[16] This work did not steal silently into the world, as is evident from the number of legendary tales, that appeared not long after its publication; and had been modelled, as the authors persuaded themselves, after the old Ballad. The Compilation was however ill suited to the then existing taste of city society; and Dr. Johnson, 'mid the little senate to which he gave laws, was not sparing in his exertions to make it an object of contempt. The critic triumphed, the legendary imitators were deservedly disregarded, and, as undeservedly, their ill-imitated models sank, in this country, into temporary neglect; while Bürger,[17] and other able writers of Germany, were translating, or imitating these Reliques and composing, with the aid of inspiration thence derived, poems which are the delight of the German nation. Dr. Percy was so abashed by the ridicule flung upon his labours from the ignorance and insensibility of the persons with whom he lived, that, though while he was writing under a mask he had not wanted resolution to follow his genius into the regions of true simplicity and genuine pathos (as is evinced by the exquisite ballad of Sir Cauline and by many other pieces), yet when he appeared in his own person and character as a poetical writer, he adopted, as in the tale of the Hermit of Warkworth, a diction scarcely in any one of its features distinguishable from the vague, the glossy, and unfeeling language of his day. I mention this remarkable fact with regret, esteeming the genius of Dr. Percy in this kind of writing superior to that of any other man by whom in modern times it has been cultivated. That even Bürger (to whom Klopstock gave, in my hearing, a commendation which he denied to Goethe and Schiller, pronouncing him to be a genuine poet,[18] and one of the few among the Germans whose works would last) had not the fine sensibility of Percy, might be shown from many passages, in which he has deserted his original only to go astray. For example,

> Now daye was gone, and night was come,
> And all were fast asleepe,
> All save the Lady Emeline,
> Who sate in her bowre to weepe:

> And soone she heard her true Love's voice
> Low whispering at the walle,
> Awake, awake my dear Ladye,
> 'Tis I thy true-love call.

Which is thus tricked out and dilated:

> Als nun die Nacht Gebirg' und Thal
> Vermummt in Rabenschatten,
> Und Hochburgs Lampen überall
> Schon ausgeflimmert hatten,
> Und alles tief entschlafen war;
> Doch nur das Fräulein immerdar,
> Voll Fieberangst, noch wachte,
> Und seinen Ritter dachte:
> Da horch! Ein süsser Liebeston
> Kam leis' empor geflogen
> "Ho, Trudchen, ho! Da bin ich schon!
> Risch auf! Dich angezogen!"[a]

[a] As evening now closed in, and dusk
Unfurled its raven wings,
And fluttering castle torches left
Their glimmer on all things,

And all lay ravelled up in sleep,
The Lady, evermore,

But from humble ballads we must ascend to heroics.

All hail, Macpherson! hail to thee, Sire of Ossain! The Phantom was begotten by the snug embrace of an impudent Highlander upon a cloud of tradition – it travelled southward, where it was greeted with acclamation, and the thin Consistence took its course through Europe, upon the breath of popular applause. The Editor of the "Reliques" had indirectly preferred a claim to the praise of invention, by not concealing that his supplementary labours were considerable! how selfish his conduct, contrasted with that of the disinterested Gael, who, like Lear, gives his kingdom away, and is content to become a pensioner upon his own issue for a beggarly pittance! – Open this far-famed Book! – I have done so at random, and the beginning of the "Epic Poem Temora," in eight Books, presents itself. "The blue waves of Ullin roll in light. The green hills are covered with day. Trees shake their dusky heads in the breeze. Grey torrents pour their noisy streams. Two green hills with aged oaks surround a narrow plain. The blue course of a stream is there. On its banks stood Cairbar of Atha. His spear supports the king; the red eyes of his fear are sad. Cormac rises on his soul with all his ghastly wounds." Precious memorandums from the pocket-book of the blind Ossian![19]

If it be unbecoming, as I acknowledge that for the most part it is, to speak disrespectfully of Works that have enjoyed for a length of time a widely-spread reputation, without at the same time producing irrefragable proofs of their unworthiness, let me be forgiven upon this occasion. – Having had the good fortune to be born and reared in a mountainous country, from my very childhood I have felt the falsehood that pervades the volumes imposed upon the world under the name of Ossian. From what I saw with my own eyes, I knew that the imagery was spurious. In nature every thing is distinct, yet nothing defined into absolute independent singleness. In Macpherson's work, it is exactly the reverse; every thing (that is not stolen) is in this manner defined, insulated, dislocated, deadened, – yet nothing distinct. It will always be so when words are substituted for things. To say that the characters never could exist, that the manners are impossible, and that a dream has more substance than the whole state of society, as there depicted, is doing nothing more than pro-

Dreamed wakefully her gentle knight
Would come, as knights of yore.

But hark! a faint, hushed, lover's call
Rose up to calm her sighs.
"Halloo, my Trudy dear, Halloo!
I'm with thee now! Arise!"

nouncing a censure which Macpherson defied; when, with the steeps of Morven before his eyes, he could talk so familiarly of his Car-borne heroes; – of Morven, which, if one may judge from its appearance at the distance of a few miles, contains scarcely an acre of ground sufficiently accommodating for a sledge to be trailed along its surface. – Mr. Malcolm Laing has ably shown that the diction of this pretended translation is a motley assemblage from all quarters; but he is so fond of making out parallel passages as to call poor Macpherson to account for his "*ands*" and his "*buts!*" and he has weakened his argument by conducting it as if he thought that every striking resemblance was a *conscious* plagiarism.[20] It is enough that the coincidences are too remarkable for its being probable or possible that they could arise in different minds without communication between them. Now as the Translators of the Bible, and Shakspeare, Milton, and Pope, could not be indebted to Macpherson, it follows that he must have owed his fine feathers to them; unless we are prepared gravely to assert, with Madame de Staël, that many of the characteristic beauties of our most celebrated English Poets are derived from the ancient Fingallian; in which case the modern translator would have been but giving back to Ossian his own.[21] – It is consistent that Lucien Buonaparte, who could censure Milton for having surrounded Satan in the infernal regions with courtly and regal splendour, should pronounce the modern Ossian to be the glory of Scotland; – a country that has produced a Dunbar, a Buchanan, a Thomson, and a Burns! These opinions are of ill omen for the Epic ambition of him who has given them to the world.[22]

Yet, much as those pretended treasures of antiquity have been admired, they have been wholly uninfluential upon the literature of the Country. No succeeding writer appears to have caught from them a ray of inspiration; no author, in the least distinguished, has ventured formally to imitate them – except the boy, Chatterton, on their first appearance. He had perceived, from the successful trials which he himself had made in literary forgery, how few critics were able to distinguish between a real ancient medal and a counterfeit of modern manufacture; and he set himself to the work of filling a magazine with *Saxon Poems*, – counterparts of those of Ossian, as like his as one of his misty stars is to another.[23] This incapability to amalgamate with the literature of the Island, is, in my estimation, a decisive proof that the book is essentially unnatural; nor should I require any other to demonstrate it to be a forgery, audacious as worthless. – Contrast, in this respect, the effect of Macpherson's publication with the Reliques of Percy, so unassuming, so modest in their pretensions! – I have already stated how much Germany is indebted to this latter work; and for our own country, its poetry has been absolutely redeemed by it. I do not think that there is an able writer in verse of the present day who would not be proud to acknowledge his obligations to the Reliques; I know that it is so with my friends; and, for myself, I am happy in this occasion to make a public avowal of my own.

Dr. Johnson, more fortunate in his contempt of the labours of Macpherson than those of his modest friend, was solicited not long after to furnish Prefaces biographical and critical for the works of some of the most eminent English Poets. The booksellers took upon themselves to make the collection; they referred probably to the most popular miscellanies, and, unquestionably, to their books of accounts; and decided upon the claim of authors to be admitted into a body of the most eminent, from the familiarity of their names with the readers of that day, and by the profits, which, from the sale of his works, each had brought and was bringing to the Trade. The Editor was allowed a limited exercise of discretion, and the Authors whom he recommended are scarcely to be mentioned without a smile. We open the volume of Prefatory Lives, and to our astonishment the *first* name we find is that of Cowley! – What is become of the morning-star of English Poetry? Where is the bright Elizabethan constellation? Or, if names be more acceptable than images, where is the ever-to-be-honoured Chaucer? where is Spenser? where Sidney? and, lastly, where he, whose rights as a poet, contradistinguished from those which he is universally allowed to possess as a dramatist, we have vindicated, – where Shakspeare?[24] – These, and a multitude of others not unworthy to be placed near them, their contemporaries and successors, we have *not*. But in their stead, we have (could better be expected when precedence was to be settled by an abstract of reputation at any given period made, as in this case before us?) Roscommon, and Stepney, and Phillips, and Walsh, and Smith, and Duke, and King, and Spratt – Halifax, Granville, Sheffield, Congreve, Broome, and other reputed Magnates – metrical writers utterly worthless and useless, except for occasions like the present, when their productions are referred to as evidence what a small quantity of brain is necessary to procure a considerable stock of admiration, provided the aspirant will accommodate himself to the likings and fashions of his day.

As I do not mean to bring down this retrospect to our own times, it may with propriety be closed at the era of this distinguished event. From the literature of other ages and countries, proofs equally cogent might have been adduced, that the opinions announced in the former part of this Essay are founded upon truth. It was not an agreeable office, nor a prudent undertaking, to declare them; but their importance seemed to render it a duty. It may still be asked, where lies the particular relation of what has been said to these Volumes? – The question will be easily answered by the discerning Reader who is old enough to remember the taste that prevailed when some of these poems were first published, seventeen years ago; who has also observed to what degree the poetry of this Island has since that period been coloured by them; and who is further aware of the unremitting hostility with which, upon some principle or other, they have each and all been opposed. A sketch of my own notion of the constitution of Fame has been given; and, as far as concerns myself, I have cause to be satisfied. The love, the admiration, the indifference, the slight, the aversion, and even the contempt, with which these Poems have been received, knowing, as I do, the source within my own mind, from which they have proceeded, and the labour and pains, which, when labour and pains appeared needful, have been bestowed upon them, must all, if I think consistently, be received as pledges and tokens, bearing the same general impression, though widely different in value; – they are all proofs that for the present time I have not laboured in vain; and afford assurances, more or less authentic, that the products of my industry will endure.

If there be one conclusion more forcibly pressed upon us than another by the review which has been given of the fortunes and fate of poetical Works, it is this, – that every author, as far as he is great and at the same time *original*, has had the task of *creating* the taste by which he is to be enjoyed: so has it been, so will it continue to be. This remark was long since made to me by the philosophical Friend[a] for the separation of whose poems from my own I have previously expressed my regret. The predecessors of an original Genius of a high order will have smoothed the way for all that he has in common with them; – and much he will have in common; but, for what is peculiarly his own, he will be called upon to clear and often to shape his own road: – he will be in the condition of Hannibal among the Alps.

And where lies the real difficulty of creating that taste by which a truly original poet is to be relished? Is it in breaking the bonds of custom, in overcoming the prejudices of false refinement, and displacing the aversions of inexperience? Or, if he labour for an object which here and elsewhere I have proposed to myself, does it consist in divesting the reader of the pride that induces him to dwell upon

[a] Coleridge

those points wherein men differ from each other, to the exclusion of those in which all men are alike, or the same; and in making him ashamed of the vanity that renders him insensible of the appropriate excellence which civil arrangements, less unjust than might appear, and Nature illimitable in her bounty, have conferred on men who may stand below him in the scale of society? Finally, does it lie in establishing that dominion over the spirits of readers by which they are to be humbled and humanised, in order that they may be purified and exalted?

If these ends are to be attained by the mere communication of *knowledge*, it does *not* lie here. – TASTE, I would remind the reader, like IMAGINATION, is a word which has been forced to extend its services far beyond the point to which philosophy would have confined them. It is a metaphor, taken from a *passive* sense of the human body, and transferred to things which are in their essence *not* passive, – to intellectual *acts* and *operations*. The word, Imagination, has been over strained, from impulses honourable to mankind, to meet the demands of the faculty which is perhaps the noblest of our nature. In the instance of Taste, the process has been reversed; and from the prevalence of dispositions at once injurious and discreditable, being no other than that selfishness which is the child of apathy, – which, as Nations decline in productive and creative power, makes them value themselves upon a presumed refinement of judging. Poverty of language is the primary cause of the use which we make of the word, Imagination; but the word, Taste, has been stretched to the sense which it bears in modern Europe by habits of self-conceit, inducing that inversion in the order of things whereby a passive faculty is made paramount among the faculties conversant with the fine arts. Proportion and congruity, the requisite knowledge being supposed, are subjects upon which taste may be trusted; it is competent to this office; – for in its intercourse with these the mind is *passive*, and is affected painfully or pleasurably as by an instinct. But the profound and the exquisite in feeling, the lofty and universal in thought and imagination; or, in ordinary language, the pathetic and the sublime; – are neither of them, accurately speaking, objects of a faculty which could ever without a sinking in the spirit of Nations have been designated by the metaphor – *Taste*. And why? Because without the exertion of a co-operating *power* in the mind of the Reader, there can be no adequate sympathy with either of these emotions: without this auxiliary impulse, elevated or profound passion cannot exist.

Passion, it must be observed, is derived from a word which signifies *suffering*; but the connection which suffering has with effort, with exertion, and *action*, is immediate and inseparable. How strikingly is this property of human nature exhibited by the fact, that, in popular language, to be in a passion, is to be angry! – But,

> "Anger in hasty *words* or *blows*
> Itself discharges on its foes."[a]

To be moved, then, by a passion, is to be excited, often to external, and always to internal, effort; whether for the continuance and strengthening of the passion, or for its suppression, accordingly as the course which it takes may be painful or pleasurable. If the latter, the soul must contribute to its support, or it never becomes vivid, – and soon languishes, and dies. And this brings us to the point. If every great poet with whose writings men are familiar, in the highest exercise of his genius, before he can be thoroughly enjoyed, has to call forth and to communicate *power*, this service, in a still greater degree, falls upon an original writer, at his first appearance in the world. – Of genius the only proof is, the act of doing well what is worthy to be done, and what was never done before: Of genius, in the fine arts, the only infallible sign is the widening the sphere of human sensibility, for the delight, honour, and benefit of human nature. Genius is the introduction of a new element into the intellectual universe: or, if that be not allowed, it is the application of powers to objects on which they had not before been exercised, or the employment of them in such a manner as to produce effects hitherto unknown. What is all this but an advance, or a conquest, made by the soul of the poet? Is it to be supposed that the reader can make progress of this kind, like an Indian prince or general – stretched on his palanquin, and borne by his slaves? No; he is invigorated and inspirited by his leader, in order that he may exert himself; for he cannot proceed in quiescence, he cannot be carried like a dead weight. Therefore to create taste is to call forth and bestow power, of which knowledge is the effect; and *there* lies the true difficulty.

As the pathetic participates of an *animal* sensation, it might seem – that, if the springs of this emotion were genuine, all men, possessed of competent knowledge of the facts and circumstances, would be instantaneously affected. And, doubtless, in the works of every true poet will be found passages of that species of excellence, which is proved by effects immediate and universal. But there are emotions of the pathetic that are simple and direct, and others – that are complex and revolutionary; some – to which the heart yields with gentleness;

---

[a] Waller, "Of Love"

others – against which it struggles with pride; these varieties are infinite as the combinations of circumstance and the constitutions of character. Remember, also, that the medium through which, in poetry, the heart is to be affected, is language; a thing subject to endless fluctuations and arbitrary associations. The genius of the poet melts these down for his purpose; but they retain their shape and quality to him who is not capable of exerting, within his own mind, a corresponding energy. There is also a meditative, as well as a human, pathos; an enthusiastic, as well as an ordinary, sorrow; a sadness that has its seat in the depths of reason, to which the mind cannot sink gently of itself – but to which it must descend by treading the steps of thought. And for the sublime, – if we consider what are the cares that occupy the passing day, and how remote is the practice and the course of life from the sources of sublimity, in the soul of Man, can it be wondered that there is little existing preparation for a poet charged with a new mission to extend its kingdom, and to augment and spread its enjoyments?

Away, then, with the senseless iteration of the word, *popular*, applied to new works in poetry, as if there were no test of excellence in this first of the fine arts but that all men should run after its productions, as if urged by an appetite, or constrained by a spell! – The qualities of writing best fitted for eager reception are either such as startle the world into attention by their audacity and extravagance; or they are chiefly of a superficial kind, lying upon the surfaces of manners; or arising out of a selection and arrangement of incidents, by which the mind is kept upon the stretch of curiosity, and the fancy amused without the trouble of thought. But in everything which is to send the soul into herself, to be admonished of her weakness, or to be made conscious of her power; – wherever life and nature are described as operated upon by the creative or abstracting virtue of the imagination; wherever the instinctive wisdom of antiquity and her heroic passions uniting, in the heart of the poet, with the meditative wisdom of later ages, have produced that accord of sublimated humanity, which is at once a history of the remote past and a prophetic enunciation of the remotest future, *there*, the poet must reconcile himself for a season to few and scattered hearers. – Grand thoughts (and Shakspeare must often have sighed over this truth), as they are most naturally and most fitly conceived in solitude, so can they not be brought forth in the midst of plaudits, without some violation of their sanctity. Go to a silent exhibition of the productions of the sister Art, and be convinced that the qualities which dazzle at first sight, and kindle the admiration of the multitude, are essentially different from those by which permanent influence is secured. Let us not shrink from following up these principles as far as they will carry us, and conclude with observing – that there never has been a period, and perhaps never will be, in which vicious poetry, of some kind or other, has not excited more zealous admiration, and been far more generally read, than good; but this advantage attends the good, that the *individual*, as well as the species, survives from age to age; whereas, of the depraved, though the species be immortal, the individual quickly *perishes*; the object of present admiration vanishes, being supplanted by some other as easily produced; which though no better, brings with it at least the irritation of novelty, – with adaptation, more or less skilful, to the changing humours of the majority of those who are most at leisure to regard poetical works when they first solicit their attention.

Is it the result of the whole, that, in the opinion of the Writer, the judgment of the People is not to be respected? The thought is most injurious; and, could the charge be brought against him, he would repel it with indignation. The People have already been justified, and their eulogium pronounced by implication, when it was said, above – that, of *good* poetry, the *individual*, as well as the species, *survives*. And how does it survive but through the People? What preserves it but their intellect and their wisdom?

> "– Past and future, are the wings
> On whose support, harmoniously conjoined,
> Moves the great Spirit of human knowledge –"[a]   MS.

The voice that issues from this Spirit, is that Vox Populi which the Deity inspires. Foolish must he be who can mistake for this a local acclamation, or a transitory outcry – transitory though it be for years, local though from a Nation. Still more lamentable is his error who can believe that there is any thing of divine infallibility in the clamour of that small though loud portion of the community, ever governed by factitious influence, which, under the name of the Public, passes itself, upon the unthinking, for the People. Towards the Public, the Writer hopes that he feels as much deference as it is entitled to: but to the People, philosophically characterised, and to the embodied spirit of their knowledge, so far as it exists and moves, at the present, faithfully supported by its two wings, the past and the future, his devout respect, his reverence, is due.[25] He offers it willingly and readily; and, this done, takes leave of his Readers, by assuring them – that, if he were not persuaded that the contents of

[a] quoting himself, *Prelude*, VI. 448–50

these Volumes, and the Work to which they are subsidiary, evince something of the "Vision and the Faculty divine;"[a] and that, both in words and things, they will operate in their degree, to extend the domain of sensibility for the delight, the honour, and the benefit of human nature, notwithstanding the many happy hours which he has employed in their composition, and the manifold comforts and enjoyments they have procured to him, he would not, if a wish could do it, save them from immediate destruction; – from becoming at this moment, to the world, as a thing that had never been.

[a] quoting himself, *Excursion*, I. 79

Charles Lamb

(1775–1834)

A native of London's Inner Temple, Charles Lamb went to school at Christ's Hospital from his seventh to his fifteenth year, and, to those who met him at a later period, he seemed to retain the mysterious geniality of the child who trusts his surroundings. In the essays he wrote under the pseudonym "Elia," Lamb himself helped to create this impression; and yet it is a very partial one, for he was neither equable by nature nor content with his fortunes. As a schoolboy he had been ambitious enough to rival his friend Coleridge, and a consciousness of these early hopes survived their disappointment. His life was broken by a single catastrophe. While still a young man, he had been helpless to prevent his sister Mary, in a mad fit, from stabbing their mother to death. After Mary's release from the asylum, Charles took her into his keeping and remained with her, except for intermittent relapses, throughout the rest of his life. This was a sorrow he could speak of to friends but seldom alluded to even with them. A style of reticence and modesty, though sometimes of mockery also, marks his writing as it did his character, and such a style can serve to recall the intimate horror it seems to repress. "Did you remember to rub it with butter," he writes to Coleridge, concerning the correct method of roasting a pig – "and gently dredge it a little, just before the crisis? Did the eyes come away kindly with no Oedipal avulsion?" The account of a familiar domestic scene evokes a monstrous domestic crime, under the pretense of conciliating an unpleasant shock with pleasant sentiments. The passage is representative of Lamb's letters, which include some of the best in English, and which bring out freely and uneasily the imaginings he buried deep in his popular essays.

Great intelligence, intense feeling, and a curious responsiveness to difficult friends, conspired to make Lamb not an intellectual satirist like Peacock, but rather a personal ironist. In conversation, he had a stammer which he knew how to use for effect, so that apparent encomiums often ended in cutting jests. "You are never sure of him," said Hazlitt, "till he gets to the end." The same holds true for his prose in general and his sentences in particular. "His jokes," Hazlitt went on with perhaps less truth, "would be the sharpest things in the world, but they are blunted by his good nature. He wants malice – which is a pity." Malice he may not show, but he has a disarming facility with morbid facts. To remove the offense of the sentences quoted on the roast pig, for example, he revised them in an essay on the subject, where the creature is said to have "wept out his pretty eyes – radiant jellies – shooting stars": a baroque conceit which, for extravagance of a grotesque kind, is hardly less disturbing than the original. Again, if he lacks the animus of satire, he can on occasion mount an attack with the weapons of mere detachment. But even in his polemics, there is always a ground note of attachment to the circumstances that have formed him. Refusing an invitation to visit Cumberland, he wrote to Wordsworth that "The crowds, the very dirt and mud, the sun shining upon houses and pavements, the print-shops, the old bookstalls, parsons cheapening books, coffee-houses, steams of soups from kitchens, the pantomimes – London itself a pantomime and a masquerade – all these things work themselves into my mind, and feed me, without a power of satiating me.... Have I not enough, without your mountains? I do not envy you. I should pity you, did I not know that the mind will make friends of anything." Charles and Mary Lamb added something palpable to the masquerade with their famous "Wednesday Evenings," at which a varied company of friends gathered to drink and play Whist, and to test each other's fancy with the improvised contests that Hazlitt described in his essay "On the Conversation of Authors."

Because Lamb, above all when he writes as Elia, is apt to portray himself as aloof or otherwise remote from present-day concerns, it is possible to think of him merely as a refined literary man. But this impression too is misleading. Almost as much as Hazlitt (to whom he was a loyal ally), Lamb considered himself the faithful offspring of Dissent, that is, of the writers, preachers, and agitators whose radicalism had migrated from religion to politics about the time of the French Revolution. Well into his middle years he contributed squibs and epigrams to journals like the *Examiner*, against the ex-radical Mackintosh, the "government critic" Gifford, or the Prince Regent on the occasion of his growing fat: "This (or else my eyesight fails), / This should be the Prince of Whales." With Godwin in particular, the hero of Dissenters in the 1790s who came to seem superannuated already in the next decade, Lamb stayed on friendly terms longer than anyone else is recorded to have done, and wrote prologues for his tragedies *Antonio* and *Faulkener*. His most eloquent defense of his own tolerance may be found in the "Letter of Elia to Robert Southey, Esq." Southey had accused Lamb of keeping up an intimacy with persons of socially questionable character, among them Hunt and Hazlitt; and Elia replied with a propriety beside which Southey's insinuations were revealed as the low cant of bigotry: "I own I could never think so considerably of myself as to decline the society of an agreeable or worthy man upon difference of opinion only." This apology also suggests two virtues of his criticism which are not often found together, namely discrimination and liberal-mindedness.

Lamb, however, wrote only a few critical essays, and by modern readers he has been more commonly known for his *Specimens* of the Elizabethan dramatists, itself an impressive work of critical intelligence. In such a work Lamb could present himself simply as an editor, captioner, and unobtrusive commentator. He was still more comfortable writing about literature from the perspective of Elia, in whose name he could affect the literate eccentricity of the dilettante; or collaborating with his sister on the *Tales from*

Shakespeare, when he knew that his readers would be children and their demands strictly fabulous. In all this there appears the conscious attitude of the original who elects to become a secondary man. The poignancy of Lamb's tone, then, comes from the strength of his self-doubt. When, by his own account, he wrote a play, *Mr. H.*, which failed to "take," he joined the audience in hissing it from the stage on the first night. Plainly a man capable of that will be incapable of certain forms of intellectual assertion – the fanciful energy of Hunt's humor, for example, or the "repeated blows" of Hazlitt's wit. But he resists self-deception, and incites a resistance to it in others, with a tact that is unrivalled. Here again some of Lamb's most interesting remarks occur in his letters, as when he discerns the jealousy that underlay Wordsworth's pedantic objections to "The Rime of the Ancient Mariner."

> For me, I was never so affected with any human tale. After first reading it, I was totally possessed with it for many days. I dislike all the miraculous part of it; but the feelings of the man under the operation of such scenery, dragged me along like Tom Pipe's magic whistle. I totally differ from your idea that the *Marinere* should have had a character and profession. This is a beauty in *Gulliver's Travels*, where the mind is kept in a placid state of little wonderments; but the *Ancient Marinere* undergoes such trials as over-whelm and bury all individuality or memory of what he was – like the state of a man in a bad dream, one terrible peculiarity of which is, that all consciousness of personality is gone.... You will excuse my remarks, because I am hurt and vexed that you should think it necessary, with a prose apology, to open the eyes of dead men that cannot see.

He is sensitive to the originality of the ballad in spite of its affinities with a humbler kind of romance – the very thing in seeking to explain which Wordsworth had blundered from one insult to the next. He is also keen to display, as Wordsworth was anxious to conceal, the general human truth of the work. For Lamb this always means that a large part of his task is to describe the sensations of reading. But if "The Rime of the Ancient Mariner" may be taken to typify the works he admired most, being "totally possessed" by books involved, for him, a threat to the self, "such trials as overwhelm and bury all individuality."

Hunt, Hazlitt, and Lamb all worked at dramatic criticism (Shaw credits them with having achieved a unique dignity in this kind of writing). But of the three, Lamb had the most expert knowledge of the actors of the last age, as well as the sharpest relish for the details of performance. What he counts as good acting is not quite the work of verisimilitude. Rather, he argues, we are aware in every performance of the element of "personation" – of the distance between actor and mask, and of how that makes us conscious too of the distance between actor and audience. Lamb favors the reverse of the modern ideal of inhabiting a part: in the essay "On the Artificial Comedy of the Last Century," he appreciates the great comic actors for their ability to detach themselves from a part. They abstracted the theatrical presence of a character from its moral reality, with the result that the audience saw a character without wanting to see through it. This Lamb takes to be the whole secret of comedy. "Translated into real life," he observes, Congreve's and Wycherley's characters would be intolerably wicked. "But we do them wrong in so translating them. No such effects are produced in *their* world. When we are among them, we are amongst a chaotic people. We are not to judge them by our usages." Thus on the one hand, the coherence of literary works is seen to be greater than the coherence of life: the rules we require for the enforcement of order in the latter realm are therefore useless in the former. On the other hand, the persons whom we meet in comedy are "chaotic" in inimitable ways: this is so patent that no danger can be foreseen to life by the infection of their example. When we go to the theatre, we go to another life.

The liberality of this judgement proves, on inspection, to apply to a single genre only, which Lamb sees as representing a place of "perfect freedom." A caricaturist like Munden shows the traits necessary to gain admission to such a place, down to the last traceable shades of expression. "A tub of butter, contemplated by him, amounts to a Platonic idea." But a very different mood pervades the essay on "The Tragedies of Shakspeare." The gravity of their poetry, Lamb says, unfits these plays for any representation at all. The trouble is that surface distractions may come to be identified with the play itself. A vivid gesture or two, a clever inflection given to an ordinary cadence, is mistaken for what the author wrote, and accordingly what the reader might take in at a glance. With its claim that performance is an enemy of reading, the essay presupposes that reading is the sole form of attention by which we feel a community of purpose with an author's imaginings. Precisely what made the comedies most impressive in the theatre – the sense of conscious distance – makes the tragedies there a forgery of the truth of intuition. Where the reader finds implications, the viewer is shown explications; it is the viewer who is satisfied, and that is his loss. In using such phrases as "the texture of Othello's mind," Lamb recalls what our language itself seems to show, that the texture of words is something more than the report of intonations. The inferiority of acting to reading is further confirmed by his observation that dramatic speeches of any sort can move an audience as much as Shakespeare's, given the right choice of tactics by the performer: "What have looks, or tones, to do with that sublime identification of [Lear's] age with that of the *heavens themselves?*" It may be conceded that the very structure of Lamb's argument is ambivalent. If the changeable artificialities of performance establish the integrity of the text alone, the existence of the text itself remains a constant temptation to performance. Still, with a curious singlemindedness, his essay makes a Rousseau-like attack on spectacle as a means of enchantment. What it defends is not a therapy of moral education through nature, but a return to the act of reading as a way of thinking and imagining.

Charles Lamb (1775–1834)

2. "On the Tragedies of Shakspeare, Considered with Reference to their Fitness for Stage Representation"

first published in *The Reflector*, October–December 1811; text of *Works* (1818),
from *Works*, ed. Thomas Hutchinson (1908), vol. 1, pp. 124–42

TAKING a turn the other day in the Abbey, I was struck with the
affected attitude of a figure, which I do not remember to have seen
before, and which upon examination proved to be a whole-length of
the celebrated Mr. Garrick.[1] Though I would not go so far with some
good catholics abroad as to shut players altogether out of consecrated
ground, yet I own I was not a little scandalized at the introduction of
theatrical airs and gestures into a place set apart to remind us of the
saddest realities. Going nearer, I found inscribed under this harlequin
figure the following lines:—

> To paint fair Nature, by divine command,
> Her magic pencil in his glowing hand,
> A Shakspeare rose: then, to expand his fame
> Wide o'er this breathing world, a Garrick came.
> Though sunk in death the forms the Poet drew,
> The Actor's genius bade them breathe anew;
> Though, like the bard himself, in night they lay,
> Immortal Garrick call'd them back to day:
> And till Eternity with power sublime
> Shall mark the mortal hour of hoary Time,
> Shakspeare and Garrick like twin-stars shall shine,
> And earth irradiate with a beam divine.

It would be an insult to my readers' understandings to attempt any
thing like a criticism on this farrago of false thoughts and nonsense.
But the reflection it led me into was a kind of wonder, how, from the
days of the actor here celebrated to our own, it should have been the
fashion to compliment every performer in his turn, that has had the
luck to please the town in any of the great characters of Shakspeare,
with the notion of possessing a *mind congenial with the poet's*: how
people should come thus unaccountably to confound the power of
originating poetical images and conceptions with the faculty of being
able to read or recite the same when put into words;[2] or what
connection that absolute mastery over the heart and soul of man,
which a great dramatic poet possesses, has with those low tricks upon
the eye and ear, which a player by observing a few general effects,
which some common passion, as grief, anger, &c. usually has upon
the gestures and exterior, can so easily compass. To know the internal

workings and movements of a great mind, of an Othello or a Hamlet for instance, the *when* and the *why* and the *how far* they should be moved; to what pitch a passion is becoming; to give the reins and to pull in the curb exactly at the moment when the drawing in or the slackening is most graceful; seems to demand a reach of intellect of a vastly different extent from that which is employed upon the bare imitation of the signs of these passions in the countenance or gesture, which signs are usually observed to be most lively and emphatic in the weaker sort of minds, and which signs can after all but indicate some passion, as I said before, anger, or grief, generally; but of the motives and grounds of the passion, wherein it differs from the same passion in low and vulgar natures, of these the actor can give no more idea by his face or gesture than the eye (without a metaphor) can speak, or the muscles utter intelligible sounds. But such is the instantaneous nature of the impressions which we take in at the eye and ear at a playhouse, compared with the slow apprehension oftentimes of the understanding in reading, that we are apt not only to sink the play-writer in the consideration which we pay to the actor, but even to identify in our minds in a perverse manner, the actor with the character which he represents. It is difficult for a frequent playgoer to disembarrass the idea of Hamlet from the person and voice of Mr. K. We speak of Lady Macbeth, while we are in reality thinking of Mrs. S.[3] Nor is this confusion incidental alone to unlettered persons, who, not possessing the advantage of reading, are necessarily dependent upon the stage-player for all the pleasure which they can receive from the drama, and to whom the very idea of *what an author is* cannot be made comprehensible without some pain and perplexity of mind: the error is one from which persons otherwise not meanly lettered, find it almost impossible to extricate themselves.

Never let me be so ungrateful as to forget the very high degree of satisfaction which I received some years back from seeing for the first time a tragedy of Shakspeare performed, in which these two great performers sustained the principal parts. It seemed to embody and realize conceptions which had hitherto assumed no distinct shape. But dearly do we pay all our life after for this juvenile pleasure, this sense of distinctness. When the novelty is past, we find to our cost that instead of realizing an idea, we have only materialized and brought down a fine vision to the standard of flesh and blood. We have let go a dream, in quest of an unattainable substance.

How cruelly this operates upon the mind, to have its free conceptions thus crampt and pressed down to the measure of a strait-lacing actuality, may be judged from that delightful sensation of freshness, with which we turn to those plays of Shakspeare which have escaped being performed, and to those passages in the acting plays of the same writer which have happily been left out in performance. How far the very custom of hearing any thing *spouted*, withers and blows upon a fine passage, may be seen in those speeches from Henry the Fifth, &c. which are current in the mouths of school-boys from their being to be found in *Enfield Speakers*,[4] and such kind of books. I confess myself utterly unable to appreciate that celebrated soliloquy in Hamlet, beginning "To be or not to be," or to tell whether it be good, bad, or indifferent, it has been so handled and pawed about by declamatory boys and men, and torn so inhumanly from its living place and principle of continuity in the play, till it is become to me a perfect dead member.

It may seem a paradox, but I cannot help being of opinion that the plays of Shakspeare are less calculated for performance on a stage, than those of almost any other dramatist whatever. Their distinguished excellence is a reason that they should be so. There is so much in them, which comes not under the province of acting, with which eye, and tone, and gesture, have nothing to do.

The glory of the scenic art is to personate passion, and the turns of passion; and the more coarse and palpable the passion is, the more hold upon the eyes and ears of the spectators the performer obviously possesses. For this reason, scolding scenes, scenes where two persons talk themselves into a fit of fury, and then in a surprising manner talk themselves out of it again, have always been the most popular upon our stage. And the reason is plain, because the spectators are here most palpably appealed to, they are the proper judges in this war of words, they are the legitimate ring that should be formed round such "intellectual prize-fighters." Talking is the direct object of the imitation here. But in all the best dramas, and in Shakspeare above all, how obvious it is, that the form of *speaking*, whether it be in soliloquy or dialogue, is only a medium, and often a highly artificial one, for putting the reader or spectator into possession of that knowledge of the inner structure and workings of mind in a character, which he could otherwise never have arrived at *in that form of composition* by any gift short of intuition. We do here as we do with novels written in the *epistolary form*. How many improprieties, perfect solecisms in letter-writing, do we put up with in Clarissa and other books, for the sake of the delight which that form upon the whole gives us.

But the practice of stage representation reduces every thing to a controversy of elocution. Every character, from the boisterous blasphemings of Bajazet to the shrinking timidity of womanhood, must play the orator. The love-dialogues of Romeo and Juliet, those silver-sweet sounds of lovers' tongues by night; the more intimate and sacred sweetness of nuptial colloquy between an Othello or a Posthumus with their married wives, all those delicacies which are so delightful in the reading, as when we read of those youthful dalliances in Paradise –

> As beseem'd
> Fair couple link'd in happy nuptial league
> Alone:[a]

by the inherent fault of stage representation, how are these things sullied and turned from their very nature by being exposed to a large assembly; when such speeches as Imogen addresses to her lord, come drawling out of the mouth of a hired actress, whose courtship, though nominally addressed to the personated Posthumus, is manifestly aimed at the spectators, who are to judge of her endearments and her returns of love.

The character of Hamlet is perhaps that by which, since the days of Betterton,[5] a succession of popular performers have had the greatest ambition to distinguish themselves. The length of the part may be one of their reasons. But for the character itself, we find it in a play, and therefore we judge it a fit subject of dramatic representation. The play itself abounds in maxims and reflexions beyond any other, and therefore we consider it as a proper vehicle for conveying moral instruction. But Hamlet himself – what does he suffer meanwhile by being dragged forth as a public schoolmaster, to give lectures to the crowd! Why, nine parts in ten of what Hamlet does, are transactions between himself and his moral sense, they are the effusions of his solitary musings, which he retires to holes and corners and the most sequestered parts of the palace to pour forth; or rather, they are the silent meditations with which his bosom is bursting, reduced to *words* for the sake of the reader, who must else remain ignorant of what is passing there. These profound sorrows, these light-and-noise-abhorring ruminations, which the tongue scarce dares utter to deaf walls and chambers, how can they be represented by a gesticulating actor, who comes and mouths them out before an audience, making four hundred people his confidants at once? I say not that it is the fault of the actor so to do; he must pronounce them *ore rotundo,*[b] he must accompany them with his eye, he must insinuate them into his auditory by some trick of eye, tone, or gesture, or he fails. *He must be*

[a] *Paradise Lost,* IV, 338–40
[b] with artfully rounded speech

thinking all the while of his appearance, because he knows that all the while the spectators are judging of it. And this is the way to represent the shy, negligent, retiring Hamlet.

It is true that there is no other mode of conveying a vast quantity of thought and feeling to a great portion of the audience, who otherwise would never earn it for themselves by reading, and the intellectual acquisition gained this way may, for aught I know, be inestimable; but I am not arguing that Hamlet should not be acted, but how much Hamlet is made another thing by being acted. I have heard much of the wonders which Garrick performed in this part; but as I never saw him, I must have leave to doubt whether the representation of such a character came within the province of his art. Those who tell me of him, speak of his eye, of the magic of his eye, and of his commanding voice: physical properties, vastly desirable in an actor, and without which he can never insinuate meaning into an auditory, – but what have they to do with Hamlet? what have they to do with intellect? In fact, the things aimed at in theatrical represen-tation, are to arrest the spectator's eye upon the form and the gesture, and so to gain a more favourable hearing to what is spoken: it is not what the character is, but how he looks; not what he says, but how he speaks it. I see no reason to think that if the play of Hamlet were written over again by some such writer as Banks or Lillo,[6] retaining the process of the story, but totally omitting all the poetry of it, all the divine features of Shakspeare, his stupendous intellect; and only taking care to give us enough of passionate dialogue, which Banks and Lillo were never at a loss to furnish; I see not how the effect could be much different upon an audience, nor how the actor has it in his power to represent Shakspeare to us differently from his representation of Banks or Lillo. Hamlet would still be a youthful accomplished prince, and must be gracefully personated; he might be puzzled in his mind, wavering in his conduct, seemingly-cruel to Ophelia, he might see a ghost, and start at it, and address it kindly when he found it to be his father; all this in the poorest and most homely language of the servilest creeper after nature that ever consul-ted the palate of an audience; without troubling Shakspeare for the matter: and I see not but there would be room for all the power which an actor has, to display itself. All the passions and changes of passion might remain: for those are much less difficult to write or act than is thought, it is a trick easy to be attained, it is but rising or falling a note or two in the voice, a whisper with a significant foreboding look to announce its approach, and so contagious the counterfeit appearance of any emotion is, that let the words be what they will, the look and tone shall carry it off and make it pass for deep skill in the passions.

It is common for people to talk of Shakspeare's plays being *so natural*; that every body can understand him. They are natural indeed, they are grounded deep in nature, so deep that the depth of them lies out of the reach of most of us. You shall hear the same persons say that George Barnwell is very natural,[7] and Othello is very natural, that they are both very deep; and to them they are the same kind of thing. At the one they sit and shed tears, because a good sort of young man is tempted by a naughty woman to commit *a trifling peccadillo*, the murder of an uncle or so,[8] that is all, and so comes to an untimely end, which is *so moving*; and at the other, because a blackamoor in a fit of jealousy kills his innocent white wife: and the odds are that ninety-nine out of a hundred would willingly behold the same catastrophe happen to both the heroes, and have thought the rope more due to Othello than to Barnwell. For of the texture of Othello's mind, the inward construction marvellously laid open with all its strengths and weaknesses, its heroic confidences and its human misgivings, its agonies of hate springing from the depths of love, they see no more than the spectators at a cheaper rate, who pay their pennies a-piece to look through the man's telescope in Leicester-fields, see into the inward plot and topography of the moon. Some dim thing or other they see, they see an actor personating a passion, of grief, or anger, for instance, and they recognize it as a copy of the usual external effects of such passions; for at least as being true to *that symbol of the emotion which passes current at the theatre for it*, for it is often no more than that: but of the grounds of the passion, its correspondence to a great or heroic nature, which is the only worthy object of tragedy, – that common auditors know any thing of this, or can have any such notions dinned into them by the mere strength of an actor's lungs, – that apprehensions foreign to them should be thus infused into them by storm, I can neither believe, nor understand how it can be possible.

We talk of Shakspeare's admirable observation of life, when we should feel, that not from a petty inquisition into those cheap and every-day characters which surrounded him, as they surround us, but from his own mind, which was, to borrow a phrase of Ben Jonson's, the very "sphere of humanity," he fetched those images of virtue and of knowledge, of which every one of us recognizing a part, think we comprehend in our natures the whole; and oftentimes mistake the powers which he positively creates in us, for nothing more than indigenous faculties of our own minds which only waited the application of corresponding virtues in him to return a full and clear echo of the same.

To return to Hamlet. – Among the distinguishing features of that wonderful character, one of the most interesting (yet painful) is that soreness of mind which makes him treat the intrusions of Polonius with harshness, and that asperity which he puts on in his interviews with Ophelia. These tokens of an unhinged mind (if they be not mixed in the latter case with a profound artifice of love, to alienate Ophelia by affected discourtesies, so to prepare her mind for the breaking off of that loving intercourse, which can no longer find a place amidst business so serious as that which he has to do) are parts of his character, which to reconcile with our admiration of Hamlet, the most patient consideration of his situation is no more than necessary; they are what we *forgive afterwards*, and explain by the whole of his character, but *at the time* they are harsh and unpleasant. Yet such is the actor's necessity of giving strong blows to the audience, that I have never seen a player in this character, who did not exaggerate and strain to the utmost these ambiguous features – these temporary deformities in the character. They make him express a vulgar scorn at Polonius which utterly degrades his gentility, and which no explanation can render palateable; they make him shew contempt, and curl up the nose at Ophelia's father, – contempt in its very grossest and most hateful form; but they get applause by it: it is natural, people say; that is, the words are scornful, and the actor expresses scorn, and that they can judge of: but why so much scorn, and of that sort, they never think of asking.

So to Ophelia. – All the Hamlets that I have ever seen, rant and rave at her as if she had committed some great crime, and the audience are highly pleased, because the words of the part are satirical, and they are enforced by the strongest expression of satirical indignation of which the face and voice are capable. But then, whether Hamlet is likely to have put on such brutal appearances to a lady whom he loved so dearly, is never thought on. The truth is, that in all such deep affections as had subsisted between Hamlet and Ophelia, there is a stock of *supererogatory love*, (if I may venture to use the expression) which in any great grief of heart, especially where that which preys upon the mind cannot be communicated, confers a kind of indulgence upon the grieved party to express itself, even to its heart's dearest object, in the language of a temporary alienation; but it is not alienation, it is a distraction purely, and so it always makes itself to be felt by that object: it is not anger, but grief assuming the appearance of anger, – love awkwardly counterfeiting hate, as sweet countenances when they try to frown: but such sternness and fierce digust as Hamlet is made to shew, is no counterfeit, but the real face of absolute aversion, – of irreconcileable alienation. It may be said he puts on the madman; but then he should only so far put on this counterfeit lunacy as his own real distraction will give him leave; that is, incompletely, imperfectly; not in that confirmed practised way, like a master of his art, or, as Dame Quickly would say, "like one of those harlotry players."[a]

I mean no disrespect to any actor, but the sort of pleasure which Shakspeare's plays give in the acting seems to me not at all to differ from that which the audience receive from those of other writers; and, *they being in themselves essentially so different from all others*, I must conclude that there is something in the nature of acting which levels all distinctions. And in fact, who does not speak indifferently of the Gamester and of Macbeth as fine stage performances, and praise the Mrs. Beverley in the same way as the Lady Macbeth of Mrs. S.? Belvidera, and Calista, and Isabella, and Euphrasia, are they less liked than Imogen, or than Juliet, or than Desdemona? Are they not spoken of and remembered in the same way? Is not the female performer as great (as they call it) in one as in the other? Did not Garrick shine, and was not he ambitious of shining in every drawling tragedy that his wretched day produced, – the productions of the Hills and the Murphys and the Browns,[9] – and shall he have that honour to dwell in our minds for ever as an inseparable concomitant with Shakspeare? A kindred mind! O who can read that affecting sonnet of Shakspeare which alludes to his profession as a player:–

> Oh for my sake do you with Fortune chide,
> The guilty goddess of my harmful deeds,
> That did not better for my life provide
> Than public means which public custom breeds –
> Thence comes it that my name receives a brand;
> And almost thence my nature is subdued
> To what it works in, like the dyer's hand –[b]

Or that other confession:–

> Alas! 'tis true, I have gone here and there,
> And made myself a motly to thy view,
> Gor'd mine own thoughts, sold cheap what is most dear –[c]

Who can read these instances of jealous self-watchfulness in our sweet Shakspeare, and dream of any congeniality between him and one that,

---

[a] *I Henry IV*, II. iv. 400 (Signet edition)   [b] Sonnet III   [c] Sonnet IIO

by every tradition of him, appears to have been as mere a player as ever existed; to have had his mind tainted with the lowest players' vices, – envy and jealousy, and miserable cravings after applause; one who in the exercise of his profession was jealous even of the women-performers that stood in his way; a manager full of managerial tricks and stratagems and finesse: that any resemblance should be dreamed of between him and Shakspeare, – Shakspeare who, in the plenitude and consciousness of his own powers, could with that noble modesty, which we can neither imitate nor appreciate, express himself thus of his own sense of his own defects:–

> Wishing me like to one more rich in hope,
> Featur'd like him, like him with friends possest;
> Desiring *this man's art, and that man's scope.*[a]

I am almost disposed to deny to Garrick the merit of being an admirer of Shakspeare. A true lover of his excellencies he certainly was not; for would any true lover of them have admitted into his matchless scenes such ribald trash as Tate and Cibber, and the rest of them, that

> With their darkness durst affront his light,[b]

have foisted into the acting plays of Shakspeare?[10] I believe it impossible that he could have had a proper reverence for Shakspeare, and have condescended to go through that interpolated scene in Richard the Third, in which Richard tries to break his wife's heart by telling her he loves another woman, and says, "if she survives this she is immortal." Yet I doubt not he delivered this vulgar stuff with as much anxiety of emphasis as any of the genuine parts; and for acting, it is as well calculated as any. But we have seen the part of Richard lately produce great fame to an actor by his manner of playing it, and it lets us into the secret of acting, and of popular judgments of Shakspeare derived from acting. Not one of the spectators who have witnessed Mr. C.'s exertions in that part,[11] but has come away with a proper conviction that Richard is a very wicked man, and kills little children in their beds, with something like the pleasure which the giants and ogres in children's books are represented to have taken in that practice; moreover, that he is very close and shrewd and devilish cunning, for you could see that by his eye.

But is in fact this the impression we have in reading the Richard of Shakspeare? Do we feel any thing like disgust, as we do at that butcher-like representation of him that passes for him on the stage? A

[a] Sonnet 29   [b] *Paradise Lost*, I. 391

horror at his crimes blends with the effect which we feel, but how is it qualified, how is it carried off, by the rich intellect which he displays, his resources, his wit, his buoyant spirits, his vast knowledge and insight into characters, the poetry of his part, – not an atom of all which is made perceivable in Mr. C.'s way of acting it. Nothing but his crimes, his actions, is visible; they are prominent and staring; the murderer stands out, but where is the lofty genius, the man of vast capacity, – the profound, the witty, accomplished Richard?

The truth is, the Characters of Shakspeare are so much the objects of meditation rather than of interest or curiosity as to their actions, that while we are reading any of his great criminal characters, – Macbeth, Richard, even Iago, – we think not so much of the crimes which they commit, as of the ambition, the aspiring spirit, the intellectual activity, which prompts them to overleap those moral fences. Barnwell is a wretched murderer; there is a certain fitness between his neck and the rope; he is the legitimate heir to the gallows; nobody who thinks at all can think of any alleviating circumstances in his case to make him a fit object of mercy. Or to take an instance from the higher tragedy, what else but a mere assassin is Glenalvon![12] Do we think of any thing but of the crime which he commits, and the rack which he deserves? That is all which we really think about him. Whereas in corresponding characters in Shakspeare so little do the actions comparatively affect us, that while the impulses, the inner mind in all its perverted greatness, solely seems real and is exclusively attended to, the crime is comparatively nothing. But when we see these things represented, the acts which they do are comparatively every thing, their impulses nothing. The state of sublime emotion into which we are elevated by those images of night and horror which Macbeth is made to utter, that solemn prelude with which he entertains the time till the bell shall strike which is to call him to murder Duncan, – when we no longer read it in a book, when we have given up that vantage-ground of abstraction which reading possesses over seeing, and come to see a man in his bodily shape before our eyes actually preparing to commit a murder, if the acting be true and impressive, as I have witnessed it in Mr. K.'s performance of that part, the painful anxiety about the act, the natural longing to prevent it while it yet seems unperpetrated, the too close pressing semblance of reality, give a pain and an uneasiness which totally destroy all the delight which the words in the book convey, where the deed doing never presses upon us with the painful sense of presence: it rather seems to belong to history, – to something past and inevitable, if it has any thing to do with time at all. The sublime images, the poetry alone, is that which is present to our minds in the reading.

So to see Lear acted, – to see an old man tottering about the stage with a walking-stick, turned out of doors by his daughters in a rainy night, has nothing in it but what is painful and disgusting. We want to take him into shelter and relieve him. That is all the feeling which the acting of Lear ever produced in me. But the Lear of Shakspeare cannot be acted. The contemptible machinery by which they mimic the storm which he goes out in, is not more inadequate to represent the horrors of the real elements, than any actor can be to represent Lear: they might more easily propose to personate the Satan of Milton upon a stage, or one of Michael Angelo's terrible figures. The greatness of Lear is not in corporal dimension, but in intellectual: the explosions of his passion are terrible as a volcano: they are storms turning up and disclosing to the bottom that sea, his mind, with all its vast riches. It is his mind which is laid bare. This case of flesh and blood seems too insignificant to be thought on; even as he himself neglects it. On the stage we see nothing but corporal infirmities and weakness, the impotence of rage; while we read it, we see not Lear, but we are Lear, – we are in his mind, we are sustained by a grandeur which baffles the malice of daughters and storms; in the aberrations of his reason, we discover a mighty irregular power of reasoning, immethodized from the ordinary purposes of life, but exerting its powers, as the wind blows where it listeth, at will upon the corruptions and abuses of mankind. What have looks, or tones, to do with that sublime identification of his age with that of the *heavens themselves*, when in his reproaches to them for conniving at the injustice of his children, he reminds them that "they themselves are old."[a] What gesture shall we appropriate to this? What has the voice or the eye to do with such things? But the play is beyond all art, as the tamperings with it shew: it is too hard and stony; it must have love-scenes, and a happy ending. It is not enough that Cordelia is a daughter, she must shine as a lover too. Tate has put his hook in the nostrils of this Leviathan, for Garrick and his followers, the showmen of the scene, to draw the mighty beast about more easily. A happy ending! – as if the living martyrdom that Lear had gone through, – that flaying of his feelings alive, did not make a fair dismissal from the stage of life the only decorous thing for him. If he is to live and be happy after, if he could sustain this world's burden after, why all this pudder and preparation, – why torment us with all this unnecessary

[a] paraphrasing and interpreting *King Lear*, II. iv. 186–89

sympathy? As if the childish pleasure of getting his gilt robes and sceptre again could tempt him to act over again his misused station, – as if at his years, and with his experience, any thing was left but to die.

Lear is essentially impossible to be represented on a stage. But how many dramatic personages are there in Shakspeare, which though more tractable and feasible (if I may so speak) than Lear, yet from some circumstance, some adjunct to their character, are improper to be shewn to our bodily eye. Othello for instance. Nothing can be more soothing, more flattering to the nobler parts of our natures, than to read of a young Venetian lady of highest extraction, through the force of love and from a sense of merit in him whom she loved, laying aside every consideration of kindred, and country, and colour, and wedding with *a coal-black Moor* – (for such he is represented, in the imperfect state of knowledge respecting foreign countries in those days, compared with our own, or in compliance with popular notions, though the Moors are now well enough known to be by many shades less unworthy of a white woman's fancy) – it is the perfect triumph of virtue over accidents, of the imagination over the senses. She sees Othello's colour in his mind. But upon the stage, when the imagination is no longer the ruling faculty, but we are left to our poor unassisted senses, I appeal to every one that has seen Othello played, whether he did not, on the contrary, sink Othello's mind in his colour; whether he did not find something extremely revolting in the courtship and wedded caresses of Othello and Desdemona; and whether the actual sight of the thing did not over-weigh all that beautiful compromise which we make in reading; – and the reason it should do so is obvious, because there is just so much reality presented to our senses as to give a perception of disagreement, with not enough of belief in the internal motives, – all that which is unseen, – to overpower and reconcile the first and obvious prejudices.[13] What we see upon a stage is body and bodily action; what we are conscious of in reading is almost exclusively the mind, and its movements: and this I think may sufficiently account for the very different sort of delight with which the same play so often affects us in the reading and the seeing.

It requires little reflection to perceive, that if those characters in Shakspeare which are within the precincts of nature, have yet something in them which appeals too exclusively to the imagination, to admit of their being made objects to the senses without suffering a change and a diminution, – that still stronger the objection must lie against representing another line of characters, which Shakspeare has introduced to give a wildness and a supernatural elevation to his scenes, as if to remove them still farther from that assimilation to common life in which their excellence is vulgarly supposed to consist. When we read the incantations of those terrible beings the Witches in Macbeth, though some of the ingredients of their hellish composition savour of the grotesque, yet is the effect upon us other than the most serious and appalling that can be imagined? Do we not feel spell-bound as Macbeth was? Can any mirth accompany a sense of their presence? We might as well laugh under a consciousness of the principle of Evil himself being truly and really present with us. But attempt to bring these beings on to a stage, and you turn them instantly into so many old women, that men and children are to laugh at. Contrary to the old saying, that "seeing is believing", the sight actually destroys the faith; and the mirth in which we indulge at their expense, when we see these creatures upon a stage, seems to be a sort of indemnification which we make to ourselves for the terror which they put us in when reading made them an object of belief, – when we surrendered up our reason to the poet, as children to their nurses and their elders; and we laugh at our fears, as children who thought they saw something in the dark, triumph when the bringing in of a candle discovers the vanity of their fears. For this exposure of supernatural agents upon a stage is truly bringing in a candle to expose their own delusiveness. It is the solitary taper and the book that generates a faith in these terrors: a ghost by chandelier light, and in good company, deceives no spectators, – a ghost that can be measured by the eye, and his human dimensions made out at leisure. The sight of a well-lighted house, and a well-dressed audience, shall arm the most nervous child against any apprehensions: as Tom Brown says of the impenetrable skin of Achilles with his impenetrable armour over it, "Bully Dawson would have fought the devil with such advantages."[14]

Much has been said, and deservedly, in reprobation of the vile mixture which Dryden has thrown into the Tempest:[15] doubtless without some such vicious alloy, the impure ears of that age would never have sate out to hear so much innocence of love as is contained in the sweet courtship of Ferdinand and Miranda. But is the Tempest of Shakspeare at all a subject for stage representation? It is one thing to read of an enchanter, and to believe the wondrous tale while we are reading it; but to have a conjuror brought before us in his conjuring-gown, with his spirits about him, which none but himself and some hundred of favoured spectators before the curtain are supposed to see, involves such a quantity of the *hateful incredible*, that all our reverence for the author cannot hinder us from perceiving such gross attempts upon the senses to be in the highest degree childish and inefficient. Spirits and fairies cannot be represented, they cannot even be painted, – they can only be believed. But the elaborate and anxious provision of scenery, which the luxury of the age demands, in these cases works a quite contrary effect to what is intended. That which in comedy, or plays of familiar life, adds so much to the life of the imitation, in plays which appeal to the higher faculties, positively destroys the illusion which it is introduced to aid. A parlour or a drawing-room, – a library opening into a garden, – a garden with an alcove in it, – a street, or the piazza of Covent-garden, does well enough in a scene; we are content to give as much credit to it as it demands; or rather, we think little about it, – it is little more than reading at the top of a page, "Scene, a Garden;" we do not imagine ourselves there, but we readily admit the imitation of familiar objects. But to think by the help of painted trees and caverns, which we know to be painted, to transport our minds to Prospero, and his island and his lonely cell;[16] or by the aid of a fiddle dexterously thrown in, in an interval of speaking, to make us believe that we hear those super-natural noises of which the isle was full: – the Orrery Lecturer at the Haymarket might as well hope, by his musical glasses cleverly stationed out of sight behind his apparatus, to make us believe that we do indeed hear the chrystal spheres ring out that chime,[17] which if it were to inwrap our fancy long, Milton thinks,

> Time would run back and fetch the age of gold,
> And speckled vanity
> Would sicken soon and die,
> And leprous Sin would melt from earthly mould;
> Yea Hell itself would pass away,
> And leave its dolorous mansions to the peering day.[a]

The Garden of Eden, with our first parents in it, is not more impossible to be shewn on a stage, than the Enchanted Isle, with its no less interesting and innocent first settlers.

The subject of Scenery is closely connected with that of the Dresses, which are so anxiously attended to on our stage. I remember the last time I saw Macbeth played, the discrepancy I felt at the changes of garment which he varied, – the shiftings and re-shiftings, like a Romish priest at mass. The luxury of stage-improvements, and the importunity of the public eye, require this. The coronation robe of the Scottish monarch was fairly a counterpart to that which our King wears when he goes to the Parliament-house, – just so full and cumbersome, and set out with ermine and pearls. And if things must

---

[a] Milton, "On the Morning of Christ's Nativity," 134–39

be represented, I see not what to find fault with in this. But in reading, what robe are we consicous of? Some dim images of royalty – a crown and sceptre, may float before our eyes, but who shall describe the fashion of it? Do we see in our mind's eye what Webb or any other robe-maker could pattern? This is the inevitable consequence of imitating every thing, to make all things natural. Whereas the reading of a tragedy is a fine abstraction. It presents to the fancy just so much of external appearances as to make us feel that we are among flesh and blood, while by far the greater and better part of our imagination is employed upon the thoughts and internal machinery of the character. But in acting, scenery, dress, the most contemptible things, call upon us to judge of their naturalness.

Perhaps it would be no bad similitude, to liken the pleasure which we take in seeing one of these fine plays acted, compared with that quiet delight which we find in the reading of it, to the different feelings with which a reviewer, and a man that is not a reviewer, reads a fine poem. The accursed critical habit, – the being called upon to judge and pronounce, must make it quite a different thing to the former. In seeing these plays acted, we are affected just as judges. When Hamlet compares the two pictures of Gertrude's first and second husband, who wants to see the pictures? But in the acting, a miniature must be lugged out; which we know not to be the picture, but only to shew how finely a miniature may be represented. This shewing of every thing, levels all things: it makes tricks, bows, and curtesies, of importance. Mrs. S. never got more fame by any thing than by the manner in which she dismisses the guests in the banquet-scene in Macbeth: it is as much remembered as any of her thrilling tones or impressive looks. But does such a trifle as this enter into the imaginations of the readers of that wild and wonderful scene? Does not the mind dismiss the feasters as rapidly as it can? Does it care about the gracefulness of the doing it? But by acting, and judging of acting, all these non-essentials are raised into an importance, injurious to the main interest of the play.

I have confined my observations to the tragic parts of Shakspeare. It would be no very difficult task to extend the enquiry to his comedies; and to shew why Falstaff, Shallow, Sir Hugh Evans, and the rest, are equally incompatible with stage representation. The length to which this Essay has run, will make it, I am afraid, sufficiently distasteful to the Amateurs of the Theatre, without going any deeper into the subject at present.

3. *"On the Acting of Munden"*

first published in *The Examiner*, November 7, 1819; text of *Elia* (1823), from *Works*, ed. Thomas Hutchinson (1908), vol. I, pp. 656–59

NOT many nights ago I had come home from seeing this extra-ordinary performer in Cockletop;[1] and when I retired to my pillow, his whimsical image still stuck by me, in a manner as to threaten sleep. In vain I tried to divest myself of it, by conjuring up the most opposite associations. I resolved to be serious. I raised up the gravest topics of life; private misery, public calamity. All would not do.

———————There the antic sate
Mocking our state —[a]

his queer visnomy – his bewildering costume – all the strange things which he had raked together – his serpentine rod, swagging about in his pocket – Cleopatra's tear, and the rest of his relics – O'Keefe's wild farce, and *his* wilder commentary – till the passion of laughter, like grief in excess, relieved itself by its own weight, inviting the sleep which in the first instance it had driven away.

But I was not to escape so easily. No sooner did I fall into slumbers, than the same image, only more perplexing, assailed me in the shape of dreams. Not one Munden, but five hundred, were dancing before me, like the faces which, whether you will or no, come when you have been taking opium – all the strange combinations, which this strangest of all strange mortals ever shot his proper countenance into, from the day he came commissioned to dry up the tears of the town for the loss of the now almost forgotten Edwin. O for the power of the pencil to have fixed them when I awoke! A season or two since there was exhibited a Hogarth gallery. I do not see why there should not be a Munden gallery. In richness and variety the latter would not fall far short of the former.

There is one face of Farley, one face of Knight, one (but what a one it is!) of Liston;[2] but Munden has none that you can properly pin down, and call *his*. When you think he has exhausted his battery of looks, in unaccountable warfare with your gravity, suddenly he sprouts out an entirely new set of features, like Hydra. He is not one, but legion. Not so much a comedian, as a company. If his name could be multiplied like his countenance, it might fill a play-bill. He, and he alone, literally *makes faces*: applied to any other person, the phrase is a mere figure, denoting certain modifications of the human counte-

[a] playing upon *Richard II*, III. ii. 162–63, "There the antic sits / Scoffing his state"

nance. Out of some invisible wardrobe he dips for faces, as his friend Suett used for wigs,[3] and fetches them out as easily. I should not be surprised to see him some day put out the head of a river horse; or come forth a pewitt, or lapwing, some feathered metamorphosis.

I have seen this gifted actor in Sir Christopher Curry – in Old Dornton[4] – diffuse a glow of sentiment which has made the pulse of a crowded theatre beat like that of one man; when he has come in aid of the pulpit, doing good to the moral heart of a people. I have seen some faint approaches to this sort of excellence in other players. But in the grand grotesque of farce, Munden stands out as single and unaccompanied as Hogarth. Hogarth, strange to tell, had no followers. The school of Munden began, and must end with himself.

Can any man *wonder*, like him? can any man *see ghosts*, like him? or *fight with his own shadow* – "SESSA" – as he does in that strangely-neglected thing, the Cobbler of Preston[5] where his alternations from the Cobbler to the Magnifico, and from the Magnifico to the Cobbler, keep the brain of the spectator in as wild a ferment, as if some Arabian Night were being acted before him. Who like him can throw, or ever attempted to throw, a preternatural interest over the commonest daily-life objects? A table, or a joint stool, in his conception, rises into a dignity equivalent to Cassiopeia's chair. It is invested with constellatory importance. You could not speak of it with more deference, if it were mounted into the firmament. A beggar in the hands of Michael Angelo, says Fuseli, rose the Patriarch of Poverty. So the gusto of Munden antiquates and ennobles what it touches. His pots and his ladles are as grand and primal as the seething-pots and hooks seen in old prophetic vision. A tub of butter, contemplated by him, amounts to a Platonic idea. He understands a leg of mutton in its quiddity. He stands wondering, amid the common-place materials of life, like primæval man with the sun and stars about him.

4. *"On the Artificial Comedy of the Last Century"*

first published as *The Old Actors*, in *The London Magazine*, April 1822; text of *Elia* (1823), from *Works*, ed. Thomas Hutchinson (1908), pp. 648–56

THE artificial Comedy, or Comedy of manners, is quite extinct on our stage. Congreve and Farquhar show their heads once in seven years only, to be exploded and put down instantly. The times cannot bear them. Is it for a few wild speeches, an occasional license of dialogue? I think not altogether. The business of their dramatic characters will not stand the moral test. We screw every thing up to that. Idle gallantry in a fiction, a dream, the passing pageant of an evening, startles us in the same way as the alarming indications of profligacy in a son or ward in real life should startle a parent or guardian. We have no such middle emotions as dramatic interests left. We see a stage libertine playing his loose pranks of two hours' duration, and of no after consequence, with the severe eyes which inspect real vices with their bearings upon two worlds. We are spectators to a plot or intrigue (not reducible in life to the point of strict morality) and take it all for truth. We substitute a real for a dramatic person, and judge him accordingly. We try him in our courts, from which there is no appeal to the *dramatis personæ*, his peers. We have been spoiled with – not sentimental comedy – but a tyrant far more pernicious to our pleasures which has succeeded to it, the exclusive and all devouring drama of common life; where the moral point is every thing; where, instead of the fictitious half-believed personages of the stage (the phantoms of old comedy) we recognise ourselves, our brothers, aunts, kinsfolk, allies, patrons, enemies, – the same as in life, – with an interest in what is going on so hearty and substantial, that we cannot afford our moral judgment, in its deepest and most vital results, to compromise or slumber for a moment. What is *there* transacting, by no modification is made to affect us in any other manner than the same events or characters would do in our relationships of life. We carry our fire-side concerns to the theatre with us. We do not go thither, like our ancestors, to escape from the pressure of reality, so much as to confirm our experience of it; to make assurance double, and take a bond of fate. We must live our toilsome lives twice over, as it was the mournful privilege of Ulysses to descend twice to the shades. All that neutral ground of character, which stood between vice and virtue; or which in fact was indifferent to neither, where neither properly was called in question; that happy breathing-place from the burthen of a perpetual moral questioning – the sanctuary and quiet Alsatia[1] of hunted casuistry – is broken up and disfranchised, as injurious to the interests of society. The privileges of the place are taken away by law. We dare not dally with images or names, of wrong. We bark like foolish dogs at shadows. We dread infection from the scenic representation of disorder; and fear a painted pustule. In our anxiety that our morality should not take cold, we wrap it up in a great blanket surtout of precaution against the breeze of sunshine.

I confess for myself that (with no great delinquencies to answer for) I am glad for a season to take an airing beyond the diocese of the strict conscience, – not to live always in the precincts of the law-courts, – but now and then, for a dream-while or so, to imagine a world with no meddling restrictions – to get into recesses, whither the hunter cannot follow me –

> ————————Secret shades
> Of woody Ida's inmost grove,
> While yet there was no fear of Jove –*a*

I come back to my cage and my restraint the fresher and more healthy for it. I wear my shackles more contentedly for having respired the breath of an imaginary freedom. I do not know how it is with others, but I feel the better always for the perusal of one of Congreve's – nay, why should I not add even of Wycherley's – comedies. I am the gayer at least for it; and I could never connect those sports of a witty fancy in any shape with any result to be drawn from them to imitation in real life. They are a world of themselves almost as much as fairy-land. Take one of their characters, male or female (with few exceptions they are alike), and place it in a modern play, and my virtuous indignation shall rise against the profligate wretch as warmly as the Catos of the pit could desire;[2] because in a modern play I am to judge of the right and the wrong. The standard of *police*[b] is the measure of *political justice*. The atmosphere will blight it, it cannot live here. It has got into a moral world, where it has no business, from which it must needs fall headlong; as dizzy, and incapable of making a stand, as a Swedenborgian bad spirit that has wandered unawares into the sphere of one of his Good Men, or Angels.[3] But in its own world do we feel the creature is so very bad? – The Fainalls and the Mirabels, the Dorimants and the Lady Touchwoods,[4] in their own sphere, do not offend my moral sense; in fact they do not appeal to it at all. They seem engaged in their proper element. They break through no laws, or conscientious restraints. They know of none. They have got out of Christendom into the land – what shall I call it? – of cuckoldry – the Utopia of gallantry, where pleasure is duty, and the manners perfect freedom. It is altogether a speculative scene of things, which has no reference whatever to the world that is. No good person can be justly offended as a spectator, because no good person suffers on the stage. Judged morally, every character in these plays – the few exceptions only are *mistakes* – is alike essentially vain and worthless. The great art of Congreve is especially shown in this, that he has entirely excluded from his scenes, – some little generosities in the part of Angelica

---

a Milton, "Il Penseroso," 28–30
b used, in an odd sense, to imply the mere regulation of life in a city

perhaps excepted,[5] – not only any thing like a faultless character, but any pretensions to goodness or good feelings whatsoever. Whether he did this designedly, or instinctively, the effect is as happy, as the design (if design) was bold. I used to wonder at the strange power which his Way of the World in particular possesses of interesting you all along in the pursuits of characters, for whom you absolutely care nothing – for you neither hate nor love his personages – and I think it is owing to this very indifference for any, that you endure the whole. He has spread a privation of moral light, I will call it, rather than by the ugly name of palpable darkness, over his creations; and his shadows flit before you without distinction or preference. Had he introduced a good character, a single gush of moral feeling, a revulsion of the judgment to actual life and actual duties, the impertinent Goshen[a] would have only lighted to the discovery of deformities, which now are none, because we think them none.

Translated into real life, the characters of his, and his friend Wycherley's dramas, are profligates and strumpets, – the business of their brief existence, the undivided pursuit of lawless gallantry. No other spring of action, or possible motive of conduct, is recognised; principles which, universally acted upon, must reduce this frame of things to a chaos. But we do them wrong in so translating them. No such effects are produced in *their* world. When we are among them, we are amongst a chaotic people. We are not to judge them by our usages. No reverend institutions are insulted by their proceedings, – for they have none among them. No peace of families is violated, – for no family ties exist among them. No purity of the marriage bed is stained, – for none is supposed to have a being. No deep affections are disquieted, – no holy wedlock bands are snapped asunder, – for affection's depth and wedded faith are not of the growth of that soil. There is neither right nor wrong, – gratitude or its opposite, – claim or duty, – paternity or sonship. Of what consequence is it to virtue, or how is she at all concerned about it, whether Sir Simon, or Dapperwit, steal away Miss Martha; or who is the father of Lord Froth's, or Sir Paul Pliant's children.[6]

The whole is a passing pageant, where we should sit as unconcerned at the issues, for life or death, as at a battle of the frogs and mice. But like Don Quixote, we take part against the puppets, and quite as impertinently. We dare not contemplate an Atlantis, a scheme, out of which our coxcombical moral sense is for a little transitory ease excluded.[7] We have not the courage to imagine a state of

---

[a] Goshen was the land of Moses and his people, who were spared the Egyptian plague of the flies; the allusion is to Exodus VIII. 22

things for which there is neither reward nor punishment. We cling to the painful necessities of shame and blame. We would indict our very dreams.

Amid the mortifying circumstances attendant upon growing old, it is something to have seen the School for Scandal in its glory. This comedy grew out of Congreve and Wycherley, but gathered some allays of the sentimental comedy which followed theirs. It is impossible that it should be now *acted*, though it continues, at long intervals to be announced in the bills. Its hero, when Palmer played it at least,[8] was Joseph Surface. When I remember the gay boldness, the graceful solemn plausibility, the measured step, the insinuating voice – to express it in a word – the downright *acted* villany of the part, so different from the pressure of conscious actual wickedness, – the hypocritical assumption of hypocrisy, – which made Jack so deservedly a favourite in that character, I must needs conclude the present generation of play-goers more virtuous than myself, or more dense. I freely confess that he divided the palm with me with his better brother; that, in fact, I liked him quite as well. Not but there are passages, – like that, for instance, where Joseph is made to refuse a pittance to a poor relation, – incongruities which Sheridan was forced upon by the attempt to join the artificial with the sentimental comedy, either of which must destroy the other – but over these obstructions Jack's manner floated him so lightly, that a refusal from him no more shocked you, than the easy compliance of Charles gave you in reality any pleasure; you got over the paltry question as quickly as you could, to get back into the regions of pure comedy, where no cold moral reigns. The highly artificial manner of Palmer in this character counteracted every disagreeable impression which you might have received from the contrast, supposing them real, between the two brothers. You did not believe in Joseph with the same faith with which you believed in Charles. The latter was a pleasant reality, the former a no less pleasant poetical foil to it. The comedy, I have said, is incongruous; a mixture of Congreve with sentimental incompatibilities: the gaiety upon the whole is buoyant; but it required the consummate art of Palmer to reconcile the discordant elements.

A player with Jack's talents, if we had one now, would not dare to do the part in the same manner. He would instinctively avoid every turn which might tend to unrealise, and so to make the character fascinating. He must take his cue from his spectators, who would expect a bad man and a good man as rigidly opposed to each other as the death-beds of those geniuses are contrasted in the prints, which I am sorry to say have disappeared from the windows of my old friend

Carrington Bowles, of St. Paul's Church-yard memory – (an exhibition as venerable as the adjacent cathedral, and almost coeval) of the bad and good man at the hour of death; where the ghastly apprehensions of the former, – and truly the grim phantom with his reality of a toasting fork is not be be despised, – so finely contrast with the meek complacent kissing of the rod, – taking it in like honey and butter, – with which the latter submits to the scythe of the gentle bleeder, Time, who wields his lancet with the apprehensive finger of a popular young ladies' surgeon.[9] What flesh, like loving grass, would not covet to meet half-way the stroke of such a delicate mower? – John Palmer was twice an actor in this exquisite part. He was playing to you all the while that he was playing upon Sir Peter and his lady. You had the first intimation of a sentiment before it was on his lips. His altered voice was meant to you, and you were to suppose that his fictitious co-flutterers on the stage perceived nothing at all of it. What was it to you if that half-reality, the husband, was over-reached by the puppetry – or the thin thing (Lady Teazle's reputation) was persuaded it was dying of a plethory? The fortunes of Othello and Desdemona were not concerned in it. Poor Jack has past from the stage in good time, that he did not live to this our age of seriousness. The pleasant old Teazle *King*, too, is gone in good time.[10] His manner would scarce have past current in our day. We must love or hate – acquit or condemn – censure or pity – exert our detestable coxcombry of moral judgment upon every thing. Joseph Surface, to go down now, must be a downright revolting villain – no compromise – his first appearance must shock and give horror – his specious plausibilities, which the pleasurable faculties of our fathers welcomed with such hearty greetings, knowing that no harm (dramatic harm even) could come, or was meant to come of them, must inspire a cold and killing aversion. Charles (the real canting person of the scene – for the hypocrisy of Joseph has its ulterior legitimate ends, but his brother's professions of a good heart centre in downright self-satisfaction) must be *loved*, and Joseph *hated*. To balance one disagreeable reality with another, Sir Peter Teazle must be no longer the comic idea of a fretful old bachelor bridegroom, whose teasings (while King acted it) were evidently as much played off at you, as they were meant to concern any body on the stage, – he must be a real person, capable in law of sustaining an injury – a person towards whom duties are to be acknowledged – the genuine crim-con antagonist of the villainous seducer Joseph. To realise him more, his sufferings under his unfortunate match must have the downright pungency of life – must (or should) make you not mirthful but uncomfortable, just as the same predicament would move you in a neighbour or old friend. The delicious scenes which give the play its name and zest, must affect you in the same serious manner as if you heard the reputation of a dear female friend attacked in your real presence. Crabteee and Sir Benjamin – those poor snakes that live but in the sunshine of your mirth – must be ripened by this hot-bed process of realization into asps or amphisbænas;* and Mrs. Candour – O! frightful! becomes a hooded serpent.[11] Oh who that remembers Parsons and Dodd – the wasp and butterfly of the School for Scandal – in those two characters; and charming natural Miss Pope, the perfect gentlewoman as distinguished from the fine lady of comedy, in this latter part – would forego the true scenic delight – the escape from life – the oblivion of consequences – the holiday barring out of the pedant Reflection – those Saturnalia of two or three brief hours, well won from the world – to sit instead at one of our modern plays – to have his coward conscience (that forsooth must not be left for a moment) stimulated with perpetual appeals – dulled rather, and blunted, as a faculty without repose must be – and his moral vanity pampered with images of notional justice, notional beneficence, lives saved without the spectators' risk, and fortunes given away that cost the author nothing?

No piece was, perhaps, ever so completely cast in all its parts as this *manager's comedy*.[12] Miss Farren had succeeded to Mrs. Abingdon in Lady Teazle; and Smith, the original Charles, had retired, when I first saw it. The rest of the characters, with very slight exceptions, remained. I remember it was then the fashion to cry down John Kemble, who took the part of Charles after Smith; but, I thought, very unjustly. Smith, I fancy, was more airy, and took the eye with a certain gaiety of person. He brought with him no sombre recollections of tragedy. He had not to expiate the fault of having pleased beforehand in lofty declamation. He had no sins of Hamlet or of Richard to atone for. His failure in these parts was a passport to success in one of so opposite a tendency. But, as far as I could judge, the weighty sense of Kemble made up for more personal incapacity than he had to answer for. His harshest tones in this part came steeped and dulcified in good humour. He made his defects a grace. His exact declamatory manner, as he managed it, only served to convey the points of his dialogue with more precision. It seemed to head the shafts to carry them deeper. Not one of his sparkling sentences was lost. I remember minutely how he delivered each in

---

* the former a poisonous snake found in Africa; the latter a mythical snake, reputedly with a head at either end

succession, and cannot by any effort imagine how any of them could be altered for the better. No man could deliver brilliant dialogue – the dialogue of Congreve or of Wycherley – because none understood it – half so well as John Kemble. His Valentine, in Love for Love, was, to my recollection, faultless. He flagged sometimes in the intervals of tragic passion. He would slumber over the level parts of an heroic character. His Macbeth has been known to nod. But he always seemed to me to be particularly alive to pointed and witty dialogue. The relaxing levities of tragedy have not been touched by any since him – the playful court-bred spirit in which he condescended to the players in Hamlet – the sportive relief which he threw into the darker shades of Richard – disappeared with him. He had his sluggish moods, his torpors – but they were the halting-stones and resting-places of his tragedy – politic savings, and fetches of the breath – husbandry of the lungs, where nature pointed him to be an economist – rather, I think, than errors of the judgment. They were, at worst, less painful than the eternal tormenting unappeasable vigilance, the "lidless dragon eyes",[a] of present fashionable tragedy.

[a] Coleridge, "Ode on the Departing Year," 145

William Hazlitt

(1778–1830)

A sketch of Hazlitt may properly begin with Leigh Hunt's eulogy in the *Tatler*: "Mr. Hazlitt was one of the profoundest writers of the day, an admirable reasoner (no one got better or sooner at the heart of a writer than he did), the best general critic, the greatest critic on art that ever appeared (his writings on that subject cast a light like a painted window), exquisite in his relish of poetry, an untameable lover of liberty, and with all his humour and irritability (of which no man had more) a sincere friend, and a generous enemy." The productions of "general criticism" to which Hunt refers were collected in several volumes which Hazlitt published in his lifetime: *The Round Table* (1817), *Characters of Shakespeare's Plays* (1817), *Lectures on the English Poets* (1818), *A View of the English Stage* (1818), *Lectures on the English Comic Writers* (1819), *Lectures on the Age of Elizabeth* (1820), and *The Spirit of the Age* (1825). As the proximity of these dates reveals, Hazlitt did most of his critical writing in an extraordinarily concentrated period of six or seven years, beginning about 1813. He had earlier published an essay on human action in which he sought to establish "the natural disinterestedness of the mind." The phrase means just what it appears to mean, provided one takes "disinterestedness" to imply a receptiveness to many different biasses, and not an ideal freedom from every bias. Hazlitt's thinking here underlies the argument of his essays in practical criticism, and is often a clue as well to his choice of themes for more personal essays. He retained to the end his fondness for such metaphysical topics as past and future, self-love and benevolence, the knowledge of character, personal identity, and "Why Distant Objects Please."

In style his lectures are very close to his essays. They register perhaps more gravely the author's obligation to impart certain facts and deliver certain opinions, with a less liberal allowance for digressions. But, for epigrammatic vigor and summary command, their nearest counterpart remains Johnson's *Lives of the Poets*. Hazlitt's chief qualification as a lecturer was his training as an independent thinker. His father had been a Dissenting minister, and Hazlitt, sent to school to a Dissenting academy, was expected to take up the same vocation. Several opportunities and interests came together to change his course: the impetus to secular radicalism given by the French Revolution; his ambition to be a painter, partly inspired by the example of his brother John; and a youthful meeting (at the age of nineteen) with Coleridge and Wordsworth. The personal power of these men, and the clear evidence of their originality, in the still unpublished ballads which they read aloud to

Hazlitt, impressed him with an idea of genius to which he would recur throughout his career. His article on *The Excursion* may still be read alongside Lamb's, as an almost unique early estimate by an appreciator who was not a disciple. After his mid-twenties, however, the affection he felt for both poets was weakened by his hatred of their politics. He looked on Coleridge and Wordsworth as apostates from the cause of liberty, whose defenses of the established order were traceable in some measure to fear, and in some measure to the affinity of poetic imagination for arbitrary power (a thought he explores in his essay on *Coriolanus*).

But even Hazlitt's dismissals are never stereotyped – they always preserve the individual traits of the thing they condemn. He writes in distinct tones, for example, of Coleridge's unsteadiness or diffuseness as a reasoner, and of Wordsworth's bigotry or "exclusionism." Thus, seeing a poem of Wordsworth's on gypsies – which had granted them a picturesque energy, but deplored "this torpid life; / Life which the very stars reprove!" – Hazlitt made his reply impulsively, in the footnote of an essay "On Manner."

> Mr. Wordsworth, who has written a sonnet to the King on the good that he has done in the last fifty years, has made an attack on a set of gipsies for having done nothing in four and twenty hours. . . . And why should they, if they were comfortable where they were? . . . We did not look for this Sunday-school philosophy from him. What had he himself been doing in these four and twenty hours? Had he been admiring a flower, or writing a sonnet? We hate the doctrine of utility, even in a philosopher, and much more in a poet.

The quickness, eloquence, and conclusiveness of this counter-attack may be taken as representative. That he should single out "utility" as the repugnant feature of Wordsworth's moralism also shows his taste for paradox – the doctrine of utility being one that Wordsworth consciously despised, so much that he would have found simply baffling the charge that he espoused it. And yet beneath the paradox there is an insight. If it was true, as Wordsworth had declared elsewhere, that men who did not wear fine clothes might nevertheless have deep feelings, then apart from utility the gypsies had as much claim to his sympathies as any other race or sect.

Hazlitt believed in the good of controversy. He has, in consequence, been regarded with ambivalence by readers who look to criticism for mediation, or resolution, or reconciliation of the controversies of taste. In his own writings, however, he failed to meet this demand because he thought it served a misunderstanding of the purposes of art. His practice as a result is difficult to characterize. Yet he does seem always to have assumed that great writers were the inspired tellers of partial truths. The critic's task therefore was to affirm the value of those truths with which he sympathized most strongly. Judgement, on this view, is related to morality in that it teaches what it requires for its own improvement, namely a spirit of tolerance, assisted by "hard thinking" and impassioned feeling. The implicit apology for literature seems to be this: that it is valuable in showing us the fates of characters whom we could not have imagined without its aid; so that its perspective resembles that of history or anthropology rather than that of theology or metaphysics. Even as it takes us out of ourselves, we cannot help using the sense of power that it gives to confirm and strengthen the powers of the self. In this respect Hazlitt articulates the poetics that Wordsworth implied in the "Essay, Supplementary."

At the same time, his *Lectures on the English Poets* reverse the plot of the very narrative of progress Wordsworth aimed to achieve. Hazlitt places Shakespeare and Milton at the head of English poets, and they also come at the start of his story. The decline that he observes has to do with a division of powers between these authors. Shakespeare stands for dramatic poetry, range of character, and an effortless immediacy of effect; Milton, for personal (or "egotistical") poetry, intensity of character, and a successful striving for effect. If Shakespeare has a successor, it is Walter Scott in prose, for in a certain sense he has left nothing to be done in poetry. Only the way of Milton now lies open while a power comparable to his is unimaginable. Poetry for a modern is the work of protestant inquest and justification: Hazlitt sometimes celebrates this outcome and sometimes laments it, but he suggests no other possibility. In its broader outlines as well as its particular defense of Wordsworth, this story had a lasting influence on Keats. As may be deduced from the essays on "Mr. Coleridge" and "Byron and Wordsworth," Hazlitt judged that beside Wordsworth, Coleridge was an exquisite poet of smaller scope, whereas Byron had done nothing in writing to earn such a comparison at all.

In the essay "Why the Arts Are Not Progressive?" Hazlitt analyzes one cause of this decline. The Enlightenment's belief in progress rested on an analogy between *refinement* in the arts and in the sciences; this analogy, it now turns out, was false. Science builds on the achievements of the past, art is dwarfed by them. "This is the peculiar distinction and privilege of each, of science and of art; of the one, never to attain its utmost summit of perfection, and of the other, to arrive at it almost at once." The unobstructed advance of science is related in another way also to the limited retrospects of art. For modern poetry has contracted its ambitions as a way of responding to the age's restless concern with practical knowledge: in the light of such a concern, its unfaciliting choice of subjects has the purity of the marginal gesture. But in making this response, necessary as it may be, poetry refuses to cooperate with the spirit of the age, which is itself on the side of enlightenment and utility. Where Peacock will rejoice, or affect to rejoice at this development, on the ground that poets are liars and flatterers whose uses are exhausted when a tribe has become a civilization, Hazlitt writes of the change elegiacally. It is not that he admires the moral character of poets: as much as Peacock, he scorns their "versatility" in the service of power. He defends poetry rather because in some fashion it has kept open the possibility of secular prophecy. This is what utilitarian thinking, for all the good it does, has risked destroying utterly. To the extent that it obliges individuals to imagine themselves as part of a multitude, it is a levelling tendency.

William Hazlitt (1778–1830)

These findings concerning the modern artist's relation to the history of his art are modified in Hazlitt's essays "On Imitation" and "On *Gusto*." Both essays remark how an artist's command derives from a temperament and a point of view. So little are the traits of any original reducible to his historical situation that a painter like Titian may be remote from most of his contemporaries and nearly allied with a successor of another nationality several hundred years later. If imitation is understood not as a routine process but as a language which anyone may learn, it follows that to be original is to say something new, intelligible, and interesting in that language, and that this aim is intrinsically no more difficult to fulfill in one age than in another. A further implication of the argument is that the work of interpretation is separate from the cumulative learning of connoisseurship. We consult art for the same reason that we consult nature: in order to assimilate – or, as Hazlitt puts it, to refine, analyze, divide and decompound – the things that interest us. This is a different thing from verifying a description of them by already familiar ground-rules. When Hazlitt says that the painter versed in nature takes the same pleasure from the object itself that the viewer takes from the painting, he means that the mind's representations come before the sense it may suppose as naturally present in things. Thus the mind is its own text. What it looks at, on the page or the canvas, in the landscape or the sky, imposes only the most general common-sense limits on what it can discern. Hazlitt's aphorism, "Art is the microscope of the mind," is a strong English precedent for the sentence that Pater quotes from Victor Hugo in the Conclusion to *The Renaissance*: "Philosophy is the microscope of thought."

The style of Hazlitt's criticism is often called "conversational." He himself called it familiar, but there is nothing wrong with the second word, so long as its sense remains precise. He wrote several essays on the differences between writing and speaking, and often noticed that those who shone in the latter very seldom had the patience, or the habits of compression required for the former. But it seems fair in thinking of him to picture a speaker who stands level with the listener, and who shows by his manner of address that he feels the listener is capable of a reply. His self-respect is contagious; and it is part of his generosity. Once, overhearing a taunt against a player at rackets who lost the hard rallies – "That is French courage" – he replied, according to his friend Procter, "The French have fought well; they have endured, too, more than enough – without your present imputation. Did you ever fight a Frenchman?" "No." "Then don't make up your mind yet to your theory: reduce it to a practice, and see if it be bullet-proof." The exchange catches a good many elements of a tone that pervades his writing: its unaccommodating likes and dislikes, and quick adjustments from defense to attack; above all, its unwillingness to settle for any but the direct hit. In this, he has no peer. The nervous and reanimating shifts of tactics may appear to consort oddly with Hazlitt's well-earned reputation for consistency of opinion. They are, in fact, the form he gave to a test of sincerity, a search for "new reasons for the faith that is in me," and new interrogations to strengthen the reasons that survived. One's impression, whether true or not, is that, as a matter of principle, he uses the word "but" more often than "and."

5. *"Why the Arts Are Not Progressive?"*

first published in *The Morning Chronicle*, January 11, 15, 1814; text from *Works*, ed. P. P. Howe (1930–34), vol. 18, pp. 5–10

IT is often made a subject of complaint and surprise, that the arts in this country, and in modern times, have not kept pace with the general progress of society and civilisation in other respects, and it has been proposed to remedy the deficiency by more carefully availing ourselves of the advantages which time and circumstances have placed within our reach, but which we have hitherto neglected, the study of the antique, the formation of academies, and the distribution of prizes.

First, the complaint itself, that the arts do not attain that progressive degree of perfection which might reasonably be expected from them, proceeds on a false notion, for the analogy appealed to in support of the regular advances of art to higher degrees of excellence, totally fails; it applies to science, not to art. Secondly, the expedients proposed to remedy the evil by adventitious means are only calculated to confirm it. The arts hold immediate communication with nature, and are only derived from that source. When that original impulse no longer exists, when the inspiration of genius is fled, all the attempts to recall it are no better than the tricks of galvanism to restore the dead to life. The arts may be said to resemble Antæus in his struggle with Hercules, who was strangled when he was raised above the ground, and only revived and recovered his strength when he touched his mother earth.

Nothing is more contrary to the fact than the supposition that in what we understand by the *fine arts*, as painting and poetry, relative perfection is only the result of repeated efforts, and that what has been once well done constantly leads to something better. What is mechanical, reducible to rule, or capable of demonstration, is progressive, and admits of gradual improvement: what is not mechanical or definite, but depends on genius, taste, and feeling, very soon becomes stationary or retrograde, and loses more than it gains by transfusion. The contrary opinion is, indeed, a common error, which has grown up, like many others, from transferring an analogy of one kind to something quite distinct, without thinking of the difference in the nature of the things, or attending to the difference of the results. For most persons, finding what wonderful advances have been made in biblical criticism, in chemistry, in mechanics, in geometry, astronomy, &c. – *i.e.* in things depending on mere inquiry and experiment, or on absolute demonstration – have been led hastily to conclude, that there was a general tendency in the efforts of the human intellect to improve by repetition, and in all other arts and institutions to grow perfect and mature by time. We look back upon the theological creed of our ancestors, and their discoveries in natural philosophy, with a smile of pity; science, and the arts connected with it, have all had their infancy, their youth, and manhood, and seem to have in them no principle of limitation or decay; and, inquiring no farther about the matter, we infer, in the height of our self-congratulation, and in the intoxication of our pride, that the same progress has been, and will continue to be, made in all other things which are the work of man. The fact, however, stares us so plainly in the face, that one would think the smallest reflection must suggest the truth, and overturn our sanguine theories. The greatest poets, the ablest orators, the best painters, and the finest sculptors that the world ever saw, appeared soon after the birth of these arts, and lived in a state of society which was, in other respects, comparatively barbarous. Those arts, which depend on individual genius and incommunicable power, have always leaped at once from infancy to manhood, from the first rude dawn of invention to their meridian height and dazzling lustre, and have in general declined ever after. This is the peculiar distinction and privilege of each, of science and of art; of the one, never to attain its utmost summit of perfection, and of the other, to arrive at it almost at once. Homer, Chaucer, Spenser, Shakspeare, Dante, and Ariosto (Milton alone was of a later age, and not the worse for it), Raphael, Titian, Michael Angelo, Correggio, Cervantes, and Boccaccio – all lived near the beginning of their arts – perfected, and all but created them. These giant sons of genius stand, indeed, upon the earth, but they tower above their fellows, and the long line of their successors does not interpose any thing to obstruct their view, or lessen their brightness. In strength and stature they are unrivalled, in grace and beauty they have never been surpassed. In after-ages, and more refined periods (as they are called), great men have arisen one by one, as it were by throes and at intervals: though in general the best of these cultivated and artificial minds were of an inferior order, as Tasso and Pope among poets, Claude Lorraine[1] and Vandyke among painters. But in the earliest stages of the arts, when the first mechanical difficulties had been got over, and the language as it were acquired, they rose by clusters and in constellations, never to rise again.

SCIENCE and the mechanic arts depend not on the force with which the mind itself is endued, or with which it contemplates given things (for this is naturally much the same), but on the number of things, successively perceived by the same or different persons, and formally arranged and registered in books or memory, which admits of being varied and augmented indefinitely. The number of objects to which the understanding may be directed is endless, and the results, so far as they are positive, tangible things, may be set down and added one to another, and made use of as occasion requires, without creating any confusion, and so as to produce a perpetual accumulation of useful knowledge. What is once gained is never lost, and may be multiplied daily, because this increase of knowledge does not depend upon increasing the force of the mind, but on directing the same force to different things, all of them in their nature definite, demonstrable, existing to the mind outwardly and by signs, less as the power than as the form of truth, and in which all the difficulty lies in the first invention, not in the subsequent communication. In like manner the mechanic parts of painting for instance, such as the mode of preparing colours, and laws of perspective, &c., which may be taught by rule and method, so that the principle being once known, every one may avail himself of it, these subordinate and instrumental parts of the art admit of uniform excellence, though from accidental causes it has happened otherwise. But it is not so in art itself, in its higher and nobler essence. "There is no shuffling," but "we ourselves compelled to give in evidence even to the teeth and forehead of our faults."[a] There is no room for the division of labour – for the accumulation of borrowed advantages; no artifical scale by which *to heaven we may ascend*; because here excellence does not depend on the quantity of representative knowledge, abstracted from a variety of subjects, but on the original force of capacity, and degree of attention, applied to the same given subject, natural feelings and images. To use the distinction of a technical philosophy, science depends on the discursive or *extensive* – art on the intuitive and *intensive* power of the mind. One chemical or mathematical discovery may be added to another, because the degree and sort of faculty required to apprehend and retain them, are in both cases the same; but no one can voluntarily add the colouring of Rubens to the expression of Raphael, till he has the same eye for colour as Rubens, and for expression as

[a] Claudius, in *Hamlet*, III. iii. 61

5. *"Why the Arts Are Not Progressive?"*

Raphael – that is, the most thorough feeling of what is profound in the one, or splendid in the other – of what no rules can teach, nor words convey – and of what the mind must possess within itself, and by a kind of participation with nature, or remain for ever destitute of it. Titian and Correggio are the only painters who united to perfect colouring a degree of expression, the one in his portraits, and the other in his histories, all but equal, if not equal, to the highest. But this union of different qualities they had from nature, and not by method. In fact, we judge of science by the number of effects produced – of art by the energy which produces them. The one is knowledge – the other power.

The arts of painting and poetry are conversant with the world of thought within us, and with the world of sense without us – with what we know, and see, and feel intimately. They flow from the sacred shrine of our own breasts, and are kindled at the living lamp of nature. The pulse of the passions assuredly beat as high, the depths and soundings of the human heart were as well understood three thousand years ago, as they are at present; the face of nature and "the human face divine," shone as bright then as they have ever done. It is this light, reflected by true genius on art, that marks out its path before it, and sheds a glory round the Muses' feet, like that which "circled Una's angel face,"

"And made a sunshine in the shady place."[a]

Nature is the soul of art. There is a strength in the imagination that reposes entirely on nature, which nothing else can supply. There is in the old poets and painters a vigour and grasp of mind, a full possession of their subject, a confidence and firm faith, a sublime simplicity, an elevation of thought, proportioned to their depth of feeling, an increasing force and impetus, which moves, penetrates, and kindles all that comes in contact with it, which seems, not theirs, but given to them. It is this reliance on the power of nature which has produced those masterpieces by the Prince of Painters,[b] in which expression is all in all, where one spirit, that of truth, pervades every part, brings down heaven to earth, mingles cardinals and popes with angels and apostles, and yet blends and harmonises the whole by the true touches and intense feeling of what is beautiful and grand in nature. It was the same trust in nature that enabled Chaucer to describe the patient sorrow of Griselda; or the delight of that young beauty in the Flower and the Leaf, shrouded in her bower, and

[a] *Faerie Queene*, Book I canto iii st. 4
[b] Raphael, with particular reference to the Cartoons and paintings for the Stanze in the Vatican

87

listening, in the morning of the year, to the singing of the nightingale, while her joy rises with the rising song, and gushes out afresh at every pause, and is borne along with the full tide of pleasure, and still increases and repeats and prolongs itself, and knows no ebb. It is thus that Boccaccio, in the divine story of the Hawk, has represented Frederigo Alberigi steadily contemplating his favourite Falcon (the wreck and remnant of his fortune), and glad to see how fat and fair a bird she is, thinking what a dainty repast she would make for his Mistress, who had deigned to visit him in his low cell. So Isabella mourns over her pot of Basile, and never asks for any thing but that. So Lear calls out for his poor fool, and invokes the heavens, for they are old like him. So Titian impressed on the countenance of that young Neapolitan nobleman in the Louvre, a look that never passed away.[a] So Nicolas Poussin describes some shepherds wandering out in a morning of the spring, and coming to a tomb with this inscription, "I also was an Arcadian."[b]

What have we left to console us for all this? Why, we have Mr. Rogers's "Pleasures of Memory," and Mr. Campbell's "Pleasures of Hope"; Mr. Westall's pictures, and all West's; Miss Burney's new novel (which is, however, some comfort), Miss Edgeworth's Fashionable Tales, Madame de Staël's next work, whatever it may be, and the praise of it in the *Edinburgh Review*, and Sir James Macintosh's *History*.[2]

6. *"On Mr. Kean's Iago"*

first published in *The Examiner*, July 24, 1814; text of *The Round Table* (1817), from *Works*, ed. P. P. Howe (1930–34), vol. 4, pp. 14–17

We certainly think Mr. Kean's[1] performance of the part of Iago one of the most extraordinary exhibitions on the stage. There is no one within our remembrance who has so completely foiled the critics as this celebrated actor: one sagacious person imagines that he must perform a part in a certain manner, – another virtuoso chalks out a different path for him; and when the time comes, he does the whole off in a way that neither of them had the least conception of, and which both of them are therefore very ready to condemn as entirely wrong. It was ever the trick of genius to be thus. We confess that Mr. Kean has thrown us out more than once. For instance, we are very much inclined to adopt the opinion of a contemporary critic,[2] that his

---

[a] *Young Man with a Glove*   [b] an allusion to Poussin's "*Et in Arcadia Ego*," in the Louvre

Richard is not gay enough, and that his *Iago* is not grave enough. This he may perhaps conceive to be the mere caprice of idle criticism; but we will try to give our reasons, and shall leave them to Mr. Kean's better judgment. It is to be remembered, then, that *Richard* was a princely villain, borne along in a sort of triumphal car of royal state, buoyed up with the hopes and privileges of his birth, reposing even on the sanctity of religion, trampling on his devoted victims without remorse, and who looked out and laughed from the high watch-tower of his confidence and his expectations on the desolation and misery he had caused around him. He held on his way, unquestioned, "hedged in with the divinity of kings,"[a] amenable to no tribunal, and abusing his power *in contempt of mankind.* But as for *Iago*, we conceive differently of him. He had not the same natural advantages. He was a mere adventurer in mischief, a pains-taking plodding knave, without patent or pedigree, who was obliged to work his up-hill way by wit, not by will, and to be the founder of his own fortune. He was, if we may be allowed a vulgar allusion, a sort of prototype of modern Jacobinism,[3] who thought that talents ought to decide the place, – a man of "morbid sensibility," (in the fashionable phrase), full of distrust, of hatred, of anxious and corroding thoughts, and who, though he might assume a temporary superiority over others by superior adroitness, and pride himself in his skill, could not be supposed to assume it as a matter of course, as if he had been entitled to it from his birth. We do not here mean to enter into the characters of the two men, but something must be allowed to the difference of their situations. There might be the same insensibility in both as to the end in view, but there could not well be the same security as to the success of the means. *Iago* had to pass through a different ordeal: he had no appliances and means to boot; no royal road to the completion of his tragedy. His pretensions were not backed by authority; they were not baptized at the font; they were not holy-waterproof. He had the whole to answer for in his own person, and could not shift the responsibility to the heads of others. Mr. Kean's *Richard* was, therefore, we think, deficient in something of that regal jollity and reeling triumph of success which the part would bear; but this we can easily account for, because it is the traditional commonplace idea of the character, that he is to "play the dog – to bite and snarl."[b] – The extreme unconcern and laboured levity of his *Iago*, on the contrary, is a refinement and original device of the actor's own mind, and therefore deserves consideration. The character of *Iago*, in fact, belongs to a class of characters common to Shakspeare, and at the same time

---

[a] an echo of *Hamlet,* IV. v. 124   [b] Richard, in *3 Henry VI,* v. vi. 77

peculiar to him – namely, that of great intellectual activity, accompanied with a total want of moral principle, and therefore displaying itself at the constant expence of others, making use of reason as a pander to will – employing its ingenuity and its resources to palliate its own crimes and aggravate the faults of others, and seeking to confound the practical distinctions of right and wrong, by referring them to some overstrained standard of speculative refinement. – Some persons, more nice than wise, have thought the whole of the character of *Iago* unnatural. Shakspeare, who was quite as good a philosopher as he was a poet, thought otherwise. He knew that the love of power, which is another name for the love of mischief, was natural to man. He would know this as well or better than if it had been demonstrated to him by a logical diagram, merely from seeing children paddle in the dirt, or kill flies for sport. We might ask those who think the character of *Iago* not natural, why they go to see it performed, but from the interest it excites, the sharper edge which it sets on their curiosity and imagination? Why do we go to see tragedies in general? Why do we always read the accounts in the newspapers of dreadful fires and shocking murders, but for the same reason? Why do so many persons frequent executions and trials, or why do the lower classes almost universally take delight in barbarous sports and cruelty to animals, but because there is a natural tendency in the mind to strong excitement, a desire to have its faculties roused and stimulated to the utmost? Whenever this principle is not under the restraint of humanity, or the sense of moral obligation, there are no excesses to which it will not of itself give rise, without the assistance of any other motive, either of passion or self-interest. *Iago* is only an extreme instance of the kind; that is, of diseased intellectual activity, with an almost perfect indifference to moral good or evil, or rather with a preference of the latter, because it falls more in with his favourite propensity, gives greater zest to his thoughts, and scope to his actions. – Be it observed, too, (for the sake of those who are for squaring all human actions by the maxims of Rochefoucault),[4] that he is quite or nearly as indifferent to his own fate as to that of others; that he runs all risks for a trifling and doubtful advantage; and is himself the dupe and victim of his ruling passion – an incorrigible love of mischief – an insatiable craving after action of the most difficult and dangerous kind. Our "Ancient"[5] is a philosopher, who fancies that a lie that kills has more point in it than an alliteration or an antithesis; who thinks a fatal experiment on the peace of a family a better thing than watching the palpitations in the heart of a flea in an air-pump;[6] who plots the ruin of his friends as an exercise for his understanding, and stabs men in the dark to prevent *ennui*. Now this, though it be sport, yet it is dreadful sport. There is no room for trifling and indifference, nor scarcely for the appearance of it; the very object of his whole plot is to keep his faculties stretched on the rack, in a state of watch and ward, in a sort of breathless suspense, without a moment's interval of repose. He has a desperate stake to play for, like a man who fences with poisoned weapons, and has business enough on his hands to call for the whole stock of his sober circumspection, his dark duplicity, and insidious gravity. He resembles a man who sits down to play at chess, for the sake of the difficulty and complication of the game, and who immediately becomes absorbed in it. His amusements, if they are amusements, are severe and saturnine – even his wit blisters. His gaiety arises from the success of his treachery; his ease from the sense of the torture he has inflicted on others. Even, if other circumstances permitted it, the part he has to play with *Othello* requires that he should assume the most serious concern, and something of the plausibility of a confessor. "His cue is villainous melancholy, with a sigh like Tom o' Bedlam."[a] He is repeatedly called "honest *Iago*," which looks as if there were something suspicious in his appearance, which admitted a different construction. The tone which he adopts in the scenes with *Roderigo, Desdemona*, and *Cassio*, is only a relaxation from the more arduous business of the play. Yet there is in all his conversation an inveterate misanthropy, a licentious keenness of perception, which is always sagacious of evil, and snuffs up the tainted scent of its quarry with rancorous delight. An exuberance of spleen is the essence of the character. The view which we have here taken of the subject (if at all correct) will not therefore justify the extreme alteration which Mr. Kean has introduced into the part. Actors in general have been struck only with the wickedness of the character, and have exhibited an assassin going to the place of execution. Mr. Kean has abstracted the wit of the character, and makes *Iago* appear throughout an excellent good fellow, and lively bottle-companion. But though we do not wish him to be represented as a monster, or fiend, we see no reason why he should instantly be converted into a pattern of comic gaiety and good-humour. The light which illumines the character should rather resemble the flashes of lightning in the mirky sky, which make the darkness more terrible. Mr. Kean's *Iago* is, we suspect, too much in the sun. His manner of acting the part would have suited better with the character of *Edmund* in *King Lear*, who, though in other respects much the same, has a spice of gallantry in his constitution, and has the favour and counte-

[a] Edmund, in *King Lear*, I. ii. 138

nance of the ladies, which always gives a man the smug appearance of a bridegroom!

7. *"On Imitation"*[1]

first published in *The Examiner*, February 18, 1816; text of *The Round Table* (1817), from *Works*, ed. P. P. Howe (1930–34), vol. 4, pp. 72–77

OBJECTS in themselves disagreeble or indifferent, often please in the imitation. A brick-floor, a pewter-table, an ugly cur barking, a Dutch boor smoking or playing at skittles, the inside of a shambles, a fishmonger's or a greengrocer's stall, have been made very interesting as pictures by the fidelity, skill, and spirit, with which they have been copied. One source of the pleasure thus received is undoubtedly the surprise or feeling of admiration, occasioned by the unexpected coincidence between the imitation and the object. The deception, however, not only pleases at first sight, or from mere novelty; but it continues to please upon farther acquaintance, and in proportion to the insight we acquire into the distinctions of nature and of art. By far the most numerous class of connoisseurs are the admirers of pictures of *still life*, which have nothing but the elaborateness of the execution to recommend them. One chief reason, it should seem then, why imitation pleases, is, because, by exciting curiosity, and inviting a comparison between the object and the representation, it opens a new field of inquiry, and leads the attention to a variety of details and distinctions not perceived before. This latter source of the pleasure derived from imitation has never been properly insisted on.

The anatomist is delighted with a coloured plate, conveying the exact appearance of the progress of certain diseases, or of the internal parts and dissections of the human body. We have known a Jennerian Professor[a] as much enraptured with a delineation of the different stages of vaccination, as a florist with a bed of tulips, or an auctioneer with a collection of Indian shells. But in this case, we find that not only the imitation pleases, – the objects themselves give as much pleasure to the professional inquirer, as they would pain to the uninitiated. The learned amateur is struck with the beauty of the coats of the stomach laid bare, or contemplates with eager curiosity the transverse section of the brain, divided on the new Spurzheim principles.[b] It is here, then, the number of the parts, their distinctions, connections, structure, uses; in short, an entire new set of ideas,

[a] after Edward Jenner (1749–1823), discoverer of the smallpox vaccine   [b] phrenology

which occupies the mind of the student, and overcomes the sense of pain and repugnance, which is the only feeling that the sight of a dead and mangled body presents to ordinary men. It is the same in art as in science. The painter of still life, as it is called, takes the same pleasure in the object as the spectator does in the imitation; because by habit he is led to perceive all those distinctions in nature, to which other persons never pay any attention till they are pointed out to them in the picture. The vulgar only see nature as it is reflected to them from art; the painter sees the picture in nature, before he transfers it to the canvass. He refines, he analyses, he remarks fifty things, which escape common eyes; and this affords a distinct source of reflection and amusement to him, independently of the beauty or grandeur of the objects themselves, or of their connection with other impressions besides those of sight. The charm of the Fine Arts, then, does not consist in any thing peculiar to imitation, even where only imitation is concerned, since *there*, where art exists in the highest perfection, namely, in the mind of the artist, the object excites the same or greater pleasure, before the imitation exists. Imitation renders an object, displeasing in itself, a source of pleasure, not by repetition of the same idea, but by suggesting new ideas, by detecting new properties, and endless shades of difference, just as a close and continued contemplation of the object itself would do. Art shows us nature, divested of the medium of our prejudices. It divides and decompounds objects into a thousand curious parts, which may be full of variety, beauty, and delicacy in themselves, though the object to which they belong may be disagreeable in its general appearance, or by association with other ideas. A painted marigold is inferior to a painted rose only in form and colour: it loses nothing in point of smell. Yellow hair is perfectly beautiful in a picture. To a person lying with his face close to the ground in a summer's day, the blades of spear-grass will appear like tall forest trees, shooting up into the sky; as an insect seen through a microscope is magnified into an elephant. Art is the microscope of the mind, which sharpens the wit as the other does the sight; and converts every object into a little universe in itself.[2] Art may be said to draw aside the veil from nature. To those who are perfectly unskilled in the practice, unimbued with the principles of art, most objects present only a confused mass. The pursuit of art is liable to be carried to a contrary excess, as where it produces a rage for the *picturesque*. You cannot go a step with a person of this class, but he stops you to point out some choice bit of landscape, or fancied improvement, and teazes you almost to death with the frequency and insignificance of his discoveries!

It is a common opinion, (which may be worth noticing here), that the study of physiognomy has a tendency to make people satirical, and the knowledge of art to make them fastidious in their taste. Knowledge may, indeed, afford a handle to ill-nature; but it takes away the principal temptation to its exercise, by supplying the mind with better resources against *ennui*. Idiots are always mischievous; and the most superficial persons are the most disposed to find fault, because they understand the fewest things. The English are more apt than any other nation to treat foreigners with contempt, because they seldom see anything but their own dress and manners; and it is only in petty provincial towns that you meet with persons who pride themselves on being satirical. In every country place in England there are one or two persons of this description who keep the whole neighbourhood in terror. It is not to be denied that the study of the *ideal* in art, if separated from the study of nature, may have the effect above stated, of producing dissatisfaction and contempt for everything but itself, as all affectation must; but to the genuine artist, truth, nature, beauty, are almost different names for the same thing.

Imitation interests, then, by exciting a more intense perception of truth, and calling out the powers of observation and comparison: wherever this effect takes place the interest follows of course, with or without the imitation, whether the object is real or artificial. The gardener delights in the streaks of a tulip, or "pansy freak'd with jet";[a] the mineralogist in the varieties of certain strata, because he understands them. Knowledge is pleasure as well as power. A work of art has in this respect no advantage over a work of nature, except inasmuch as it furnishes an additional stimulus to curiosity. Again, natural objects please in proportion as they are uncommon, by fixing the attention more steadily on their beauties or differences. The same principle of the effect of novelty in exciting the attention, may account, perhaps, for the extraordinary discoveries and lies told by travellers, who, opening their eyes for the first time in foreign parts, are startled at every object they meet.

Why the excitement of intellectual activity pleases, is not here the question; but that it does so, is a general and acknowledged law of the human mind. We grow attached to the mathematics only from finding out their truth; and their utility chiefly consists (at present) in the contemplative pleasure they afford to the student. Lines, points, angles, squares, and circles are not interesting in themselves; they

[a] The quotation uses Milton, *Lycidas*, 144 against Johnson, *Rasselas*, chapter 10: "The business of a poet ... is to examine, not the individual, but the species ... he does not number the streaks of the tulip."

become so by the power of mind exerted in comprehending their properties and relations. People dispute for ever about Hogarth.[3] The question has not in one respect been fairly stated. The merit of his pictures does not so much depend on the nature of the subject, as on the knowledge displayed of it, on the number of ideas they excite, on the fund of thought and observation contained in them. They are to be looked on as works of science; they gratify our love of truth; they fill up the void of the mind: they are a series of plates of natural history, and also of that most interesting part of natural history, the history of man. The superiority of high art over the common or mechanical consists in combining truth of imitation with beauty and grandeur of subject. The historical painter is superior to the flower-painter, because he combines or ought to combine human interests and passions with the same power of imitating external nature; or, indeed, with greater, for the greatest difficulty of imitation is the power of imitating expression. The difficulty of copying increases with our knowledge of the object; and that again with the interest we take in it. The same argument might be applied to shew that the poet and painter of imagination are superior to the mere philosopher or man of science, because they exercise the powers of reason and intellect combined with nature and passion. They treat of the highest categories of the human soul, pleasure and pain.

From the foregoing train of reasoning, we may easily account for the too great tendency of art to run into pedantry and affection. There is "a pleasure in art which none but artists feel."[a] They see beauty where others see nothing of the sort, in wrinkles, deformity, and old age. They see it in Titian's Schoolmaster as well as in Raphael's Galatea; in the dark shadows of Rembrandt as well as in the splendid colours of Rubens; in an angel's or in a butterfly's wings. They see with different eyes from the multitude. But true genius, though it has new sources of pleasure opened to it, does not lose its sympathy with humanity. It combines truth of imitation with effect, the parts with the whole, the means with the end. The mechanic artist sees only that which nobody else sees, and is conversant only with the technical language and difficulties of his art. A painter, if shewn a picture, will generally dwell upon the academic skill displayed in it, and the knowledge of the received rules of composition. A musician, if asked to play a tune, will select that which is the most difficult and the least intelligible. The poet will be struck with the harmony of versification, or the elaborateness of the arrangement in a composition. The

[a] adapted from Cowper, *The Task*, II. 285–86: "There is a pleasure in poetic pains, / Which only poets know"

conceits in Shakspeare were his greatest delight; and improving upon this perverse method of judging, the German writers, Goethe and Schiller, look upon Werter and The Robbers as the worst of all their works, because they are the most popular. Some artists among ourselves have carried the same principle to a singular excess.[4] If professors themselves are liable to this kind of pedantry, connoisseurs and dilettanti, who have less sensibility and more affectation, are almost wholly swayed by it. They see nothing in a picture but the execution. They are proud of their knowledge in proportion as it is a secret. The worst judges of pictures in the United Kingdom are, first, picture-dealers; next, perhaps, the Directors of the British Institution; and after them, in all probability, the Members of the Royal Academy.[5]

8. "*On* Gusto"[1]

first published in *The Examiner*, May 26, 1816; text of *The Round Table* (1817), from *Works*, ed. P. P. Howe (1930–34), vol. 4, pp. 77–80

GUSTO in art is power or passion defining any object. It is not so difficult to explain this term in what relates to expression (of which it may be said to be the highest degree) as in what relates to things without expression, to the natural appearances of objects, as mere colour or form. In one sense, however, there is hardly any object entirely devoid of expression, without some character of power belonging to it, some precise association with pleasure or pain: and it is in giving this truth of character from the truth of feeling, whether in the highest or the lowest degree, but always in the highest degree of which the subject is capable, that gusto consists.

There is a gusto in the colouring of Titian. Not only do his heads seem to think – his bodies seem to feel. This is what the Italians mean by the *morbidezza*[a] of his flesh-colour. It seems sensitive and alive all over; not merely to have the look and texture of flesh, but the feeling in itself. For example, the limbs of his female figures have a luxurious softness and delicacy, which appears conscious of the pleasure of the beholder. As the objects themselves in nature would produce an impression on the sense, distinct from every other object, and having something divine in it, which the heart owns and the imagination consecrates, the objects in the picture preserve the same impression, absolute, unimpaired, stamped with all the truth of passion, the pride of the eye, and the charm of beauty. Rubens makes his flesh-colour

[a] a life-like delicacy, or tangible vividness to the eye

like flowers; Albano's is like ivory; Titian's is like flesh, and like nothing else. It is as different from that of other painters, as the skin is from a piece of white or red drapery thrown over it. The blood circulates here and there, the blue veins just appear, the rest is distinguished throughout only by that sort of tingling sensation to the eye, which the body feels within itself. This is gusto. Vandyke's flesh-colour, though it has great truth and purity, wants gusto. It has not the internal character, the living principle in it. It is a smooth surface, not a warm, moving mass. It is painted without passion, with indifference. The hand only has been concerned. The impression slides off from the eye, and does not, like the tones of Titian's pencil, leave a sting behind it in the mind of the spectator. The eye does not acquire a taste or appetite for what it sees. In a word, gusto in painting is where the impression made on one sense excites by affinity those of another.

Michael Angelo's forms are full of gusto. They everywhere obtrude the sense of power upon the eye. His limbs convey an idea of muscular strength, of moral grandeur, and even of intellectual dignity: they are firm, commanding, broad, and massy, capable of executing with ease the determined purposes of the will. His faces have no other expression than his figures, conscious power and capacity. They appear only to think what they shall do, and to know that they can do it. This is what is meant by saying that his style is hard and masculine. It is the reverse of Correggio's, which is effeminate. That is, the gusto of Michael Angelo consists in expressing energy of will without proportionable sensibility, Correggio's in expressing exquisite sensibility without energy of will. In Correggio's faces as well as figures we see neither bones nor muscles, but then what a soul is there, full of sweetness and of grace – pure, playful, soft, angelical! There is sentiment enough in a hand painted by Correggio to set up a school of history painters. Whenever we look at the hands of Correggio's women or of Raphael's, we always wish to touch them.

Again, Titian's landscapes have a prodigious gusto, both in the colouring and forms. We shall never forget one that we saw many years ago in the Orleans Gallery of Acteon hunting. It had a brown, mellow, autumnal look. The sky was of the colour of stone. The winds seemed to sing through the rustling branches of the trees, and already you might hear the twanging of bows resound through the tangled mazes of the wood. Mr. West,[2] we understand, has this landscape. He will know if this description of it is just. The landscape back-ground of the St. Peter Martyr is another well known instance of the power of this great painter to give a romantic interest and an appropriate character to the objects of his pencil, where every circumstance adds to the effect of the scene, – the bold trunks of the tall forest trees, the trailing ground plants, with that tall convent spire rising in the distance, amidst the blue sapphire mountains and the golden sky.[3]

Rubens has a great deal of gusto in his Fauns and Satyrs, and in all that expresses motion, but in nothing else. Rembrandt has it in everything; everything in his pictures has a tangible character. If he puts a diamond in the ear of a burgomaster's wife, it is of the first water; and his furs and stuffs are proof against a Russian winter. Raphael's gusto was only in expression; he had no idea of the character of anything but the human form. The dryness and poverty of his style in other respects is a phenomenon in the art. His trees are like sprigs of grass stuck in a book of botanical specimens. Was it that Raphael never had time to go beyond the walls of Rome? That he was always in the streets, at church, or in the bath? He was not one of the Society of Arcadians.[4]

Claude's landscapes, perfect as they are, want gusto. This is not easy to explain. They are perfect abstractions of the visible images of things; they speak the visible language of nature truly. They resemble a mirror or a microscope. To the eye only they are more perfect than any other landscapes that ever were or will be painted; they give more of nature, as cognisable by one sense alone; but they lay an equal stress on all visible impressions. They do not interpret one sense by another; they do not distinguish the character of different objects as we are taught, and can only be taught, to distinguish them by their effect on the different senses. That is, his eye wanted imagination: it did not strongly sympathise with his other faculties. He saw the atmosphere, but he did not feel it. He painted the trunk of a tree or a rock in the foreground as smooth – with as complete an abstraction of the gross, tangible impression, as any other part of the picture. His trees are perfectly beautiful, but quite immovable; they have a look of enchantment. In short, his landscapes are unequalled imitations of nature, released from its subjection to the elements, as if all objects were become a delightful fairy vision, and the eye had rarefied and refined away the other senses.

The gusto in the Greek statues is of a very singular kind.[5] The sense of perfect form nearly occupies the whole mind, and hardly suffers it to dwell on any other feeling. It seems enough for them *to be*, without acting or suffering. Their forms are ideal, spiritual. Their beauty is power. By their beauty they are raised above the frailties of pain or passion; by their beauty they are deified.

The infinite quantity of dramatic invention in Shakspeare takes from his gusto. The power he delights to show is not intense, but discursive. He never insists on anything as much as he might, except a quibble. Milton has great gusto. He repeats his blows twice; grapples with and exhausts his subject. His imagination has a double relish of its objects, an inveterate attachment to the things he describes, and to the words describing them.

> – "Or where Chineses drive
> With sails and wind their *cany* waggons *light*."
> . . .
> "Wild above rule or art, *enormous* bliss."[a]

There is a gusto in Pope's compliments, in Dryden's satires, and Prior's tales; and among prose writers Boccacio and Rabelais had the most of it. We will only mention one other work which appears to us to be full of gusto, and that is the *Beggar's Opera*. If it is not, we are altogether mistaken in our notions on this delicate subject.

9. "Coriolanus"

first published in *The Examiner*, December 15, 1816; text of *Characters of Shakespear's Plays* (1817), from *Works*, ed. P. P. Howe (1930–34), vol. 4, pp. 214–16

SHAKESPEAR has in this play shewn himself well versed in history and state-affairs. CORIOLANUS is a store-house of political common-places. Any one who studies it may save himself the trouble of reading Burke's Reflections, or Paine's Rights of Man, or the Debates in both Houses of Parliament since the French Revolution or our own. The arguments for and against aristocracy or democracy, on the privileges of the few and the claims of the many, on liberty and slavery, power and the abuse of it, peace and war, are here very ably handled, with the spirit of a poet and the acuteness of a philosopher. Shakespear himself seems to have had a leaning to the arbitrary side of the question, perhaps from some feeling of contempt for his own origin; and to have spared no occasion of baiting the rabble. What he says of them is very true: what he says of their betters is also very true, though he dwells less upon it. – The cause of the people is indeed but little calculated as a subject for poetry: it admits of rhetoric, which goes into argument and explanation, but it presents no immediate or distinct images to the mind, "no jutting frieze, buttress, or coigne of

---

[a] *Paradise Lost*, III. 438–39 and V. 297

99

vantage" for poetry "to make its pendant bed and procreant cradle in."[a] The language of poetry naturally falls in with the language of power. The imagination is an exaggerating and exclusive faculty: it takes from one thing to add to another: it accumulates circumstances together to give the greatest possible effect to a favourite object. The understanding is a dividing and measuring faculty: it judges of things not according to their immediate impression on the mind, but according to their relations to one another.[1] The one is a mono-polising faculty, which seeks the greatest quantity of present excite-ment by inequality and disproportion; the other is a distributive faculty, which seeks the greatest quantity of ultimate good, by justice and proportion. The one is an aristocratical, the other a republican faculty. The principle of poetry is a very anti-levelling principle. It aims at effect, it exists by contrast. It admits of no medium. It is every thing by excess. It rises above the ordinary standard of sufferings and crimes. It presents a dazzling appearance. It shows its head turretted, crowned, and crested. Its front is gilt and blood-stained. Before it "it carries noise, and behind it leaves tears."[b] It has its altars and its victims, sacrifices, human sacrifices. Kings, priests, nobles are its train-bearers, tyrants and slaves its executioners. – "Carnage is its daughter."[c] – Poetry is right-royal. It puts the individual for the species, the one above the infinite many, might before right. A lion hunting a flock of sheep or a herd of wild asses is a more poetical object than they; and we even take part with the lordly beast, because our vanity or some other feeling makes us disposed to place ourselves in the situation of the strongest party. So we feel some concern for the poor citizens of Rome when they meet together to compare their wants and grievances till Coriolanus comes in and with blows and big words drives this set of "poor rats,"[d] this rascal scum, to their homes and beggary before him. There is nothing heroical in a multitude of miserable rogues not wishing to be starved, or complaining that they are like to be so: but when a single man comes forward to brave their cries and to make them submit to the last indignities, from mere pride and self-will, our admiration of his prowess is immediately converted into contempt for their pusillanimity. The insolence of power is stronger than the plea of necessity. The tame submission to usurped authority or even the natural resistance to it has nothing to excite or flatter the imagination: it is the assumption of a right to insult or

[a] *Macbeth*, I. vi. 6–8   [b] *Coriolanus*, II. i. 163
[c] Wordsworth, "Ode: 1815", 108; said, in the original context, of God rather than "the principle of poetry"; Wordsworth deleted the line in his 1845 edition
[d] *Coriolanus*, I. i. 250

oppress others that carries an imposing air of superiority with it. We had rather be the oppressor than the oppressed. The love of power in ourselves and the admiration of it in others are both natural to man: the one makes him a tyrant, the other a slave. Wrong dressed out in pride, pomp, and circumstance, has more attraction than abstract right. – Coriolanus complains of the fickleness of the people: yet, the instant he cannot gratify his pride and obstinacy at their expense, he turns his arms against his country. If his country was not worth defending, why did he build his pride on its defence? He is a conquerer and a hero; he conquers other countries, and makes this a plea for enslaving his own; and when he is prevented from doing so, he leagues with its enemies to destroy his country. He rates the people "as if he were a God to punish, and not a man of their infirmity."[a] He scoffs at one of their tribunes for maintaining their rights and franchises: "Mark you his absolute *shall*?"[b] not marking his own absolute *will* to take every thing from them, his impatience of the slightest opposition to his own pretensions being in proportion to their arrogance and absurdity. If the great and powerful had the beneficence and wisdom of Gods, then all this would have been well: if with a greater knowledge of what is good for the people, they had as great a care for their interest as they have themselves, if they were seated above the world, sympathising with the welfare, but not feeling the passions of men, receiving neither good nor hurt from them, but bestowing their benefits as free gifts on them, they might then rule over them like another Providence. But this is not the case. Coriolanus is unwilling that the senate should shew their "cares" for the people, lest their "cares" should be construed into "fears," to the subversion of all due authority; and he is no sooner disappointed in his schemes to deprive the people not only of the cares of the state, but of all power to redress themselves, than Volumnia is made madly to exclaim,

> "Now the red pestilence strike all trades in Rome,
> And occupations perish."[c]

This is but natural: it is but natural for a mother to have more regard for her son than for a whole city; but then the city should be left to take some care of itself. The care of the state cannot, we here see, be safely entrusted to maternal affection, or to the domestic charities of high life. The great have private feelings of their own, to which the interests of humanity and justice must courtesy. Their interests are so far from being the same as those of the community,

[a] *Coriolanus*, III. i. 81–82   [b] *Coriolanus*, III. i. 89   [c] *Coriolanus*, IV. i. 13–14

that they are in direct and necessary opposition to them; their power is at the expense of *our* weakness; their riches of *our* poverty; their pride of *our* degradation; their splendour of *our* wretchedness; their tyranny of *our* servitude. If they had the superior knowledge ascribed to them (which they have not) it would only render them so much more formidable; and from Gods would convert them into devils. The whole dramatic moral of CORIOLANUS is that those who have little shall have less, and that those who have much shall take all that others have left.[2] The people are poor; therefore they ought to be starved. They are slaves; therefore they ought to be beaten. They work hard; therefore they ought to be treated like beasts of burden. They are ignorant; therefore they ought not to be allowed to feel that they want food, or clothing, or rest, that they are enslaved, oppressed, and miserable. This is the logic of the imagination and the passions; which seek to aggrandize what excites admiration and to heap contempt on misery, to raise power into tyranny, and to make tyranny absolute; to thrust down that which is low still lower, and to make wretches desperate: to exalt magistrates into kings, kings into gods; to degrade subjects to the rank of slaves, and slaves to the condition of brutes. The history of mankind is a romance, a mask, a tragedy, constructed upon the principles of *poetical justice*; it is a noble or royal hunt, in which what is sport to the few is death to the many, and in which the spectators halloo and encourage the strong to set upon the weak, and cry havoc in the chase though they do not share in the spoil. We may depend upon it that what men delight to read in books, they will put in practice in reality. . . .

10. *"On the Periodical Essayists"*

first published in *Lectures on the English Comic Writers* (1819); text from *Works*, ed. P. P. Howe (1930–34), vol. 6, pp. 99–102

. . . The dramatic and conversational turn which forms the distinguishing feature and greatest charm of the Spectator and Tatler, is quite lost in the Rambler by Dr. Johnson. There is no reflected light thrown on human life from an assumed character, nor any direct one from a display of the author's own. The Tatler and Spectator are, as it were, made up of notes and memorandums of the events and incidents of the day, with finished studies after nature, and characters fresh from the life, which the writer moralises upon, and turns to account as they come before him: the Rambler[1] is a collection of moral Essays, or scholastic theses, written on set subjects, and of which the individual characters and incidents are merely artificial illustrations, brought in to give a pretended relief to the dryness of didactic discussion. The Rambler is a splendid and imposing common-place-book of general topics, and rhetorical declamation on the conduct and business of human life. In this sense, there is hardly a reflection that had been suggested on such subjects which is not to be found in this celebrated work, and there is, perhaps, hardly a reflection to be found in it which had not been already suggested and developed by some other author, or in the common course of conversation. The mass of intellectual wealth here heaped together is immense, but it is rather the result of gradual accumulation, the produce of the general intellect, labouring in the mine of knowledge and reflection, than dug out of the quarry, and dragged into the light by the industry and sagacity of a single mind. I am not here saying that Dr. Johnson was a man without originality, compared with the ordinary run of men's minds, but he was not a man of original thought or genius, in the sense in which Montaigne or Lord Bacon was. He opened no new vein of precious ore, nor did he light upon any single pebbles of uncommon size and unrivalled lustre. We seldom meet with any thing to "give us pause;" he does not set us thinking for the first time. His reflections present themselves like reminiscences; do not disturb the ordinary march of our thoughts; arrest our attention by the stateliness of their appearance, and the costliness of their garb, but pass on and mingle with the throng of our impressions. After closing the volumes of the Rambler, there is nothing that we remember as a new truth gained to the mind, nothing indelibly stamped upon the memory; nor is there any passage that we wish to turn to as embodying any known principle or observation, with such force and beauty that justice can only be done to the idea in the author's own words. Such, for instance, are many of the passages to be found in Burke, which shine by their own light, belong to no class, have neither equal nor counterpart, and of which we say that no one but the author could have written them! There is neither the same boldness of design, nor mastery of execution in Johnson. In the one, the spark of genius seems to have met with its congenial matter: the shaft is sped; the forked lightning dresses up the face of nature in ghastly smiles, and the loud thunder rolls far away from the ruin that is made. Dr. Johnson's style, on the contrary, resembles rather the rumbling of mimic thunder at one of our theatres; and the light he throws upon a subject is like the dazzling effect of phosphorus, or an *ignis fatuus*[a] of words. There is a wide

[a] delusive fire or *will-o'-the-wisp*

difference, however, between perfect originality and perfect common-place: neither ideas nor expressions are trite or vulgar because they are not quite new. They are valuable, and ought to be repeated, if they have not become quite common; and Johnson's style both of reasoning and imagery holds the middle rank between startling novelty and vapid common-place. Johnson has as much originality of thinking as Addison; but then he wants his familiarity of illustration, knowledge of character, and delightful humour. – What most distinguishes Dr. Johnson from other writers is the pomp and uniformity of his style. All his periods are cast in the same mould, are of the same size and shape, and consequently have little fitness to the variety of things he professes to treat of. His subjects are familiar, but the author is always upon stilts. He has neither ease nor simplicity, and his efforts at playfulness, in part, remind one of the lines in Milton: –

> "————The elephant
> To make them sport wreath'd his proboscis lithe."[a]

His Letters from Correspondents, in particular, are more pompous and unwieldy than what he writes in his own person.[2] This want of relaxation and variety of manner has, I think, after the first effects of novelty and surprise were over, been prejudicial to the matter. It takes from the general power, not only to please, but to instruct. The monotony of style produces an apparent monotony of ideas. What is really striking and valuable, is lost in the vain ostentation and circumlocution of the expression; for when we find the same pains and pomp of diction bestowed upon the most trifling as upon the most important parts of a sentence or discourse, we grow tired of distinguishing between pretension and reality, and are disposed to confound the tinsel and bombast of the phraseology with want of weight in the thoughts. Thus, from the imposing and oracular nature of the style, people are tempted at first to imagine that our author's speculations are all wisdom and profundity: till having found out their mistake in some instances, they suppose that there is nothing but common-place in them, concealed under verbiage and pedantry; and in both they are wrong. The fault of Dr. Johnson's style is, that it reduces all things to the same artificial and unmeaning level. It destroys all shades of difference, the association between words and things. It is a perpetual paradox and innovation. He condescends to the familiar till we are ashamed of our interest in it: he expands the little till it looks big. "If he were to write a fable of little fishes," as

---

[a] *Paradise Lost*, IV. 345–47

Goldsmith said of him, "he would make them speak like great whales."[a] We can no more distinguish the most familiar objects in his descriptions of them, than we can a well-known face under a huge painted mask. The structure of his sentences, which was his own invention, and which has been generally imitated since his time, is a species of rhyming in prose, where one clause answers to another in measure and quantity, like the tagging of syllables at the end of a verse; the close of the period follows as mechanically as the oscillation of a pendulum, the sense is balanced with the sound; each sentence, revolving round its centre of gravity, is contained with itself like a couplet, and each paragraph forms itself into a stanza. Dr. Johnson is also a complete balance-master in the topics of morality. He never encourages hope, but he counteracts it by fear; he never elicits a truth, but he suggests some objection in to answer to it.[3] He seizes and alternately quits the clue of reason, lest it should involve him in the labyrinths of endless error: he wants confidence in himself and his fellows. He dares not trust himself with the immediate impressions of things, for fear of compromising his dignity; or follow them into their consequences, for fear of committing his prejudices. His timidity is the result, not of ignorance, but of morbid apprehension. "He runs the great circle, and is still at home."[b] No advance is made by his writings in any sentiment, or mode of reasoning. Out of the pale of established authority and received dogmas, all is sceptical, loose, and desultory: he seems in imagination to strengthen the domain of prejudice, as he weakens and dissipates that of reason; and round the rock of faith and power, on the edge of which he slumbers blindfold and uneasy, the waves and billows of uncertain and dangerous opinion roar and heave for evermore. His Rasselas is the most melancholy and debilitating moral speculation that ever was put forth. Doubtful of the faculties of his mind, as of his organs of vision, Johnson trusted only to his feelings and his fears. He cultivated a belief in witches as an out-guard to the evidences of religion; and abused Milton, and patronised Lauder, in spite of his aversion to his countrymen, as a step to secure the existing establishment in church and state.[4] This was neither right feeling nor sound logic....

11. *"On the Picturesque and Ideal: A Fragment"*[1]

first published in *Table-Talk; or, Original Essays* (1821); text from *Works*, ed. P. P. Howe (1930–34), vol. 8, pp. 317–21

[a] Boswell, *Life of Johnson*, Thursday, April 29, 1773   [b] Cowper, *The Task*, IV. 119

William Hazlitt (1778–1830)

THE natural in visible objects is whatever is ordinarily presented to the senses: the picturesque is that which stands out, and catches the attention by some striking peculiarity: the *ideal* is that which answers to the preconceived imagination and appetite in the mind for love and beauty. The picturesque depends chiefly on the principle of discrimination or contrast; the *ideal* on harmony and continuity of effect: the one surprises, the other satisfies the mind; the one starts off from a given point, the other reposes on itself; the one is determined by an excess of form, the other by a concentration of feeling.

The picturesque may be considered as something like an excrescence on the face of nature. It runs imperceptibly into the fantastical and grotesque. Fairies and satyrs are picturesque; but they are scarcely *ideal*. They are an extreme and unique conception of a certain thing, but not of what the mind delights in, or broods fondly over. The image created by the artist's hand is not moulded and fashioned by the love of good and yearning after grace and beauty, but rather the contrary: that is, they are ideal deformity, not ideal beauty. Rubens was perhaps the most picturesque of painters; but he was almost the least *ideal*. So Rembrandt was (out of sight) the most picturesque of colourists; as Correggio was the most *ideal*. In other words, his composition of light and shade is more a whole, more in unison, more blended into the same harmonious feeling than Rembrandt's, who staggers by contrast, but does not soothe by gradation. Correggio's forms, indeed, had a picturesque air; for they often incline (even when most beautiful) to the quaintness of caricature. Vandyke, I think, was at once the least picturesque and least *ideal* of all the great painters. He was purely natural, and neither selected from outward forms nor added any thing from his own mind. He owes every thing to perfect truth, clearness, and transparency; and though his productions certainly arrest the eye, and strike in a room full of pictures, it is from the contrast they present to other pictures, and from being stripped quite naked of all artificial advantages. They strike almost as a piece of white paper would, hung up in the same situation. – I began with saying that whatever stands out from a given line, and as it were projects upon the eye, is picturesque; and this holds true (comparatively) in form and colour. A rough terrier-dog, with the hair bristled and matted together, is picturesque. As we say, there is a decided character in it, a marked determination to an extreme point. A shock-dog is odd and disagreeable, but there is nothing picturesque in its appearance: it is a mere mass of flimsy confusion. A goat with projecting horns and pendent beard is a picturesque animal: a sheep is not. A horse is only picturesque from opposition of colour; as in Mr.

Northcote's[2] study of Gadshill, where the white horse's head coming against the dark scowling face of the man makes as fine a contrast as can be imagined. An old stump of a tree with rugged bark, and one or two straggling branches, a little stunted hedge-row line, marking the boundary of the horizon, a stubble-field, a winding path, a rock seen against the sky, are picturesque, because they have all of them prominence and a distinctive character of their own. They are not objects (to borrow Shakespear's phrase) "Of no mark or likelihood."[a] A country may be beautiful, romantic, or sublime, without being picturesque. The Lakes in the North of England are not picturesque, though certainly the most interesting sight in this country. To be a subject for painting, a prospect must present sharp striking points of view or singular forms, or one object must relieve and set off another. There must be distinct stages and salient points for the eye to rest upon or start from, in its progress over the expanse before it. The distance of a landscape will often-times look flat or heavy, that the trunk of a tree or a ruin in the foreground would immediately throw into perspective and turn to air. Rembrandt's landscapes are the least picturesque in the world, except from the strait lines and sharp angles, the deep incision and dragging of his pencil, like a harrow over the ground, and the broad contrast of earth and sky. Earth, in his copies, is rough and hairy; and Pan has struck his hoof against it! – A camel is a picturesque ornament in a landscape or history-piece. This is not merely from its romantic and oriental character; for an elephant has not the same effect, and if introduced as a necessary appendage, is also an unwieldy incumbrance. A negro's head in a group is picturesque from contrast: so are the spots on a panther's hide. This was the principle that Paul Veronese went upon, who said the rule for composition was *black upon white, and white upon black*. He was a pretty good judge. His celebrated picture of the Marriage of Cana is in all likelihood the completest piece of workmanship extant in the art. When I saw it, it nearly covered one side of a large room in the Louvre (being itself forty feet by twenty) – and it seemed as if that side of the apartment was thrown open, and you looked out at the open sky, at buildings, marble pillars, galleries with people in them, emperors, female slaves, Turks, negroes, musicians, all the famous painters of the time, the tables loaded with viands, goblets, and dogs under them – a sparkling, overwhelming confusion, a bright, unexpected reality – the only fault you could find was that no miracle was going on in the faces of the spectators: the only miracle there was the picture itself! A French gentleman, who showed me this "triumph of

<hr>

[a] *1 Henry IV*, III. ii. 45

painting" (as it has been called), perceiving I was struck with it, observed, "My wife admires it exceedingly for the facility of the execution." I took this proof of sympathy for a compliment. It is said that when Humboldt, the celebrated traveller and naturalist,[3] was introduced to Buonaparte, the Emperor addressed him in these words – *"Vous aimez la botanique, Monsieur"* – and on the other's replying in the affirmative, added – *"Et ma femme aussi!"[a]* This has been found fault with as a piece of brutality and insolence in the great man by bigoted critics, who do not know what a thing it is to get a Frenchwoman to agree with them in any point. For my part, I took the observation as it was meant, and it did not put me out of conceit with myself or the picture that Madame M— liked it as well as *Monsieur l'Anglois.* Certainly, there could be no harm in that. By the side of it happened to be hung two allegorical pictures of Rubens (and in such matters he too was "no baby") – I don't remember what the figures were, but the texture seemed of wool or cotton. The texture of the Paul Veronese was not wool or cotton, but stuff, jewels, flesh, marble, air, whatever composed the essence of the varied subjects, in endless relief and truth of handling. If the Fleming had seen his two allegories hanging where they did, he would, without a question, have wished them far enough.

I imagine that Rubens's landscapes are picturesque: Claude's are *ideal.* Rubens is always in extremes: Claude in the middle. Rubens carries some one peculiar quality or feature of nature to the utmost verge of probability: Claude balances and harmonises different forms and masses with laboured delicacy, so that nothing falls short, no one thing overpowers another. Rainbows, showers, partial gleams of sunshine, moon-light, are the means with which Rubens produces his most gorgeous and enchanting effects: there are neither rainbows, nor showers, nor sudden bursts of sunshine, nor glittering moon-beams in Claude. He is all softness and proportion; the other is all spirit and brilliant excess. The two sides (for example) of one of Claude's landscapes balance one another, as in a scale of beauty: in Rubens the several objects are grouped and thrown together with capricious wantonness. Claude has more repose: Rubens more gaiety and extravagance. And here it might be asked, Is a rainbow a picturesque or an *ideal* object? It seems to me to be both. It is an accident in nature; but it is an inmate of the fancy. It startles and surprises the sense, but it soothes and tranquillises the spirit. It makes the eye glisten to behold it, but the mind turns to it long after it has faded from its place in the sky. It has both properties then of giving an

[a] "You are fond of botany, Sir. So is my wife!"

extraordinary impulse to the mind by the singularity of its appearance, and of riveting the imagination by its intense beauty. I may just notice here in passing, that I think the effect of moon-light is treated in an *ideal* manner in the well-known line in Shakespear –

"See how the moonlight *sleeps* upon yon bank!"[a]

The image is heightened by the exquisiteness of the expression beyond its natural beauty, and it seems as if there could be no end to the delight taken in it. – A number of sheep coming to a pool of water to drink, with shady trees in the back-ground, the rest of the flock following them, and the shepherd and his dog left carelessly behind, is surely the *ideal* in landscape-composition, if the *ideal* has its source in the interest excited by a subject, in its power of drawing the affections after it linked in a golden chain, and in the desire of the mind to dwell on it for ever. The *ideal*, in a word, is the height of the pleasing, that which satisfies and accords with the inmost longing of the soul: the picturesque is merely a sharper and bolder impression of reality. A morning mist drawing a slender veil over all objects is at once picturesque and *ideal*: for it in the first place excites immediate surprise and admiration, and in the next a wish for it to continue, and a fear lest it should be too soon dissipated. Is the Cupid riding on a lion in the ceiling at Whitehall, and urging him with a spear over a precipice, with only clouds and sky beyond, most picturesque or *ideal*? It has every effect of startling contrast and situation, and yet inspires breathless expectation and wonder for the event. Rembrandt's Jacob's Dream, again, is both – fearful to the eye, but realising that loftiest vision of the soul.[4] Take two faces in Leonardo da Vinci's Last Supper, the Judas and the St. John; the one is all strength, repulsive character, the other is all divine grace and mild sensibility. The individual, the characteristic in painting, is that *which is* in a marked manner – the *ideal* is that which we wish any thing to be, and to contemplate without measure and without end. The first is truth, the last is good. The one appeals to the sense and understanding, the other to the will and the affections. The truly beautiful and grand attracts the mind to it by instinctive harmony, is absorbed in it, and nothing can ever part them afterwards. Look at a Madonna of Raphael's: what gives the *ideal* character to the expression – the insatiable purpose of the soul, or its measureless content in the object of its contemplation? A portrait of Vandyke's is mere indifference and still-life in the comparison: it has not in it the principle of growing and still unsatisfied desire. In the *ideal* there is no fixed stint or limit

[a] *The Merchant of Venice*, v. i. 54

but the limit of possibility: it is the infinite with respect to human capacities and wishes. Love is for this reason an *ideal* passion. We give to it our all of hope, of fear, of present enjoyment, and stake our last chance of happiness wilfully and desperately upon it. A good authority puts into the mouth of one of his heroines –

> "My bounty is as boundless as the sea,
> My love as deep!" – [a]

How many fair catechumens will there be found in all ages to repeat as much after Shakespear's Juliet!

12. *"Mr. Coleridge"*

first published in *The Spirit of the Age: or Contemporary Portraits* (1825); text from *Works*, ed. P. P. Howe (1930–34), vol. II, pp. 28–38

THE present is an age of talkers, and not of doers; and the reason is, that the world is growing old. We are so far advanced in the Arts and Sciences, that we live in retrospect, and doat on past achievements. The accumulation of knowledge has been so great, that we are lost in wonder at the height it has reached, instead of attempting to climb or add to it; while the variety of objects distracts and dazzles the looker-on. What *niche* remains unoccupied? What path untried? What is the use of doing anything, unless we could do better than all those who have gone before us? What hope is there of this? We are like those who have been to see some noble monument of art, who are content to admire without thinking of rivalling it; or like guests after a feast, who praise the hospitality of the donor "and thank the bounteous Pan"[b] – perhaps carrying away some trifling fragments; or like the spectators of a mighty battle, who still hear its sound afar off, and the clashing of armour and the neighing of the war-horse and the shout of victory is in their ears, like the rushing of innumerable waters!

Mr. Coleridge has "a mind reflecting ages past";[c] his voice is like the echo of the congregated roar of the "dark rearward and abyss"[d] of thought. He who has seen a mouldering tower by the side of a chrystal lake, hid by the mist, but glittering in the wave below, may conceive the dim, gleaming, uncertain intelligence of his eye: he who

---

[a] *Romeo and Juliet*, II. ii. 133–34   [b] Milton, *Comus*, 176
[c] first line of verses "On the Worthy Master Shakespeare and his Poems" (prefixed to the Second Folio), which Coleridge attributed to Milton
[d] *The Tempest*, I. ii. 50

has marked the evening clouds uprolled (a world of vapours), has seen the picture of his mind, unearthly, unsubstantial, with gorgeous tints and ever-varying forms –

> "That which was now a horse, even with a thought
> The rack dislimns, and makes it indistinct
> As water is in water."[a]

Our author's mind is (as he himself might express it) *tangential*. There is no subject on which he has not touched, none on which he has rested. With an understanding fertile, subtle, expansive, "quick, forgetive, apprehensive," beyond all living precedent, few traces of it will perhaps remain. He lends himself to all impressions alike; he gives up his mind and liberty of thought to none. He is a general lover of art and science, and wedded to no one in particular. He pursues knowledge as a mistress, with outstretched hands and winged speed; but as he is about to embrace her, his Daphne turns – alas! not to a laurel! Hardly a speculation has been left on record from the earliest time, but it is loosely folded up in Mr. Coleridge's memory, like a rich, but somewhat tattered piece of tapestry: we might add (with more seeming than real extravagance), that scarce a thought can pass through the mind of man, but its sound has at some time or other passed over his head with rustling pinions. On whatever question or author you speak, he is prepared to take up the theme with advantage – from Peter Abelard down to Thomas Moore, from the subtlest metaphysics to the politics of the *Courier*.[b] There is no man of genius, in whose praise, he descants, but the critic seems to stand above the author, and "what in him is weak, to strengthen, what is low, to raise and support":[c] nor is there any work of genius that does not come out of his hands like an illuminated Missal, sparkling even in its defects. If Mr. Coleridge had not been the most impressive talker of his age, he would probably have been the finest writer; but he lays down his pen to make sure of an auditor, and mortgages the admiration of posterity for the stare of an idler. If he had not been a poet, he would have been a powerful logician; if he had not dipped his wing in the Unitarian controversy,[1] he might have soared to the very summit of fancy. But in writing verse, he is trying to subject the Muse to *transcendental* theories:[2] in his abstract reasoning, he misses his way by strewing it with flowers. All that he has done of moment, he had done twenty years ago: since then, he may be said to have lived on the sound of his own voice. Mr. Coleridge is too rich in intellectual wealth, to need to

[a] *Antony and Cleopatra*, IV. xiv. 9–11
[b] newspaper to which Coleridge contributed many anti-Napoleonic articles
[c] *Paradise Lost*, I. 23–24

task himself to any drudgery: he has only to draw the sliders of his imagination, and a thousand subjects expand before him, startling him with their brilliancy, or losing themselves in endless obscurity –

> "And by the force of blear illusion,
> They draw him on to his confusion."[a]

What is the little he could add to the stock, compared with the countless stores that lie about him, that he should stoop to pick up a name, or to polish an idle fancy? He walks abroad in the majesty of an universal understanding, eyeing the "rich strond," or golden sky above him, and "goes sounding on his way," in eloquent accents, uncompelled and free!

Persons of the greatest capacity are often those, who for this reason do the least; for surveying themselves from the highest point of view, amidst the infinite variety of the universe, their own share in it seems trifling, and scarce worth a thought, and they prefer the contemplation of all that is, or has been, or can be, to the making a coil about doing what, when done, is no better than vanity. It is hard to concentrate all our attention and efforts on one pursuit, except from ignorance of others; and without this concentration of our faculties, no great progress can be made in any one thing. It is not merely that the mind is not capable of the effort; it does not think the effort worth making. Action is one; but thought is manifold. He whose restless eye glances through the wide compass of nature and art, will not consent to have "his own nothings monstered": but he must do this before he can give his whole soul to them. The mind, after "letting contemplation have its fill," or

> "Sailing with supreme dominion
> Through the azure deep of air,"[b]

sinks down on the ground, breathless, exhausted, powerless, inactive; or if it must have some vent to its feelings, seeks the most easy and obvious; is soothed by friendly flattery, lulled by the murmur of immediate applause, thinks as it were aloud, and babbles in its dreams! A scholar (so to speak) is a more disinterested and abstracted character than a mere author. The first looks at the numberless volumes of a library, and says, "All these are mine": the other points to a single volume (perhaps it may be an immortal one) and says, "My name is written on the back of it." This is a puny and groveling ambition, beneath the lofty amplitude of Mr. Coleridge's mind. No, he revolves in his wayward soul, or utters to the passing wind, or

---

[a] mixing *Macbeth*, III. v. 28–29 with Milton, *Comus*, 155   [b] Gray, "The Progress of Poesy," 116

discourses to his own shadow, things mightier and more various! –
Let us draw the curtain, and unlock the shrine.

Learning rocked him in his cradle, and while yet a child,

> "He lisped in numbers, for the numbers came."[a]

At sixteen he wrote his *Ode on Chatterton*, and he still reverts to that
period with delight, not so much as it relates to himself (for that
string of his own early promise of fame rather jars than otherwise) but
as exemplifying the youth of a poet. Mr. Coleridge talks of himself,
without being an egotist, for in him the individual is always merged
in the abstract and general. He distinguished himself at school and at
the University by his knowledge of the classics, and gained several
prizes for Greek epigrams. How many men are there (great scholars,
celebrated names in literature) who having done the same thing in
their youth, have no other idea all the rest of their lives but on this
achievement, of a fellowship and dinner, and who, installed in
academic honours, would look down on our author as a mere
strolling bard! At Christ's Hospital, where he was brought up, he was
the idol of those among his schoolfellows, who mingled with their
bookish studies the music of thought and of humanity; and he was
usually attended round the cloisters by a group of these (inspiring and
inspired) whose hearts, even then, burnt within them as he talked,
and where the sounds yet linger to mock ELIA[b] on his way, still
turning pensive to the past! One of the finest and rarest parts of
Mr. Coleridge's conversation, is when he expatiates on the Greek
tragedians (not that he is not well acquainted, when he pleases,
with the epic poets, or the philosophers, or orators, or historians of
antiquity) – on the subtle reasonings and melting pathos of Euripides, on the harmonious gracefulness of Sophocles, tuning his love-
laboured song, like sweetest warblings from a sacred grove; on the
high-wrought trumpet-tongued eloquence of Æschylus, whose
Prometheus, above all, is like an Ode to Fate, and a pleading with
Providence, his thoughts being let loose as his body is chained on his
solitary rock, and his afflicted will (the emblem of mortality)

> "Struggling in vain with ruthless destiny."[c]

As the impassioned critic speaks and rises in his theme, you would
think you heard the voice of the Man hated by the Gods, contending

---

[a] Pope, "Epistle to Dr. Arbuthnot," 128
[b] Charles Lamb, a schoolmate of Coleridge's who remembered him in an essay on "Christ's Hospital Five and Thirty Years Ago"
[c] Wordsworth, *The Excursion*, VI. 557

with the wild winds as they roar, and his eye glitters with the spirit of Antiquity!

Next, he was engaged with Hartley's tribes of mind, "etherial braid, thought-woven,"[a] – and he busied himself for a year or two with vibrations and vibratiuncles and the great law of association that binds all things in its mystic chain, and the doctrine of Necessity (the mild teacher of Charity) and the Millennium, anticipative of a life to come – and he plunged deep into the controversy on Matter and Spirit, and, as an escape from Dr. Priestley's Materialism, where he felt himself imprisoned by the logician's spell, like Ariel in the cloven pine-tree, he became suddenly enamoured of Bishop Berkeley's fairy-world,[3] and used in all companies to build the universe, like a brave poetical fiction, of fine words – and he was deep-read in Malebranche, and in Cudworth's Intellectual System (a huge pile of learning, unwieldy, enormous) and in Lord Brook's hieroglyphic theories, and in Bishop Butler's Sermons, and in the Duchess of Newcastle's fantastic folios, and in Clarke and South and Tillotson, and all the fine thinkers and masculine reasoners of that age – and Leibnitz's *Pre-Established Harmony* reared its arch above his head, like the rainbow in the cloud, covenanting with the hopes of man – and then he fell plump, ten thousand fathoms down (but his wings saved him harmless) into the *hortus siccus*[b] of Dissent, where he pared religion down to the standard of reason and stripped faith of mystery, and preached Christ crucified and the Unity of the Godhead, and so dwelt for a while in the spirit with John Huss and Jerome of Prague and Socinus and the old John Zisca, and ran through Neal's History of the Puritans, and Calamy's Non-Conformists' Memorial, having like thoughts and passions with them – but then Spinoza became his God, and he took up the vast chain of being in his hand, and the round world became the centre and the soul of all things in some shadowy sense, forlorn of meaning, and around him he beheld the living traces and the sky-pointing proportions of the mighty Pan – but poetry redeemed him from this spectral philosophy, and he bathed his heart in beauty, and gazed at the golden light of heaven, and drank of the spirit of the universe, and wandered at eve by fairy-stream or fountain,

> "————When he saw nought but beauty,
> When he heard the voice of that Almighty One
> In every breeze that blew, or wave that murmured" –[c]

[a] Collins, "Ode to Evening," 7
[b] sterile garden; a phrase applied to Dissent in the opening pages of Burke's *Reflections on the Revolution in France*
[c] Coleridge, *Remorse*, IV. ii. 101–03

and wedded with truth in Plato's shade, and in the writings of Proclus and Plotinus saw the ideas of things in the eternal mind, and unfolded all mysteries with the Schoolmen and fathomed the depths of Duns Scotus and Thomas Aquinas, and entered the third heaven with Jacob Behmen, and walked hand in hand with Swedenborg through the pavilions of the New Jerusalem, and sung his faith in the promise and in the word in his *Religious Musings* – and lowering himself from that dizzy height, poised himself on Milton's wings, and spread out his thoughts in charity with the glad prose of Jeremy Taylor, and wept over Bowles's Sonnets, and studied Cowper's blank verse, and betook himself to Thomson's Castle of Indolence, and sported with the wits of Charles the Second's days and of Queen Anne, and relished Swift's style and that of the John Bull (Arbuthnot's we mean, not Mr. Croker's), and dallied with the British Essayists and Novelists, and knew all qualities of more modern writers with a learned spirit, Johnson, and Goldsmith, and Junius, and Burke, and Godwin, and the Sorrows of Werter, and Jean Jacques Rousseau, and Voltaire, and Marivaux, and Crebillon, and thousands more – now "laughed with Rabelais in his easy chair"[a] or pointed to Hogarth, or afterwards dwelt on Claude's classic scenes, or spoke with rapture of Raphael, and compared the women at Rome to figures that had walked out of his pictures, or visited the Oratory of Pisa, and described the works of Giotto and Ghirlandaio and Massaccio, and gave the moral of the picture of the Triumph of Death,[b] where the beggars and the wretched invoke his dreadful dart, but the rich and mighty of the earth quail and shrink before it; and in that land of siren sights and sounds, saw a dance of peasant girls, and was charmed with lutes and gondolas, – or wandered into Germany and lost himself in the labyrinths of the Hartz Forest and of the Kantean philosophy, and amongst the cabalistic names of Fichte and Schelling and Lessing, and God knows who[4] – this was long after, but all the former while, he had nerved his heart and filled his eyes with tears, as he hailed the rising orb of liberty, since quenched in darkness and in blood, and had kindled his affections at the blaze of the French Revolution, and sang for joy when the towers of the Bastile and the proud places of the insolent and the oppressor fell, and would have floated his bark, freighted with fondest fancies, across the Atlantic wave with Southey and others to seek for peace and freedom –

[a] Pope, *Dunciad*, I. 22   [b] by Giotto

William Hazlitt (1778–1830)

"In Philarmonia's undivided dale!"[a]

Alas! "Frailty, thy name is *Genius!*" – What is become of all this mighty heap of hope, of thought, of learning, and humanity? It has ended in swallowing doses of oblivion[b] and in writing paragraphs in the *Courier*. – Such, and so little is the mind of man!

It was not to be supposed that Mr. Coleridge could keep on at the rate he set off; he could not realize all he knew or thought, and less could not fix his desultory ambition; other stimulants supplied the place, and kept up the intoxicating dream, the fever and the madness of his early impressions. Liberty (the philosopher's and the poet's bride) had fallen a victim, meanwhile, to the murderous practices of the hag, Legitimacy. Proscribed by court-hirelings, too romantic for the herd of vulgar politicians, our enthusiast stood at bay, and at last turned on the pivot of a subtle casuistry to the *unclean side*:[5] but his discursive reason would not let him trammel himself into a poet-laureate or stamp-distributor,[c] and he stopped, ere he had quite passed that well-known "bourne from whence no traveller returns"[d] – and so has sunk into torpid, uneasy repose, tantalized by useless resources, haunted by vain imaginings, his lips idly moving, but his heart for ever still, or, as the shattered chords vibrate of themselves, making melancholy music to the ear of memory! Such is the fate of genius in an age, when in the unequal contest with sovereign wrong, every man is ground to powder who is not either a born slave, or who does not willingly and at once offer up the yearnings of humanity and the dictates of reason as a welcome sacrifice to besotted prejudice and loathsome power.

Of all Mr. Coleridge's productions, the *Ancient Mariner* is the only one that we could with confidence put into any person's hands, on whom we wished to impress a favourable idea of his extraordinary powers. Let whatever other objections be made to it, it is unquestionably a work of genius – of wild, irregular, overwhelming imagination, and has that rich, varied movement in the verse, which gives a distant idea of the lofty or changeful tones of Mr. Coleridge's voice. In the *Christabel*, there is one splendid passage on divided friendship. The *Translation of Schiller's Wallenstein* is also a masterly production in its kind, faithful and spirited. Among his smaller pieces there are occasional bursts of pathos and fancy, equal to what we might expect

---

[a] quoting from memory an early draft of a poem by Coleridge, concerning his design of founding with Southey a utopian community of equals ("pantisocracy"), in the Susquehannah Valley in America
[b] laudanum [c] Southey had become poet-laureate, and Wordsworth a stamp-distributor.
[d] *Hamlet*, III. i. 79–80

from him; but these form the exception, and not the rule. Such, for instance, is his affecting Sonnet to the author of the Robbers.[a]

"Schiller! that hour I would have wish'd to die,
    If through the shudd'ring midnight I had sent
    From the dark dungeon of the tower time-rent,
That fearful voice, a famish'd father's cry –
That in no after-moment aught less vast
    Might stamp me mortal! A triumphant shout
    Black horror scream'd, and all her goblin rout
From the more with'ring scene diminish'd pass'd.
Ah! Bard tremendous in sublimity!
    Could I behold thee in thy loftier mood,
Wand'ring at eve, with finely frenzied eye,
    Beneath some vast old tempest-swinging wood!
    Awhile, with mute awe gazing, I would brood,
Then weep aloud in a wild ecstasy."

His Tragedy, entitled *Remorse*, is full of beautiful and striking passages, but it does not place the author in the first rank of dramatic writers. But if Mr. Coleridge's works do not place him in that rank, they injure instead of conveying a just idea of the man, for he himself is certainly in the first class of general intellect.

If our author's poetry is inferior to his conversation, his prose is utterly abortive. Hardly a gleam is to be found in it of the brilliancy and richness of those stores of thought and language that he pours out incessantly, when they are lost like drops of water in the ground. The principal work, in which he has attempted to embody his general view of things, is the FRIEND,[b] of which, though it contains some noble passages and fine trains of thought, prolixity and obscurity are the most frequent characteristics.

No two persons can be conceived more opposite in character or genius than the subject of the present and of the preceding sketch.[6] Mr. Godwin, with less natural capacity, and with fewer acquired advantages, by concentrating his mind on some given object, and doing what he had to do with all his might, has accomplished much, and will leave more than one monument of a powerful intellect behind him; Mr. Coleridge, by dissipating his, and dallying with every subject by turns, has done little or nothing to justify to the world or to posterity, the high opinion which all who have ever heard him converse, or known him intimately, with one accord entertain of him. Mr. Godwin's faculties have kept at home, and plied their task in

[a] *The Robbers*, a tragedy by Friedrich Schiller
[b] an irregular periodical, incorporating essays in criticism, politics, metaphysics and aesthetic theory, which Coleridge wrote in 1809–10 and collected in 1818

the workshop of the brain, diligently and effectually: Mr. Coleridge's have gossiped away their time, and gadded about from house to house, as if life's business were to melt the hours in listless talk. Mr. Godwin is intent on a subject, only as it concerns himself and his reputation; he works it out as a matter of duty, and discards from his mind whatever does not forward his main object as impertinent and vain. Mr. Coleridge, on the other hand, delights in nothing but episodes and digressions, neglects whatever he undertakes to perform, and can act only on spontaneous impulses, without object or method. "He cannot be constrained by mastery." While he should be occupied with a given pursuit, he is thinking of a thousand other things; a thousand tastes, a thousand objects tempt him, and distract his mind, which keeps open house, and entertains all comers; and after being fatigued and amused with morning calls from idle visitors, finds the day consumed and its business unconcluded. Mr. Godwin, on the contrary, is somewhat exclusive and unsocial in his habits of mind, entertains no company but what he gives his whole time and attention to, and wisely writes over the doors of his understanding, his fancy, and his senses – "No admittance except on business." He has none of that fastidious refinement and false delicacy, which might lead him to balance between the endless variety of modern attainments. He does not throw away his life (nor a single half-hour of it) in adjusting the claims of different accomplishments, and in choosing between them or making himself master of them all. He sets about his task, (whatever it may be) and goes through it with spirit and fortitude. He has the happiness to think an author the greatest character in the world, and himself the greatest author in it. Mr. Coleridge, in writing an harmonious stanza, would stop to consider whether there was not more grace and beauty in a *Pas de trois,*[a] and would not proceed till he had resolved this question by a chain of metaphysical reasoning without end. Not so Mr. Godwin. That is best to him, which he can do best. He does not waste himself in vain aspirations and effeminate sympathies. He is blind, deaf, insensible to all but the trump of Fame. Plays, operas, painting, music, ball-rooms, wealth, fashion, titles, lords, ladies, touch him not – all these are no more to him than to the magician in his cell, and he writes on to the end of the chapter, through good report and evil report. *Pingo in eternitatem*[b] – is his motto. He neither envies nor admires what others are, but is contented to be what he is, and strives to do the utmost he can. Mr. Coleridge has flirted with the Muses as with a set of mistresses: Mr. Godwin has been married twice, to Reason and to

[a] dance of three   [b] I paint for eternity

Fancy, and has to boast no short-lived progeny by each. So to speak, he has *valves* belonging to his mind, to regulate the quantity of gas admitted into it, so that like the bare, unsightly, but well-compacted steam-vessel, it cuts its liquid way, and arrives at its promised end: while Mr. Coleridge's bark, "taught with the little nautilus to sail," the sport of every breath, dancing to every wave,

"Youth at its prow, and Pleasure at its helm,"[a]

flutters its gaudy pennons in the air, glitters in the sun, but we wait in vain to hear of its arrival in the destined harbour. Mr. Godwin, with less variety and vividness, with less subtlety and susceptibility both of thought and feeling, has had firmer nerves, a more determined purpose, a more comprehensive grasp of his subject, and the results are as we find them. Each has met with his reward: for justice has, after all, been done to the pretensions of each; and we must, in all cases, use means to ends!

It was a misfortune to any man of talent to be born in the latter end of the last century. Genius stopped the way of Legitimacy, and therefore it was to be abated, crushed, or set aside as a nuisance.[7] The spirit of the monarchy was at variance with the spirit of the age. The flame of liberty, the light of intellect was to be extinguished with the sword – or with slander, whose edge is sharper than the sword. The war between power and reason was carried on by the first of these abroad – by the last at home. No quarter was given (then or now) by the Government-critics,[b] the authorised censors of the press, to those who followed the dictates of independence, who listened to the voice of the tempter, Fancy. Instead of gathering fruits and flowers, immortal fruits and amaranthine flowers, they soon found themselves beset not only by a host of prejudices, but assailed with all the engines of power, by nicknames, by lies, by all the arts of malice, interest and hypocrisy, without the possibility of their defending themselves "from the pelting of the pitiless storm,"[c] that poured down upon them from the strong-holds of corruption and authority. The philosophers, the dry abstract reasoners, submitted to this reverse pretty well, and armed themselves with patience "as with triple steel"[d] to bear discomfiture, persecution, and disgrace. But the poets, the creatures of sympathy, could not stand the frowns both of king and people. They did not like to be shut out when places and pensions, when the critic's praises, and the laurel-wreath were about

[a] Gray, *The Bard*, 74   [b] literary or ideological hired guns of an established power
[c] *King Lear*, III. v. 29
[d] Milton, *Paradise Lost*, II. 569

to be distributed. They did not stomach being *sent to Coventry*, and Mr. Coleridge sounded a retreat for them by the help of casuistry, and a musical voice. – "His words were hollow, but they pleased the ear"[a] of his friends of the Lake School, who turned back disgusted and panic-struck from the dry desert of unpopularity, like Hassan the camel driver,

> "And curs'd the hour, and curs'd the luckless day,
> When first from Shiraz' walls they bent their way."[b]

They are safely inclosed there, but Mr. Coleridge did not enter with them; pitching his tent upon the barren waste without, and having no abiding place nor city of refuge.

13. *"Byron and Wordsworth"*

first published in *The London Weekly Review*, April 5, 1828; text from *Works*, ed. P. P. Howe (1930–34), vol. 20, pp. 155–57

I AM much surprised at Lord Byron's haste to return a volume of Spenser, which was lent him by Mr. Hunt,[c] and at his apparent indifference to the progress and (if he pleased) *advancement* of poetry up to the present day. Did he really think that all genius was concentrated in his own time, or in his own bosom? With his pride of ancestry, had he no curiosity to explore the heraldry of intellect? or did he regard the Muse as an upstart – a mere modern *blue-stocking* and fine lady? I am afraid that high birth and station, instead of being (as Mr. Burke predicates), "a cure for a narrow and selfish mind,"[d] only make a man more full of himself, and, instead of enlarging and refining his views, impatient of any but the most inordinate and immediate stimulus. I do not recollect, in all Lord Byron's writings, a single recurrence to a feeling or object that had ever excited an interest before; there is no display of natural affection – no twining of the heart round any object: all is the restless and disjointed effect of first impressions, of novelty, contrast, surprise, grotesque costume, or sullen grandeur. *His* beauties are the *houris* of Paradise, the favourites of a seraglio, the changing visions of a feverish dream. His poetry, it is true, is stately and dazzling, arched like a rainbow, of bright and lovely hues, painted on the cloud of his own gloomy temper –

---

[a] adapting *Paradise Lost*, II. 112–17   [b] Collins, *Persian Eclogues*, II. 29   [c] Leigh Hunt
[d] paraphrasing Burke, *Reflections on the Revolution in France*, on "the spirit of a gentleman"

perhaps to disappear as soon! It is easy to account for the antipathy between him and Mr. Wordsworth. Mr Wordsworth's poetical mistress is a Pamela;[a] Lord Byron's an Eastern princess or a Moorish maid. It is the extrinsic, the uncommon that captivates him, and all the rest he holds in sovereign contempt. This is the obvious result of pampered luxury and high-born sentiments. The mind, like the palace in which it has been brought up, admits none but new and costly furniture. From a scorn of homely simplicity, and a surfeit of the artificial, it has but one resource left in exotic manners and preternatural effect. So we see in novels, written by ladies of quality, all the marvellous allurements of a fairy tale, jewels, quarries of diamonds, giants, magicians, condors and ogres. The author of the Lyrical Ballads describes the lichen on the rock, the withered fern, with some peculiar feeling that he has about them: the author of Childe Harold describes the stately cypress, or the fallen column, with the feeling that every schoolboy has about them. The world is a grown schoolboy, and relishes the latter most. When Rousseau called out – "*Ah! voila de la pervenche!*"[b] in a transport of joy at sight of the periwinkle, because he had first seen this little blue flower in company with Madame Warens thirty years before, I cannot help thinking, that any astonishment expressed at the sight of a palm-tree, or even of Pompey's Pillar,[c] is vulgar compared to this! Lord Byron, when he does not saunter down Bond-street, goes into the East: when he is not occupied with the passing topic, he goes back two thousand years, at one poetic, gigantic stride! But instead of the sweeping mutations of empire, and the vast lapses of duration, shrunk up into an antithesis, commend me to the "slow and creeping foot of time,"[d] in the commencement of Ivanhoe, where the jester and the swineherd watch the sun going down behind the low-stunted trees of the forest, and their loitering and impatience make the summer's day seem so long, that we wonder how we have ever got to the end of the six hundred years that have passed since! That where the face of nature has changed, time should have rolled on its course, is but a common-place discovery; but that where all seems the same (the long rank grass, and the stunted oaks, and the innocent pastoral landscape), all should have changed – this is to me the burthen and the mystery.[e] The ruined pile is a memento and a monument to him that

[a] heroine of Richardson's *Pamela*, who successfully defends her virginity
[b] "Ah! look at the periwinkle!"
[c] granite column erected in A.D. 302 at Alexandria; here typifying Byron's use of ancient monuments as emblems of personal sensibility, in *Childe Harold's Pilgrimage* and elsewhere
[d] *As You Like It*, II. vii. 111   [e] paraphrasing Wordsworth, "Tintern Abbey," 38

reared it – oblivion has here done but half its work; but what yearnings, what vain conflicts with its fate come over the soul in the other case, which makes man seem like a grasshopper – an insect of the hour, and all that he is, or that others have been – nothing!

Leigh Hunt

(1784–1859)

Leigh Hunt was an adolescent prodigy in the writing of verse, and the poetry by which he came to be known in his mid-twenties retained a youthful power to startle, to vivify, and to embarrass. By that time Hunt had mastered as well a flexible middle style of prose – a style which he would find appropriate to criticism, topographical or descriptive writing, biographical essays and a two-volume autobiography. In the penetration of his satire and in a certain persistent plainness of statement, Hunt may be felt to resemble Swift, whom he acknowledged as a model. But he is closer to Goldsmith in his mischief, his energy at observation, and his customary good nature. By all of these traits he was well qualified to serve, together with his brother, John, as editor of the *Examiner*, a weekly paper concerned with politics and the arts. From its founding in 1808, through the popular upheavals of 1819, to Hunt's departure for Italy in 1822, the *Examiner* set a standard of public discourse unrivalled by other journals. In part this was because it had a coherent audience: the mixed company of republicans and reformers who have since come to be called middle-class radicals. Hunt, as a rule, attended to the "Theatrical Examiner" and other departments of cultural commentary, leaving the political direction of the paper to his brother. But he made a fateful exception in an article on the Prince Regent which disputed the portrait of him by his liberal allies as an "Adonis in Loveliness." Hunt called him instead "a corpulent man of fifty ... a violator of his word, a libertine over head and ears in disgrace, a despiser of domestic ties, the companion of gamblers and demireps, a man who has just closed half a century without one single claim on the gratitude of his country or the respect of posterity." The article provoked the Tory ministry to prosecute both Hunts on charges of seditious libel, and they were sentenced to two years in prison.

In his *Autobiography* Hunt writes poignantly of the melancholy that assailed him throughout the time of his confinement. But the ministry's action had the effect of making him, at least for a period, something of a hero among the dissident men and women of his generation. Even Byron paid court to him in prison, and there began a friendship which would lead eventually to the founding of a magazine, *The Liberal*. Apart from inculcating a degree of prudence in the expression of his opinions, Hunt's imprisonment seems to have had few outward effects on his life. The *Examiner* kept on appearing and Hunt remained a voice of individual protest against corruption. He would describe himself in later years as a monarchist with a sentimental leaning to "the religion of the heart," that is, to the cause of common humanity. He embarked alone on several ventures in periodicial journalism, his preferred manner here being that of Richard Steele, as his choice of titles indicates: "The Indicator," "The Reflector," "The Tatler," "The Companion." He became a familiar author, however, for Victorian writers like Dickens and Macaulay, chiefly with the anthologies of his last years: of the English comic dramatists; of the Italian poets; of Imagination and Fancy; of Wit and Humour. These projects were sometimes successful or satisfying to Hunt, but they were generated by the anxieties of book-making. "The commonest rules of arithmetic," he says, "were, by a singular chance, omitted in my education." In consequence, a defining fact of his existence was an imperviousness to financial practicalities, which was apt to wear the look of a complacent dependence on others. This colored Byron's later opinion of his character and may have contributed unwarrantably to the decline of his reputation.

Hunt's personal introduction to Keats, his publication of Keats's early poems and his assumption of the role of mentor, date from October 1816, shortly after his release from prison. From the first he treated the younger man as an equal, and shared with him the discoveries of his own generous taste in poetry. Before Keats's death Hunt had implicitly recognized him as the greater poet. What *good* (modern critics have asked) could Hunt have done Keats? The answer is that Keats was familiar with *The Story of Rimini*, with its frank sensuality and pert clarity of statement, and that the presence of these qualities in Hunt belonged to a risky originality that made him interesting. To judge by the *Hyperion*, Keats had also studied Hunt's masque *The Descent of Liberty*; and Hunt's *jeux d'esprit*, "Ultra-Crepidarius" and *The Feast of the Poets*, may have emboldened Keats in the way that Hazlitt's "Letter to William Gifford" did. Among the cockneyisms for which Keats was attacked were certain more equivocal gifts from Hunt: the habit, for example, of converting nouns to adjectives with a terminal "y" (*massy, streaky, balmy, glary*); and a taste for such good–bad lines as "The two divinest things this world has got, / A lovely woman in a rural spot." The texture of Hunt's mind, as his friends are likely to have known it in person, is best encountered now in his anthologies, which consist of specimens with short commentaries. He can be a subtle analyst of the music of verse – as when he writes of the vowel sounds in the ninth stanza of "To a Skylark," or the comparative values of "ordain" and "decree" in "Kubla Kahn." At the same time he reads poetry as an incitement to moral and psychological observation. The phrase "flattered to tears," in "The Eve of St. Agnes," prompts him to write: "This 'flattered' is exquisite.... [In it] is the whole theory of the secret of tears; which are the tributes, more or less worthy, of self-pity to self-love. Whenever we shed tears, we take pity on ourselves; and we feel, if we do not consciously say so, that we deserve to have the pity taken." Other comments in this vein may be found in *Imagination and Fancy* (1844), the anthology in which Hunt canonized his usual practice of giving brief selections under appropriate headings, with the lines or phrases of pure poetry set in italics.

As such a practice suggests, he thought of poetry as a distillment of passion, to be known in isolation from the interlarded matter of argumentative writing. His idea of eloquence gives him the conscious delicacy of the aesthetic critic; it also makes him a close reader in something like the modern sense. This was a necessary strength for an introducer and early advocate of poetry by Keats, Shelley, and, to a lesser extent, Coleridge. But it leads Hunt even more than his contemporaries to rely on quotations of great bulk, to set the scene for his criticism. His inquiries may therefore deviate on occasion into a fastidious sampling of artistic sensations. But as a rule Hunt is among the least mannered writers of prose; and, in detail, he is the most incisive of all romantic critics of poetry. This care for detail may be the most important thing he taught Keats. The injunction that Keats urged on Shelley, to "curb your magnanimity, and be more of an artist, and load every rift of your subject with ore," he could have learned from a single favorite word of Hunt's, "unsuperfluousness." Yet it was not by favorite words but by the sustained force of his quotations and analysis that Hunt became a leader in the revival of Spenser, Boccaccio, and the early Milton. For these achievements many of the literate men and women of the age felt specially indebted to his guidance.

The review printed here, of Keats's *Poems* of 1817, is remarkable for the accuracy with which it points out the faults of Keats's first manner. Though he admires Keats as a poet ideally gifted with fancy, Hunt warns him against the "superabundance of detail" that may be crowded into some poems as a diversion from commonplace. It is a quality, he observes, itself "as faulty and unseasonable" as commonplace. Still, he credits Keats with an imagination that rises, above fancy, to "an intense feeling of external beauty in its most natural and least expressible simplicity." The assertion is then proved with a well-chosen sequence of passages: a method fortunate for Keats at this stage, since it gives a unique setting to felicities which were original in kind, while making little of the compositional economy that he lacked. As for Hunt's opening paragraphs on poetry in general, they are a fine instance of *ad hoc* history in the service of a new movement in art. If the praise of the Lake School is not quite persuasive, the reason may be that it is not quite Hunt's own. His friends Lamb and Hazlitt had only lately talked him out of a prejudice against Wordsworth, and his subsequent appreciations of Coleridge were a response to "Christabel," "Kubla Khan," and other poems which had not yet been published.

"On the Realities of Imagination" is, in its very title, a fair clue to Keats's *Endymion*. The essay teaches not so much that one may awake from dreams to find them true, as that experience is a record of dreamlike truths available to the discerning. Hunt seeks, in short, to correct the notion that there is any reality more immediate, purely sensory, or vivid than the realities of imagination. His paradox is that something must have been imagined in order to be real for us: "whatever touches us, whatever moves us, does touch and does move us," whether it is the sight of an ox knocked down in the street, or the way a poem has made us look at the horizon. The words, "touch" and "move," have both a physical sense and an emotional one, and it is in the nature of the mind to pass between these two kinds of sense. The brute fact has to be picked out by the imagination before it can signify at all. The refined idea is tested by the weight of things before it carries conviction. Similarly, Hunt uses the word "impression" for the sake of its double weight, for the realities he speaks of are neither perceptions nor thoughts. They are rather the combinations of pleasure and pain by which we give an intelligible shape to life.

A vital element in Hunt's thinking is the belief that such realities are plural. A given reality may exist as the effect of a point of view (what is now called a perspective), or of a special intensity of feeling (what is now called an affect). So a difference between realities is equally a difference between persons, or between aspects or moods of a single person. In either case it is made real simply by its results in feeling, and it is judged significant by the endurance of those results. Having questioned the distinction between reality and imagination and between physical and mental life, Hunt ends by associating more strongly than ever before the feelings we learn from experience and the feelings we learn from poetry. Here his essay draws upon the argument of Hazlitt's "On Imitation," and yet it makes its claim more explicitly. The powerful particulars or abstractions by which poetry is brought home to us Hunt describes as "intellectual objects." It is as such objects that the gods of ancient myth are to be understood; and, with them, the natural personifications and allegories of a later poetry (as may be seen in such characters as Ariel and Caliban). Hunt's last paragraph moves naturally from an association imparted to objects by literary invention, to an association imparted by human interest, without registering where the first leaves off and the second begins. In keeping with this design, his naming of particulars affords an echo of Wordsworth's sonnet "Composed upon Westminster Bridge," but an echo of which one is hardly conscious apart from the feeling of the things themselves.

14. *"Poems by John Keats"*

first published in *The Examiner*, June 1, July 6 and 13, 1817

THIS is the production of the young writer, whom we had the pleasure of announcing to the public a short time since, and several of whose Sonnets have appeared meanwhile in the *Examiner* with the signature of J. K. From these and stronger evidences in the book itself, the readers will conclude that the author and his critic are personal friends; and they are so, – made however, in the first instance, by nothing but his poetry, and at no greater distance of time than the announcement above-mentioned. We had published one of his Sonnets in our paper, without knowing more of him than any other anonymous correspondent; but at the period in question, a friend brought us one morning some copies of verses, which he said were from the pen of a youth. We had not been led, generally speaking, by a good deal of experience in these matters, to expect pleasure from introductions of the kind, so much as pain; but we had not read more than a dozen lines, when we recognised "a young poet indeed."

It is no longer a new observation, that poetry has of late years undergone a very great change, or rather, to speak properly, poetry has undergone no change, but something which was not poetry has made way for the return of something which is. The school which existed till lately since the restoration of Charles the 2d, was rather a school of wit and ethics in verse, than anything else; nor was the verse, with the exception of Dryden's, of the best order. The authors, it is true, are to be held in great honour. Great wit there certainly was, excellent satire, excellent sense, pithy sayings; and Pope distilled as much real poetry as could be got from the drawing-room world in which the art then lived, – from the flowers and luxuries of artificial life, – into that exquisite little toilet-bottle of essence, the *Rape of the Lock*. But there was little imagination, of a higher order, no intense feeling of nature, no sentiment, no real music or variety. Even the writers who gave evidences meanwhile of a truer poetical faculty, Gray, Thomson, Akenside, and Collins himself, were content with a great deal of second-hand workmanship, and with false styles made up of other languages and a certain kind of inverted cant.[1] It has been thought that Cowper was the first poet who re-opened the true way to nature and a natural style; but we hold this to be a mistake, arising merely from certain negations on the part of that amiable but by no means powerful writer. Cowper's style is for the most part as inverted and artificial as that of the others; and we look upon him to have been by nature not so great a poet as Pope: but Pope, from certain infirmities on his part, was thrown into the society of the world, and thus had to get what he could out of an artificial sphere: – Cowper, from other and distressing infirmities, (which by the way the wretched superstition that undertook to heal, only burnt in upon him) was confined to a still smaller though more natural sphere, and in truth did not much with it, though quite as much perhaps as was to be expected from an organisation too sore almost to come in contact with any thing.

It was the Lake Poets in our opinion (however grudgingly we say it, on some accounts) that were the first to revive a true taste for nature; and like most Revolutionists, especially of the cast which they have since turned out to be, they went to an extreme, calculated rather at first to make the readers of poetry disgusted with originality and adhere with contempt and resentment to their magazine common-places. This had a bad effect also in the way of re-action; and none of those writers have ever since been able to free themselves from certain stubborn affectations, which having been ignorantly confounded by others with the better part of them, have been retained by their self-love with a still less pardonable want of wisdom. The greater part indeed of the poetry of Mr. Southey, a weak man in all respects, is really made up of little else. Mr. Coleridge still trifles with his poetical as he has done with his metaphysical talent. Mr. Lamb, in our opinion, has a more real tact of humanity, a modester, Shakespearean wisdom, than any of them; and had he written more, might have delivered the school victoriously from all its defects. But it is Mr. Wordsworth who has advanced it the most, and who in spite of some morbidities as well as mistaken theories in other respects, has opened upon us a fund of thinking and imagination, that ranks him as the successor of the true and abundant poets of the older time. Poetry, like Plenty, should be represented with a cornucopia, but it should be a real one; not swelled out and insidiously *optimized* at the top, like Mr. Southey's stale strawberry baskets, but fine and full to the depth, like a heap from the vintage. Yet from the time of Milton till lately, scarcely a tree had been planted that could be called a poet's own. People got shoots from France, that ended in nothing but a little barren wood, from which they made flutes for young gentlemen and fan-sticks for ladies. The rich and enchanted ground of real poetry, fertile with all that English succulence could produce, bright with all that Italian sunshine could lend, and haunted with exquisite humanities, had become invisible to mortal eyes like the garden of Eden:—

"And from that time those Graces were not found."

These Graces, however, are re-appearing; and one of the greatest evidences is the little volume before us; for the work is not one of mere imitation, or a compilation of ingenious and promising things that merely announce better, and that after all might only help to keep up a bad system; but here is a young poet giving himself up to his own impressions, and revelling in real poetry for its own sake. He has had his advantages, because others have cleared the way into those happy bowers; but it shews the strength of his natural tendency, that he has not been turned aside by the lingering enticements of a former system, and by the self-love which interests others in enforcing them. We do not, of course, mean to say, that Mr. Keats has as much talent as he will have ten years hence, or that there are no imitations in his book, or that he does not make mistakes common to inexperience; – the reverse is inevitable at his time of life.[a] In proportion to our ideas, or impressions of the images of things, must be our acquaintance with the things themselves. But our author has all the sensitiveness of temperament requisite to receive these impressions; and wherever he has turned hitherto, he has evidently felt them deeply.

The very faults indeed of Mr. Keats arise from a passion for beauties, and a young impatience to vindicate them; and as we have mentioned these, we shall refer to them at once. They may be comprised in two; – first, a tendency to notice every thing too indiscriminately and without an eye to natural proportion and effect; and second, a sense of the proper variety of versification without a due consideration of its principles.

The former error is visible in several parts of the book, but chiefly though mixed with great beauties in the Epistles, and more between pages 28 and 47, where are collected the author's earliest pieces, some of which, we think, might have been omitted, especially the string of magistrate-interrogatories about a shell and a copy of verses.[b] See also (p. 61) a comparison of wine poured out in heaven to the appearance of a falling star, and (p. 62) the sight of far-seen fountains in the same region to "silver streaks across a dolphin's fin."[c] It was by thus giving way to every idea that came across him, that Marino,[d] a man of real poetical fancy, but no judgment, corrupted the poetry of Italy; a catastrophe, which however we by no means anticipate from our author, who with regard to this point is much more deficient in age than in good taste. We shall presently have to notice passages of a reverse nature, and these are by far the most numerous. But we warn him against a fault, which is the more tempting to a young writer of genius, inasmuch as it involves something so opposite to the contented commonplace and vague generalities of the late school of poetry. There is a super-abundance of detail, which, though not so wanting, of course, in power of perception, is as faulty and unseasonable sometimes as common-place. It depends upon circumstances, whether we are to consider ourselves near enough, as it were, to the subject we are describing to grow microscopical upon it. A person basking in a landscape for instance, and a person riding through it, are in two very different situations for the exercise of their eyesight; and even where the license is most allowable, care must be taken not to

[a] Keats was twenty-one   [b] "On Receiving a Curious Shell, and a Copy of Verses"
[c] Epistle "To My Brother George," 42, 50
[d] Giovanni Battista Marino (1569–1625), Italian poet of baroque extravagance

give to small things and great, to nice detail and to general feeling, the same proportion of effect. Errors of this kind in poetry answer to a want of perspective in painting, and of a due distribution of light and shade. To give an excessive instance in the former art, there was Denner, who copied faces to a nicety amounting to a horrible want of it, like Brobdignagian visages encountered by Gulliver; and who, according to the facetious Peter Pindar,[2]

> Made a bird's beak appear at twenty mile.

And the same kind of specimen is afforded in poetry by Darwin,[a] a writer now almost forgotten and deservedly, but who did good in his time by making unconscious caricatures of all the poetical faults in vogue, and flattering himself that the sum total went to the account of his original genius. Darwin would describe a dragon-fly and a lion in the same terms of proportion. You did not know which he would have scrambled from the sooner. His pictures were like the two-penny sheets which the little boys buy, and in which you see J Jackdaw and K King, both of the same dimensions.

Mr. Keats's other fault, the one in his versification, arises from a similar cause, – that of contradicting over-zealously the fault on the opposite side. It is this which provokes him now and then into mere roughnesses and discords for their own sake, not for that of variety and contrasted harmony. We can manage, by substituting a greater feeling for a smaller, a line like the following:–

> I shall roll on the grass with two-fold ease;[b]

but by no contrivance of any sort can we prevent this from jumping out of the heroic measure into mere rhythmicality, –

> How many bards gild the lapses of time![c]

We come now however to the beauties; and the reader will easily perceive that they not only outnumber the faults a hundred fold, but that they are of a nature decidedly opposed to what is false and inharmonious. Their characteristics indeed are a fine ear, a fancy and imagination at will, and an intense feeling of external beauty in its most natural and least expressible simplicity.

We shall give some specimens of the last beauty first, and conclude with a noble extract or two that will shew the second, as well as the powers of our young poet in general. The harmony of his verses will appear throughout.

[a] Erasmus Darwin (1731–1802), author of the *Botanic Garden*
[b] "To Charles Cowden Clarke," 79   [c] "How Many Bards," 1

14. *"Poems by John Keats"*

The first poem consists of a piece of luxury in a rural spot, ending with an allusion to the story of Endymion and to the origin of other lovely tales of mythology, on the ground suggested by Mr. Wordsworth in a beautiful passage of his *Excursion*.[3] Here, and in the other largest poem, which closes the book, Mr. Keats is seen to his best advantage, and displays all that fertile power of association and imagery which constitutes the abstract poetical faculty as distinguished from every other. He wants age for a greater knowledge of humanity, but evidences of this also bud forth here and there. – To come however to our specimens:–

The first page of the book presents us with a fancy, founded, as all beautiful fancies are, on a strong sense of what really exists or occurs. He is speaking of

> *A Gentle Air in Solitude.*[a]
> There crept
> A little noiseless noise among the leaves,
> Born of the very sigh that silence heaves.[b]

> *Young Trees.*
> There too should be
> The frequent chequer of a youngling tree,
> That with a score of light green brethren shoots
> From the quaint mossiness of aged roots;
> Round which is heard a spring-head of clear waters.[c]

Any body who has seen a throng of young beeches, furnishing those natural clumpy seats at the root, must recognise the truth and grace of this description. The remainder of this part of the poem, especially from –

> Open afresh your round of starry folds,
> Ye ardent marigolds! – [d]

down to the bottom of page 5, affords an exquisite proof of close observation of nature as well as the most luxuriant fancy.

> *The Moon.*
> Lifting her silver rim
> Above a cloud, and with a gradual swim
> Coming into the blue with all her light.[e]

> *Fir Trees.*
> Fir trees grow around,
> Aye dropping their hard fruit upon the ground.[f]

---

[a] This and the headings that follow are Hunt's own. [b] "I stood tip-toe," 10–12
[c] "I stood tip-toe," 37–41 [d] "I stood tip-toe," 47–48
[e] "I stood tip-toe," 113–15 [f] "Calidore," 40–41

This last line is in the taste of the Greek simplicity.

A Starry Sky.
The dark silent blue
With all its diamonds trembling through and through.[a]

Sound of a Pipe.
And some are hearing eagerly the wild
Thrilling liquidity of dewy piping.[b]

The *Specimen of an Induction to a Poem*, and the fragment of the
Poem itself entitled *Calidore*, contain some very natural touches on
the human side of things; as when speaking of a lady who is anxiously
looking out on the top of a tower for her defender, he describes her as
one

Who cannot feel for cold her tender feet;[c]

and when Calidore has fallen into a fit of amorous abstraction, he says
that

– The kind voice of good Sir Clerimond
Came to his ear, as something from beyond
His present being.[d]

The Epistles, the Sonnets, and indeed the whole of the book,
contain strong evidences of warm and social feelings, but particularly
the Epistle to Charles Cowden Clarke, and the Sonnet to his own
Brothers, in which the "faint cracklings" of the coal-fire are said to be

Like whispers of the household gods that keep
A gentle empire o'er fraternal souls.[e]

The Epistle to Mr. Clarke is very amiable as well as poetical, and
equally honourable to both parties, – to the young writer who can be
so grateful towards his teacher, and to the teacher who had the sense
to perceive his genius, and the qualities to call forth his affection. It
consists chiefly of recollections of what his friend had pointed out to
him in poetry and in general taste; and the lover of Spenser will
readily judge of his preceptor's qualifications, even from a single
triplet, in which he is described, with a deep feeling of simplicity, as
one

Who had beheld Belphoebe in a brook,
And lovely Una in a leafy nook,
And Archimago leaning o'er his book.[f]

---

[a] Epistle "To My Brother George," 57–58   [b] "Sleep and Poetry," 370–71
[c] "Specimen of an Induction to a Poem," 14
[d] "Calidore," 99–101   [e] "To My Brothers," 3–4   [f] "To Charles Cowden Clarke," 35–37

The Epistle thus concludes:—

Picture of Companionship.

But many days have past —
Since I have walked with you through shady lanes,
That freshly terminate in open plains,
And revell'd in a chat that ceased not,
When at night-fall among your books we got;
No, nor when supper came, — nor after that, —
Nor when reluctantly I took my hat;
No, nor till cordially you shook my hand
Midway between our homes: — your accents bland
Still sounded in my ears, when I no more
Could hear your footsteps touch the gravelly floor.
Sometimes I lost them, and then found again,
You changed the footpath for the grassy plain.
In those still moments I have wished you joys
That well you know to honour: — "Life's very toys
With him," said I, "will take a pleasant charm;
It cannot be that ought will work him harm."[a]

And we can only add, without any disrespect to the graver warmth of our young poet, that if Ought attempted it, Ought would find he had stout work to do with more than one person.

The following passage in one of the Sonnets passes, with great happiness, from the mention of physical associations to mental; and concludes with a feeling which must have struck many a contemplative mind, that has found the sea-shore like a border, as it were, of existence. He is speaking of

The Ocean.

The Ocean with its vastness, its blue green,
Its ships, its rocks, its caves, — its hopes, its fears, —
Its voice mysterious, which whoso hears
Must think on what will be, and what has been.[b]

We have read somewhere the remark of a traveller, who said that when he was walking alone at night-time on the sea-shore, he felt conscious of the earth, not as the common every day sphere it seems, but as one of the planets, rolling round with him in the mightiness of space. The same feeling is common to imaginations that are not in need of similar local excitements.

The best poem is certainly the last and longest, entitled *Sleep and Poetry*. It originated in sleeping in a room adorned with busts and pictures,[c] and is a striking specimen of the restlessness of the young

---

[a] "To Charles Cowden Clarke," 114–30   [b] Sonnet "To My Brother George," 5–8
[c] The room, which is described in the poem itself, was at Hunt's residence.

poetical appetite, obtaining its food by the very desire of it, and glancing for fit subjects of creation "from earth to heaven." Nor do we like it the less for an impatient, and as it may be thought by some irreverent assault upon the late French school of criticism and monotony, which has held poetry chained long enough to render it somewhat indignant when it got free.

The following ardent passage is highly imaginative:–

An Aspiration after Poetry.

O Poesy! for thee I grasp my pen
That am not yet a glorious denizen
Of thy wide heaven; yet to my ardent prayer,
Yield from thy sanctuary some clear air,
Smoothed for intoxication by the breath
Of flowering bays, that I may die a death
Of luxury, and my young spirit follow
The morning sun-beams to the great Apollo
Like a fresh sacrifice; or, if I can bear
The o'erwhelming sweets, 'twill bring to me the fair
Visions of all places: a bowery nook
Will be elysium – an eternal book
Whence I may copy many a lovely saying
About the leaves, and flowers – about the playing
Of nymphs in woods and fountains; and the shade
Keeping a silence round a sleeping maid;
And many a verse from so strange influence
That we must ever wonder how and whence
It came. Also imaginings will hover
Round my fire-side, and haply there discover
Vistas of solemn beauty, where I'd wander
In happy silence, like the clear Meander
Through its lone vales; and where I found a spot
Of awfuller shade, or an enchanted grot,
Or a green hill o'erspread with chequered dress
Of flowers, and fearful from its loveliness,
Write on my tablets all that was permitted,
All that was for our human senses fitted.
Then the events of this wide world I'd seize
Like a strong giant, and my spirit tease
Till at its shoulders it should proudly see
Wings to find out an immortality.[a]

Mr. Keats takes an opportunity, though with very different feelings towards the school than he has exhibited towards the one above-mentioned, to object to the morbidity that taints the productions of the Lake Poets. They might answer perhaps, generally, that they

[a] "Sleep and Poetry," 53–84

chuse to grapple with what is unavoidable, rather than pretend to be blind to it; but the more smiling Muse may reply, that half of the evils alluded to are produced by brooding over them; and that it is much better to strike at as many *causes* of the rest as possible, than to pretend to be satisfied with them in the midst of the most evident dissatisfaction.

> *Happy Poetry Preferred.*
> These things are doubtless: yet in truth we've had
> Strange thunders from the potency of song;
> Mingled indeed with what is sweet and strong,
> From majesty: but in clear truth the themes
> Are ugly clubs, the Poets Polyphemes
> Disturbing the grand sea. A drainless shower
> Of light is poesy; 'tis the supreme of power;
> 'Tis might half slumbering on its own right arm.
> The very archings of her eye-lids charm
> A thousand willing agents to obey.
> And still she governs with the mildest sway:
> But strength alone though of the Muses born
> Is like a fallen angel; trees uptorn,
> Darkness, and worms, and shrouds, and sepulchres
> Delight it; for it feeds upon the burrs
> And thorns of life; forgetting the great end
> Of poesy, that it should be a friend
> To soothe the cares, and lift the thoughts of man.[a]

We conclude with the beginning of the paragraph which follows this passage, and which contains an idea of as lovely and powerful a nature in embodying an abstraction, as we ever remember to have seen put into words:—

> Yet I rejoice: a myrtle fairer than
> E'er grew in Paphos, from the bitter weeds
> Lifts its sweet head into the air, *and feeds*
> *A silent space with ever sprouting green.*[b]

Upon the whole, Mr. Keats's book cannot be better described than in a couplet written by Milton when he too was young, and in which he evidently alludes to himself. It is a little luxuriant heap of

> Such sights as youthful poets dream
> On summer eves by haunted stream.[c]

---

[a] "Sleep and Poetry," 230–47   [b] "Sleep and Poetry," 248–51
[c] Milton, "L'Allegro," 129–30

Leigh Hunt (1784–1859)

15. "On the Realities of Imagination"[1]

first published in *The Indicator*, March 22, 1820; text from *The Indicator* (1822), pp. 185–92, with cuts

THERE is not a more unthinking way of talking, than to say such and such pains and pleasures are only imaginary, and therefore to be got rid of or undervalued accordingly. There is nothing imaginary, in the common acceptation of the word. The logic of Moses in the *Vicar of Wakefield* is good argument here: – "Whatever is, is." Whatever touches us, whatever moves us, does touch and does move us. We recognise the reality of it, as we do that of a hand in the dark. We might as well say that a sight which makes us laugh, or a blow which brings tears to our eyes, is imaginary, as that any thing else is imaginary which makes us laugh or weep. We can only judge of things by their effects. Our perception constantly deceives us, in things with which we suppose ourselves perfectly conversant; but our reception of their effect is a different matter. Whether we are materialists or immaterialists, whether things be about us or within us, whether we think the sun is a substance, or only the image of a divine thought, an idea, a thing imaginary, we are equally agreed as to the notion of its warmth. But on the other hand, as this warmth is felt differently by different temperaments, so what we call imaginary things affect different minds. What we have to do is not to deny their effect, because we do not feel in the same proportion, or whether we even feel it at all; but to see whether our neighbours may not be moved. If they are, there is, to all intents and purposes, a moving cause. But we do not see it? No; – neither perhaps do they. They only feel it; they are only sentient, – a word which implies the sight given to the imagination by the feelings. But what do you mean, we may ask in return, by seeing? Some rays of light come in contact with the eye; they bring a sensation to it; in a word, they touch it; and the impression left by this touch we call sight. How far does this differ in effect from the impression left by any other touch, however mysterious? An ox knocked down by a butcher, and a man knocked down by a fit of apoplexy, equally feel themselves compelled to drop. The tickling of a straw and of a comedy equally move the muscles about our mouth. The look of a beloved eye will so thrill the whole frame, that old philosophers have had recourse to a doctrine of beams and radiant particles flying from one sight to another. In fine, what is contact itself, and why does it affect us? There is no one cause more mysterious than another, if we look into it.

Nor does the question concern us like moral causes. We may be content to know the earth by its fruits; but how to increase and improve them is a more attractive study. If instead of saying that the causes which moved in us this or that pain or pleasure were imaginary, people were to say that the causes themselves were removable, they would be nearer the truth. When a stone trips us up, we do not fall to disputing its existence: we put it out of the way. In like manner, when we suffer from what is called an imaginary pain, our business is not to canvass the reality of it. Whether there is any cause or not in that or any other perception, or whether every thing consist not in what is called effect, it is sufficient for us that the effect is real. Our sole business is to remove those second causes, which always accompany the original idea. As in deliriums for instance, it would be idle to go about persuading the patient that he did not behold the figures he says he does. He might reasonably ask us, if he could, how we know any thing about the matter; or how we can be sure, that in the infinite wonders of the universe, certain realities may not become apparent to certain eyes, whether diseased or not. Our business would be to put him into that state of health, in which human beings are not diverted from their offices and comforts by a liability to such imaginations. The best reply to his question would be, that such a morbidity is clearly no more a fit state for a human being, than a disarranged or incomplete state of works is for a watch; and that seeing the general tendency of nature to this completeness or state of comfort, we naturally conclude that the imaginations in question, whether substantial or not, are at least not of the same lasting or prevailing description.

We do not profess metaphysics. We are indeed so little conversant with the masters of that art, that we are never sure whether we are using even its proper terms. All that we may know on the subject comes to us from some reflection and some experience; and this all may be so little as to make a metaphysician smile; which if he be a true one, he will do good-naturedly. The pretender will take occasion from our very confession, to say that we know nothing. Our faculty, such as it is, is rather instinctive than reasoning; rather physical than metaphysical; rather wise because it loves much, than because it knows much; rather calculated by a certain retention of boyhood, and by its wanderings in the green places of thought, to light upon a piece of the old golden world, than to tire ourselves, and conclude it unattainable, by too wide and scientific a search. We pretend to see farther than none but the worldly and the malignant. And yet those who see farther, may not all see so well. We do not blind our eyes with looking upon the sun in the heavens. We believe it to be there, but we find its light upon earth also; and we would lead humanity, if we could, out of misery and coldness into the shine of it. Pain might still be there; must be so, as long as we are mortal;

For oft we still must weep, since we are human:[a]

but it should be pain for the sake of others, which is noble; not unnecessary pain inflicted by or upon them, which it is absurd not to remove. The very pains of mankind struggle towards pleasures; and such pains as are proper for them have this inevitable accompaniment of true humanity, – that they cannot but realise a certain gentleness of enjoyment. Thus the true bearer of pain would come round to us; and he would not grudge us a share of his burden, though in taking from his trouble it might diminish his pride. Pride is but a bad pleasure at the expense of others. The great object of humanity is to enrich every body. If it is a task destined not to succeed, it is a good one from its very nature; and fulfils at least a glad destiny of its own. To look upon it austerely is in reality the reverse of austerity. It is only such an impatience of the want of pleasure as leads us to grudge it in others; and this impatience itself, if the sufferer knew how to use it, is but another impulse, in the general yearning, towards an equal wealth of enjoyment.

But we shall be getting into other discussions. – The ground-work of all happiness is health. Take care of this ground; and the doleful imaginations that come to warn us against its abuse, will avoid it. Take care of this ground, and let as many glad imaginations throng to it as possible. Read the magical works of the poets, and they will come. If you doubt their existence, ask yourself whether you feel pleasure at the idea of them; whether you are moved into delicious smiles, or tears as delicious. If you are, the result is the same to you, whether they exist or not. It is not mere words to say, that he who goes through a rich man's park, and sees things in it which never bless the mental eyesight of the possessor, is richer than he. He is richer. More results of pleasure come home to him. The ground is actually more fertile to him: the place haunted with finer shapes. He has more servants to come at his call, and administer to him with full hands. Knowledge, sympathy, imagination, are all Divining Rods, with which he discovers treasure. Let a painter go through the grounds, and he will see not only the general colours of green and brown, but all their combinations and contrasts, and all the modes in which they might again be combined and contrasted. He will also put figures in

[a] Shelley, *The Revolt of Islam*, 2232

the landscape if there are none there, flocks and herds, or a solitary spectator, or Venus lying with her white body among the violets and primroses. Let a musician go through, and he will hear "differences discreet" in the notes of the birds and the lapsing of the water-fall. He will fancy a serenade of wind instruments in the open air at the lady's window, with a voice rising through it; or the horn of the hunter; or the musical cry of the hounds,

> Matched in mouth like bells,
> Each under each;[a]

or a solitary voice in a bower, singing for an expected lover; or the chapel organ, waking up like the fountain of the winds. Let a poet go through the grounds, and he will heighten and increase all these sounds and images. He will bring the colours from heaven, and put an unearthly meaning into the voice. He will have stories of the sylvan inhabitants; will shift the population through infinite varieties; will put a sentiment upon every sight and sound; will be human, romantic, supernatural; will make all nature send tribute into that spot. . . .

We may say of the Love of Nature, what Shakspeare says of another love, that it

> Adds a precious seeing to the eye.[b]

And we may say also, upon the like principle, that it adds a precious hearing to the ear. This and Imagination, which ever follows upon it, are the two purifiers of our sense, which rescue us from the deafening babble of common cares, and enable us to hear all the affectionate voices of earth and heaven. The starry orbs, lapsing about in their smooth and sparkling dance, sing to us. The brooks talk to us of solitude. The birds are the animal spirits of nature, carolling in the air, like a careless lass.

> The gentle gales,
> Fanning their odoriferous wings, dispense
> Native perfumes; and whisper whence they stole
> Those balmy spoils. – *Paradise Lost*, B. IV.

The poets are called creators (ποιηταί, Makers), because with their magical words, they bring forth to our eyesight the abundant images and beauties of creation. They put them there, if the reader pleases; and so are literally creators. But whether put there or discovered, whether created or invented, (for invention means nothing but

---

[a] *Midsummer Night's Dream*, IV. i. 124–25   [b] *Love's Labor's Lost*, IV. iii. 330

finding out), there they are. If they touch us, they exist to as much purpose as any thing else which touches us. If a passage in King Lear brings the tears into our eyes, it is real as the touch of a sorrowful hand. If the flow of a song of Anacreon's intoxicates us, it is as true to a pulse within us as the wine he drank. We hear not their sounds with ears, nor see their sights with eyes; but we hear and see both so truly, that we are moved with pleasure; and the advantage, nay, even the test, of seeing and hearing, at any time, is not in the seeing and hearing, but in the ideas we realise, and the pleasure we derive. Intellectual objects therefore, inasmuch as they come home to us, are as true a part of the population of nature, as visible ones; and they are infinitely more abundant. Between the tree of a country clown, and the tree of a Milton or Spenser, what a difference in point of productiveness! Between the plodding of a sexton through a church-yard, and the walk of a Gray, what a difference! What a difference between the Bermudas of a ship-builder, and the Bermoothes of Shakespeare; the isle

> Full of noises,
> Sounds, and sweet airs, that give delight, and hurt not;[a]

the isles of elves and fairies, that chased the tide to and fro on the sea-shore; of coral-bones, and the knells of sea-nymphs; of spirits dancing on the sands, and singing amidst the hushes of the wind; of Caliban, whose brute nature enchantment had made poetical; of Ariel, who lay in cowslip bells, and rode upon the bat; of Miranda, who wept when she saw Ferdinand work so hard, and begged him to let her help; telling him,

> I am your wife, if you will marry me;
> If not, I'll die your maid. To be your fellow
> You may deny me; but I'll be your servant,
> Whether you will or no.[b]

Such are the discoveries which the poets make for us; – worlds, to which that of Columbus was but a handful of brute matter. It began to be richer for us the other day, when Humboldt[c] came back and told us of its luxuriant and gigantic vegetation; of the myriads of shooting lights, which revel at evening in the southern sky; and of that grand constellation, at which Dante seems to have made so remarkable a guess (Purgatorio, cant. i., v. 22). The natural warmth of the Mexican and Peruvian genius, set free from despotism, will soon do all the rest

---

[a] *The Tempest*, III. ii. 138–39   [b] *The Tempest*, III. i. 83–86
[c] See note 3 to Hazlitt's "On the Picturesque and Ideal."

for it; awaken the sleeping riches of its eyesight, and call forth the glad music of its affections. . . .

Imagination enriches every thing. A great library contains not only books, but

> The assembled souls of all that men held wise. DAVENANT.[a]

The moon is Homer's and Shakespeare's moon, as well as the one we look at. The sun comes out of his chamber in the east, with a sparkling eye, "rejoicing like a bridegroom."[b] The commonest thing becomes like Aaron's rod, that budded. Pope called up the spirits of the Cabala to wait upon a lock of hair, and justly gave it the honours of a constellation; for he has hung it, sparkling for ever, in the eyes of posterity. A common meadow is a sorry thing to a ditcher or a coxcomb; but by the help of its dues from imagination and the love of nature, the grass brightens for us, the air soothes us, we feel as we did in the daisied hours of childhood. Its verdures, its sheep, its hedge-row elms, – all these, and all else which sight, and sound, and association can give it, are made to furnish a treasure of pleasant thoughts. Even brick and mortar are vivified, as of old, at the harp of Orpheus. A metropolis becomes no longer a mere collection of houses or of trades. It puts on all the grandeur of its history, and its literature; its towers, and rivers; its art, and jewellery, and foreign wealth; its multitude of human beings all intent upon excitement, wise or yet to learn; the huge and sullen dignity of its canopy of smoke by day; the wide gleam upwards of its lighted lustre at night-time; and the noise of its many chariots, heard, at the same hour, when the wind sets gently towards some quiet suburb.[2]

[a] William Davenant (1605–68), dramatist and author of the epic *Gondibert*
[b] an echo of Isaiah LXII: 5 and *As You Like It* V. iv. 178–79

Thomas De Quincey

(1785–1859)

Thomas De Quincey was born and reared in Manchester, the son of a merchant who died when Thomas was seven but left the family with a secure fortune. As a child De Quincey showed a precocious gift for the classical languages, and in his *Confessions of an English Opium Eater* he would quote with pride his master's verdict in recommending him to a stranger: "That boy could harangue an Athenian mob better than you or I could an English one." But he felt oppressed by the regimen of his grammar school; and in 1802 he ran away to London. There he formed the companionship with a prostitute, Anne, which he describes at length in the *Confessions*. By De Quincey's account she saved his life once, reviving him from a starvation faint with a glass of wine purchased by her last sixpence. She disappeared soon after without a trace. De Quincey for his part eventually legitimated himself once more with his guardians, and was able to attend Oxford, though on insufficiently conventional terms to earn a degree. He studied Hebrew and German on his own; and about this time he began to take opium. It was as an opium dreamer that he was to make his reputation in writing many years later. Indeed, outside of literary criticism, his most characteristic prose was opium-inspired. And yet the sprawling reverie, *Suspiria de Profundis*, on which he believed his fame would rest, appeared only in fragments during his lifetime, and has yet to be gathered together according to his design. He treated his addiction at times as a source of esoteric authority, pronouncing "the doctrine of the true church on the subject of opium; of which church I acknowledge myself to be the Pope (consequently infallible)." But he laid to the effects of opium the abortive pattern of his career.

As an essayist De Quincey's most pervasive debt is to the gothic mode in fiction. Like the romances of Radcliffe and Godwin, his narratives often depend on the absorbing power of a secret (a fact whose essence may appear at once reductively literal and insolubly figurative). His critical essays are no different in this respect: they always seem to hesitate before the immensity of a long-foreseen disclosure. His judgements, very elaborately prepared for, are delivered in so scattered a fashion that the sense of an untold mystery may survive its revelation. Something of this style De Quincey probably learned from Coleridge, whom he met in 1807 and who exerted a continuous influence on his thinking. If De Quincey's criticism leaves a more coherent impression than Coleridge's, that is because his attempts are sustained with fewer interruptions. But his single great theme – the power of the mind to unify and reconcile outward life with inward thought and feeling – is

Coleridgean. And the smaller topics out of which he likes to make digressions of any size – the distinction between fancy and imagination, the superiority of German metaphysics to French politics – are among the usual themes of Coleridge's prose and conversation alike. Still, De Quincey's intellectual loyalties, together with his sensitivity (almost vulnerability) to powerful impressions as a reader, help to make him the idealist critic that Coleridge himself promised to be. He has one fault everywhere, a weak instinct for truth. But he can be a vehement and effective polemicist for the taste in poetry inculcated by the Lake School, and for the revised estimates of earlier poetry which the success of that taste implied. He has the enthusiasms and even, in places, the earnestness of the second-generation disciple.

Apart from autobiography, personal confession, "dream fugue" and romance, De Quincey explored the whole range of subjects available to a writer for the quarterlies. This included historical narratives like "The Revolt of the Tartars," and contentious articles on political economy; sketches of the great English authors, and of recent German philosophers and critics; dicta on the uses of classical rhetoric, and memoirs of the Lake poets. All of these writings are occasionally impressive and occasionally "appalling" in De Quincey's favorable sense of the word. They wield, with the correct quantum of dignity, the weapon of prose forged by the *Quarterly* review, when not by a higher model. But, to a degree almost unique among the writers of great prose, De Quincey stops short of an effort to bind his deeper impressions to each other. His critical essays particularly show an argumentative flatness and a tactical indecisiveness that belie their customary fluency. He resists the epigram – on principle, one feels, as a cultivator of *rhythmus* – but perhaps from necessity also, as he would resist any token of self-trust. His recourse to classical words or phrases – often to no precise purpose, since they have good English equivalents which he decides to give afterwards – comes to seem a form of ostentation. (It is typical of him to speak of "the French anabasis to Moscow.") With a full set of opinions and a resonant memory, he brings almost no temperamental interest to the conduct of an argument. Rather, he trusts the present state of controversy to take him forward into battle, to the enhancement of one side or the other. Over long stretches of exposition he is deliberately ponderous, scholastic, unindividuated.

Every other author in this volume may be considered as in some measure an inheritor of the Enlightenment. De Quincey's language echoes theirs; his impulses carry him in an opposite direction. He was fond of the lore of secret societies and hermetic sects, and, for all his researches into German idealism, he treated its leading doctrines as still another branch of esoteric knowledge. A contempt for common sense marks all his writings. Indeed, genuine as his sympathy is for the thinkers he knows best, he has a good deal of the costume of the man of intellect, with very little of the passion. An author familiar with him in his later years, James Hogg, recorded that "of all the subjects which exercised a permanent fascination over De Quincey, I would place first in order Thuggism in India and the Gagots of Spain and France." He was obsessed with murder, above all with murder as a stimulus to the imagination, and his celebrated essay "On Murder Considered as One of the Fine Arts" gives a fair impression of his talent for intensifying the stimulus. In such performances the dandyish tone is sometimes a misleading clue to the awe with which De Quincey has contemplated his subject.

A great essay in criticism and a dangerous exercise of sympathy, "On the Knocking at the Gate in *Macbeth*" joins to De Quincey's own speculations the superstitious horror of the scene after Duncan's murder. It is noteworthy that the essay should be written in the first person and as if from a particular point of view. For if we ask whose perspective in the play it represents, the answer is somewhat perplexing. The vast pause that De Quincey supposes cannot belong to the mind of Macbeth: his response to the crime and its aftermath, as Shakespeare presents it, is dreadfully haunted but never quite as conscious as that of De Quincey's narrator. By contrast Lady Macbeth is pragmatic, and contents herself at the time with remarks on the unexpected quantity of blood and on Duncan's resemblance to her father: her imaginative response to these things is deferred to a much later moment in the play. Nor can De Quincey's reflections be identified with the Porter, or with some spirit of the drama unmentioned by Shakespeare. What we are reading is the critic's affective response to the total suspension of "human things, human purposes, human desires" which he associates with murder. He uses here the same analogy that he uses in the essay "On Murder Considered as One of the Fine Arts," comparing the dead halt of the action with a pause in the traffic of a metropolis. Thus his own imaginings assign to the focus of one passage a larger feeling which the play has dispersed into many parts: Macbeth's speeches at the beginning of I. vii, for example, and at the end of III. ii. De Quincey reads the dramatic poetry of *Macbeth* as one would read a lyric poem. He achieves his homage at the price of a deformation, by concentrating the play's sublimities into a single recognition that belongs to no single character.

The energies that the mind can bring to such a scene are again De Quincey's concern in the part of his essay on Pope that distinguishes the literature of power from the literature of knowledge. These categories are not derived from the author's intention, or the chosen or assignable genre of the work, or its formal properties, or its figurative richness. Power comes rather from the existence of uncanny moments in a text – moments, De Quincey believes, which in themselves the mind can do nothing with, but which point to the tremendousness of its activity and the necessity of its dreamwork. Literature as it is commonly defined (works of poetry, fiction, drama, and perhaps a few biographies and histories; excluding all criticism, metaphysics, social commentary and moral philosophy, sermons, and most biographies and histories) has nothing to do with "the literature of power." What are called literary works may fail to have power and what are called non-literary works may have power. *Power* itself is defined as a "deep sympathy with truth," by which De Quincey means a truth not yet discovered, and therefore unsusceptible of conscious statement. It is for that matter a kind of truth, in a line, a scene, or a sentiment impossible to locate, which we cannot encounter again without feeling that it is still to be discovered. It seems an accurate extension of De Quincey's thought to say that power makes knowledge endurable by making it seem always incomplete.

De Quincey's essay "On Wordsworth's Poetry" is the work of a man who had admired Wordsworth from the time of his first great publications. He had lived to witness the ascent of Wordsworth first to the select appreciation of a coterie and then to the established honor of the poet laureateship, and he chose this moment to write his criticism. De Quincey gives more space than need have been expected to a rehearsal of Wordsworth's salutary departures from the eighteenth-century idiom of Dryden and Pope – the same ground that Hunt thought it proper to cover three decades earlier, at the start of his first review of Keats. Again, he offers some intelligent strictures on Words-worth's understanding of "the real language of men," more to summarize than to modify the verdict of earlier critics. And he is waylaid by a rather peevish objection to the narrator of Book I of *The Excursion*, who makes a show of imaginative sympathy where the case seems to require literal charity. The objection may not be unfair to Wordsworth's story, but it would apply with equal force to virtually any representation of economic distress. Nevertheless this remains a well-balanced estimate, with a notably original choice of poems for quotation. As for the weight given to *The Excursion*, it may be explained by the absence of any published version of *The Prelude*. By 1845 De Quincey feels justified in asserting that the moral depth of Words-worth's poetry has been generally acknowledged. This makes a contrast with Hazlitt's finding only fifteen years earlier, in "Byron and Wordsworth": the world was "a grown schoolboy" and it relished Byron the most, so that Wordsworth still seemed altogether a special taste in need of a personal defense. For De Quincey he is a poet whose inmost eccentricities have now become canonical. The essay picks as a touchstone of Wordsworth's genius his power of abstraction, and exemplifies it with a single metaphor, "frozen by distance." By itself this seems to earn the conclusion that for Wordsworth "the fact has also a profound meaning as a hieroglyphic." With its sense of the connection between "the hyperphysical character" of things and "those spiritual and shadowy foundations which alone are enduring," the essay both sums up the great romantic considerations of Wordsworth and suggests the burden of later inquiries into the egotistical sublime.

16. *"On the Knocking at the Gate in* Macbeth"

first published in the *London Magazine*, October 1823; text from *Works*, ed. David Masson (1890), vol. 10, pp. 389–95

FROM my boyish days I had always felt a great perplexity on one point in *Macbeth*. It was this: – The knocking at the gate which succeeds to the murder of Duncan[a] produced to my feelings an effect for which I never could account. The effect was that it reflected back upon the murderer a peculiar awfulness and a depth of solemnity; yet, however obstinately I endeavoured with my understanding to comprehend this, for many years I never could see *why* it should produce such an effect.

Here I pause for one moment, to exhort the reader never to pay any attention to his understanding when it stands in opposition to any other faculty of his mind. The mere understanding, however useful and indispensable, is the meanest faculty in the human mind, and the most to be distrusted; and yet the great majority of people trust to nothing else, – which may do for ordinary life, but not for philosophical purposes. Of this out of ten thousand instances that I might produce I will cite one. Ask of any person whatsoever who is not previously prepared for the demand by a knowledge of the perspective to draw in the rudest way the commonest appearance which depends upon the laws of that science, – as, for instance, to represent the effect of two walls standing at right angles to each other, or the appearance of the houses on each side of a street as seen by a person looking down the street from one extremity. Now, in all cases, unless the person has happened to observe in pictures how it is that artists produce these effects, he will be utterly unable to make the smallest approximation to it. Yet why? For he has actually seen the effect every day of his life. The reason is that he allows his understanding to overrule his eyes. His understanding, which includes no intuitive knowledge of the laws of vision, can furnish him with no reason why a line which is known and can be proved to be a horizontal line should not *appear* a horizontal line: a line that made any angle with the perpendicular less than a right angle would seem to him to indicate that his houses were all tumbling down together. Accordingly, he makes the line of his houses a horizontal line, and fails, of course, to produce the effect demanded. Here, then, is one instance out of many in which not only the understanding is allowed to overrule the eyes, but where the understanding is positively allowed to obliterate the eyes, as it were; for not only does the man believe the evidence of his understanding in opposition to that of his eyes, but (what is monstrous) the idiot is not aware that his eyes ever gave such evidence. He does not know that he has seen (and therefore *quoad*[b] his consciousness has *not* seen) that which he *has* seen every day of his life.[1]

But to return from this digression. My understanding could

[a] Act II, scene iii   [b] with respect to

furnish no reason why the knocking at the gate in Macbeth should produce any effect, direct or reflected. In fact, my understanding said positively that it could *not* produce any effect. But I knew better; I felt that it did; and I waited and clung to the problem until further knowledge should enable me to solve it. At length, in 1812, Mr. Williams made his *début* on the stage of Ratcliffe Highway, and executed those unparalleled murders which have procured for him such a brilliant and undying reputation.[2] On which murders, by the way, I must observe that in one respect they have had an ill effect, by making the connoisseur in murder very fastidious in his taste, and dissatisfied by anything that has been since done in that line. All other murders look pale by the deep crimson of his; and, as an amateur once said to me in a querulous tone, "There has been absolutely nothing *doing* since his time, or nothing that's worth speaking of." But this is wrong; for it is unreasonable to expect all men to be great artists, and born with the genius of Mr. Williams. Now, it will be remembered that in the first of these murders (that of the Marrs) the same incident (of a knocking at the door soon after the work of extermination was complete) did actually occur which the genius of Shakspere has invented; and all good judges, and the most eminent dilettanti, acknowledged the felicity of Shakspere's suggestion as soon as it was actually realized. Here, then, was a fresh proof that I was right in relying on my own feeling, in opposition to my understanding; and I again set myself to study the problem. At length I solved it to my own satisfaction; and my solution is this:– Murder, in ordinary cases, where the sympathy is wholly directed to the case of the murdered person, is an incident of coarse and vulgar horror; and for this reason, – that it flings the interest exclusively upon the natural but ignoble instinct by which we cleave to life: an instinct which, as being indispensable to the primal law of self-preservation, is the same in kind (though different in degree) amongst all living creatures. This instinct, therefore, because it annihilates all distinctions, and degrades the greatest of men to the level of "the poor beetle that we tread on,"[a] exhibits human nature in its most abject and humiliating attitude. Such an attitude would little suit the purposes of the poet. What then must he do? He must throw the interest on the murderer. Our sympathy must be with *him* (of course I mean a sympathy of comprehension, a sympathy by which we enter into his feelings, and are made to understand them, – not a sympathy of pity or appro-bation). In the murdered person, all strife of thought, all flux and reflux of passion and of purpose, are crushed by one overwhelming

[a] *Measure for Measure*, III. i. 78

panic; the fear of instant death smites him "with its petrific mace."*a*
But in the murderer, such a murderer as a poet will condescend to,
there must be raging some great storm of passion, – jealousy,
ambition, vengeance, hatred, – which will create a hell within him;
and into this hell we are to look.

In *Macbeth*, for the sake of gratifying his own enormous and
teeming faculty of creation, Shakspere has introduced two murderers: and as usual in his hands, they are remarkably discriminated:
but, – though in Macbeth the strife of mind is greater than in his wife,
the tiger spirit not so awake, and his feelings caught chiefly by
contagion from her, – yet, as both were finally involved in the guilt of
murder, the murderous mind of necessity is finally to be presumed in
both. This was to be expressed; and, on its own account, as well as to
make it a more proportionable antagonist to the unoffending nature
of their victim, "the gracious Duncan," and adequately to expound
"the deep damnation of his taking off," this was to be expressed with
peculiar energy. We were to be made to feel that the human nature, –
i.e. the divine nature of love and mercy, spread through the hearts of
all creatures, and seldom utterly withdrawn from man, – was gone,
vanished, extinct, and that the fiendish nature had taken its place.
And, as this effect is marvellously accomplished in the *dialogues* and
soliloquies themselves, so it is finally consummated by the expedient
under consideration; and it is to this that I now solicit the reader's
attention. If the reader has ever witnessed a wife, daughter, or sister in
a fainting fit, he may chance to have observed that the most affecting
moment in such a spectacle is *that* in which a sigh and a stirring
announce the recommencement of suspended life. Or, if the reader
has ever been present in a vast metropolis on the day when some great
national idol was carried in funeral pomp to his grave, and, chancing
to walk near the course through which it passed, has felt powerfully,
in the silence and desertion of the streets, and in the stagnation of
ordinary business, the deep interest which at that moment was
possessing the heart of man, – if all at once he should hear the
death-like stillness broken up by the sound of wheels rattling away
from the scene, and making known that the transitory vision was
dissolved, he will be aware that at no moment was his sense of the
complete suspension and pause in ordinary human concerns so full
and affecting as at that moment when the suspension ceases, and the
goings-on of human life are suddenly resumed. All action in any
direction is best expounded, measured, and made apprehensible, by
reaction. Now, apply this to the case in *Macbeth*. Here, as I have said,

a Paradise Lost, x. 274

the retiring of the human heart and the entrance of the fiendish heart was to be expressed and made sensible. Another world has stept in; and the murderers are taken out of the region of human things, human purposes, human desires. They are transfigured: Lady Macbeth is "unsexed"; Macbeth has forgot that he was born of woman; both are conformed to the image of devils; and the world of devils is suddenly revealed. But how shall this be conveyed and made palpable? In order that a new world may step in, this world must for a time disappear. The murderers and the murder must be insulated — cut off by an immeasurable gulf from the ordinary tide and succession of human affairs — locked up and sequestered in some deep recess; we must be made sensible that the world of ordinary life is suddenly arrested, laid asleep, tranced, racked into a dread armistice; time must be annihilated, relation to things without abolished; and all must pass self-withdrawn into a deep syncope and suspension of earthly passion.[3] Hence it is that, when the deed is done, when the work of darkness is perfect, then the world of darkness passes away like a pageantry in the clouds: the knocking at the gate is heard, and it makes known audibly that the reaction has commenced; the human has made its reflux upon the fiendish; the pulses of life are beginning to beat again; and the re-establishment of the goings-on of the world in which we live first makes us profoundly sensible of the awful parenthesis that had suspended them.

O mighty poet! Thy works are not as those of other men, simply and merely great works of art, but are also like the phenomena of nature, like the sun and the sea, the stars and the flowers, like frost and snow, rain and dew, hail-storm and thunder, which are to be studied with entire submission of our own faculties, and in the perfect faith that in them there can be no too much or too little, nothing useless or inert, but that, the farther we press in our discoveries, the more we shall see proofs of design and self-supporting arrangement where the careless eye had seen nothing but accident!

17. *"On Wordsworth's Poetry"*

first published in *Tait's Magazine*, September 1845; text of 1857, from *Works*, ed. David Masson (1890), vol. II, pp. 294–322

HERETOFORE, upon one impulse or another, I have retraced fugitive memorials of several persons celebrated in our own times; but I have never undertaken an examination of any man's writings. The one labour is, comparatively, without an effort; the other is both difficult, and, with regard to contemporaries, is invidious. In genial moments the characteristic remembrances of men expand as fluently as buds travel into blossoms; but criticism, if it is to be conscientious and profound, and if it is applied to an object so unlimited as poetry, must be almost as unattainable by any hasty effort as fine poetry itself. "Thou hast convinced me," says Rasselas to Imlac, "that it is impossible to be a poet"; so vast had appeared to be the array of qualifications.[a] But, with the same ease, Imlac might have convinced the prince that it was impossible to be a critic. And hence it is that, in the sense of absolute and philosophic criticism, we have little or none; for, before *that* can exist, we must have a good psychology, whereas, at present, we have none at all.

If, however, it is more difficult to write critical sketches than sketches of personal recollections, often it is much less connected with painful scruples. Of books, so long as you rest only on grounds which, in sincerity, you believe to be true, and speak without anger or scorn, you can hardly say the thing which *ought* to be taken amiss. But of men and women you dare not, and must not, tell all that chance may have revealed to you. Sometimes you are summoned to silence by pity for that general human infirmity which you also, the writer, share. Sometimes you are checked by the consideration that perhaps your knowledge of the case was originally gained under opportunities allowed only by confidence, or by unsuspecting carelessness. Sometimes the disclosure would cause quarrels between parties now at peace. Sometimes it would inflict pain, such as you could not feel any right to inflict, upon people not directly but collaterally interested in the exposure. Sometimes, again, if right to be told, it might be difficult to prove. Thus, for one cause or another, some things are sacred, and some things are perilous, amongst any *personal* revelations that else you might have it in your power to make. And seldom, indeed, is your own silent retrospect of close personal connexions with distinguished men altogether happy. "Put not your trust in princes, nor in the sons of princes" – this has been the warning – this has been the farewell moral, winding up and pointing the experience of dying statesmen. Not less truly it might be said – "Put not your trust in the intellectual princes of your age"; form no connexions too close with any who live only in the atmosphere of admiration and praise. The love or the friendship of such people rarely contracts itself into the narrow circle of individuals. You, if you are brilliant like themselves, or in any degree standing upon intellectual pretensions,

[a] Johnson, *Rasselas*, chapter ii

such men will hate; you, if you are dull, they will despise. Gaze, therefore, on the splendour of such idols as a passing stranger. Look for a moment as one sharing in the idolatry; but pass on before the splendour has been sullied by human frailty, or before your own generous admiration has been confounded with offerings of weeds, or with the homage of the sycophantic.[1]

Safer, then, it is to scrutinise the works of eminent poets than long to connect yourself with themselves, or to revive your remembrances of them in any personal record. Now, amongst all works that have illustrated our own age, none can more deserve an earnest notice than those of the Laureate;[a] and on some grounds, peculiar to themselves, none so much. Their merit in fact is not only supreme, but unique; not only supreme in their general class, but unique as in a class of their own. And there is a challenge of a separate nature to the curiosity of the readers in the remarkable contrast between the first stage of Wordsworth's acceptation with the public and that which he enjoys at present.

One original obstacle to the favourable impression of the Wordsworthian poerty, and an obstacle purely self-created, was his theory of Poetic Diction.[2] The diction itself, without the theory, was of less consequence; for the mass of readers would have been too blind or too careless to notice it. But the preface to the second edition of his Poems (2 vols 1799–1800)[b] compelled all readers to notice it. Nothing more injudicious was ever done by man. An unpopular truth would, at any rate, have been a bad inauguration for what, on *other* accounts, the author had announced as "an experiment." His poetry was already, and confessedly, an experiment as regarded the quality of the subjects selected, and as regarded the mode of treating them. That was surely trial enough for the reader's untrained sensibilities, without the unpopular novelty besides as to the quality of the diction. But, in the meantime, this novelty, besides being unpopular, was also in part false; it was true, and it was *not* true. And it was not true in a double way. Stating broadly, and allowing it to be taken for his meaning, that the diction of ordinary life (in his own words, "the very language of men") was the proper diction for poetry, the writer meant no such thing; for only a *part* of this diction, according to his own subsequent restriction, was available for such a use. And, secondly, as his own subsequent practice showed, even this part was available only for peculiar classes of poetry. In his own exquisite "Laodamia," in his "Sonnets," in his "Excursion," few are his obligations to the idiomatic language of life, as distinguished from

---

[a] Wordsworth became Poet Laureate in 1843. 　　[b] Preface to *Lyrical Ballads*

that of books, or of perspective usage. Coleridge remarked, justly, that the "Excursion" bristles beyond most poems with what are called "dictionary" words, – that is, polysyllabic words of Latin or Greek origin.[a] And so it must ever be in meditative poetry upon solemn philosophic themes. The gamut of ideas needs a corresponding gamut of expressions; the scale of the thinking which ranges through *every* key exacts, for the artist, an unlimited command over the entire scale of the instrument which he employs. Never, in fact, was there a more erroneous direction – one falser in its grounds, or more ruinous in its tendency – than that given by a modern Rector[b] of the Glasgow University to the students – viz. that they should cultivate the Saxon part of our language rather than the Latin part. Nonsense. Both are indispensable; and, speaking generally, without stopping to distinguish as to subjects, both are *equally* indispensable. Pathos, in situations which are homely, or at all connected with domestic affections, naturally moves by Saxon words. Lyrical emotion of every kind, which (to merit the name *lyrical*) must be in the state of flux and reflux, or, generally, of agitation, also requires the Saxon element of our language. And why? Because the Saxon is the aboriginal element, – the basis, and not the superstructure; consequently it comprehends all the ideas which are natural to the heart of man, and to the *elementary* situations of life. And, although the Latin often furnishes us with duplicates of these ideas, yet the Saxon, or monosyllabic part, has the advantage of precedency in our use and knowledge; for it is the language of the NURSERY, whether for rich or poor, – in which great philological academy no toleration is given to words in "*osity*" or "*ation*." There is, therefore, a great advantage, as regards the consecration to our feelings, settled, by usage and custom, upon the Saxon strands in the mixed yarn of our native tongue. And, universally, this may be remarked – that, wherever the passion of a poem is of that sort which *uses*, *presumes*, or *postulates* the ideas, without seeking to extend them, Saxon will be the "cocoon" (to speak by the language applied to silkworms) which the poem spins for itself. But, on the other hand, where the motion of the feeling is *by* and *through* the ideas, where (as in religious or meditative poetry – Young's, for instance, or Cowper's) the sentiment creeps and kindles underneath the very tissues of the thinking, there the Latin will predominate; and so much so that, whilst the flesh, the blood, and the muscle, will be often almost exclusively Latin, the articulations or hinges of connexion and transition will be Anglo-Saxon.

[a] The remark occurs in the *Biographia Literaria*, in the last paragraph of chapter 20.
[b] Lord Brougham, in his 1825 address on being elected to the Lord Rectorship

But a blunder, more perhaps from thoughtlessness and careless reading than from malice, on the part of the professional critics ought to have roused Wordsworth into a firmer feeling of the entire question. These critics had fancied that, in Wordsworth's estimate, whatsoever was plebeian was also poetically just in diction – not as though the impassioned phrase were sometimes the vernacular phrase, but as though the vernacular phrase were universally the impassioned. They naturally went on to suggest, as a corollary which Wordsworth (as they fancied) could not refuse, that Dryden and Pope must be translated into the flash diction of prisons and the slang of streets before they could be regarded as poetically costumed. Now, so far as these critics were concerned, the answer would have been simply to say that much in the poets mentioned, but especially of the racy Dryden, actually *is* in that vernacular diction for which Wordsworth contended, and, for the other part, which is *not*, frequently it *does* require the very purgation (if *that* were possible) which the critics were presuming to be so absurd. In Pope, and sometimes in Dryden, there is much of the unfeeling and the prescriptive diction which Wordsworth denounced. During the eighty years between 1660 and 1740 grew up that scrofulous taint in our diction which was denounced by Wordsworth as technically received for "poetic language"; and, if Dryden and Pope were less infected than others, this was merely because their understandings were finer. Much there is in both poets, as regards diction, which *does* require correction, and correction of the kind presumed by the Wordsworth theory. And, if, *so* far, the critics should resist Wordsworth's principle of reform, not he, but they, would have been found the patrons of deformity. This course would soon have turned the tables upon the critics. For the poets, or the class of poets, whom they unwisely selected as models susceptible of no correction, happen to be those who chiefly require it. But *their* foolish selection ought not to have intercepted or clouded the true question when put in another shape, since in this shape it opens into a very troublesome dilemma. Spenser, Shakspere, the Bible of 1611, and Milton – how say you, William Wordsworth – are these sound and true as to diction, or are they not? If you say they *are*, then what is it that you are proposing to change? What room for a revolution? Would you, as Sancho says, have "better bread than is made of wheat"? But, if you say *No*, they are *not* sound, then, indeed, you open a fearful range to your own artillery, but in a war greater than you could, by possibility, have contemplated. In the first case, – that is, if the leading classics of the English literature are, in quality of diction and style, loyal to the canons of sound taste, – then you cut away the *locus standi*[a] for yourself as a reformer: the reformation applies only to secondary and recent abuses. In the second case, if they also are faulty, you undertake an *onus* of hostility so vast that you will be found fighting against stars.

It is clear, therefore, that Wordsworth thus far erred, and caused needless embarrassment, equally to the attack and to the defence, by not assigning the names of the parties offending whom he had specially contemplated. The bodies of the criminals should have been had into court. But much more he erred in another point, where his neglect cannot be thought of without astonishment. The whole appeal turned upon a comparison between two modes of phraseology; each of which, the bad and the good, should have been extensively illustrated; and until that were done the whole dispute was an aerial subtlety, equally beyond the grasp of the best critic and the worst. How *could* a man so much in earnest, and so deeply interested in the question, commit so capital an oversight? *Tantamne rem tam negligenter?* (What! treat a matter so weighty in a style so slight and slipshod?) The truth is that at this day, after a lapse of forty-seven years and much discussion, the whole question moved by Wordsworth is still a *res integra* (a case untouched). And for this reason, – that no sufficient specimen has ever been given of the particular phraseology which each party contemplates as good or bad; no man, in this dispute, steadily understands even himself; and, if he did, no other person understands him, for want of distinct illustrations. Not only the answer, therefore, is still entirely in arrear, but even the question is still in arrear: it has not yet practically explained itself so as that an answer to it could be possible.

Passing from the diction of Wordsworth's poetry to its matter, the least plausible objection ever brought against it was that of Mr. Hazlitt. "One would suppose," he said, "from the tenor of his subjects, that on this earth there was neither marrying nor giving in marriage." But as well might it be said of Aristophanes: "One would suppose that in Athens no such thing had been known as sorrow and weeping." Or Wordsworth himself might say reproachfully to some of Mr. Hazlitt's more favoured poets: "Judging by *your* themes, a man must believe that there is no such thing on our planet as fighting and kicking." Wordsworth has written many memorable poems (for instance, "On the Tyrolean and the Spanish Insurrections," "On the Retreat from Moscow," "On the Feast of Brougham Castle") all sympathising powerfully with the martial spirit. Other poets, favourites of Mr. Hazlitt, have never struck a solitary note from this

[a] standing place

Tyrtæan lyre;ᵃ and who blames them? Surely, if every man breathing finds his powers limited, every man would do well to respect this silent admonition of nature by not travelling out of his appointed walk through any coxcombry of sporting a spurious versatility. And, in this view, what Mr. Hazlitt made the reproach of the poet is amongst the first of his praises. But there is another reason why Wordsworth could not meddle with festal raptures like the glory of a wedding-day. These raptures are not only too brief, but (which is worse) they tend downwards: even for as long as they last, they do not move upon an ascending scale. And even *that* is not their worst fault: they do not diffuse or communicate themselves; the wretches chiefly interested in a marriage are so selfish that they keep all the rapture to themselves. Mere joy that does not linger and reproduce itself in reverberations and endless mirrors is not fitted for poetry. What would the sun be itself, if it were a mere blank orb of fire that did not multiply its splendours through millions of rays refracted and reflected, or if its glory were not endlessly caught, splintered, and thrown back by atmospheric repercussions?

There is, besides, a still subtler reason (and one that ought not to have escaped the acuteness of Mr. Hazlitt) why the muse of Wordsworth could not glorify a wedding festival. Poems no longer than a sonnet he *might* derive from such an impulse; and one such poem of his there really is. But whosoever looks searchingly into the characteristic genius of Wordsworth will see that he does not willingly deal with a passion in its direct aspect, or presenting an unmodified contour, but in forms more complex and oblique, and when passing under the shadow of some secondary passion. Joy, for instance, that wells up from constitutional sources, joy that is ebullient from youth to age, and cannot cease to sparkle, he yet exhibits, in the person of Matthew,³ the village schoolmaster, as touched and overgloomed by memories of sorrow. In the poem of "We are Seven," which brings into day for the first time a profound fact in the abysses of human nature – viz. that the mind of an infant cannot admit the idea of death, cannot comprehend it, any more than the fountain of light can comprehend the aboriginal darkness (a truth on which Mr. Ferrier⁴ has since commented beautifully in his "Philosophy of Consciousness") – the little mountaineer who furnishes the text for this lovely strain, she whose fulness of life could not brook the gloomy faith in a grave, is yet (for the effect upon the reader) brought into connexion with the reflex shadows of the grave; and, if she herself has *not*, the

---

ᵃ after Tyrtaeus, Spartan elegiac poet of the seventh century B.C., whose patriotic compositions were sung by soldiers at their camp fires

reader *has*, and through this very child, the gloom of that contemplation obliquely irradiated, as raised in relief upon his imagination even by *her*. That same infant, which subjectively could not tolerate death, being by the reader contemplated objectively, flashes upon us the tenderest images of death. Death and its sunny antipole are forced into connexion. I remember, again, to have heard a man complain that in a little poem of Wordsworth's having for its very subject the universal diffusion (and the gratuitous diffusion) of joy –

> "Pleasure is spread through the earth
> In stray gifts to be claimed by whoever shall find" –

a picture occurs which overpowered him with melancholy. It was this –

> "In sight of the spires
> All alive with the fires
> Of the sun going down to his rest,
> In the broad open eye of the solitary sky
> They dance – there are three, as jocund as free,
> While they dance on the calm river's breast."[a]

Undeniably there is (and without ground for complaint there is) even here, where the spirit of gaiety is professedly invoked, an oblique though evanescent image flashed upon us of a sadness that lies deep behind the laughing figures, and of a solitude that is the real possessor in fee of all things, but is waiting an hour or so for the dispossession of the dancing men and maidens who for that transitory hour are the true, but, alas! the fugitive tenants.

An inverse case, as regards the three just cited, is found in the poem of "Hart-leap well," over which the mysterious spirit of the noonday Pan seems to brood. Out of suffering there is evoked the image of peace. Out of the cruel leap, and the agonising race through thirteen hours – out of the anguish in the perishing brute, and the headlong courage of his final despair,

> "Not unobserved by sympathy divine" –

out of the ruined lodge and the forgotten mansion, bowers that are trodden under foot, and pleasure-houses that are dust – the poet calls up a vision of *palingenesis* (or restorative resurrection); he interposes his solemn images of suffering, of decay, and ruin, only as a visionary haze through which gleams transpire of a trembling dawn far off, but surely even now on the road: –

---

[a] "Stray Pleasures," 27–28, 13–18

"The pleasure-house is dust: behind, before,
This is no common waste, no common gloom;
But Nature in due course of time once more
Shall here put on her beauty and her bloom.

She leaves these objects to a slow decay,
That what we are, and have been, may be known;
But, at the coming of the milder day,
These monuments shall all be overgrown."

This influx of the joyous into the sad, and of the sad into the joyous –
this reciprocal entanglement of darkness in light, and of light in
darkness – offers a subject too occult for popular criticism; but merely
to have suggested it may be sufficient to account for Wordsworth's
not having chosen a theme of pure garish sunshine, such as the hurry
of a wedding-day, so long as others, more picturesque or more plastic
to a subtle purpose of creation, were to be had. A wedding-day is, in
many a life, the sunniest of its days. But, unless it is overcast with
some event more tragic than could be wished, its uniformity of blaze,
without shade or relief, makes it insipid to the mere bystander. It
must not be forgotten that a wedding is pre-eminently that sort of
festival which swamps all individuality of sentiment or character. The
epithalamia of Edmund Spenser are the most impassioned that exist;
but nobody reads them.

But far beyond these causes of repulsiveness to ordinary readers
was the class of subjects selected, and the mode of treating them. The
earliest line of readers, the van in point of time, always includes a
majority of the young, the commonplace, and the unimpassioned.
Subsequently these are sifted and winnowed, as the rear-ranks come
forward in succession. But at first it was sure to ruin any poems if the
situations treated are not those which reproduce to the fancy of
readers their own hopes and prospects. The meditative are interested
by all that has an interest for human nature; but what cares a young
lady, dreaming of lovers kneeling at her feet, for the agitations of a
mother forced into resigning her child? or for the sorrow of a
shepherd at eighty parting for ever amongst mountain solitudes with
an only son of seventeen, innocent and hopeful, whom soon afterwards the guilty town seduces into ruin irreparable? Romances and
novels in verse constitute the poetry which is *immediately* successful;
and that is a poetry, it may be added, which, being successful through
one generation, afterwards is unsuccessful for ever.

But from this theme, as too extensive, let us pass to the separate
works of Wordsworth; and, in deference to the opinion of the world,
let us begin with the "Excursion." This poem, as regards its opening,

seems to require a recast. The inaugurating story of Margaret is in a wrong key, and rests upon a false basis. It is a case of sorrow from desertion. So at least it is represented. Margaret loses, in losing her husband (parted from her by mere stress of poverty), the one sole friend of her heart. And the Wanderer, who is the presiding philosopher of the poem, in retracing her story, sees nothing in the case but a wasting away through sorrow, natural in its kind, but preternatural in its degree.

There is a story somewhere told of a man who complained, and his friends also complained, that his face looked almost always dirty. The man explained this strange affection out of a mysterious idiosyncrasy in the face itself, upon which the atmosphere so acted as to force out stains or masses of gloomy suffusion, just as it does upon some qualities of stone in rainy or vapoury weather. But, said his friend, had you no advice for this strange affection? Oh yes: surgeons had prescribed; chemistry had exhausted its secrets upon the case; magnetism had done its best; electricity had done its worst. His friend mused for some time, and then asked – "Pray, amongst these painful experiments, did it ever happen to you to try one that I have read of – viz. a basin of soap and water?" And perhaps, on the same principle, it might be allowable to ask the philosophic wanderer who washes the case of Margaret with so many coats of metaphysical varnish, but ends with finding all unavailing, "Pray, amongst your other experiments, did you ever try the effect of a guinea?" Supposing this, however, to be a remedy beyond his fortitude, at least he might have offered a little rational advice, which costs no more than civility. Let us look steadily at the case. The particular calamity under which Margaret groaned was the loss of her husband, who had enlisted – not into the horse marines, too unsettled in their headquarters, but into our British Army. There is something, even on the husband's part, in this enlistment to which the reader can hardly extend his indulgence. The man had not gone off, it is true, as a heartless deserter of his family, or in profligate quest of pleasure. Cheerfully he would have staid and worked, had trade been good; but, as it was *not*, he found it impossible to support the spectacle of domestic suffering. He takes the bounty of a recruiting sergeant, and off he marches with his regiment. Nobody reaches the summit of heartlessness at once; and, accordingly, in this early stage of his desertion, we are not surprised to find that part (but why part?) of the bounty had been silently conveyed to his wife. So far we are barely not indignant; but as time wears on we become highly so, for no letter does he ever send to his poor forsaken partner, either of tender excuse, or of encouraging prospects. Yet, if he *had* done this, still we must condemn him. Millions have supported (and supported without praise or knowledge of man) that trial from which he so weakly fled. Even in this, and going no further, he was a voluptuary. Millions have heard, and acknowledged as a secret call from Heaven, the summons not only to take their own share of household suffering, as a mere sacrifice to the spirit of manliness, but also to stand the far sterner trial of witnessing the same privations in a wife and little children. To evade this, to slip his neck out of the yoke, when God summons a poor man to such a trial, is the worst form of cowardice. And Margaret's husband, by adding to this cowardice subsequently an entire neglect of his family, not so much as intimating the destination of the regiment, forfeits his last hold upon our lingering sympathy. But with *him*, it will be said, the poet has not connected the leading thread of the interest. Certainly not; though, in some degree, by a reaction from *his* character depends the respectability of Margaret's grief. And it is impossible to turn away from *his* case entirely, because from the act of the enlistment is derived the whole movement of the story. Here it is that we must tax the wandering philosopher with treason to his obvious duty. He found so luxurious a pleasure in contemplating a pathetic *phthisis* of heart in the abandoned wife that the one obvious word of counsel in her particular distress, which dotage could not have overlooked, he suppresses. And yet this one word in the revolution of a week would have brought her effectual relief. Surely the regiment into which her husband had enlisted bore some number: it was the king's "dirty half-hundred," or the rifle brigade, or some corps known to men and the Horse Guards. Instead, therefore, of suffering poor Margaret to loiter at a gate, looking for answers to her questions from vagrant horsemen, a process which reminds one of a sight sometimes extorting at once smiles and deep pity in the crowded thoroughfares of London – viz. a little child innocently asking with tearful eyes from strangers for the mother whom it has lost in that vast wilderness – the Wanderer should at once have inquired for the station of that particular detachment which had enlisted him. This *must* have been in the neighbourhood. Here he would have obtained all the particulars. That same night he might have written to the War-Office; and in a very few days an official answer, bearing the indorsement *On H. M.'s Service*, would have placed Margaret in communication with her truant. To have overlooked a point of policy so broadly apparent as this vitiates and nullifies the very basis of the story. Even for a romance it will not do, far less for a philosophic poem, dealing with intense realities. No such case of distress could have lived for one fortnight; nor could it have survived a single interview with the rector, the curate, or the parish-clerk, with the schoolmaster, the doctor, the attorney, the innkeeper, or the exciseman.

But, apart from the vicious mechanism of the incidents, the story is far more objectionable by the doubtful quality of the leading character from which it derives its pathos. Had any one of us the readers discharged the duties of coroner in her neighbourhood, he would have found it his duty to hold an inquest upon the body of her infant. This child, as every reader could depose (*now* when the case has been circumstantially reported by the poet), died of neglect, – not originating in direct cruelty, but in criminal self-indulgence. Self-indulgence in what? Not in liquor, yet not altogether in fretting. Sloth, and the habit of gadding abroad, were most in fault. The Wanderer*a* himself might have been called, as a witness for the crown, to prove that the infant was left to sleep in solitude for hours: the key even was taken away, as if to intercept the possibility (except through burglary) of those tender attentions from some casual stranger which the thoughtless and vagrant mother had withdrawn. The child absolutely awoke whilst the philosopher was listening at the door. It cried, but finally hushed itself to sleep. That looks like a case of Dalby's carminative.[5] But this solution of the case (the soothing into sleep) could not have been relied on. Tragical catastrophes arise from neglected crying: ruptures in the first place, a very common result in infants; rolling out of bed, followed by dislocation of the neck; fits, and other short cuts to death. It is hardly any praise to Margaret that she carried the child to that consummation by a more lingering road.

This first tale, therefore, must, and will, if Mr. Wordsworth retains energy for such recasts of a laborious work, be cut away from its connexion with the "Excursion." Such an amputation is the more to be expected from a poet aware of his own importance, and anxious for the perfection of his works, because nothing in the following books depends upon this narrative. No timbers or main beams need to be sawed away; it is but a bolt that is to be slipped, a rivet to be unscrewed. And yet, on the other hand, if the connexion is slight, the injury is great; for we all complain heavily of entering a temple dedicated to new combinations of truth through a vestibule of falsehood. And the falsehood is double: falsehood in the adjustment of the details (however separately possible); falsehood in the character which, wearing the mask of profound sentiment, does apparently repose upon dyspepsy and sloth.

a the sage of *The Excursion*, who serves as expositor of Wordsworth's doctrine

Far different in value and in principle of composition is the next tale in the "Excursion." This occupies the fourth book, and is the impassioned record from the infidel solitary of those heart-shaking chapters in his own life which had made him what the reader finds him. Once he had not been a solitary; once he had not been an infidel; now he is both. He lives in a little urn-like valley (a closet-recess from Little Langdale, to judge by the description), amongst the homely household of a yeoman; he has become a bitter cynic, – and not against man alone, or society alone, but against the laws of hope or fear upon which both repose. If he endures the society with which he is now connected, it is because, being dull, that society is of few words; it is because, being tied to hard labour, that society goes early to bed, and packs up its dulness at eight P.M. in blankets; it is because, under the acute inflictions of Sunday, or the chronic inflictions of the Christmas holidays, that dull society is easily laid into a magnetic sleep by three passes of metaphysical philosophy. The narrative of this misanthrope is grand and impassioned, – not creeping by details and minute touches, but rolling through capital events, and uttering its pathos through great representative abstractions. Nothing can be finer than when, upon the desolation of his household, upon the utter emptying of his domestic chambers by the successive deaths of children and youthful wife, just at that moment the mighty phantom of the French Revolution rises solemnly above the horizon. Even then, even by this great vision, new earth and new heavens are promised to human nature; and suddenly the solitary man, translated by the frenzy of human grief into the frenzy of supernatural hopes, adopts these radiant visions for the darlings whom he has lost –

> "Society becomes his glittering bride,
> And airy hopes his children."

Yet it is a misfortune in the fate of this fine tragic movement, rather than its structure, that it tends to collapse; the latter strains, coloured deeply by disappointment, do not correspond with the grandeur of the first. And the hero of the record becomes even more painfully a contrast to himself than the tenor of the incidents to their own earlier stages. Sneering and querulous comments upon so broad a field as human folly make poor compensation for the magnificence of youthful enthusiasm. But may not this defect be redressed in a future section of the poem? It is probable, from a hint dropped by the author, that one collateral object of the philosophical discussions is the reconversion of the splenetic infidel to his ancient creed in some higher form, and to his ancient temper of benignant hope; in which case, what *now* we feel to be a cheerless depression will sweep round into a noble reascent, quite on a level with the aspirations of his youth, and differing, not in degree, but only in quality of enthusiasm. Yet, if this is the poet's plan, it seems to rest upon a misconception. For how should the sneering sceptic, who has actually found solace in Voltaire's "Candide," be restored to the benignities of faith and hope by argument? It was not in this way that he lost his station amongst Christian believers. No false philosophy it had been which wrecked his Christian spirit of hope; but, in the very inverse order, his bankruptcy in hope it was which wrecked his Christian philosophy. Here, therefore, the poet will certainly find himself in an "almighty fix"; because any possible treatment which could restore the solitary's former self, such as a course of tonic medicines or sea-bathing, could not interest the reader, and, reversely, any successful treatment through argument that could interest the philosophic reader would not, under the circumstances, seem a plausible restoration commensurate with the case.

What is it that has made the recluse a sceptic? Is it the reading of bad books? In that case he may be reclaimed by the arguments of those who have read better. But not at all. He has become the unbelieving cynic that he is, first, through his own domestic calamities predisposing him to *gloomy* views of human nature, and, secondly, through the overclouding of his high-toned expectations from the French Revolution; which overclouding has disposed him, in a spirit of revenge for his own disappointment, to *contemptuous* views of human nature. Now, surely the dejection which supports his gloom, and the despondency which supports his contempt, are not of a nature to give way before philosophic reasonings. Make him happy by restoring what he has lost, and his genial philosophy will return of itself. Make him triumphant by realising what had seemed to him the golden promises of the French Revolution, and his political creed will moult her sickly feathers. Do this, and he is still young enough for hope; but less than this restoration of his morning visions will not call back again his morning happiness; and breaking spears with him in logical tournaments will injure his temper without bettering his hopes.

Indirectly, besides, it ought not to be overlooked that, as respects the French Revolution, the whole college of philosophy in the "Excursion," who are gathered together upon the case of the recluse, make the same mistake that *he* makes. Why is the recluse disgusted with the French Revolution? Because it had not fulfilled many of his expectations; and, of those which it *had* fulfilled, some had soon been darkened by reverses. But really this was childish impatience. If a man depends for the exuberance of his harvest upon the splendour of the coming summer, we do not excuse him for taking prussic acid because it rains cats and dogs through the first ten days of April. All in good time, we say; take it easy; make acquaintance with May and June before you do anything rash. The French Revolution has not even yet (1845) come into full action. This mighty event was the explosion of a prodigious volcano, which scattered its lava over every kingdom of every continent, silently manuring them for social struggles; this lava is gradually fertilising all soils in all countries; the revolutionary movement is moving onwards at this hour as inexorably as ever. Listen, if you have ears for such spiritual sounds, to the mighty tide even now slowly coming up from the sea to Milan, to Rome, to Naples, to Vienna. Hearken to the ominous undulations already breaking against the steps of that golden throne which stretches from St. Petersburg to Astrakan; tremble at the hurricanes which have long been mustering about the pavilions of the Ottoman Padishah.*ª* All these are long swells setting in from the original impulses and fermentations of the French Revolution. Even as regards France herself, that which gave the mortal offence to the sympathies of Wordsworth's "Solitary" was the Reign of Terror. But how thoughtless to measure the cycles of vast national revolutions by metres that would not stretch round an ordinary human career. Even to a frail sweetheart you would grant more indulgence than to be off in a pet because some momentary cloud arose between you. The Reign of Terror was a mere fleeting and transitional phasis. The Napoleon dynasty was nothing more. Even that very Napoleon scourge which was supposed by many to have consummated and superseded the Revolution has itself passed away upon the wind – has itself been superseded – leaving no wreck, relic, or record behind, except precisely those changes which it worked, *not in its character of an enemy of the Revolution* (which also it was), *but as its servant and its tool.* See, even whilst we speak, the folly of that cynical sceptic who would not allow time for great natural processes of purification to travel onwards to their birth, or wait for the evolution of natural results: the storm that shocked him has wheeled away; the frost and the hail that offended him have done their office; the rain is over and gone; happier days have descended upon France; the voice of the turtle is heard in all her forests; once again, after two thousand years of serfdom, man walks with his head erect; bastiles are no more; every cottage is searched by the golden light of law; and the privileges of

ª Turkish Sultan

religious conscience have been guaranteed and consecrated for ever and ever.

Here, then, the poet himself, the philosophic Wanderer, the learned Vicar, are all equally in fault with the solitary Sceptic; for they all agree in treating his disappointment as sound and reasonable in itself, but blamable only in relation to those exalted hopes which he never ought to have encouraged. Right (they say) to consider the French Revolution now as a failure: but *not* right originally to have expected that it should succeed. Whereas, in fact, gentlemen blockheads, it *has* succeeded; it is far beyond the reach of ruinous reactions; it is propagating its life; it is travelling on to new births – conquering, and yet to conquer.

It is not easy to see, therefore, how the Laureate can avoid making some change in the constitution of his poem, were it only to rescue his philosophers, and therefore his own philosophy, from the imputation of precipitancy in judgment. They charge the sceptic with rash judgment *a parte ante*; and, meantime, they themselves are very much more liable to that charge *a parte post*.[a] If he, at the first, hoped too much (which is not clear, but only that he hoped too impatiently), they afterwards recant too rashly. And this error they will not themselves fail to acknowledge, as soon as they awaken to the truth that the French Revolution did not close on the 18th Brumaire 1799,[b] – at which time it suffered eclipse but not final eclipse, at which time it entered a cloud but not the cloud of death, at which time its vital movement was arrested by a military traitor, – but that this Revolution is still mining under ground, like the ghost in Hamlet, through every quarter of the globe.[6]

In paying so much attention to the "Excursion" (of which, in any more extended notice, the two books entitled "The Churchyard amongst the Mountains" would have claimed the profoundest attention), I yield less to my own opinion than to that of the public. Or, perhaps, it is not so much the public as the vulgar opinion, governed entirely by the consideration that the "Excursion" is very much the longest poem of its author, and, secondly, that it bears currently the title of a *philosophic* poem, – on which account it is presumed to have a higher dignity. The big name and the big size of the particular volume are allowed to settle its rank. But in this there is much delusion. In the very scheme and movement of the "Excursion" there are two defects which interfere greatly with its power to act upon the mind with any vital effect of unity, – so that, infallibly, it will be read by future

[a] *a parte ante*: from the part before; *a parte post*: from the part after
[b] date of Napoleon's assumption of power

generations in parts and fragments; and, being thus virtually dismembered into many small poems, it will scarcely justify men in allowing it the rank of a long one. One of these defects is the *undulatory* character of the course pursued by the poem, – which does not ascend uniformly, or even keep one steady level, but trespasses, as if by forgetfulness or chance, into topics yielding a very humble inspiration, and not always closely connected with the presiding theme. In part this arises from the accident that a slight tissue of narrative connects the different sections; and to this movement of the narrative the fluctuations of the speculative themes are in part obedient: the succession of the incidents becomes a law for the succession of the thoughts, as oftentimes it happens that these incidents are the proximate occasions of the thoughts. Yet, as the narrative is not of a nature to be moulded by any determinate principle of controlling passion, but bends easily to the caprices of chance and the moment, unavoidably it stamps, by reaction, a desultory or even incoherent character upon the train of the philosophic discussions. You know not what is coming next as regards the succession of the incidents; and, when the next movement *does* come, you do not always know *why* it comes. This has the effect of crumbling the poem into separate segments, and causes the whole (when loked at *as* a whole) to appear a rope of sand. A second defect lies in the colloquial form which the poem sometimes assumes. It is dangerous to conduct a philosophic discussion by *talking*. If the nature of the argument could be supposed to roll through logical quillets*or metaphysical conundrums, so that, on putting forward a problem, the interlocutor could bring matters to a crisis by saying "Do you give it up?" in that case there might be a smart reciprocation of dialogue, of asserting and denying, giving and taking, butting, rebutting and "surrebutting"; and this would confer an interlocutory or *amœbean* character upon the process of altercation. But, the topics and the quality of the arguments being *moral*, – in which always the reconciliation of the feelings is to be secured by gradual persuasion, rather than the understanding to be floored by a solitary blow, – inevitably it becomes impossible that anything of this brilliant conversational swordplay, cut-and-thrust, "carte" and "tierce," can make for itself an opening. Mere decorum requires that the speakers should be prosy. And you yourself, though sometimes disposed to say "Do now, dear old soul, cut it short," are sensible that very often he *cannot* cut it short. Disquisitions, in a certain key, can no more turn round within the compass of a sixpence than a coach-and-six. They must have

a niceties or refinements

sea-room to "wear" ship, and to tack. This in itself is often tedious; but it leads to a worse tediousness: a practised eye sees from afar the whole evolution of the coming argument. And this *second* blemish, unavoidable if the method of dialogue is adopted, becomes more painfully apparent through a *third*, almost inalienable from the natural constitution of the subjects concerned. It is that in cases where a large interest of human nature is treated, such as the position of man in this world, his duties, his difficulties, many parts become necessary as transitional or connecting links which *per se* are not attractive, nor can by any art be made so. Treating the whole theme *in extenso*, the poet is, therefore, driven into discussions that would not have been chosen by his own taste, but dictated by the logic of the question, and by the impossibility of evading any one branch of a subject which is essential to the integrity of the speculation simply because it is irreconcilable with poetic brilliancy of treatment.

Not, therefore, in the "Excursion" must we look for that reversionary influence which awaits Wordsworth with posterity. It is the vulgar superstition in behalf of big books and sounding pretensions that must have prevailed upon Coleridge and others to undervalue, by comparison with the direct philosophic poetry of Wordsworth, those earlier poems which are all short, but generally scintillating with gems of far profounder truth. I speak of that truth which strengthens into solemnity an impression very feebly acknowledged previously, or truth which suddenly unveils a connexion between objects hitherto regarded as irrelate and independent. In astronomy, to gain the rank of discoverer, it is not required that you should reveal a star absolutely new: find out with respect to an old star some new affection – as, for instance, that it has an ascertainable parallax – and immediately you bring it within the verge of a human interest; or, with respect to some old familiar planet, that its satellites suffer periodical eclipses, and immediately you bring it within the verge of terrestrial uses. Gleams of steadier vision that brighten into certainty appearances else doubtful, or that unfold relations else unsuspected, are not less discoveries of truth than the downright revelations of the telescope, or the absolute conquests of the diving-bell. It is astonishing how large a harvest of new truths would be reaped simply through the accident of a man's feeling, or being made to feel, more *deeply* than other men. He sees the same objects, neither more nor fewer, but he sees them engraved in lines far stronger and more determinate: and the difference in the strength makes the whole difference between consciousness and subconsciousness. And in questions of the mere understanding we see the same fact illustrated.

The author who wins notice the most is not he that perplexes men by truths drawn from fountains of absolute novelty, – truths as yet unsunned, and from that cause obscure, – but he that awakens into illuminated consciousness ancient lineaments of truth long slumbering in the mind, although too faint to have extorted attention. Wordsworth has brought many a truth into life, both for the eye and for the understanding, which previously had slumbered indistinctly for all men.

For instance, as respects the eye, who does not acknowledge instantaneously the magical strength of truth in his saying of a cataract seen from a station two miles off that it was "frozen by distance"? In all nature there is not an object so essentially at war with the stiffening of frost as the headlong and desperate life of a cataract; and yet notoriously the effect of distance is to lock up this frenzy of motion into the most petrific column of stillness. This effect is perceived at once when pointed out; but how few are the eyes that ever *would* have perceived it for themselves! Twilight, again – who before Wordsworth ever distinctly noticed its *abstracting* power? – that power of removing, softening, harmonising, by which a mode of obscurity executes for the eye the same mysterious office which the mind so often, within its own shadowy realms, executes for itself. In the dim interspace between day and night all disappears from our earthly scenery, as if touched by an enchanter's rod, which is either mean or inharmonious, or unquiet, or expressive of temporary things. Leaning against a column of rock, looking down upon a lake or river, and at intervals carrying your eyes forward through a vista of mountains, you become aware that your sight rests upon the very same spectacle, unaltered in a single feature, which once at the same hour was beheld by the legionary Roman from his embattled camp, or by the roving Briton in his "wolf-skin vest," lying down to sleep, and looking

> "Through some leafy bower,
> Before his eyes were closed."[a]

How magnificent is the summary or abstraction of the elementary features in such a scene, as executed by the poet himself, in illustration of this abstraction daily executed by Nature through her handmaid Twilight! Listen, reader, to the closing strain, solemn as twilight is solemn, and grand as the spectacle which it describes: –

> "By him [*i.e.* the roving Briton] was seen
> The self-same vision which *we* now behold,

[a] "Hail Twilight," 8–9

At thy meek bidding, shadowy Power, brought forth;
These mighty barriers and the gulf between;
The flood, the stars – a spectacle as old
As the beginning of the heavens and earth."[a]

Another great field there is amongst the pomps of nature which, if Wordsworth did not first notice, he certainly has noticed most circumstantially. I speak of cloud-scenery, or those pageants of sky-built architecture which sometimes in summer, at noonday, and in all seasons about sunset, arrest or appal the meditative; "perplexing monarchs" with the spectacle of armies manœuvring, or deepening the solemnity of evening by towering edifices that mimic – but which also in mimicking mock – the transitory grandeurs of man. It is singular that these gorgeous phenomena, not less than those of the *Aurora Borealis*, have been so little noticed by poets. The *Aurora* was naturally neglected by the southern poets of Greece and Rome, as not much seen in their latitudes. But the cloud-architecture of the daylight belongs alike to north and south. Accordingly, I remember one notice of it in Hesiod, – a case where the clouds exhibited

"The beauteous semblance of a flock at rest."

Another there is, a thousand years later, in Lucan: amongst the portents which that poet notices as prefiguring the dreadful convulsions destined to shake the earth at Pharsalia, I remember some fiery coruscation of arms in the heavens; but, so far as I recollect, the appearances might have belonged equally to the workmanship of the clouds or the Aurora. Up and down the next eight hundred years are scattered evanescent allusions to these vapoury appearances; in "Hamlet" and elsewhere occur gleams of such allusions; but I remember no distinct sketch of such an appearance before that in the "Antony and Cleopatra" of Shakspere, beginning,

"Sometimes we see a cloud that's dragonish."[b]

Subsequently to Shakspere, these notices, as of all phenomena whosoever that demanded a familiarity with nature in the spirit of love, became rarer and rarer. At length, as the eighteenth century was winding up its accounts, forth stepped William Wordsworth; of whom, as a reader of all pages in nature, it may be said that, if we except Dampier, the admirable buccaneer, the gentle *flibustier*,[c] and some few professional naturalists, he first and he last looked at natural objects with the eye that neither will be dazzled from without nor cheated by preconceptions from within. Most men look at nature in

[a] "Hail Twilight," 9–14   [b] *Antony and Cleopatra*, IV. xiv. 2   [c] freebooter

the hurry of a confusion that distinguishes nothing; *their* error is from without. Pope, again, and many who live in towns,[7] make such blunders as that of supposing the moon to tip with silver the hills *behind* which she is rising, not by erroneous use of their eyes (for they use them not at all), but by inveterate preconceptions. Scarcely has there been a poet with what could be called a learned eye, or an eye *extensively* learned, before Wordsworth. Much affectation there has been of that sort since *his* rise, and at all times much counterfeit enthusiasm; but the sum of the matter is this, – that Wordsworth had his passion for nature fixed in his blood; it was a necessity, like that of the mulberry-leaf to the silkworm; and through his commerce with nature did he live and breathe. Hence it was – viz. from the *truth* of his love – that his knowledge grew; whilst most others, being merely hypocrites in their love, have turned out merely sciolists in their knowledge. This chapter, therefore, of *sky*-scenery may be said to have been revivified amongst the resources of poetry by Wordsworth – rekindled, if not absolutely kindled. The sublime scene indorsed upon the draperies of the storm in the fourth book of the "Excursion" – that scene again witnessed upon the passage of the Hamilton Hills in Yorkshire – the solemn "sky prospect" from the fields of France – are unrivalled in that order of composition; and in one of these records Wordsworth has given first of all the true key-note of the sentiment belonging to these grand pageants. They are, says the poet, speaking in a case where the appearance had occurred towards night,

> "Meek nature's evening comment on the shows
> And all the fuming vanities of earth."[a]

Yes, that is the secret moral whispered to the mind. These mimicries express the laughter which is in heaven at earthly pomps. Frail and vapoury are the glories of man, even as the visionary parodies of those glories are frail, even as the scenical copies of those glories are frail, which nature weaves in clouds.

As another of those natural appearances which must have haunted men's eyes since the Flood, but yet had never forced itself into *conscious* notice until arrested by Wordsworth, I may notice an effect of *iteration* daily exhibited in the habits of cattle:–

> "The cattle are grazing,
> Their heads never raising;
> There are forty feeding like one."[b]

---

[a] "Sky Prospect – From the Plain of France," 12, 14; the missing line is: "That for oblivion take their daily birth"
[b] "Written in March while Resting on the Bridge at the Foot of Brother's Water," 8–10

Now, merely as a *fact*, and if it were nothing more, this characteristic appearance in the habits of cows, when all repeat the action of each, ought not to have been overlooked by those who profess themselves engaged in holding up a mirror to nature. But the fact has also a profound meaning as a hieroglyphic. In all animals which live under the protection of man a life of peace and quietness, but do not share in his labours or in his pleasures, what we regard is the species, and not the individual. Nobody but a grazier ever looks at one cow amongst a field of cows, or at one sheep in a flock. But, as to those animals which are more closely connected with man, not passively connected, but actively, being partners in his toils, and perils, and recreations – such as horses, dogs, falcons – they are regarded as individuals, and are allowed the benefit of an individual interest. It is not that cows have not a differential character, each for herself; and sheep, it is well known, have all a separate physiognomy for the shepherd who has cultivated their acquaintance. But men generally have no opportunity or motive for studying the individualities of creatures, however otherwise respectable, that are too much regarded by all of us in the reversionary light of milk, and beef, and mutton. Far otherwise it is with horses, who share in man's martial risks, who sympathise with man's frenzy in hunting, who divide with man the burdens of noonday. Far otherwise it is with dogs, that share the hearths of man, and adore the footsteps of his children. These man loves; of these he makes dear, though humble, friends. These often fight for *him*; and for *them* he reciprocally will sometimes fight. Of necessity, therefore, every horse and every dog is an individual – has a sort of personality that makes him *separately* interesting – has a beauty and a character of his own. Go to Melton, therefore, on some crimson morning, and what will you see? Every man, every horse, every dog, glorying in the plenitude of life, is in a different attitude, motion, gesture, action. It is not there the sublime unity which you must seek, where forty are like one; but the sublime infinity, like that of ocean, like that of Flora, like that of nature, where no repetitions are endured, no leaf is the copy of another leaf, no absolute identity, and no painful tautologies. This subject might be pursued into profounder recesses; but in a popular discussion it is necessary to forbear.

A volume might be filled with such glimpses of novelty as Wordsworth has first laid bare, even to the apprehension of the *senses*. For the *understanding*, when moving in the same track of human sensibilities, he has done only not so much. How often (to give an instance or two) must the human heart have felt the case, and yearned for an expression of the case, when there are sorrows which descend far below the region in which tears gather; and yet who has ever given utterance to this feeling until Wordsworth came with his immortal line:—

"Thoughts that do often lie too deep for tears"?

This sentiment, and others that might be adduced (such as "The child is father to the man"), have even passed into the popular heart, and are often quoted by those who know not *whom* they are quoting. Magnificent, again, is the sentiment, and yet an echo to one which lurks amongst all hearts, in relation to the frailty of merely human schemes for working good, which so often droop and collapse through the unsteadiness of human energies —

"Foundations must be laid
In heaven."[a]

How? Foundations laid in realms that are *above*? But *that* is impossible; *that* is at war with elementary physics; foundations must be laid *below*. Yes; and even so the poet throws the mind yet more forcibly on the hyperphysical character — on the grandeur transcending all physics — of those spiritual and shadowy foundations which alone are enduring.

But the great distinction of Wordsworth, and the pledge of his increasing popularity, is the extent of his sympathy with what is *really* permanent in human feelings, and also the depth of this sympathy. Young and Cowper, the two earlier leaders in the province of meditative poetry, are too circumscribed in the range of their sympathies, too narrow, too illiberal, and too exclusive. Both these poets manifested the quality of their strength in the quality of their public reception. Popular in some degree from the first, they entered upon the inheritance of their fame almost at once. Far different was the fate of Wordsworth; for in poetry of this class, which appeals to what lies deepest in man, in proportion to the native power of the poet, and his fitness for permanent life, is the strength of resistance in the public taste. Whatever is too original will be hated at the first. It must slowly mould a public for itself; and the resistance of the early thoughtless judgments must be overcome by a counter-resistance to itself in a better audience slowly mustering against the first. Forty and seven years it is since William Wordsworth first appeared as an author. Twenty of those years he was the scoff of the world, and his poetry a byword of scorn. Since then, and more than once, senates have rung with acclamations to the echo of his name. Now, at this

[a] "Malham Cove," 10–11

moment, whilst we are talking about him, he has entered upon his seventy-sixth year. For himself, according to the course of nature, he cannot be far from his setting; but his poetry is only now clearing the clouds that gathered about its rising. Meditative poetry is perhaps that province of literature which will ultimately maintain most power amongst the generations which are coming; but in this department, at least, there is little competition to be apprehended by Wordsworth from anything that has appeared since the death of Shakspere.

18. *"The Poetry of Pope"*

first published in the *North British Review*, August 1848; text of 1858, from *Works* (1890), ed. David Masson, vol. II, pp. 51–60, 88–95

EVERY great classic in our native language should from time to time be reviewed anew; and especially if he belongs in any considerable extent to that section of the literature which connects itself with manners, and if his reputation originally, or his style of composition, is likely to have been much influenced by the transient fashions of his own age. The withdrawal, for instance, from a dramatic poet, or a satirist, of any false lustre which he has owed to his momentary connexion with what we may call the *personalities* of a fleeting generation, or of any undue shelter to his errors which may have gathered round them from political bias, or from intellectual infirmities amongst his partisans, will sometimes seriously modify, after a century or so, the fairest *original* appreciation of a fine writer. A window composed of Claude Lorraine glasses spreads over the landscape outside a disturbing effect, which not the most practised eye can evade. The *eidola theatri*[a] affect us all. No man escapes the contagion from his contemporary bystanders. And the reader may see further on that, had Pope been merely a satiric poet, he must in these times have laid down much of the splendour which surrounds him in our traditional estimate of his merit. Such a renunciation would be a forfeit – not always to errors in himself, but sometimes to errors in that stage of English society which forced the ablest writer into a collusion with its own meretricious tastes. The antithetical prose "characters," as they were technically termed, which circulated amongst the aristocracy in the early part of the last century, the style of the dialogue in such comedy as was then popular,[1] and much of the occasional poetry in that age, expose an immoderate craving for

[a] idols of the theatre

glittering effects from contrasts too harsh to be natural, too sudden to be durable, and too fantastic to be harmonious. To meet this vicious taste, – from which (as from any diffusive taste) it is vain to look for *perfect* immunity in any writer lying immediately under its beams, – Pope sacrificed, in *one* mode of composition, the simplicities of nature and sincerity; and, had he practised no other mode, we repeat that *now* he must have descended from his pedestal. To some extent he is degraded even as it is; for the reader cannot avoid whispering to himself – What quality of thinking must *that* be which allies itself so naturally (as will be shown) with distortions of fact or of philosophic truth? But, had his whole writings been of that same cast, he must have been degraded altogether, and a star would have fallen from our English galaxy of poets.

We mention this particular case as a reason generally for renewing by intervals the examination of great writers, and liberating the verdict of their contemporaries from the casual disturbances to which every age is liable in its judgments and in its tastes. As books multiply to an unmanageable excess, selection becomes more and more a necessity for readers, and the power of selection more and more a desperate problem for the busy part of readers. The possibility of selecting wisely is becoming continually more hopeless as the necessity for selection is becoming continually more pressing. Exactly as the growing weight of books overlays and stifles the power of comparison, *pari passu*[a] is the call for comparison the more clamourous; and thus arises a duty correspondingly more urgent of searching and revising until everything spurious has been weeded out from amongst the Flora of our highest literature, and until the waste of time for those who have so little at their command is reduced to a *minimum*. For, where the good cannot be read in its twentieth part, the more requisite it is that no part of the bad should steal an hour of the available time; and it is not to be endured that people without a minute to spare should be obliged first of all to read a book before they can ascertain whether in fact it is *worth* reading. The public cannot read by proxy as regards the good which it is to appropriate, but it *can* as regards the poison which it is to escape. And thus, as literature expands, becoming continually more of a household necessity, the duty resting upon critics (who are the vicarious readers for the public) becomes continually more urgent – of reviewing all works that may be supposed to have benefited too much or too indiscriminately by the superstition of a name. The *prægustatores*[b] should have tasted of every cup, and reported its quality, before the public call for

[a] keeping pace   [b] foretasters

it; and, above all, they should have done this in all cases of the higher literature, – that is, of literature properly so called.

What is it that we mean by *literature*? Popularly, and amongst the thoughtless, it is held to include everything that is printed in a book. Little logic is required to disturb *that* definition. The most thoughtless person is easily made aware that in the idea of *literature* one essential element is some relation to a general and common interest of man, – so that what applies only to a local, or professional, or merely personal interest, even though presenting itself in the shape of a book, will not belong to Literature. So far the definition is easily narrowed; and it is as easily expanded. For not only is much that takes a station in books not literature; but inversely, much that really *is* literature never reaches a station in books. The weekly sermons of Christendom, that vast pulpit literature which acts so extensively upon the popular mind – to warn, to uphold, to renew, to comfort, to alarm – does not attain the sanctuary of libraries in the ten-thousandth part of its extent. The Drama again, – as, for instance, the finest of Shakspere's plays in England, and all leading Athenian plays in the noontide of the Attic stage, – operated as a literature on the public mind, and were (according to the strictest letter of that term) *published* through the audiences that witnessed their representation some time before they were published as things to be read; and they were published in this scenical mode of publication with much more effect than they could have had as books during ages of costly copying or of costly printing.

Books, therefore, do not suggest an idea coextensive and inter-changeable with the idea of Literature; since much literature, scenic, forensic, or didactic (as from lecturers and public orators), may never come into books, and much that *does* come into books may connect itself with no literary interest. But a far more important correction, applicable to the common vague idea of literature, is to be sought not so much in a better definition of literature as in a sharper distinction of the two functions which it fulfils. In that great social organ which, collectively, we call literature, there may be distinguished two separate offices that may blend and often *do so*, but capable, severally, of a severe insulation, and naturally fitted for reciprocal repulsion. There is, first, the literature of *knowledge*; and, secondly, the literature of *power*. The function of the first is – to *teach*; the function of the second is – to *move*: the first is a rudder; the second, an oar or a sail. The first speaks to the *mere* discursive understanding; the second speaks ultimately, it may happen, to the higher understanding or reason, but always *through* affections of pleasure and sympathy.[2] Remotely, it may travel towards an object seated in what Lord Bacon calls *dry* light,[3] but, proximately, it does and must operate, – else it ceases to be a literature of *power*, – on and through that *humid* light which clothes itself in the mists and glittering *iris* of human passions, desires, and genial emotions. Men have so little reflected on the higher functions of literature as to find it a paradox if one should describe it as a mean or subordinate purpose of books to give information. But this is a paradox only in the sense which makes it honourable to be paradoxical. Whenever we talk in ordinary language of seeking information or gaining knowledge, we understand the words as connected with something of absolute novelty. But it is the grandeur of all truth which *can* occupy a very high place in human interests that it is never absolutely novel to the meanest of minds: it exists eternally by way of germ or latent principle in the lowest as in the highest, needing to be developed, but never to be planted. To be capable of transplantation is the immediate criterion of a truth that ranges on a lower scale. Besides which, there is a rarer thing than truth, – namely, *power* or deep sympathy with truth. What is the effect, for instance, upon society, of children? By the pity, by the tenderness, and by the peculiar modes of admiration, which connect themselves with the helplessness, with the innocence, and with the simplicity of children, not only are the primal affections strengthened and continually renewed but the qualities which are dearest in the sight of heaven, – the frailty, for instance, which appeals to forbearance, the innocence which symbolises the heavenly, and the simplicity which is most alien from the worldly, – are kept up in perpetual remembrance, and their ideals are continually refreshed. A purpose of the same nature is answered by the higher literature, viz. the literature of power. What do you learn from "Paradise Lost"? Nothing at all. What do you learn from a cookery-book? Something new, something that you did not know before, in every paragraph. But would you therefore put the wretched cookery-book on a higher level of estimation than the divine poem? What you owe to Milton is not any knowledge, of which a million separate items are still but a million of advancing steps on the same earthly level; what you owe is *power*, – that is, exercise and expansion to your own latent capacity of sympathy with the infinite, where every pulse and each separate influx is a step upwards, a step ascending as upon a Jacob's ladder from earth to mysterious altitudes above the earth. *All* the steps of knowledge, from first to last, carry you further on the same plane, but could never raise you one foot above your ancient level of earth: whereas the very *first* step in power is a flight – is an ascending movement into another element where earth is forgotten.

Were it not that human sensibilities are ventilated and continually called out into exercise by the great phenomena of infancy, or of real life as it moves through chance and change, or of literature as it recombines these elements in the mimicries of poetry, romance, &c., it is certain that, like any animal power or muscular energy falling into disuse, all such sensibilities would gradually droop and dwindle. It is in relation to these great *moral* capacities of man that the literature of power, as contradistinguished from that of knowledge, lives and has its field of action. It is concerned with what is highest in man; for the Scriptures themselves never condescended to deal by suggestion or co-operation with the mere discursive understanding: when speaking of man in his intellectual capacity, the Scriptures speak not of the understanding, but of *"the understanding heart,"*[a] – making the heart, *i.e.* the great *intuitive* (or non-discursive) organ, to be the inter-changeable formula for man in his highest state of capacity for the infinite. Tragedy, romance, fairy tale, or epopee,[b] all alike restore to man's mind the ideals of justice, of hope, of truth, of mercy, of retribution, which else (left to the support of daily life in its realities) would languish for want of sufficient illustration. What is meant, for instance, by *poetic justice*? – It does not mean a justice that differs by its object from the ordinary justice of human jurisprudence; for then it must be confessedly a very bad kind of justice; but it means a justice that differs from common forensic justice by the degree in which it *attains* its object, a justice that is more omnipotent over its own ends, as dealing – not with the refractory elements of earthly life, but with the elements of its own creation, and with materials flexible to its own purest preconceptions. It is certain that, were it not for the Literature of Power, these ideals would often remain amongst us as mere arid notional forms; whereas, by the creative forces of man put forth in literature, they gain a vernal life of restoration, and germinate into vital activities. The commonest novel, by moving in alliance with human fears and hopes, with human instincts of wrong and right, sustains and quickens those affections. Calling them into action, it rescues them from torpor. And hence the pre-eminency over all authors that merely *teach* of the meanest that *moves*, or that teaches, if at all, indirectly *by* moving. The very highest work that has ever existed in the Literature of Knowledge is but a *provisional* work: a book upon trial and sufferance, and *quamdiu bene se gesserit.*[c] Let its teaching be even partially revised, let it be but expanded, – nay, even

<hr>

[a] I Kings III. 9   [b] epic poem   [c] as long as it sustains itself

let its teaching be but placed in a better order, – and instantly it is superseded. Whereas the feeblest works in the Literature of Power, surviving at all, survive as finished and unalterable amongst men. For instance, the *Principia* of Sir Isaac Newton was a book *militant* on earth from the first. In all stages of its progress it would have to fight for its existence: 1st, as regards absolute truth; 2dly, when that combat was over, as regards its form or mode of presenting the truth. And as soon as a La Place, or anybody else, builds higher upon the foundations laid by this book, effectually he throws it out of the sunshine into decay and darkness;[4] by weapons won from this book he superannuates and destroys this book, so that soon the name of Newton remains as a mere *nominis umbra*,[a] but his book, as a living power, has transmigrated into other forms. Now, on the contrary, the Iliad, the Prometheus of Æschylus, the Othello or King Lear, the Hamlet or Macbeth, and the Paradise Lost, are not militant, but triumphant for ever as long as the languages exist in which they speak or can be taught to speak.[5] They never *can* transmigrate into new incarnations. To reproduce *these* in new forms, or variations, even if in some things they should be improved, would be to plagiarise. A good steam-engine is properly superseded by a better. But one lovely pastoral valley is not superseded by another, nor a statue of Praxiteles by a statue of Michael Angelo. These things are separated not by imparity, but by disparity. They are not thought of as unequal under the same standard, but as different in *kind*, and, if otherwise equal, as equal under a different standard. Human works of immortal beauty and works of nature in one respect stand on the same footing: they never absolutely repeat each other, never approach so near as not to differ; and they differ not as better and worse, or simply by more and less: they differ by undecipherable and incommunicable differences, that cannot be caught by mimicries, that cannot be reflected in the mirror of copies, that cannot become ponderable in the scales of vulgar comparison.

Applying these principles to Pope as a representative of fine literature in general, we would wish to remark the claim which he has, or which any equal writer has, to the attention and jealous winnowing of those critics in particular who watch over public morals. Clergymen, and all organs of public criticism put in motion by clergymen, are more especially concerned in the just appreciation of such writers, if the two canons are remembered which we have endeavoured to illustrate, viz. that all works in this class, as opposed to those in the literature of knowledge, 1st, work by far deeper

[a] shadow of a name

agencies, and, 2dly, are more permanent; in the strictest sense they are κτήματα ἐς ἀει:[a] and what evil they do, or what good they do, is commensurate with the national language, sometimes long after the nation has departed. At this hour, five hundred years since their creation, the tales of Chaucer, never equalled on this earth for their tenderness, and for life of picturesqueness, are read familiarly by many in the charming language of their natal day, and by others in the modernisations of Dryden, of Pope, and Wordsworth. At this hour, one thousand eight hundred years since their creation, the Pagan tales of Ovid, never equalled on this earth for the gaiety of their movement and the capricious graces of their narrative, are read by all Christendom. This man's people and their monuments are dust; but *he* is alive: he has survived them, as he told us that he had it in his commission to do, by a thousand years; "and *shall* a thousand more."

All the literature of knowledge builds only ground-nests, that are swept away by floods, or confounded by the plough; but the literature of power builds nests in aërial altitudes of temples sacred from violation, or of forests inaccessible to fraud. *This* is a great prerogative of the *power* literature; and it is a greater which lies in the mode of its influence. The *knowledge* literature, like the fashion of this world, passeth away. An Encyclopædia is its abstract; and, in this respect, it may be taken for its speaking symbol – that before one generation has passed an Encyclopædia is superannuated; for it speaks through the dead memory and unimpassioned understanding, which have not the repose of higher faculties, but are continually enlarging and varying their phylacteries. But all literature properly so called – literature κατ' ἐξοχην,[b] – for the very same reason that it is so much more durable than the literature of knowledge, is (and by the very same proportion it is) more intense and electrically searching in its impressions. The directions in which the tragedy of this planet has trained our human feelings to play, and the combinations into which the poetry of this planet has thrown our human passions of love and hatred, of admiration and contempt, exercise a power for bad or good over human life that cannot be contemplated, when stretching through many generations, without a sentiment allied to awe.[6] And of this let every one be assured – that he owes to the impassioned books which he has read many a thousand more of emotions than he can consciously trace back to them. Dim by their origination, these emotions yet arise in him, and mould him through life, like forgotten incidents of his childhood. . . .

What *is* didactic poetry? What does "didactic" mean when applied

[a] possessions for ever   [b] at the head of its kind

as a distinguishing epithet to such an idea as a poem? The predicate destroys the subject: it is a case of what logicians call *contradictio in adjecto*[a] – the unsaying by means of an attribute the very thing which is the subject of that attribute you have just affirmed. No poetry can have the function of teaching. It is impossible that a variety of species should contradict the very purpose which contradistinguishes its *genus*. The several species differ partially, but not by the whole idea which differentiates their class. Poetry, or any one of the fine arts (all of which alike speak through the genial nature of man and his excited sensibilities), can teach only as nature teaches, as forests teach, as the sea teaches, as infancy teaches, – viz. by deep impulse, by hieroglyphic suggestion. Their teaching is not direct or explicit, but lurking, implicit, masked in deep incarnations. To teach formally and professedly is to abandon the very differential character and principle of poetry. If poetry could condescend to teach anything, it would be truths moral or religious. But even these it can utter only through symbols and actions. The great moral, for instance, the last result, of the Paradise Lost is once formally announced, – viz. *to justify the ways of God to man*; but it teaches itself only by diffusing its lesson through the entire poem in the total succession of events and purposes: and even this succession teaches it only when the whole is gathered into unity by a reflex act of meditation, just as the pulsation of the physical heart can exist only when all the parts in an animal system are locked into one organisation.

To address the *insulated* understanding is to lay aside the Prospero's robe of poetry. The objection, therefore, to didactic poetry, as vulgarly understood, would be fatal even if there were none but this logical objection derived from its definition. To be in self-contradiction is, for any idea whatever, sufficiently to destroy itself. But it betrays a more obvious and practical contradiction when a little searched. If the true purpose of a man's writing a didactic poem were to teach, by what suggestion of idiocy should he choose to begin by putting on fetters? wherefore should the simple man volunteer to handcuff and manacle himself, were it only by the encumbrances of metre, and perhaps of rhyme? But these he will find the very least of his encumbrances. A far greater exists in the sheer necessity of omitting in any poem a vast variety of details, and even capital sections of the subject, unless they will bend to purposes of ornament. Now this collision between two purposes, – the purpose of use in mere teaching, and the purpose of poetic delight, – shows, by the uniformity of its solution, which of the two is the true purpose, and

[a] contradiction in terms

which the merely ostensible purpose. Had the true purpose been instruction, the moment that this was found incompatible with a poetic treatment, as soon as it was seen that the sound education of the reader-pupil could not make way without loitering to gather poetic flowers, the stern cry of "duty" would oblige the poet to remember that he had dedicated himself to a didactic mission, and that he differed from other poets, as a monk from other men, by his vows of self-surrender to harsh ascetic functions. But, on the contrary, in the very teeth of this rule, wherever such a collision does really take place, and one or other of the supposed objects must give way, it is always the vulgar object of *teaching* (the pedagogue's object) which goes to the rear, whilst the higher object of poetic emotion moves on triumphantly. In reality not one didactic poet has ever yet attempted to use any parts or processes of the particular art which he made his theme, unless in so far as they seemed susceptible of poetic treatment, and only *because* they seemed so. Look at the poem of *Cyder* by Philips, of the *Fleece* by Dyer,[7] or (which is a still weightier example) at the *Georgics* of Virgil, – does any of these poets show the least anxiety for the correctness of your principles, or the delicacy of your manipulations, in the worshipful arts they affect to teach? No; but they pursue these arts through every stage that offers any attractions of beauty. And, in the very teeth of all anxiety for teaching, if there existed traditionally any very absurd way of doing a thing which happened to be eminently picturesque, and if, opposed to this, there were some improved mode that had recommended itself to poetic hatred by being dirty and ugly, the poet (if a good one) would pretend never to have heard of this disagreeable improvement. Or, if obliged, by some rival poet, not absolutely to ignore it, he would allow that such a thing could be done, but hint that it was hateful to the Muses or Graces, and very likely to breed a pestilence.

This subordination of the properly didactic function to the poetic, – which leaves the old essential distinction of poetry (viz. its sympathy with the genial motions of man's heart) to override all accidents of special variation, and shows that the essence of poetry never can be set aside by its casual modifications, – will be compromised by some loose thinkers, under the idea that in didactic poetry the element of instruction is, in fact, one element, though subordinate and secondary. Not at all. What we are denying is that the element of instruction enters *at all* into didactic poetry. The subject of the Georgics, for instance, is Rural Economy as practised by Italian farmers; but Virgil not only *omits* altogether innumerable points of instruction insisted on as articles of religious necessity by Varro,

Cato, Columella, &c., but, even as to those instructions which he *does* communicate, he is careless whether they are made technically intelligible or not. He takes very little pains to keep you from capital mistakes in *practising* his instructions; but he takes good care that you shall not miss any strong impression for the eye or the heart to which the rural process, or rural scene, may naturally lead. He pretends to give you a lecture on farming, in order to have an excuse for carrying you all round the beautiful farm. He pretends to show you a good plan for a farm-house, as the readiest means of veiling his impertinence in showing you the farmer's wife and her rosy children. It is an excellent plea for getting a peep at the bonny milkmaids to propose an inspection of a model dairy. You pass through the poultry-yard, under whatever pretence, in reality to see the peacock and his harem. And so, on to the very end, the pretended instruction is but in secret the connecting tie which holds together the laughing flowers going off from it to the right and to the left; whilst, if ever at intervals this prosy thread of pure didactics is brought forward more obtrusively, it is so by way of foil, to make more effective upon the eye the prodigality of the floral magnificence.

We affirm, therefore, that the didactic poet is so far from seeking even a secondary or remote object in the particular points of information which he may happen to communicate, that much rather he would prefer the having communicated none at all. We will explain ourselves by means of a little illustration from Pope, which will at the same time furnish us with a miniature type of what we ourselves mean by a didactic poem, both in reference to what it *is* and to what it is *not*. In the Rape of the Lock there is a game at cards played, and played with a brilliancy of effect and felicity of selection, applied to the circumstances, which make it a sort of gem within a gem.[a] This game was not in the first edition of the poem, but was an afterthought of Pope's, laboured therefore with more than usual care. We regret that *ombre*, the game described, is no longer played, so that the entire skill with which the mimic battle is fought cannot be so fully appreciated as in Pope's days. The strategics have partly perished; which really Pope ought not to complain of, since he suffers only as Hannibal, Marius, Sertorius, suffered before him.[8] Enough, however, survives of what will tell its own story. For what is it, let us ask, that a poet has to do in such a case, supposing that he were disposed to weave a didactic poem out of a pack of cards, as Vida has out of the chess-board?[9] In describing any particular game he does not seek to *teach* you that game – he postulates it as *already* known to you; but he

[a] Canto III, lines 25–100

relies upon separate resources. 1st, He will revive in the reader's eye, for picturesque effect, the well-known personal distinctions of the several kings, knaves, &c., their appearances and their powers. 2dly, He will choose some game in which he may display a happy selection applied to the chances and turns of fortune, to the manœuvres, to the situations of doubt, of brightening expectation, of sudden danger, of critical deliverance, or of final defeat. The interest of a war will be rehearsed: *lis est de paupere regno*[a] – that is true; but the depth of the agitation on such occasions, whether at chess, at draughts, or at cards, is not measured of necessity by the grandeur of the stake; he selects, in short, whatever fascinates the eye or agitates the heart by mimicry of life; but, so far from *teaching*, he presupposes the reader already *taught*, in order that he may go along with the movement of the descriptions.

Now, in treating a subject so vast as that which Pope chose for his Essay, viz. MAN, this eclecticism ceases to be possible. Every part depends upon every other part: in such a *nexus* of truths, to insulate is to annihilate. Severed from each other, the parts lose their support, their coherence, their very meaning; you have no liberty to reject or choose. Besides, in treating the ordinary themes proper for what is called didactic poetry – say, for instance, that it were the art of rearing silkworms or bees, or suppose it to be horticulture, landscape-gardening, hunting, or hawking – rarely does there occur anything polemic; or, if a slight controversy *does* arise, it is easily hushed asleep – it is stated in a line, it is answered in a couplet. But in the themes of Lucretius and Pope *everything* is polemic – you move only through dispute, you prosper only by argument and never-ending controversy. There is not positively one capital proposition or doctrine about Man, about his origin, his nature, his relations to God, or his prospects, but must be fought for with energy, watched at every turn with vigilance, and followed into endless mazes, not under the choice of the writer, but under the inexorable dictation of the argument.

Such a poem, so unwieldy, whilst at the same time so austere in its philosophy, together with the innumerable polemic parts essential to its good faith and even to its evolution, would be absolutely unmanageable from excess and from disproportion, since often a secondary demur would occupy far more space than a principal section. Here lay the impracticable dilemma for Pope's Essay on Man. To satisfy the demands of the subject was to defeat the objects of poetry. To evade the demands in the way that Pope has done is to offer us a ruin for a palace. The very same dilemma existed for

---

[a] the dispute is for a trifling gain

Lucretius, and with the very same result. The *De Rerum Naturâ*[a] (which might, agreeably to its theme, have been entitled *De Omnibus Rebus*[b]) and the Essay on Man (which might equally have borne the Lucretian title *De Rerum Naturâ*), are both, and from the same cause, fragments that could not have been completed. Both are accumulations of diamond-dust without principles of coherency. In a succession of pictures, such as usually form the materials of didactic poems, the slightest thread of interdependency is sufficient. But, in works essentially and everywhere argumentative and polemic, to omit the connecting links, as often as they are insusceptible of poetic effect, is to break up the unity of the parts, and to undermine the foundations, in what expressly offers itself as a systematic and architectural whole. Pope's poem has suffered even more than that of Lucretius from this want of cohesion. It is indeed the realisation of anarchy; and one amusing test of this may be found in the fact that different commentators have deduced from it the very opposite doctrines. In some instances this apparent antinomy is doubtful, and dependent on the ambiguities or obscurities of the expression. But in others it is fairly deducible; and the cause lies in the elliptical structure of the work: the ellipsis, or (as sometimes it may be called) the chasm, may be filled up in two different modes essentially hostile; and he that supplies the *hiatus* in effect determines the bias of the poem this way or that — to a religious or to a sceptical result. In this edition the commentary of Warburton has been retained; which ought certainly to have been dismissed. The essay is, in effect, a Hebrew word with the vowel-points omitted; and Warburton supplies one set of vowels, whilst Crousaz sometimes with equal right supplies a contradictory set .... [10]

---

[a] concerning the nature of things   [b] concerning everything

Thomas Love Peacock

(1785–1866)

The typical characters of the Regency years – political economists, utilitarian philosophers, romantic poets, country squires, philanthropic ladies – all found their proper satirist in Thomas Love Peacock. He knew his targets well and almost seems in retrospect to have cultivated their acquaintance for the sake of checking the accuracy of his portraits. Yet Peacock's sympathies are so generous that one suspects him of having been a member of every group he satirized. It would, in fact, be fair to call him, as it would be fair to call no other writer of the period, at once a romantic and a utilitarian. Even down to individual traits, his novels record his continuing interest in persons as divergent as Shelley and Malthus. Thus the protagonist of *Nightmare Abbey*, Scythrop, a character manifestly based on Shelley, provoked an admiring comment from Shelley himself:

> I know not how to praise sufficiently the lightness, the chastity, and strength of the language of the whole. It perhaps exceeds all your works in this. The catastrophe is excellent. I suppose the moral is contained in what Falstaff says – "For God's sake, talk like a man of this world"; and yet, looking deeper into it, is not the misdirected enthusiasm of Scythrop what J. C. calls "the salt of the earth"?

That such a response should be possible for a *victim* of Peacock's satire points to the singularity of his gift. His novels practice the serious truth-telling about human nature by a fallible participant in human nature, for which earlier moralists reserved the word "candor." His intelligence, in short, while it leaves nothing shining quite as imposingly as it once did, still manages somehow to leave nothing tarnished.

Peacock experimented in both poetry and prose, and freely blended what less original minds took to be the properties of discrete genres. The sort of novel he repeated most often was a mingling of limpid prose narrative, Theophrastan character, and comedy of humors, varied by passages of straight dialogue, but without stage-directions except for muttered signals of assent or reprobation, and the spontaneous interludes where an entire company breaks into a drinking song. In the work of intellectual portraiture, Peacock makes every detail tell; as, for example, in his opening description of Mr. Flosky, an anti-Jacobin mystic loosely based on Coleridge:

> He dreamed with his eyes open, and saw ghosts dancing round him at noontide. He had been in his youth an enthusiast for liberty, and had

hailed the dawn of the French Revolution as the promise of a day that was to banish war and slavery, and every form of vice and misery, from the face of the earth. Because all this was not done, he deduced that nothing was done; and from this deduction, according to his system of logic, he drew a conclusion that worse than nothing was done; that the overthrow of the feudal fortresses of tyranny and superstition was the greatest calamity that had ever befallen mankind; and that their only hope now was to rake the rubbish together, and rebuild it without any of those loopholes by which the light had originally crept in.

The points are lost or scored in his writing even more implicitly than in Jane Austen's. It is assumed that we will learn all we need to know about Mr. Flosky from the phrase, "He dreamed with his eyes open" – suggesting an unexpected craftiness, as well as a condition of wakeful stupor – with the result that Peacock's remarkable insight into the psychology of political reaction can be condensed into one intricate sentence. Often, as in this passage, Peacock's style hovers delicately between verbal parody and intellectual cartoon. When the occasion requires either mode in its pure state, his mastery is faultless.

It was Peacock's distrust of all pretensions to otherworldliness that gave him the strength for an unintimidated friendship with Shelley. He was also a considerable literary influence on Shelley, in at least two directions: he encouraged an appreciation of classical authors, and confirmed an already existing bias toward the vocabulary of empiricism. One effect of this may have been to cool Shelley's idolatry of Godwin. Another was certainly to teach that a care for the aggregate destinies of mankind did not necessitate a faith in the abstraction *Man.* Peacock believed in tolerance – in the disclosing of truths, not the revelation of truth – and in the authority of human needs, as distinct from principles. His skepticism offered a resistance to Shelley which never seemed uncongenial. As an illustrative anecdote, Peacock tells of having once been informed of a plot Shelley had discovered by his own father and uncle, "to entrap me and lock me up." The informant was a man named Williams, with whom, Shelley said, he had taken a walk. What hat did you wear? asked Peacock. Shelley picked one up that covered his face, and then remonstrated with Peacock for his faithlessness. "If I do not know that I saw Williams, how do I know that I see you?" "An idea," Peacock replied, "may have the force of a sensation; but the oftener a sensation is repeated, the greater is the probability of its origin in reality. You saw me today, and will see me to-morrow." It is the same tone with which he successfully provokes Shelley in "The Four Ages of Poetry."

How far Peacock in this essay may have meant to take the side of utility against poetry, is no easier to determine than the degree of sympathy he felt for the characters he ridiculed. But he treats some characters with more respect than others; and in "The Four Ages of Poetry" utility has the better of the argument. Peacock supposes that for a person of advanced intelligence in the beginning of the nineteenth century, the case against poetry is as powerful as it has ever been. More particularly, he takes advantage of an irony in the situation of the romantic poet. For in the age of Wordsworth, poets are making greater claims on their audience than ever before: their province, they argue, is not to imitate the real but to represent its hidden and ideal aspects; the reader is accordingly asked to admire not the fidelity but the expressiveness of the result. It is only a step further for poets to assume the burden – as Wordsworth does in his "Essay, Supplementary" – of showing how readers may be "humbled and humanised, in order that they may be purified and exalted." This honor poets grant themselves the more readily, because they see their works as cooperating prophetically with the spirit of the age. Now, Peacock observes, since one thing we know about the spirit of the age is that it is utilitarian, let us inquire a little into the utility of poetry. Poets have their uses in an earlier state of society, when a king wants "an organ to disseminate the fame of his achievements and the extent of his possessions; and this organ he finds in a bard, who is always ready to celebrate the strength of his arm, being first duly inspired by that of his liquor." Viewed in this way, poetry is not so much a calling as a social function, for which the need wears out with the advent of historians more refined than the poet. Poetry indeed is only useful in this primitive stage of its development, which Peacock calls the iron age. By contrast, the golden age of poetry "finds its materials in the age of iron"; so that, at the very height of its achievement, poetry is already retrospective and already useless. Peacock leaves us with the suggestion that poetry is a branch of flattery and lying, and that its four ages may be reduced to two main divisions: a time when its products were mistaken for truth and valued accordingly; and a later time, when they were seen for what they were. The puzzle therefore is how poetry can interest any citizen of such a later time.

As history competes with poetry, improves itself and becomes less poetical (a progress illustrated by the succession of Thucydides to Herodotus), so poetry itself becomes more fanciful, until the bard of a golden age sings the family and history of a character he has inherited from the iron age. Following these elaborations of subject are the elaborations of surface which Peacock associates with the silver age. Throughout this part of his account, he implies that only the incompetence of poets as historians has driven them back on earlier forms of expression. The invention of "literature," self-conscious in its ambitions, comes with the age of brass. Peacock has in mind Alexandrian poetry but also alexandrianism in a more general sense: the decadence of invention, half concealed by the sophistications of aimless talent. He calls this the second childhood of poetry. And he adds that modern poetry repeats the same sequence, with the Lake poets bringing up the rear. From the premise that "poetry was the mental rattle that awakened the attention of intellect in the infancy of civil society," Peacock concludes that "a poet in our times is a semi-barbarian in a civilized community." The audience for poetry now consists of those "who are indifferent to any thing beyond being charmed, moved, excited, affected, and exalted: charmed by harmony, moved by sentiment, excited by passion, affected by pathos, and exalted by sublimity: harmony, which is language on the rack of Procrustes;

sentiment, which is canting egotism in the mask of refined feeling; passion, which is the commotion of a weak and selfish mind; pathos, which is the whining of an unmanly spirit; and sublimity, which is the inflation of an empty head." That sentence, executed with the methodical regularity of Bentham, is in fact a parody of Sidney's *Apology for Poetry*. It makes an *ethical* attack in the original sense of the word, that is, an attack on the sort of people who care for poetry. At least one passage of Shelley's "Defence of Poetry" offers a direct response to this challenge – the phrase in which Shelley speaks of poetry as a record of "the best and happiest moments of the happiest and best minds." Peacock's curious echo of the *Apology* may also have prompted Shelley to reread that work.

Poetry in the "Four Ages" stands condemned as venal, retrograde, artificial, and non-utilitarian. It must be all of these things, in the present state of society. Even, however, in the absence of other evidence, Peacock's "Essay on Fashionable Literature" alone would show that he looked on such traits as the vices of poetry and not its necessary attributes. The essay was planned as a defence of "Christabel" and "Kubla Khan," and was never completed according to Peacock's design. Much of it has great interest nevertheless. For, in the course of explaining the originality of these poems, Peacock anatomizes the whole system of publishing and reviewing that had fostered a public taste capable of rejecting them as trifles. The system depended on an idea of the fashionable public, an idea which was itself the creation of the quarterlies. But the quarterlies for their part reflected the opinions of readers much less than they did each other's prejudices. The worst vices of contemporary fashion Peacock associates with official moralism on one side and Byronic affectation on the other. (Like Hazlitt, he cherished a distant respect for Byron's celebrity, with a ready skepticism about his writings.) Yet for all Peacock's appreciation of those whose genius lies outside the understanding of fashion, the concessions of this "Essay" do not neutralize the accusations of "The Four Ages of Poetry." Whether one reads the latter as a sincere protest or a piece of ventriloquy, the trick of Peacock's adventure in utilitarian criticism is that it is answerable by none of the stock defenses of poetry, which speak of "enrichment" or "enlargement" but admit common pleasure to be something quite different. For Shelley, the virtue of the attack was that it returned him to first premises; and the final words ought to be his, from the description of Peacock in his "Letter to Maria Gisborn": "his fine wit / Makes such a wound, the knife is lost in it; / A strain too learned for this shallow age, / Too wise. . . . "

19. *"An Essay on Fashionable Literature"*

written in 1818; text from *Works*, ed. H. B. F. Brett-Smith and C. E. Jones (1926), vol. 8, pp. 263–82, 289–91, with cuts

I. The fashionable metropolitan winter, which begins in spring and ends in autumn, is the season of happy re-union to those ornamental varieties of the human species who live to be amused for the benefit of social order. It is the period of the general muster, the levy *en masse* of gentlemen in stays and ladies in short petticoats against their arch enemy Time. It is the season of operas and exhibitions, of routs and concerts, of dinners at midnight and suppers at sunrise. But these are the arms with which they assail the enemy in battalion: there are others with which in moments of morning solitude they are compelled to encounter him single-handed: and one of these weapons is the reading of light and easy books which command attention without the labour of application, and amuse the idleness of fancy without disturbing the sleep of understanding.

II. This species of literature, which aims only to amuse and must be very careful not to instruct, had never so many purveyors as at present: for there never was any state of society in which there were so many idle persons as there are at present in England, and it happens that these idle persons are for the most part so circumstanced that they can do nothing if they would, and in the next place that they are united in the links of a common interest which, being based in delusion, makes them even more averse than the well-dressed vulgar always are from the free exercise of reason and the bold investigation of truth.

III. That the faculty of amusing should be the only passport of a literary work into the hands of general readers is not very surprising, more especially when we consider that the English is the most thinking people in the universe: but that the faculty of amusing should be as transient as the gloss of a new coat does seem at first view a little singular: for though all fashionable people read (gentlemen who have been at college excepted), yet as the soul of fashion is novelty, the books and the dress of the season go out of date together; and to be amused this year by that which amused others twelve months ago would be to plead guilty to the heinous charge of having lived out of the world.

IV. The stream of new books, therefore, floats over the parlour window, the boudoir sofa, and the drawing-room table to furnish a ready answer to the question of Mr. Donothing as to what Mrs. Dolittle and her daughters are reading, and having served this purpose, and that of putting the monster Time to a temporary death, flows peacefully on towards the pool of Lethe.

V. The nature of this lighter literature, and the changes which it has undergone with the fashions of the last twenty years, deserve consideration for many reasons, and afford a subject of speculation which may be amusing, and I would add instructive, were I not fearful of terrifying my readers in the outset. As every age has its own character, manners, and amusements, which are influenced even in their lightest forms by the fundamental features of the time, the moral and political character of the age or nation may be read by an attentive observer even in its lightest literature, how remote soever *prima facie* from morals and politics.

VI. The newspaper of the day, the favorite magazine of the month, the review of the quarter, the tour, the novel, and the poem which are most recent in date and most fashionable in name, furnish forth the morning table of the literary dilettante. The spring tide of metropolitan favor floats these intellectual *deliciæ* into every minor town and village in the kingdom, where they circle through their little day in the eddies of reading societies.

VII. It may be questioned how far the favor of fashionable readers is a criterion of literary merit. It is certain that no work attracts any great share of general attention, which does not possess considerable originality and great power to interest and amuse. But originality will sometime attract notice for a little space, as Mr. Romeo Coates attracted some three or four audiences by the mere force of excessive absurdity: and the records of the Minerva press will shew that a considerable number of readers can be both interested and amused by works completely expurgated of all the higher qualities of mind.[1] And without dragging reluctant dullness back to day, let us only consider the names of Monk Lewis and of Kotzebue,[2] from what acclamations of popular applause they have sunk in a few years into comparative oblivion, and we shall see that the condition of a fashionable author differs very little in stability from that of a political demagogue.

[VIII. Mr. Walter Scott seems an exception to this. Having long occupied the poetical throne, he seems indeed to have been deposed by Lord Byron, but he has risen with redoubled might as a novelist, and has thus continued, from the publication of the *Lay of the Last Minstrel*, the most popular writer of his time; perhaps the most universally successful in his own day of any writer that ever lived. He has the rare talent of pleasing all ranks and classes of men, from the peer to the peasant, and all orders and degrees of mind from the philosopher to the manmilliner, of whom nine make a taylor. On the arrival of *Rob Roy*, as formerly on that of *Marmion*, the scholar lays aside his Plato, the statesman suspends his calculations, the young lady deserts her harp, the critic smiles as he trims his lamp, the lounger thanks God for his good fortune, and the weary artisan resigns his sleep for the refreshment of the magic page. But we must not anticipate.]

IX. Periodical publications form a very prominent feature in this transitory literature:– To any one who will compare the Reviews and Magazines of the present day with those of thirty years ago, it must be obvious that there is a much greater diffusion of general talent through them all, and more instances of great individual talent in the present than at the former period: and at the same time it must be equally obvious that there is much less literary honesty, much more illiberality and exclusiveness, much more subdivision into petty gangs and factions, much less classicality and very much less philosophy. The stream of knowledge seems spread over a wider superficies, but what it has gained in breadth it has lost in depth. There is more dictionary learning, more scientific smattering, more of that kind of knowledge which is calculated for shew in general society, to produce a brilliant impression on the passing hour of literature, and less, far less, of that solid and laborious research which builds up in the silence of the closet, and in the disregard of perishable fashions of mind, the strong and permanent structure of history and philosophy.

X. The two principal periodical publications of the time – the *Edinburgh* and *Quarterly Reviews* – are the organs and oracles of the two great political factions, the Whigs and Tories; and their extensive circulation is less ascribable to any marked superiority, either of knowledge or talent, which they possess over their minor competitors, than to the curiosity of the public in general to learn or divine from these semi-official oracles what the said two factions are meditating....

XII. The *country gentlemen*[3] appear to be in the habit of considering reviews as the joint productions of a body of men who meet at a sort of green board, where all new literary productions are laid before them for impartial consideration, and the merits of each having been fairly canvassed, some aged and enlightened censor records the opinion of the council and promulgates its definitive judgment to the world. The solitary quack becomes a medical board. The solitary play-frequenter becomes a committee of amateurs of the drama. The elector of Old Sarum[4] is a respectable body of constituents. This is an all-pervading quackery. Plurality is its essence. The mysterious *we* of the invisible assassin converts his poisoned dagger into a host of legitimate broadswords. Nothing, however, can be more remote from the facts. Of the ten or twelve articles which compose the *Edinburgh Review*, one is manufactured on the spot, another comes from Aberdeen, another from Islington, another from Herefordshire, another from the coast of Devon, another from bonny Dundee, *etc.*, *etc.*, *etc.*, without any one of the contributors even knowing the names of his brethren, or having any communication with any one but the editor. The only point of union among them is respect for the magic circle drawn by the compasses of faction and nationality, within which dullness and ignorance is secure of favor, and without which genius and knowledge are equally certain of neglect or persecution.

XIII. The case is much the same with the *Quarterly Review* except that the contributors are more in contact, being all more or less hired slaves of the Government, and for the most part gentlemen pensioners clustering round a common centre in the tangible shape of their paymaster Mr. Gifford.[a] This publication contains more talent and less principle than it would be easy to believe coexistent.

XIV. The monthly publications are so numerous that the most indefatigable reader of desultory literature could not get through the whole of their contents in a month: a very happy circumstance no doubt for that not innumerous class of persons who make the reading of reviews and magazines the sole business of their lives.

XV. All these have their own little exclusive circles of favor and faction, and it is very amusing to trace in any one of them half a dozen favored names circling in the preeminence of glory in that little circle, and scarcely named or known out of it. Glory, it is said, is like a circle in the water, that grows feebler and feebler as it recedes from the centre and expands with a wider circumference: but the glory of these little idols of little literary factions is like the many circles produced by the simultaneous splashing of a multitude of equal-sized pebbles, which each throws out for a few inches its own little series of concentric circles, limiting and limited by the small rings of its brother pebbles, [while in the midst of all this petty splashing in the pool of public favor Scott or Byron plunges a ponderous fragment in the centre and effaces them all with its eddy: but the disturbing power ceases: the splashings recommence, and the pebbles dance with joy in the rings of their self-created fame.] . . .

XVIII. There is a systematical cant in criticism which passes with many for the language of superior intelligence; such, for instance, is that which pronounces unintelligible whatever is in any degree obscure, more especially if it be really matter of deeper sense than the critic likes to be molested with. A critic is bound to study for an author's meaning, and not to make his own stupidity another's reproach. (The *Edinburgh Review* and *Excursion* and *Christabel*.) – How very ill Pindar would have fared with these gentlemen, we may

[a] William Gifford, editor of the *Quarterly*

readily imagine; nay, we have sufficiently seen, in the memorable instance in which he appeared *incognito* before a renowned Græculus[a] of the critical corps.

XIX. This instance occurred in an article on one of the most admirable pieces of philosophical criticism that has appeared in any language: Knight's *Principles of Taste.*[b] One of the best metaphysical and one of the best moral treatises in our language appeared at the same time. The period seemed to promise the revival of philosophy: but it has since fallen into deeper sleep than ever, and even classical literature seems sinking into the same repose. The favorite journals of the day, only within a very few years, were seldom without a classical and a philosophical article for the grace of keeping up appearances: but now we have volume after volume without either, and almost without any thing to remind us that such things were.

XX. Sir William Drummond[5] complains that philosophy is neglected at the universities from an exclusive respect for classical literature. I wish the reason were so good. Philosophy is discouraged from fear of itself, not from love of the classics. There would be too much philosophy in the latter for the purposes of public education, were it not happily neutralised by the very ingenious process of academical chemistry which separates reason from grammar, taste from prosody, philosophy from philology, and absorbs all perception of the charms of the former in tedium and disgust at the drudgery of the latter. Classical literature, thus disarmed of all power to shake the dominion of venerable mystery and hoary imposture, is used merely as a stepping-stone to church preferment, and there, God knows,

> Small skill in Latin and still less in Greek
> Is more than adequate to all we seek. –

XXI. If periodical criticism were honestly and conscientiously conducted, it might be a question how far it has been beneficial or injurious to literature: but being, as it is, merely a fraudulent and exclusive tool of party and partiality, that it is highly detrimental to it none but a trading critic will deny. The success of a new work is made to depend, in a great measure, not on the degree of its intrinsic merit, but on the degree of interest the publisher may have with the periodical press. Works of weight and utility, indeed, aided by the great counterpoise Time, break through these flimsy obstacles; but on the light and transient literature of the day its effect is almost omnipotent. Personal or political alliance being the only passports to

---

[a] pipsqueak classicist
[b] Richard Payne Knight, *Analytical Inquiry into the Principles of Taste* (1805)

critical notice, the independence and high thinking, that keeps an individual aloof from all the petty subdivisions of faction, makes every several gang his foe: and of this the *late* Mr. Wordsworth is a striking example.[6]

XXII. There is a common influence to which the periodical press is subservient: it has many ultras on the side of power, but none on the side of liberty (one or two *weekly* publications excepted). And this is not from want of sufficient liberty of the press, which is ample to all purposes; it is from want of an audience. There is a degree of spurious liberty, a Whiggish moderation with which many will go hand in hand; but few have the courage to push enquiry to its limits.

XXIII. Now though there is no censorship of the press, there is an influence widely diffused and mighty in its operation that is almost equivalent to it. The whole scheme of our government is based in influence, and the immense number of genteel persons, who are maintained by the taxes, gives this influence an extent and complication from which few persons are free. They shrink from truth, for it shews those dangers which they dare not face. The *legatur*[a] of corruption must be stamped upon a work before it can be admitted to fashionable circulation.

XXIV. In orthodox families that have the advantage of being acquainted with such a phænomenon as a reading parson (which is fortunately as rare as the Atropos Belladonna – a hunting parson, on the other hand, a much more innocent variety, being as common as the Solanum Nigrum –)[b] or any tolerably literate variety of political and theological orthodoxy – the reading of the young ladies is very much influenced by his advice. He is careful not to prohibit, unless in extreme cases – Voltaire, for example – who is by many well-meaning grown ladies and gentlemen in leading-strings considered little better than a devil incarnate. He is careful not to prohibit, for prohibition is usually accompanied with longing for forbidden fruit – it is much more easy to exclude by silence, and pre-occupy by counter-recommendation. Young ladies read only for amusement: the best recommendation a work of fancy can have is that it should inculcate no opinions at all, but implicitly acquiesce in all the assumptions of worldly wisdom. The next best is that it should be well-seasoned with *petitiones principii*[c] in favor of things as they are.

XXV. Fancy indeed treads on dangerous ground when she trespasses on the land of opinion – the soil is too slippery for her glass slippers, and the atmosphere too heavy for her filmy wings. But she is

---

[a] official seal   [b] the former a deadly, the latter a common, nightshade   [c] begged questions

a degenerate spirit if she be contented within the limits of her own empire, and keep the mind continually gazing upon phantasms without pointing to more important realities. Her province is to awaken the mind, not to enchain it. Poetry precedes philosophy, but true poetry prepares its path. – See Forsyth. – [7]

XXVI. Cervantes – Rabelais – Swift – Voltaire – Fielding – have led fancy against opinion with a success that no other names can parallel. Works of mere amusement, that teach nothing, may have an accidental and transient success, but cannot of course have influence on their own times, and will certainly not pass to posterity. Mr. Scott's success has been attributed in a great measure to his keeping clear of opinion. [But he is far from being a writer who teaches nothing. On the contrary, he communicates great and valuable information. He is a painter of manners. He is the historian of a peculiar and remote class of our own countrymen, who within a few years have completely passed away. He offers materials to the philosopher in depicting, with the truth of life, the features of human nature in a peculiar state of society, before comparatively little known.] . . .

XXVIII. The article of the Edinburgh Reviewers on Mr. Coleridge's *Christabel* affords a complete specimen of the manner in which criticism is now conducted, and certainly nothing but the most implicit contempt for their readers, and the most absolute reliance on the prostration of public judgment before the throne of criticism, could have induced them to put forth such a tissue of ignorance, folly, and *fraud*.[8] The last is a grave charge, but it is the worst and the most prominent feature of modern criticism: for as to ignorance and folly, they are by no means criminal, and are perhaps indispensable in critical journals, for whose *non integra lignea*[a] wisdom and learning would be too heavy ballast. But neither ignorance nor folly, nor any thing but the most unblushing fraud, could have dictated the following passage. *Crimine ab uno disce omnes.*[b]

"One word as to the metre of Christabel, or, as Mr. Coleridge terms it, '*the* Christabel' – happily enough; for indeed we doubt if the peculiar force of the definite article was ever more strongly exemplified.[9] He says, that though the reader may fancy there prevails a great *irregularity* in the metre, some lines being of four, others of twelve syllables, yet in reality it is quite regular; only that it is 'founded on a new principle, namely, that of counting in each line the accents, not the syllables.' We say nothing of the monstrous assurance of any man coming forward coolly at this time of day, and telling the readers of English poetry, whose ear has been tuned to the lays of Spenser, Milton, Dryden, and Pope, that he makes his metre 'on a new principle!' but we utterly deny the truth of the assertion, and defy him to show us *any* principle

[a] rickety craft   [b] From one crime learn all the rest.

upon which his lines can be conceived to tally. We give two or three specimens, to confound at once this miserable piece of coxcombry and shuffling. Let our 'wild, and singularly original and beautiful' author, show us how these lines agree either in number of accents or of feet.

> 'Ah wel-a-day!' –
> 'For this is alone in – '
> 'And didst bring her home with thee in love and in charity' –
> 'I pray you drink this cordial wine' –
> 'Sir Leoline' –
> 'And found a bright lady surpassingly fair' –
> 'Tu–whit!—Tu–whoo!' "

Now Mr. Coleridge expressly says: Though the syllables may vary from *seven* to *twelve* the number of accents will be found always the same: *i.e.* four. If the reviewer had had the common candor which characterises even the lowest of mankind (reviewers excepted), he would have stated Mr. Coleridge's assertion truly, and then have disproved it if it had appeared erroneous. Mr. Coleridge asserts that lines of any number of syllables from seven to twelve contain alike four accents, and nothing can be more true:[10] and how does the reviewer disprove this assertion: He first omits the limitation, and makes him say what he never said, that all his lines contain the same number of accents; and then placing lines of four and fourteen syllables in contact. Can any one suppose that the suppression was not wilful? That a man would copy one half of a sentence, the whole of which he could not disprove, and argue against the half as if it were the whole? Could any man do this under any supposition but that of wilful and fraudulent misrepresentation? Or would any man have ventured to do it if he had not felt conscious that in his capacity of critical purveyor he was catering not for liberality and taste but for envy and malignity?

xxix. Reviews have been published in this country seventy years: eight hundred and forty months: and if we reckon only on an average four numbers to a month, we shall find that in that period three thousand three hundred and sixty numbers have been published: three thousand three hundred and sixty numbers, two hundred thousand pages, of sheer criticism, every page of which is now in existence. What a treasury of information! What a repertory of excellent jokes to be cracked on an unhappy author and his unfavored publications! So it would seem. Yet on examination these excellent jokes reduce themselves to some half dozen, which have been repeated through every number of every review of the bulk of periodical criticism to the present day (and were stale in the first instance), without apparently losing any portion of what Miss Edgeworth[a] would call the raciness of their humour. They were borrowed in the first instance from Pope, who himself took one or two of them at second hand. They have an everlasting gloss, like the three coats in the *Tale of a Tub*.[11]

xxx. One of these is the profundity of the Bathos. There is in the lowest deep a lower still, and the author in question (be he who he may) has plunged lower than any one before him. Another is that the work in question is a narcotic, and sets the unfortunate critic to sleep. A third is that it is unintelligible, and that true no-meaning puzzles more than wit. A fourth, that the author is insane. It cannot be denied that this is super-excellent wit which can bear so much repetition without palling, for there is not any number of any review which does not contain them all at least once, and sometimes six or seven times: but taking them only at an average of one in a number, they have been repeated three thousand three hundred and sixty times in seventy years, and so far it is demonstrated that they are three thousand three hundred and sixty times better than the best joke in Joseph Miller, whose brightest recorded repartees will not bear a second repetition....[b]

xxxii. Lord Byron had, it seems, in a singularly original collocation of words, characterised Christabel as a "wild and singularly original and beautiful poem."[c] This unfortunate phrase proved a tid-bit for the critics, who rung the changes upon it with infinite whim.

> "'Tis the middle of night by the castle clock,
> And the owls have awaken'd the crowing cock;
> Tu–whit!—tu–whoo!
> And hark, again! the crowing cock.
> How drowsily it crew.'
> 'Sir Leoline, the Baron rich,
> Hath a toothless mastiff bitch;
> From her kennel beneath the rock
> She makes answer to the clock,
> Four for the quarters, and twelve for the hour;
> Ever and aye, moonshine or shower,
> Sixteen short howls, not over loud;
> Some say she sees my lady's shroud.'
> 'Is the night chilly and dark?
> The night is chilly, but not dark.'

[a] Maria Edgeworth (1767–1849), author of *Castle Rackrent*, *The Absentee* and other novels
[b] Joseph Miller (1684–1738), comic actor, better known in Peacock's time as collector of the posthumous *Joe Miller's Jests* (1739), an anthology of homely repartees, *bon mots*, and occasional humorous remarks which dated very badly
[c] a phrase quoted in advertisements for the poem, at its first publication in 1816

It is probable that Lord Byron may have had this passage in his eye, when he called the poem 'wild' and 'original;' but how he discovered it to be 'beautiful,' is not quite so easy for us to imagine."

The critic does not condescend to alledge any reason for his disapprobation: he knew well that his readers would not require any, but on his magisterial affirmation would take it for granted that the passage was naught, without exercising a grain of judgment for themselves. – But with all due deference to this Aristarchus,[a] let us examine the culprit on whom he thus summarily pronounces. Christabel is a ballad romance, a tale of wonder and mystery told with the simplicity of our elder minstrels, who depict every scene as it were passing under their eyes, and narrate their most marvellous legends with an unaffected *bonne foi*, that shews a mind fully impressed with the truth of its own tale. They never destroyed the appearance of self-persuasion by too much minuteness of detail, and a perpetual pausing to explain and account for every thing. They seem to tell us as much as they know, and leave it to be supposed that there is much more of which they are ignorant. Their language is always that of circumstantial evidence, never of complete and positive testimony. (Note. *Sir Patrick Spence*).[12] Their style is at once simple and energetic, unincumbered with extraneous ornaments; the natural expression of distinctly conceived imagery, rising and falling with the elevation or homeliness of the subject. Such is the style and the language of *Christabel*. The poet relates a tale of magic and mystery, as one who is himself perplexed by the dark wonders which have passed under his own knowledge. The poem is a succession of scenes, and every succession or change presents as many visible or audible circumstances as the fancy can comprehend at once without vacancy from their fewness or confusion from their multitude (note Homer Milton *etc.* as opposed to Chaucer and his modern imitators.)[13] The first scene, the castle at midnight, is characterised by a few circumstances at once original and true to nature. And the regular howl of the dog, under some unknown supernatural influence, prepares the reader at once for a supernatural tale. . . .

> A damsel with a dulcimer
> In a vision once I saw:
> It was an Abyssinian maid
> And on her dulcimer she play'd,
> Singing of Mount Abora.
> Could I revive within me
> Her symphony and song,

[a] Greek grammarian of the second century B.C.

To such a deep delight 'twould win me,
That with music loud and long,
I would build that dome in air,
That sunny dome! those caves of ice!
And all who heard should see them there,
And all should cry, Beware! Beware!
His flashing eyes, his floating hair!
Weave a circle round him thrice,
And close your eyes with holy dread:
For he on honey-dew hath fed.

It is extremely probable that Mr. Coleridge, being a very visionary
gentleman, has somewhat deceived himself respecting the origin of
Kubla Khan; and as the story of its having been composed in his sleep
must necessarily, by all who are acquainted with his manner of
narrating matter of fact, be received with a certain degree of scepticism, its value as a psychological curiosity is nothing, and whatever
value it has is in its poetic merit alone. But from its having been
asserted by the author to have been produced in sleep, it was to be
foreseen that the third standard joke would present itself to the critics
too naturally to be passed by; that the poem itself would be
pronounced to be a narcotic, and to smell strongly of the anodyne,
etc. etc.; and accordingly, in every review which I have seen of
Christabel, this very exquisite joke has been duly cracked over the head
of *Kubla Khan*. It has been uniformly pronounced unintelligible,
especially that passage beginning "a damsel with a dulcimer" *etc.* As
the poem is short, and the manner in which the critics have treated it
affords throughout an excellent standard of critical taste and sagacity,
I will insert the whole of it, prefixing a number to each sentence as a
reference to the following observations.[14]

> In Xanadu did Kubla Khan
> A stately pleasure-dome decree:
> Where Alph, the sacred river, ran
> Through caverns measureless to man
> Down to a sunless sea.

I have read this poem several times over to discover what is
unintelligible in it, as intending to explain it for the benefit of the
critics, in the hope that when they have got their lesson, and learned
to understand it, some of them will condescend to tell us anew what
they think of it. For that a man should pass judgment without
understanding what is in itself intelligible, is as if a judge should take a
nap during the latter half of [a] trial, and waking to give his charge
should say to the jury: "Gentlemen, I do not understand the

defendant's evidence; therefore, you will do well to find for the plaintiff." The jury, if not a special jury, would naturally say, "My lord, if you do not understand the evidence, we do; and are therefore better qualified to give judgment on it than your lordship." I do not believe that to any person of ordinary comprehension, who will take the pains to read this poem twice over, there will appear any thing unintelligible or incoherent in it: indeed there are very few specimens of lyrical poetry so plain, so consistent, so completely *simplex et unum*[a] from first to last.

20. *"The Four Ages of Poetry"*

first published in *Ollier's Literary Magazine* No. 1 (1820); text from *Works*, ed. H. B. F. Brett-Smith and C. E. Jones (1926), vol. 8, pp. 3–25

> Qui inter hæc nutriuntur non magis sapere possunt, quam bene olere qui in culinâ habitant. — PETRONIUS.[b]

POETRY, like the world, may be said to have four ages, but in a different order: the first age of poetry being the age of iron; the second, of gold; the third, of silver; and the fourth, of brass.

The first, or iron age of poetry, is that in which rude bards celebrate in rough numbers the exploits of ruder chiefs, in days when every man is a warrior, and when the great practical maxim of every form of society, "to keep what we have and to catch what we can," is not yet disguised under names of justice and forms of law, but is the naked motto of the naked sword, which is the only judge and jury in every question of *meum* and *tuum*. In these days, the only three trades flourishing (besides that of priest which flourishes always) are those of king, thief, and beggar: the beggar being for the most part a king deject, and the thief a king expectant. The first question asked of a stranger is, whether he is a beggar or a thief: the stranger, in reply, usually assumes the first, and waits a convenient opportunity to prove his claim to the second appellation.

The natural desire of every man to engross to himself as much power and property as he can acquire by any of the means which might makes right, is accompanied by the no less natural desire of making known to as many people as possible the extent to which he has been a winner in this universal game. The successful warrior

---

[a] simple and one
[b] *Satyricon*, second paragraph: "People brought up in such surroundings can no more taste than people who live in kitchens can smell properly."

becomes a chief; the successful chief becomes a king: his next want is an organ to disseminate the fame of his achievements and the extent of his possessions; and this organ he finds in a bard, who is always ready to celebrate the strength of his arm, being first duly inspired by that of his liquor. This is the origin of poetry, which, like all other trades, takes its rise in the demand for the commodity, and flourishes in proportion to the extent of the market.

Poetry is thus in its origin panegyrical. The first rude songs of all nations appear to be a sort of brief historical notices, in a strain of tumid hyperbole, of the exploits and possessions of a few pre-eminent individuals. They tell us how many battles such an one has fought, how many helmets he has cleft, how many breastplates he has pierced, how many widows he has made, how much land he has appropriated, how many houses he has demolished for other people, what a large one he has built for himself, how much gold he has stowed away in it, and how liberally and plentifully he pays, feeds, and intoxicates the divine and immortal bards, the sons of Jupiter, but for whose everlasting songs the names of heroes would perish.

This is the first stage of poetry before the invention of written letters. The numerical modulation is at once useful as a help to memory, and pleasant to the ears of uncultured men, who are easily caught by sound: and from the exceeding flexibility of the yet unformed language, the poet does no violence to his ideas in subjecting them to the fetters of number. The savage indeed lisps in numbers,[a] and all rude and uncivilized people express themselves in the manner which we call poetical.

The scenery by which he is surrounded, and the superstitions which are the creed of his age, form the poet's mind. Rocks, mountains, seas, unsubdued forests, unnavigable rivers, surround him with forms of power and mystery, which ignorance and fear have peopled with spirits, under multifarious names of gods, goddesses, nymphs, genii, and dæmons. Of all these personages marvellous tales are in existence: the nymphs are not indifferent to handsome young men, and the gentlemen-genii are much troubled and very troublesome with a propensity to be rude to pretty maidens: the bard therefore finds no difficulty in tracing the genealogy of his chief to any of the deities in his neighbourhood with whom the said chief may be most desirous of claiming relationship.

In this pursuit, as in all others, some of course will attain a very marked pre-eminence; and these will be held in high honour, like Demodocus in the *Odyssey*, and will be consequently inflated with

[a] adapted from Pope, "Epistle to Dr. Arbuthnot": "I lisp'd in Numbers, for the Numbers came"

boundless vanity, like Thamyris in the *Iliad*. Poets are as yet the only historians and chroniclers of their time, and the sole depositories of all the knowledge of their age; and though this knowledge is rather a crude congeries of traditional phantasies than a collection of useful truths, yet, such as it is, they have it to themselves. They are observing and thinking, while others are robbing and fighting: and though their object be nothing more than to secure a share of the spoil, yet they accomplish this end by intellectual, not by physical, power: their success excites emulation to the attainment of intellectual eminence: thus they sharpen their own wits and awaken those of others, at the same time that they gratify vanity and amuse curiosity. A skilful display of the little knowledge they have, gains them credit for the possession of much more which they have not. Their familiarity with the secret history of gods and genii obtains for them, without much difficulty, the reputation of inspiration; thus they are not only historians but theologians, moralists, and legislators: delivering their oracles *ex cathedrâ*, and being indeed often themselves (as Orpheus and Amphion) regarded as portions and emanations of divinity: building cities with a song, and leading brutes with a symphony; which are only metaphors for the faculty of leading multitudes by the nose.

The golden age of poetry finds its materials in the age of iron. This age begins when poetry begins to be retrospective; when something like a more extended system of civil polity is established; when personal strength and courage avail less to the aggrandising of their possessor and to the making and marring of kings and kingdoms, and are checked by organised bodies, social institutions, and hereditary successions. Men also live more in the light of truth and within the interchange of observation; and thus perceive that the agency of gods and genii is not so frequent among themselves as, to judge from the songs and legends of past time, it was among their ancestors. From these two circumstances, really diminished personal power, and apparently diminished familiarity with gods and genii, they very easily and naturally deduce two conclusions: 1st, That men are degenerated, and 2nd, That they are less in favour with the gods. The people of the petty states and colonies, which have now acquired stability and form, which owed their origin and first prosperity to the talents and courage of a single chief, magnify their founder through the mists of distance and tradition, and perceive him achieving wonders with a god or goddess always at his elbow. They find his name and his exploits thus magnified and accompanied in their traditionary songs, which are their only memorials. All that is said of him is in this character. There is nothing to contradict it. The man and his exploits and his tutelary deities are mixed and blended in one invariable association. The marvellous too is very much like a snow-ball: it grows as it rolls downward, till the little nucleus of truth which began its descent from the summit is hidden in the accumulation of super-induced hyperbole.

When tradition, thus adorned and exaggerated, has surrounded the founders of families and states with so much adventitious power and magnificence, there is no praise which a living poet can, without fear of being kicked for clumsy flattery, address to a living chief, that will not still leave the impression that the latter is not so great a man as his ancestors. The man must in this case be praised through his ancestors. Their greatness must be established, and he must be shown to be their worthy descendant. All the people of a state are interested in the founder of their state. All states that have harmonized into a common form of society, are interested in their respective founders. All men are interested in their ancestors. All men love to look back into the days that are past. In these circumstances traditional national poetry is reconstructed and brought like chaos into order and form. The interest is more universal: understanding is enlarged: passion still has scope and play: character is still various and strong: nature is still unsubdued and existing in all her beauty and magnificence, and men are not yet excluded from her observation by the magnitude of cities or the daily confinement of civic life: poetry is more an art: it requires greater skill in numbers, greater command of language, more extensive and various knowledge, and greater comprehensiveness of mind. It still exists without rivals in any other department of literature; and even the arts, painting and sculpture certainly, and music probably, are comparatively rude and imperfect. The whole field of intellect is its own. It has no rivals in history, nor in philosophy, nor in science. It is cultivated by the greatest intellects of the age, and listened to by all the rest. This is the age of Homer, the golden age of poetry. Poetry has now attained its perfection: it has attained the point which it cannot pass: genius therefore seeks new forms for the treatment of the same subjects: hence the lyric poetry of Pindar and Alcæus, and the tragic poetry of Æschylus and Sophocles. The favour of kings, the honour of the Olympic crown, the applause of present multitudes, all that can feed vanity and stimulate rivalry, await the successful cultivator of this art, till its forms become exhausted, and new rivals arise around it in new fields of literature, which gradually acquire more influence as, with the progress of reason and civilization, facts become more interesting than fiction: indeed the maturity of poetry may be considered the infancy of history. The transition from Homer to Herodotus is scarcely more remarkable than that from Herodotus to Thucydides: in the gradual dereliction of fabulous incident and ornamented language, Herodotus is as much a poet in relation to Thucydides as Homer is in relation to Herodotus. The history of Herodotus is half a poem: it was written while the whole field of literature yet belonged to the Muses, and the nine books of which it was composed were therefore of right, as well as courtesy, super-inscribed with their nine names.

Speculations, too, and disputes, on the nature of man and of mind; on moral duties and on good and evil; on the animate and inanimate components of the visible world; begin to share attention with the eggs of Leda and the horns of Io, and to draw off from poetry a portion of its once undivided audience.

Then comes the silver age, or the poetry of civilized life. This poetry is of two kinds, imitative and original. The imitative consists in recasting, and giving an exquisite polish to, the poetry of the age of gold: of this Virgil is the most obvious and striking example. The original is chiefly comic, didactic, or satiric: as in Menander, Aristophanes, Horace, and Juvenal. The poetry of this age is characterised by an exquisite and fastidious selection of words, and a laboured and somewhat monotonous harmony of expression: but its monotony consists in this, that experience having exhausted all the varieties of modulation, the civilized poetry selects the most beautiful, and prefers the repetition of these to ranging through the variety of all. But the best expression being that into which the idea naturally falls, it requires the utmost labour and care so to reconcile the inflexibility of civilized language and the laboured polish of versification with the idea intended to be expressed, that sense may not appear to be sacrificed to sound. Hence numerous efforts and rare success.

This state of poetry is however a step towards its extinction. Feeling and passion are best painted in, and roused by, ornamental and figurative language; but the reason and the understanding are best addressed in the simplest and most unvarnished phrase. Pure reason and dispassionate truth would be perfectly ridiculous in verse, as we may judge by versifying one of Euclid's demonstrations. This will be found true of all dispassionate reasoning whatever, and of all reasoning that requires comprehensive views and enlarged combinations. It is only the more tangible points of morality, those which command assent at once, those which have a mirror in every mind, and in which the severity of reason is warmed and rendered palatable by being mixed up with feeling and imagination, that are applicable even to what is called moral poetry: and as the sciences of morals and of mind advance towards perfection, as they become more enlarged and comprehensive in their views, as reason gains the ascendancy in them over imagination and feeling, poetry can no longer accompany them in their progress, but drops into the background, and leaves them to advance alone.

Thus the empire of thought is withdrawn from poetry, as the empire of facts had been before. In respect of the latter, the poet of the age of iron celebrates the achievements of his contemporaries; the poet of the age of gold celebrates the heroes of the age of iron; the poet of the age of silver re-casts the poems of the age of gold: we may here see how very slight a ray of historical truth is sufficient to dissipate all the illusions of poetry. We know no more of the men than of the gods of the *Iliad*; no more of Achilles than we do of Thetis; no more of Hector and Andromache than we do of Vulcan and Venus: these belong altogether to poetry; history has no share in them: but Virgil knew better than to write an epic about Cæsar; he left him to Livy; and travelled out of the confines of truth and history into the old regions of poetry and fiction.

Good sense and elegant learning, conveyed in polished and somewhat monotonous verse, are the perfection of the original and imitative poetry of civilized life. Its range is limited, and when exhausted, nothing remains but the *crambe repetita*ᵃ of commonplace, which at length becomes thoroughly wearisome, even to the most indefatigable readers of the newest new nothings.

It is now evident that poetry must either cease to be cultivated, or strike into a new path. The poets of the age of gold have been imitated and repeated till no new imitation will attract notice: the limited range of ethical and didactic poetry is exhausted: the associations of daily life in an advanced state of society are of very dry, methodical, unpoetical matters-of-fact: but there is always a multitude of listless idlers, yawning for amusement, and gaping for novelty: and the poet makes it his glory to be foremost among their purveyors.

Then comes the age of brass, which, by rejecting the polish and the learning of the age of silver, and taking a retrograde stride to the barbarisms and crude traditions of the age of iron, professes to return to nature and revive the age of gold. This is the second childhood of poetry. To the comprehensive energy of the Homeric Muse, which, by giving at once the grand outline of things, presented to the mind a vivid picture in one or two verses, inimitable alike in simplicity and magnificence, is substituted a verbose and minutely-detailed descrip-

---

ᵃ rehash

tion of thoughts, passions, actions, persons, and things, in that loose rambling style of verse, which any one may write, *stans pede in uno,*[a] at the rate of two hundred lines in an hour. To this age may be referred all the poets who flourished in the decline of the Roman Empire. The best specimen of it, though not the most generally known, is the *Dionysiaca* of Nonnus, which contains many passages of exceeding beauty in the midst of masses of amplification and repetition.

The iron age of classical poetry may be called the bardic; the golden, the Homeric; the silver, the Virgilian; and the brass, the Nonnic.

Modern poetry has also its four ages: but "it wears its rue with a difference."[b]

To the age of brass in the ancient world succeeded the dark ages, in which the light of the Gospel began to spread over Europe, and in which, by a mysterious and inscrutable dispensation, the darkness thickened with the progress of the light. The tribes that overran the Roman Empire brought back the days of barbarism, but with this difference, that there were many books in the world, many places in which they were preserved, and occasionally some one by whom they were read, who indeed (if he escaped being burned *pour l'amour de Dieu,*) generally lived an object of mysterious fear, with the reputation of magician, alchymist, and astrologer. The emerging of the nations of Europe from this superinduced barbarism, and their settling into new forms of polity, was accompanied, as the first ages of Greece had been, with a wild spirit of adventure, which, co-operating with new manners and new superstitions, raised up a fresh crop of chimæras, not less fruitful, though far less beautiful, than those of Greece. The semi-deification of women by the maxims of the age of chivalry, combining with these new fables, produced the romance of the middle ages. The founders of the new line of heroes took the place of the demi-gods of Grecian poetry. Charlemagne and his Paladins, Arthur and his knights of the round table, the heroes of the iron age of chivalrous poetry, were seen through the same magnifying mist of distance, and their exploits were celebrated with even more extravagant hyperbole. These legends, combined with the exaggerated love that pervades the songs of the troubadours, the reputation of magic that attached to learned men, the infant wonders of natural philosophy, the crazy fanaticism of the crusades, the power and privileges of the great feudal chiefs, and the holy mysteries of monks and nuns, formed a state of society in which no two laymen could meet without fighting, and in which the three staple ingredients of lover, prize-

---

[a] standing on one foot   [b] *Hamlet,* IV. v. 183

fighter, and fanatic, that composed the basis of the character of every true man, were mixed up and diversified, in different individuals and classes, with so many distinctive excellencies, and under such an infinite motley variety of costume, as gave the range of a most extensive and picturesque field to the two great constituents of poetry, love and battle.

From these ingredients of the iron age of modern poetry, dispersed in the rhymes of minstrels and the songs of the troubadours, arose the golden age, in which the scattered materials were harmonized and blended about the time of the revival of learning; but with this peculiar difference, that Greek and Roman literature pervaded all the poetry of the golden age of modern poetry, and hence resulted a heterogeneous compound of all ages and nations in one picture; an infinite licence, which gave to the poet the free range of the whole field of imagination and memory. This was carried very far by Ariosto, but farthest of all by Shakespeare and his contemporaries, who used time and locality merely because they could not do without them, because every action must have its when and where: but they made no scruple of deposing a Roman Emperor by an Italian Count, and sending him off in the disguise of a French pilgrim to be shot with a blunderbuss by an English archer.[a] This makes the old English drama very picturesque, at any rate, in the variety of costume, and very diversified in action and character; though it is a picture of nothing that ever was seen on earth except a Venetian carnival.

The greatest of English poets, Milton, may be said to stand alone between the ages of gold and silver, combining the excellencies of both; for with all the energy, and power, and freshness of the first, he united all the studied and elaborate magnificence of the second.

The silver age succeeded; beginning with Dryden, coming to perfection with Pope, and ending with Goldsmith, Collins, and Gray.

Cowper divested verse of its exquisite polish; he thought in metre, but paid more attention to his thoughts than his verse. It would be difficult to draw the boundary of prose and blank verse between his letters and his poetry.

The silver age was the reign of authority; but authority now began to be shaken, not only in poetry but in the whole sphere of its dominion. The contemporaries of Gray and Cowper were deep and elaborate thinkers. The subtle scepticism of Hume, the solemn irony of Gibbon, the daring paradoxes of Rousseau, and the biting ridicule of Voltaire, directed the energies of four extraordinary minds to shake every portion of the reign of authority. Enquiry was roused, the

[a] a parody plot-summary of *Cymbeline*

activity of intellect was excited, and poetry came in for its share of the general result. The changes had been rung on lovely maid and sylvan shade, summer heat and green retreat, waving trees and sighing breeze, gentle swains and amorous pains, by versifiers who took them on trust, as meaning something very soft and tender, without much caring what: but with this general activity of intellect came a necessity for even poets to appear to know something of what they professed to talk of. Thomson and Cowper looked at the trees and hills which so many ingenious gentlemen had rhymed about so long without looking at them at all, and the effect of the operation on poetry was like the discovery of a new world. Painting shared the influence, and the principles of picturesque beauty were explored by adventurous essayists with indefatigable pertinacity. The success which attended these experiments, and the pleasure which resulted from them, had the usual effect of all new enthusiasms, that of turning the heads of a few unfortunate persons, the patriarchs of the age of brass, who, mistaking the prominent novelty for the all-important totality, seem to have ratiocinated much in the following manner: "Poetical genius is the finest of all things, and we feel that we have more of it than any one ever had. The way to bring it to perfection is to cultivate poetical impressions exclusively. Poetical impressions can be received only among natural scenes: for all that is artificial is anti-poetical. Society is artificial, therefore we will live out of society. The mountains are natural, therefore we will live in the mountains. There we shall be shining models of purity and virtue, passing the whole day in the innocent and amiable occupation of going up and down hill, receiving poetical impressions, and communicating them in immortal verse to admiring generations." To some such perversion of intellect we owe that egregious confraternity of rhymesters, known by the name of the Lake Poets;[a] who certainly did receive and communicate to the world some of the most extraordinary poetical impressions that ever were heard of, and ripened into models of public virtue, too splendid to need illustration. They wrote verses on a new principle; saw rocks and rivers in a new light; and remaining studiously ignorant of history, society, and human nature, cultivated the phantasy only at the expense of the memory and the reason; and contrived, though they had retreated from the world for the express purpose of seeing nature as she was, to see her only as she was not, converting the land they lived in into a sort of fairy-land, which they peopled with mysticisms and chimæras. This gave what is called a new tone to poetry, and conjured up a herd of

[a] Wordsworth, Coleridge, and Southey

desperate imitators, who have brought the age of brass prematurely to its dotage.

The descriptive poetry of the present day has been called by its cultivators a return to nature. Nothing is more impertinent than this pretension. Poetry cannot travel out of the regions of its birth, the uncultivated lands of semi-civilized men. Mr. Wordsworth, the great leader of the returners to nature, cannot describe a scene under his own eyes without putting into it the shadow of a Danish boy or the living ghost of Lucy Gray, or some similar phantastical parturition of the moods of his own mind.[1]

In the origin and perfection of poetry, all the associations of life were composed of poetical materials. With us it is decidedly the reverse. We know too that there are no Dryads in Hyde-park nor Naiads in the Regent's-canal. But barbaric manners and supernatural interventions are essential to poetry. Either in the scene, or in the time, or in both, it must be remote from our ordinary perceptions. While the historian and the philosopher are advancing in, and accelerating, the progress of knowledge, the poet is wallowing in the rubbish of departed ignorance, and raking up the ashes of dead savages to find gewgaws and rattles for the grown babies of the age. Mr. Scott digs up the poachers and cattle-stealers of the ancient border. Lord Byron cruizes for thieves and pirates on the shores of the Morea[a] and among the Greek islands. Mr. Southey wades through ponderous volumes of travels and old chronicles, from which he carefully selects all that is false, useless, and absurd, as being essentially poetical; and when he has a commonplace book full of monstrosities, strings them into an epic. Mr. Wordsworth picks up village legends from old women and sextons; and Mr. Coleridge, to the valuable information acquired from similar sources, superadds the dreams of crazy theologians and the mysticisms of German metaphysics, and favours the world with visions in verse, in which the quadruple elements of sexton, old woman, Jeremy Taylor,[b] and Emanuel Kant, are harmonized into a delicious poetical compound. Mr. Moore presents us with a Persian, and Mr. Campbell with a Pennsylvanian tale,[c] both formed on the same principle as Mr. Southey's epics, by extracting from a perfunctory and desultory perusal of a collection of voyages and travels, all that useful investigation would not seek for and that common sense would reject.

These disjointed relics of tradition and fragments of second-hand

---

[a] a peninsula of southern Greece
[b] English author and divine (1613–67), celebrated for the Latinate intricacy of his sermons
[c] *Lalla Rookh* and *Gertrude of Wyoming*

observation, being woven into a tissue of verse, constructed on what Mr. Coleridge calls a new principle (that is, no principle at all), compose a modern-antique compound of frippery and barbarism, in which the puling sentimentality of the present time is grafted on the misrepresented ruggedness of the past into a heterogeneous congeries of unamalgamating manners, sufficient to impose on the common readers of poetry, over whose understandings the poet of this class possesses that commanding advantage, which, in all circumstances and conditions of life, a man who knows something, however little, always possesses over one who knows nothing.

A poet in our times is a semi-barbarian in a civilized community. He lives in the days that are past. His ideas, thoughts, feelings, associations, are all with barbarous manners, obsolete customs, and exploded superstitions. The march of his intellect is like that of a crab, backward. The brighter the light diffused around him by the progress of reason, the thicker is the darkness of antiquated barbarism, in which he buries himself like a mole, to throw up the barren hillocks of his Cimmerian labours. The philosophic mental tranquillity which looks round with an equal eye on all external things, collects a store of ideas, discriminates their relative value, assigns to all their proper place, and from the materials of useful knowledge thus collected, appreciated, and arranged, forms new combinations that impress the stamp of their power and utility on the real business of life, is diametrically the reverse of that frame of mind which poetry inspires, or from which poetry can emanate. The highest inspirations of poetry are resolvable into three ingredients: the rant of unregulated passion, the whine of exaggerated feeling, and the cant of factitious sentiment: and can therefore serve only to ripen a splendid lunatic like Alexander, a puling driveller like Werter,[a] or a morbid dreamer like Wordsworth. It can never make a philosopher, nor a statesman, nor in any class of life an useful or rational man. It cannot claim the slightest share in any one of the comforts and utilities of life of which we have witnessed so many and so rapid advances. But though not useful, it may be said it is highly ornamental, and deserves to be cultivated for the pleasure it yields. Even if this be granted, it does not follow that a writer of poetry in the present state of society is not a waster of his own time, and a robber of that of others. Poetry is not one of those arts which, like painting, require repetition and multiplication, in order to be diffused among society. There are more good poems already existing than are sufficient to employ that portion of life which any mere reader and recipient of poetical impressions should devote to them,

[a] hero of Goethe's *Sorrows of Young Werther*, always excessive in his display of sensibility

and these having been produced in poetical times, are far superior in all the characteristics of poetry to the artificial reconstructions of a few morbid ascetics in unpoetical times. To read the promiscuous rubbish of the present time to the exclusion of the select treasures of the past, is to substitute the worse for the better variety of the same mode of enjoyment.

But in whatever degree poetry is cultivated, it must necessarily be to the neglect of some branch of useful study: and it is a lamentable spectacle to see minds, capable of better things, running to seed in the specious indolence of these empty aimless mockeries of intellectual exertion. Poetry was the mental rattle that awakened the attention of intellect in the infancy of civil society: but for the maturity of mind to make a serious business of the playthings of its childhood, is as absurd as for a full-grown man to rub his gums with coral, and cry to be charmed to sleep by the jingle of silver bells.

As to that small portion of our contemporary poetry, which is neither descriptive, nor narrative, nor dramatic, and which, for want of a better name, may be called ethical, the most distinguished portion of it, consisting merely of querulous, egotistical rhapsodies, to express the writer's high dissatisfaction with the world and every thing in it, serves only to confirm what has been said of the semi-barbarous character of poets, who from singing dithyrambics and "Io Triumphe,"[a] while society was savage, grow rabid, and out of their element, as it becomes polished and enlightened.[2]

Now, when we consider that it is not to the thinking and studious, and scientific and philosophical part of the community, not to those whose minds are bent on the pursuit and promotion of permanently useful ends and aims, that poets must address their minstrelsy, but to that much larger portion of the reading public, whose minds are not awakened to the desire of valuable knowledge, and who are indifferent to any thing beyond being charmed, moved, excited, affected, and exalted: charmed by harmony, moved by sentiment, excited by passion, affected by pathos, and exalted by sublimity: harmony, which is language on the rack of Procrustes; sentiment, which is canting egotism in the mask of refined feeling; passion, which is the commotion of a weak and selfish mind; pathos, which is the whining of an unmanly spirit; and sublimity, which is the inflation of an empty head: when we consider that the great and permanent interests of human society become more and more the main spring of intellectual pursuit; that in proportion as they become so, the subordinacy of the ornamental to the useful will be more and more seen and ack-

[a] "Hail triumph"

nowledged; and that therefore the progress of useful art and science, and of moral and political knowledge, will continue more and more to withdraw attention from frivolous and unconducive, to solid and conducive studies: that therefore the poetical audience will not only continually diminish in the proportion of its number to that of the rest of the reading public, but will also sink lower and lower in the comparison of intellectual acquirement: when we consider that the poet must still please his audience, and must therefore continue to sink to their level, while the rest of the community is rising above it: we may easily conceive that the day is not distant, when the degraded state of every species of poetry will be as generally recognized as that of dramatic poetry has long been: and this not from any decrease either of intellectual power, or intellectual acquisition, but because intellectual power and intellectual acquisition have turned themselves into other and better channels, and have abandoned the cultivation and the fate of poetry to the degenerate fry of modern rhymesters, and their olympic judges, the magazine critics, who continue to debate and promulgate oracles about poetry, as if it were still what it was in the Homeric age, the all-in-all of intellectual progression, and as if there were no such things in existence as mathematicians, astronomers, chemists, moralists, metaphysicians, historians, politicians, and political economists, who have built into the upper air of intelligence a pyramid, from the summit of which they see the modern Parnassus far beneath them, and, knowing how small a place it occupies in the comprehensiveness of their prospect, smile at the little ambition and the circumscribed perceptions with which the drivellers and mountebanks upon it are contending for the poetical palm and the critical chair.

Percy Bysshe Shelley

(1792–1822)

An aristocrat by birth and a radical by conviction, Shelley throughout his life was an agitator for political and economic reforms. By the age of nineteen he had been expelled from University College, Oxford, for the advocacy of atheism in a pamphlet of which he was both co-author and publisher. He was already the disciple of William Godwin, a believer in his doctrine of philosophical necessity and a proselytizer for his anti-cooperative ideal of utopian individualism. In 1812 he wrote an adulatory letter to Godwin, and soon after began to visit his household. There he met Godwin's daughter Mary (whose mother was Mary Wollstonecraft), with whom he eloped in 1815. On being denied the custody of his children by an earlier marriage, and finding his character personally assaulted at the trial by Lord Chancellor Eldon, he left England for permanent exile in Italy. Shelley's hatred for bigotry of every sort and his more than national sympathies thus derived from his experience as much as from his reading. With more justification than Byron, he could claim to have been hounded out of England. As late as 1934 a modern Shelleyan, Bertrand Russell, pointed out that whereas Byron was still indulgently deplored as a rake, Shelley had never been forgiven by the aristocracy, and was looked on as a traitor to his class. This betrayal was by Shelley's lights an act of solidarity with something at once larger and more definite. He calls it by many names in his poetry. In the "Defence of Poetry," the great prose work of his last years, he sums up an argument that he had advanced from his first lyrics, and calls it simply poetry. As his examples show, however, poetry to Shelley is synonymous with making, and it denotes every work of thought, feeling, and expression which changes what we consider as possible to thought or feeling or expression.

Language may be provisionally defined as anything that communicates from person to person and from age to age. Poetry, then, exists through the medium of language, and on Shelley's view it is the principle of revision or reform in language. In this way the existence of poetry is a precondition for all the other reforms that may occur in society. In his "Ode to the West Wind," a poem written in late 1819 – only a little before the "Defence" – Shelley commanded the spirit of change itself to be his spirit:

> Drive my dead thoughts over the universe
> Like withered leaves to quicken a new birth!
> And, by the incantation of this verse,
>
> Scatter, as from an unextinguished hearth,
> Ashes and sparks, my words among mankind.

Here, as in the "Defence," dead thoughts cannot be judged dead, apart from the success or failure of the words that represent them. And success or failure in this sense can only mean: to be remembered, whether as the author wished to be remembered or for reasons he could not possibly have foreseen. At any rate the memory of words is greater than, though it brings in its train, the memory of the author who produced them. What is preserved as a result may seem an accident or even a cheat. But it is no more so than history – which, like language, depends for its recoveries on the unforeseeable volitions of men and women. Such volitions, Shelley believed, are not less necessary for having been chosen.

Shelley's incitement to compose the "Defence" came from his reading of "The Four Ages of Poetry"; and one part of his reply to Peacock is implicit in his understanding of language. It turns out that poetry is less easy to despise than the "Four Ages" had presumed. Rather, its achievements co-incide with everything admirable in human life – everything above the level of animal reflexes or powers, and the inertia of personal habits. Peacock had appeared to confine poetry to works concerned with verbal invention, and tending to excite the passions of readers. One can see how far Shelley has broken free of this definition by remarking that his instances of sublime poetry include the sayings of Plato, Jesus Christ, and Francis Bacon, and the legal institutions of ancient Rome, as well as the works of Dante and Shake-speare. Yet Shelley felt all of Peacock's reservations about the idea of poetry as a language to itself. Several months before the appearance of the "Four Ages," he had written in a letter to its author: "I consider Poetry very sub-ordinate to moral and political science, and if I were well, certainly I should aspire to the latter; for I can conceive a great work, embodying the discover-ies of all ages, and harmonising the contending creeds by which mankind have been ruled." In the career of Wordsworth, which he pondered often, he saw an example of a questing originality that had narrowed into "ultra-legitimate dullness." Still, it was the promise of Wordsworth's early work that he had most nearly in view, when he thought of the great things poetry might do. The "Defence" echoes in particular certain words of the Preface to *Lyrical Ballads*, which characterize the poet as "the rock of defence for human nature; an upholder and preserver, carrying everywhere with him relationship and love." It may be felt that Shelley's own ideal is less amelio-rative than Wordsworth's; but for the same reason it is better fortified against disappointment. It asserts that "Poetry redeems from decay the visitations of the divinity in Man." Equally, it warns that "[Poetry's] foot-steps are like those of a wind over a sea, which the coming calm erases, and whose traces remain only, as on the wrinkled sand which paves it." Of the spirit that inspired it only the text of the poem remains as a positive trace or inscription. Its sense may vanish with the mortality of the author. But its power may revive nevertheless, under a different and unfamiliar aspect, at the coming of later authors and readers who find that the traces concern them after all.

More steadily even than Wordsworth, Shelley insists on the connection between imagination and sympathy. "The great secret of morals," he writes, "is love; or a going out of our nature, and an identification of ourselves with the beautiful which exists in thought, action, or person, not our own. . . . The great instrument of moral good is the imagination; and poetry administers to the effect by acting upon the cause." The role here given to imagination, as an instrument on which poetry acts in order to effect a moral good, seems to imply that it is a subordinate or merely passive faculty. In keeping with this suggestion, the "Defence" has sometimes been read as arguing that poetry executes a remedial function in the service of morals. It needs to be recalled, however, that in the sentences just quoted Shelley's starting point is neither morals nor poetry, but what he calls "our nature," or "ourselves." Poetry does indeed command our attention only by its relation with such things. But, in this, its claim is not smaller than that of philosophy or religion. The sayings of Jesus Christ, for example, like the record of his life, have been subject to revision and therefore to distortion, in the same way that poetry is: "The scattered fragments preserved to us by the biographers of this extraordinary person, are all instinct with the most vivid poetry. But his doctrines seem to have been quickly distorted." Poetry continues beyond the decay of the beliefs that first animated it, so long as its words show the actions and passions of a life we can still recognize as ours.

Considered as an argument, the "Defence" exhibits several theses in an overlapping progression. The most important is that poetry foreshadows the complete imagination of the true and the good which mankind exists to realize. In making this claim, Shelley uses the Platonic images of mirror and shadow in an anti-Platonic way. For him, the mirror of imagination does not reflect an object more substantial than itself; the shadow is not the counterfeit of something solid, but the penumbra of something otherwise unknowable. Thus "poetry," he writes, "is a mirror which makes beautiful that which is distorted"; and again, poets are "the mirrors of the gigantic shadows which futurity casts upon the present." This brings us to a second thesis, that the poet is one who beholds the future in the present – that is, a prophet in the true sense, an interpreter rather than a projector. Shelley holds that poetry is intimately related to the age in which it was produced (of which it becomes for later ages the most telling history). All the defects of poetry are chargeable to the circumstances of its making, and yet its power rises above the force of those circumstances. Hence we are right to forget the vices of a poet's life when we read his poetry: by virtue of its survival alone, it is, whatever it may seem, "the record of the best and happiest moments of the happiest and best minds." A final thesis follows from this. If the end of all corrupt moral systems is to destroy our susceptibility to pleasure, the end of poetry, Shelley believes, is to renew that susceptibility. Underlying his belief is a complex idea of pleasure which challenges Peacock's utilitarian assurance. "There are two modes or degrees of pleasure," Shelley observes, "one durable, universal, and permanent; the other transitory and particular. Utility may either express the means of producing the former or the latter. In the former sense, whatever strengthens and purifies the affections, enlarges the imagination, and adds spirit to sense, is useful. But the meaning in which the Author of the Four

Ages of Poetry seems to have employed the word utility is the narrower one." Even so, he allows that utility in the narrower sense promotes such goods as the alleviation of extreme misery, the uprooting of superstition, and the creation of the conditions for social tolerance. To the extent that such goods are achieved, they take their pattern from the suggestions of poetry.

When Shelley writes that "the freedom of women produced the poetry of sexual love," he implies a development of the following sort. An existing circumstance prompts the expression of a truth about it, which in turn brings about a mutation in the thoughts and feelings of persons. Women (as Shelley assumes we will grant) were beginning to free themselves imaginatively, before that fact could be registered anywhere except in poetry. But the poetry that expressed their changing condition was about sexual love; and the consciousness of sexual love itself gave a larger scope to their freedom. Evidently, there is nothing mystical in Shelley's understanding of the origins of poetry: his bias on the contrary is historical and empirical. What remains mysterious about poetry is that its effects cannot be regulated, and they cannot be known in all their extent at any time. To see why this should be so we have to recur to this essay's account of language. All the other arts, says Shelley, are obliged to deal with "materials, instruments, and conditions" (pigments, woodwinds, and an amphitheatre, for instance) which have "relations among each other, which limit and interpose between conception and expression." Language, on the other hand, though it is "arbitrarily produced," has "relation to thoughts alone." This makes it the uniquely human medium. Once we have admitted the sense of the assertion, we may realize more plainly what is involved in Shelley's belief that individual poems are "episodes to that great poem, which all poets, like the cooperating thoughts of one great mind, have built up since the beginning of the world." The process he refers to is the process by which metaphors are created.

Of the language of poets in general, Shelley writes that it "marks the before unapprehended relations of things and perpetuates their apprehension, until the words which represent them become, through time, signs for portions or classes of thoughts instead of pictures of integral thoughts; and then, if no new poets should arise to create afresh the associations which have been thus disorganized, language will be dead to all the nobler purposes of human intercourse." Every unconscious use of a dead metaphor thus participates in the decay of language; and it may be expected of poets that they should renounce their vocation rather than abuse words. The point will be clarified by two illustrations from Wordsworth, whose poetry Shelley seems to have thought of anyway in this context. In a line of verse like, "I feel the weight of chance-desires," he was vitally metaphorical. But when he translated his idea of sublimity on crossing the Alps into "the features / Of the same face, blossoms upon one tree; / Characters of the great Apocalypse," he was giving signs for portions or classes of thoughts rather than pictures of integral thoughts. In this aspect of the "Defence," Shelley is perhaps a moralist of language. But that is another way of stating his belief that the reaction of words upon each other affects the reaction of words upon things. He does not regard language as imitative (derived from given materials whose nature is already known); or as creative (derived from ideas whose nature is undetermined by material conditions). Rather language is constructive of the apprehension of life, for, in the very process of construing, it builds.

In sustained vigor of argument and in imaginative accuracy, Shelley's "Defence" stands alone among the essays of the romantic period. It has affinities with Hazlitt's essay "On Imitation" and with Hunt's "On the Realities of Imagination"; yet it urges the value of poetry in a manner both more exalted and more matter-of-fact than its predecessors. One feels this even in the most controversial phrase of the essay, the very last one, which calls poets "the unacknowledged legislators of the world." In a sense this was only another reply to Peacock, who had represented poets at the height of their worldly power as nothing but flatterers of the great, the composers of drinking songs for tribal chieftains – in short, contemptible but all-too-fully acknowledged companions of the true legislators. Earlier in the "Defence," too, Shelley had conceded that "The fame of legislators and founders of religions, so long as their institutions last, alone seems to exceed that of poets in the restricted sense." But, subtracting from their reputation "the celebrity which their flattery of the gross opinions of the vulgar usually conciliates," he had found that what survived of the legislators themselves was only what they bore of the "higher character of poets." Legislators are poets in the measure that they shape a people's destiny through laws and deeds which successfully bind their past to their future. Poets, then, are legislators in the measure that their words shape the destiny of all who share their language. They are "unacknowledged" not because they are obscure or uncelebrated, but because language exerts an influence on life that is indeterminate as well as pervasive. If aesthetics is the defense of the individual poem, on the grounds of its autonomy, freedom from all interest, and inward relations with itself, then Shelley cannot be counted among the aesthetic theorists. If poetry is the set of all powerful utterances – questions, assertions, petitions, commands, comparisons – made at different times for different purposes, which have outlived their times and come to seem more important than their purposes, then Shelley is the greatest defender of poetry that ever lived.

21. *"A Defence of Poetry"*

written in 1821; text from *Works*, ed. Roger Ingpen and Walter E. Peck (1926–30), vol. 7, pp. 109–40

Part I

ACCORDING to one mode of regarding those two classes of mental action, which are called reason and imagination, the former may be considered as mind contemplating the relations borne by one thought to another, however produced; and the latter, as mind acting upon those thoughts so as to colour them with its own light, and composing from them, as from elements, other thoughts, each containing within itself the principle of its own integrity. The one is the τὸ ποιειν, or the principle of synthesis, and has for its objects those forms which are common to universal nature and existence itself; the other is the τὸ λογιζειν, or principle of analysis, and its action regards the relations of things, simply as relations; considering thoughts, not in their integral unity, but as the algebraical representations which conduct to certain general results. Reason is the enumeration of quantities, already known; imagination is the perception of the value of those quantities, both separately and as a whole. Reason respects the differences, and imagination the similitudes of things. Reason is to imagination as the instrument to the agent, as the body to the spirit, as the shadow to the substance.

Poetry, in a general sense, may be defined to be "the expression of the imagination": and poetry is connate with the origin of man. Man is an instrument over which a series of external and internal impressions are driven, like the alternations of an ever-changing wind over an Æolian lyre, which move it by their motion to ever-changing melody.[1] But there is a principle within the human being, and perhaps within all sentient beings, which acts otherwise than in the lyre, and produces not melody, alone, but harmony, by an internal adjustment of the sounds or motions thus excited to the impressions which excite them. It is as if the lyre could accommodate its chords to the motions of that which strikes them, in a determined proportion of sound; even as the musician can accommodate his voice to the sound of the lyre. A child at play by itself will express its delight by its voice and motions; and every inflexion of tone and every gesture will bear exact relation to a corresponding antitype in the pleasurable impressions which awakened it; it will be the reflected image of that impression; and as the lyre trembles and sounds after the wind has died away, so the child seeks, by prolonging in its voice and motions the duration of the effect, to prolong also a consciousness of the cause. In relation to the objects which delight a child, these expressions are, what poetry is to higher objects. The savage (for the savage is to ages what the child is to years) expresses the emotions produced in him by surrounding objects in a similar manner; and language and gesture, together with plastic or pictorial imitation, become the image of the combined effect of those objects, and of his apprehension of them. Man in society, with all his passions and his pleasures, next becomes the object of the passions and pleasures of man; an additional class of emotions produces an augmented treasure of expressions; and language, gesture, and the imitative arts, become at once the representation and the medium, the pencil and the picture, the chisel and the statue, the chord and the harmony. The social sympathies, or those laws from which, as from its elements, society results, begin to develop themselves from the moment that two human beings coexist; the future is contained within the present, as the plant within the seed; and equality, diversity, unity, contrast, mutual dependence, become the principles alone capable of affording the motives according to which the will of a social being is determined to action, inasmuch as he is social; and constitute pleasure in sensation, virtue in sentiment, beauty in art, truth in reasoning, and love in the intercourse of kind. Hence men, even in the infancy of society, observe a certain order in their words and actions, distinct from that of the objects and the impressions represented by them, all expression being subject to the laws of that from which it proceeds. But let us dismiss those more general considerations which might involve an inquiry into the principles of society itself, and restrict our view to the manner in which the imagination is expressed upon its forms.

In the youth of the world, men dance and sing and imitate natural objects, observing in these actions, as in all others, a certain rhythm or order. And, although all men observe a similar, they observe not the same order, in the motions of the dance, in the melody of the song, in the combinations of language, in the series of their imitations of natural objects. For there is a certain order or rhythm belonging to each of these classes of mimetic representation, from which the hearer and the spectator receive an intenser and purer pleasure than from any other: the sense of an approximation to this order has been called taste by modern writers. Every man in the infancy of art, observes an order which approximates more or less closely to that from which this highest delight results: but the diversity is not sufficiently marked, as that its gradations should be sensible, except in those instances where the predominance of this faculty of approximation to the beautiful (for so we may be permitted to name the relation between this highest pleasure and its cause) is very great. Those in whom it exists in excess are poets, in the most universal sense of the word; and the pleasure resulting from the manner in which they express the influence of society or nature upon their own minds, communicates itself to others, and gathers a sort of reduplication from that community. Their language is vitally metaphorical; that is, it marks the before unapprehended relations of things and perpetuates their apprehension, until the words which represent them, become, through time, signs for portions or classes of thoughts instead of pictures of integral thoughts; and then if no new poets should arise to create afresh the associations which have been thus disorganised, language will be dead to all the nobler purposes of human intercourse. These similitudes or relations are finely said by Lord Bacon to be "the same footsteps of nature impressed upon the various subjects of the world"[a] – and he considers the faculty which perceives them as the storehouse of axioms common to all knowledge. In the infancy of society every author is necessarily a poet, because language itself is poetry; and to be a poet is to apprehend the true and the beautiful, in a word, the good which exists in the relation, subsisting, first between existence and perception, and secondly between perception and expression. Every original language near to its source is in itself the chaos of a cyclic poem: the copiousness of lexicography and the distinctions of grammar are the works of a later age, and are merely the catalogue and the form of the creations of poetry.

But the poets, or those who imagine and express this indestructible order, are not only the authors of language and of music, of the dance and architecture, and statuary, and painting; they are the institutors of laws, and the founders of civil society, and the inventors of the arts of life, and the teachers, who draw into a certain propinquity with the beautiful and the true, that partial apprehension of the agencies of the invisible world which is called religion. Hence all original religions are allegorical, or susceptible of allegory, and, like Janus, have a double face of false and true. Poets, according to the circumstances of the age and nation in which they appeared, were called, in the earlier epochs of the world, legislators, or prophets: a poet essentially comprises and unites both these characters. For he not only beholds intensely the present as it is and discovers those laws according to which present things ought to be ordered, but he beholds the future in the present, and his thoughts are the germs of the flower and the fruit of latest time. Not that I assert poets to be prophets in the gross sense of the word, or that they can foretell the form as surely as they foreknow the spirit of events: such is the pretence of superstition, which would make poetry an attribute of prophecy, rather than prophecy an attribute of poetry. A poet participates in the eternal, the infinite, and the one; as far as relates to his conceptions, time and place and number are not. The grammatical forms which express the moods of time, and the difference of persons, and the distinction of

[a] Shelley's own translation of *De Augmentis Scientiarum*, III. i; rendered in *The Advancement of Learning* as: "the same footsteps of nature, treading or printing upon several subjects or matters"

place, are convertible with respect to the highest poetry without injuring it as poetry;[2] and the choruses of Æschylus, and the book of Job, and Dante's Paradise, would afford, more than any other writings, examples of this fact, if the limits of this essay did not forbid citation. The creations of sculpture, painting, and music, are illustrations still more decisive.

Language, colour, form, and religious and civil habits of action, are all the instruments and materials of poetry; they may be called poetry by that figure of speech which considers the effect as a synonyme of the cause. But poetry in a more restricted sense expresses those arrangements of language, and especially metrical language, which are created by that imperial faculty, whose throne is curtained within the invisible nature of man. And this springs from the nature itself of language, which is a more direct representation of the actions and passions of our internal being, and is susceptible of more various and delicate combinations, than colour, form, or motion, and is more plastic and obedient to the control of that faculty of which it is the creation. For language is arbitrarily produced by the imagination, and has relation to thoughts alone; but all other materials, instruments, and conditions of art, have relations among each other, which limit and interpose between conception and expression. The former is as a mirror which reflects, the latter as a cloud which enfeebles, the light of which both are mediums of communication. Hence the fame of sculptors, painters, and musicians, although the intrinsic powers of the great masters of these arts may yield in no degree to that of those who have employed language as the hieroglyphic of their thoughts, has never equalled that of poets in the restricted sense of the term; as two performers of equal skill will produce unequal effects from a guitar and a harp. The fame of legislators and founders of religions, so long as their institutions last, alone seems to exceed that of poets in the restricted sense; but it can scarcely be a question, whether, if we deduct the celebrity which their flattery of the gross opinions of the vulgar usually conciliates, together with that which belonged to them in their higher character of poets, any excess will remain.

We have thus circumscribed the meaning of the word Poetry within the limits of that art which is the most familiar and the most perfect expression of the faculty itself. It is necessary, however, to make the circle still narrower, and to determine the distinction between measured and unmeasured language; for the popular division into prose and verse is inadmissible in accurate philosophy.

Sounds as well as thoughts have relation both between each other and towards that which they represent, and a perception of the order of those relations has always been found connected with a perception of the order of those relations of thoughts. Hence the language of poets has ever affected a certain uniform and harmonious recurrence of sound, without which it were not poetry, and which is scarcely less indispensable to the communication of its action, than the words themselves, without reference to that peculiar order. Hence the vanity of translation; it were as wise to cast a violet into a crucible that you might discover the formal principle of its colour and odour, as seek to transfuse from one language into another the creations of a poet. The plant must spring again from its seed, or it will bear no flower – and this is the burthen of the curse of Babel.

An observation of the regular mode of the recurrence of this harmony in the language of poetical minds, together with its relation to music, produced metre, or a certain system of traditional forms of harmony of language. Yet it is by no means essential that a poet should accommodate his language to this traditional form, so that the harmony, which is its spirit, be observed. The practice is indeed convenient and popular, and to be preferred, especially in such composition as includes much form and action: but every great poet must inevitably innovate upon the example of his predecessors in the exact structure of his peculiar versification. The distinction between poets and prose writers is a vulgar error. The distinction between philosophers and poets has been anticipated. Plato was essentially a poet – the truth and splendour of his imagery, and the melody of his language, is the most intense that it is possible to conceive. He rejected the measure of the epic, dramatic, and lyrical forms, because he sought to kindle a harmony in thoughts divested of shape and action, and he forbore to invent any regular plan of rhythm which should include, under determinate forms, the varied pauses of his style. Cicero sought to imitate the cadence of his periods, but with little success. Lord Bacon was a poet. His language has a sweet and majestic rhythm, which satisfies the sense, no less than the almost superhuman wisdom of his philosophy satisfies the intellect; it is a strain which distends, and then bursts the circumference of the hearer's mind, and pours itself forth together with it into the universal element with which it has perpetual sympathy. All the authors of revolutions in opinion are not only necessarily poets as they are inventors, nor even as their words unveil the permanent analogy of things by images which participate in the life of truth; but as their periods are harmonious and rhythmical, and contain in themselves the elements of verse; being the echo of the eternal music. Nor are those supreme poets, who have employed traditional forms of rhythm on account of the form and action of their subjects, less capable of perceiving and teaching the truth of things, than those who have omitted that form. Shakspeare, Dante, and Milton (to confine ourselves to modern writers) are philosophers of the very loftiest power.

A poem is the image of life expressed in its eternal truth. There is this difference between a story and a poem, that a story is a catalogue of detached facts, which have no other bond of connexion than time, place, circumstance, cause and effect; the other is the creation of actions according to the unchangeable forms of human nature, as existing in the mind of the creator, which is itself the image of all other minds. The one is partial, and applies only to a definite period of time, and a certain combination of events which can never again recur; the other is universal, and contains within itself the germ of a relation to whatever motives or actions have place in the possible varieties of human nature. Time, which destroys the beauty and the use of the story of particular facts, stript of the poetry which should invest them, augments that of poetry, and for ever develops new and wonderful applications of the eternal truth which it contains. Hence epitomes have been called the moths of just history; they eat out the poetry of it. The story of particular facts is a mirror which obscures and distorts that which should be beautiful: Poetry is a mirror which makes beautiful that which is distorted.[3]

The parts of a composition may be poetical, without the composition as a whole being a poem. A single sentence may be considered as a whole, though it be found in a series of unassimilated portions; a single word even may be a spark of inextinguishable thought. And thus all the great historians, Herodotus, Plutarch, Livy, were poets; and although the plan of these writers, especially that of Livy, restrained them from developing this faculty in its highest degree, they make copious and ample amends for their subjection, by filling all the interstices of their subjects with living images.

Having determined what is poetry, and who are poets, let us proceed to estimate its effects upon society.

Poetry is ever accompanied with pleasure: all spirits on which it falls open themselves to receive the wisdom which is mingled with its delight. In the infancy of the world, neither poets themselves nor their auditors are fully aware of the excellence of poetry: for it acts in a divine and unapprehended manner, beyond and above consciousness; and it is reserved for future generations to contemplate and measure the mighty cause and effect in all the strength and splendour of their union. Even in modern times, no living poet ever arrived at the fulness of his fame; the jury which sits in judgment upon a poet, belonging as he does to all time, must be composed of his peers: it must be impanneled by Time from the selectest of the wise of many generations. A Poet is a nightingale, who sits in darkness and sings to cheer its own solitude with sweet sounds; his auditors are as men entranced by the melody of an unseen musician, who feel that they are moved and softened, yet know not whence or why. The poems of Homer and his contemporaries were the delight of infant Greece; they were the elements of that social system which is the column upon which all succeeding civilization has reposed. Homer embodied the ideal perfection of his age in human character; nor can we doubt that those who read his verses were awakened to an ambition of becoming like to Achilles, Hector, and Ulysses: the truth and beauty of friendship, patriotism, and persevering devotion to an object, were unveiled to the depths in these immortal creations: the sentiments of the auditors must have been refined and enlarged by a sympathy with such great and lovely impersonations, until from admiring they imitated, and from imitation they identified themselves with the objects of their admiration. Nor let it be objected, that these characters are remote from moral perfection, and that they can by no means be considered as edifying patterns for general imitation. Every epoch, under names more or less specious, has deified its peculiar errors; Revenge is the naked Idol of the worship of a semi-barbarous age; and Self-deceit is the veiled Image of unknown evil, before which luxury and satiety lie prostrate. But a poet considers the vices of his contemporaries as the temporary dress in which his creations must be arrayed, and which cover without concealing the eternal proportions of their beauty. An epic or dramatic personage is understood to wear them around his soul, as he may the antient armour or the modern uniform around his body; whilst it is easy to conceive a dress more graceful than either. The beauty of the internal nature cannot be so far concealed by its accidental vesture, but that the spirit of its form shall communicate itself to the very disguise, and indicate the shape it hides from the manner in which it is worn. A majestic form and graceful motions will express themselves through the most barbarous and tasteless costume. Few poets of the highest class have chosen to exhibit the beauty of their conceptions in its naked truth and splendour; and it is doubtful whether the alloy of costume, habit, &c., be not necessary to temper this planetary music for mortal ears.

The whole objection, however, of the immorality of poetry rests upon a misconception of the manner in which poetry acts to produce the moral improvement of man. Ethical science arranges the elements which poetry has created, and propounds schemes and proposes examples of civil and domestic life: nor is it for want of admirable doctrines that men hate, and despise, and censure, and deceive, and subjugate one another. But Poetry acts in another and diviner manner. It awakens and enlarges the mind itself by rendering it the receptacle of a thousand unapprehended combinations of thought. Poetry lifts the veil from the hidden beauty of the world, and makes familiar objects be as if they were not familiar; it reproduces all that it represents, and the impersonations clothed in its Elysian light stand thenceforward in the minds of those who have once contemplated them, as memorials of that gentle and exalted content which extends itself over all thoughts and actions with which it coexists. The great secret of morals is love; or a going out of our own nature, and an identification of ourselves with the beautiful which exists in thought, action, or person, not our own. A man, to be greatly good, must imagine intensely and comprehensively; he must put himself in the place of another and of many others; the pains and pleasures of his species must become his own. The great instrument of moral good is the imagination; and poetry administers to the effect by acting upon the cause. Poetry enlarges the circumference of the imagination by replenishing it with thoughts of ever new delight, which have the power of attracting and assimilating to their own nature all other thoughts, and which form new intervals and interstices whose void for ever craves fresh food. Poetry strengthens that faculty which is the organ of the moral nature of man, in the same manner as exercise strengthens a limb. A Poet therefore would do ill to embody his own conceptions of right and wrong, which are usually those of his place and time, in his poetical creations, which participate in neither. By this assumption of the inferior office of interpreting the effect, in which perhaps after all he might acquit himself but imperfectly, he would resign the glory in a participation in the cause. There was little danger that Homer, or any of the eternal Poets, should have so far misunderstood themselves as to have abdicated this throne of their widest dominion. Those in whom the poetical faculty, though great, is less intense, as Euripides, Lucan, Tasso, Spenser, have frequently affected a moral aim, and the effect of their poetry is diminished in exact proportion to the degree in which they compel us to advert to this purpose.

Homer and the cyclic poets were followed at a certain interval by the dramatic and lyrical Poets of Athens, who flourished contemporaneously with all that is most perfect in the kindred expressions of the poetical faculty; architecture, painting, music, the dance, sculpture, philosophy, and we may add, the forms of civil life. For although the scheme of Athenian society was deformed by many imperfections which the poetry existing in Chivalry and Christianity have erased from the habits and institutions of modern Europe; yet never at any other period has so much energy, beauty, and virtue, been developed; never was blind strength and stubborn form so disciplined and rendered subject to the will of man, or that will less repugnant to the dictates of the beautiful and the true, as during the century which preceded the death of Socrates. Of no other epoch in the history of our species have we records and fragments stamped so visibly with the image of the divinity in man. But it is Poetry alone, in form, in action, or in language, which has rendered this epoch memorable above all others, and the storehouse of examples to everlasting time. For written poetry existed at that epoch simultaneously with the other arts, and it is an idle enquiry to demand which gave and which received the light, which all, as from a common focus, have scattered over the darkest periods of succeeding age. We know no more of cause and effect than a constant conjunction of events: Poetry is ever found to coexist with whatever other arts contribute to the happiness and perfection of man. I appeal to what has already been established to distinguish between the cause and the effect.

It was at the period here adverted to, that the Drama had its birth; and however a succeeding writer may have equalled or surpassed those few great specimens of the Athenian drama which have been preserved to us, it is indisputable that the art itself never was understood or practised according to the true philosophy of it, as at Athens. For the Athenians employed language, action, music, painting, the dance, and religious institutions, to produce a common effect in the representation of the loftiest idealisms of passion and of power; each division in the art was made perfect in its kind by artists of the most consummate skill, and was disciplined into a beautiful proportion and unity one towards another. On the modern stage a few only of the elements capable of expressing the image of the poet's conception are employed at once. We have tragedy without music and dancing; and music and dancing without the high impersonations of which they are the fit accompaniment, and both without religion and solemnity; religious institution has indeed been usually banished from the stage. Our system of divesting the actor's face of a mask, on which the many expressions appropriated to his dramatic character might be moulded into one permanent and unchanging expression, is favourable only to a partial and inharmonious effect; it is fit for nothing but a monologue, where all the attention may be directed to some great master of ideal mimicry. The modern practice of blending comedy with tragedy, though liable to great abuse in point of practice, is undoubtedly an extension of the dramatic circle; but the comedy should be as in King Lear, universal, ideal, and sublime. It is perhaps the intervention of this principle which determines the balance in favour of King Lear against the Œdipus Tyrannus or the Agamemnon, or, if you will the trilogies with which they are connected; unless the intense power of the choral poetry, especially that of the latter, should be considered as restoring the equilibrium. King Lear, if it can sustain this comparison, may be judged to be the most perfect specimen of the dramatic art existing in the world; in spite of the narrow conditions to which the poet was subjected by the ignorance of the philosophy of the drama which has prevailed in modern Europe. Calderon, in his religious Autos,[a] has attempted to fulfil some of the high conditions of dramatic representation neglected by Shakspeare; such as the establishing a relation between the drama and religion, and the accommodating them to music and dancing; but he omits the observation of conditions still more important, and more is lost than gained by a substitution of the rigidly-defined and ever-repeated idealisms of a distorted superstition for the living impersonations of the truth of human passion.

But we digress. – The Author of the Four Ages of Poetry has prudently omitted to dispute on the effect of the Drama upon life and manners. For, if I know the Knight by the device of his shield, I have only to inscribe Philoctetes or Agamemnon or Othello upon mine to put to flight the giant sophisms which have enchanted him, as the mirror of intolerable light though on the arm of one of the weakest of the Paladines could blind and scatter whole armies of necromancers and pagans. The connexion of scenic exhibitions with the improvement or corruption of the manners of men, has been universally recognised: in other words, the presence or absence of poetry in its most perfect and universal form, has been found to be connected with good and evil in conduct and habit. The corruption which has been imputed to the drama as an effect, begins, when the poetry employed in its constitution ends: I appeal to the history of manners whether the gradations of the growth of the one and the decline of the other have not corresponded with an exactness equal to any other example of moral cause and effect.[4]

[a] The *autos sacramentales* of the Spanish dramatist Calderón (1600–81) were allegorical representations of the Catholic theology.

The drama at Athens, or wheresoever else it may have approached to its perfection, coexisted with the moral and intellectual greatness of the age. The tragedies of the Athenian poets are as mirrors in which the spectator beholds himself, under a thin disguise of circumstance, stript of all but the ideal perfection and energy which every one feels to be the internal type of all that he loves, admires, and would become. The imagination is enlarged by a sympathy with pains and passions so mighty, that they distend in their conception the capacity of that by which they are conceived; the good affections are strengthened by pity, indignation, terror and sorrow; and an exalted calm is prolonged from the satiety of this high exercise of them into the tumult of familiar life: even crime is disarmed of half its horror and all its contagion by being represented as the fatal consequence of the unfathomable agencies of nature; error is thus divested of its wilfulness; men can no longer cherish it as the creation of their choice. In a drama of the highest order there is little food for censure or hatred; it teaches rather self-knowledge and self-respect. Neither the eye nor the mind can see itself, unless reflected upon that which it resembles. The drama, so long as it continues to express poetry, is as a prismatic and many-sided mirror, which collects the brightest rays of human nature and divides and reproduces them from the simplicity of these elementary forms, and touches them with majesty and beauty, and multiplies all that it reflects, and endows it with the power of propagating its like wherever it may fall.

But in periods of the decay of social life, the drama sympathises with that decay. Tragedy becomes a cold imitation of the form of the great masterpieces of antiquity, divested of all harmonious accompaniment of the kindred arts; and often the very form misunderstood, or a weak attempt to teach certain doctrines, which the writer considers as moral truths, and which are usually no more than specious flatteries of some gross vice or weakness, with which the author, in common with his auditors, are infected. Hence what has been called the classicial and domestic drama. Addison's "Cato" is a specimen of the one; and would it were not superfluous to cite examples of the other! To such purposes poetry cannot be made subservient. Poetry is a sword of lightning, ever unsheathed, which consumes the scabbard that would contain it. And thus we observe that all dramatic writings of this nature are unimaginative in a singular degree; they affect sentiment and passion, which divested of imagination, are other names for caprice and appetite. The period in our own history of the grossest degradation of the drama is the reign of Charles II., when all forms in which poetry had been accustomed to be expressed became hymns to the triumph of kingly power over liberty and virtue. Milton stood alone illuminating an age unworthy of him. At such periods the calculating principle pervades all the forms of dramatic exhibition, and poetry ceases to be expressed upon them. Comedy loses its ideal universality: wit succeeds to humour; we laugh from self complacency and triumph, instead of pleasure; malignity, sarcasm and contempt, succeed to sympathetic merriment; we hardly laugh, but we smile. Obscenity, which is ever blasphemy against the divine beauty in life, becomes, from the very veil which it assumes, more active if less disgusting: it is a monster for which the corruption of society for ever brings forth new food, which it devours in secret.

The drama being that form under which a greater number of modes of expression of poetry are susceptible of being combined than any other, the connexion of poetry and social good is more observable in the drama than in whatever other form. And it is indisputable that the highest perfection of human society has ever corresponded with the highest dramatic excellence; and that the corruption or the extinction of the drama in a nation where it has once flourished, is a mark of a corruption of manners, and an extinction of the energies which sustain the soul of social life. But, as Machiavelli says of political institutions, that life may be preserved and renewed, if men should arise capable of bringing back the drama to its principles. And this is true with respect to poetry in its most extended sense; all language institution and form, require not only to be produced but to be sustained: the office and character of a poet participates in the divine nature as regards providence, no less than as regards creation.

Civil war, the spoils of Asia, and the fatal predominance first of the Macedonian, and then of the Roman arms, were so many symbols of the extinction or suspension of the creative faculty in Greece. The bucolic writers,[a] who found patronage under the lettered tyrants of Sicily and Egypt, were the latest representatives of its most glorious reign. Their poetry is intensely melodious; like the odour of the tuberose, it overcomes and sickens the spirit with excess of sweetness; whilst the poetry of the preceding age was as a meadow-gale of June, which mingles the fragrance of all the flowers of the field, and adds a quickening and harmonising spirit of its own which endows the sense with a power of sustaining its extreme delight. The bucolic and erotic delicacy in written poetry is correlative with that softness in statuary, music, and the kindred arts, and even in manners and institutions, which distinguished the epoch to which we now refer. Nor is it the

---

[a] Alexandrian poets, at least one of whom (Theocritus) is prominently named below

poetical faculty itself, or any misapplication of it, to which this want of harmony is to be imputed. An equal sensibility to the influence of the senses and the affections is to be found in the writings of Homer and Sophocles: the former, especially, has clothed sensual and pathetic images with irresistible attractions. Their superiority over these succeeding writers consists in the presence of those thoughts which belong to the inner faculties of our nature, not in the absence of those which are connected with the external: their incomparable perfection consists in an harmony of the union of all. It is not what the erotic writers have, but what they have not, in which their imperfection consists. It is not inasmuch as they were Poets, but inasmuch as they were not Poets, that they can be considered with any plausibility as connected with the corruption of their age. Had that corruption availed so as to extinguish in them the sensibility to pleasure, passion, and natural scenery, which is imputed to them as an imperfection, the last triumph of evil would have been achieved. For the end of social corruption is to destroy all sensibility to pleasure; and, therefore, it is corruption. It begins at the imagination and the intellect at the core, and distributes itself thence as a paralysing venom, through the affections into the very appetites, till all become a torpid mass in which sense hardly survives. At the approach of such a period, Poetry ever addresses itself to those faculties which are the last to be destroyed, and its voice is heard, like the footsteps of Astræa,[a] departing from the world. Poetry ever communicates all the pleasure which men are capable of receiving: it is ever still the light of life; the source of whatever of beautiful or generous or true can have place in an evil time. It will readily be confessed that those among the luxurious citizens of Syracuse and Alexandria, who were delighted with the poems of Theocritus, were less cold, cruel, and sensual than the remnant of their tribe. But corruption must have utterly destroyed the fabric of human society before poetry can ever cease. The sacred links of that chain have never been entirely disjoined, which descending through the minds of many men is attached to those great minds, whence as from a magnet the invisible effluence is sent forth, which at once connects, animates and sustains the life of all. It is the faculty which contains within itself the seeds at once of its own and of social renovation. And let us not circumscribe the effects of the bucolic and erotic poetry within the limits of the sensibility of those to whom it was addressed. They may have perceived the beauty of those immortal compositions, simply as fragments and isolated portions: those who are more finely organised, or born in a happier

[a] goddess of justice; when the world grew corrupt, she took her place among the stars, as Virgo

age, may recognise them as episodes to that great poem, which all poets, like the co-operating thoughts of one great mind, have built up since the beginning of the world.

The same revolutions within a narrower sphere had place in antient Rome; but the actions and forms of its social life never seem to have been perfectly saturated with the poetical element. The Romans appear to have considered the Greeks as the selectest treasuries of the selectest forms of manners and of nature, and to have abstained from creating in measured language, sculpture, music, or architecture, any thing which might bear a particular relation to their own condition, whilst it might bear a general one to the universal constitution of the world. But we judge from partial evidence, and we judge perhaps partially. Ennius, Varro, Pacuvius, and Accius, all great poets, have been lost. Lucretius is in the highest, and Virgil in a very high sense, a creator. The chosen delicacy of the expressions of the latter, are as a mist of light which conceal from us the intense and exceeding truth of his conceptions of nature. Livy is instinct with poetry. Yet Horace, Catullus, Ovid, and generally the other great writers of the Virgilian age, saw man and nature in the mirror of Greece. The institutions also, and the religion of Rome, were less poetical than those of Greece, as the shadow is less vivid than the substance. Hence poetry in Rome, seemed to follow, rather than accompany, the perfection of political and domestic society. The true poetry of Rome lived in its institutions; for whatever of beautiful, true, and majestic, they contained, could have sprung only from the faculty which creates the order in which they consist. The life of Camillus, the death of Regulus; the expectation of the Senators, in their godlike state, of the victorious Gauls; the refusal of the Republic to make peace with Hannibal, after the battle of Cannæ, were not the consequences of a refined calculation of the probable personal advantage to result from such a rhythm and order in the shews of life, to those who were at once the poets and the actors of these immortal dramas. The imagination beholding the beauty of this order, created it out of itself according to its own idea; the consequence was empire, and the reward ever-living fame. These things are not the less poetry, *quia carent vate sacro.*[a] They are the episodes of that cyclic poem written by Time upon the memories of men. The Past, like an inspired rhapsodist, fills the theatre of everlasting generations with their harmony.

At length the antient system of religion and manners had fulfilled the circle of its revolution. And the world would have fallen into utter

---

[a] because they lack a sacred oracle (loosely, "because they are not *called* poetry"), from Horace, *Odes*, Book IV, ix, line 28

anarchy and darkness, but that there were found poets among the authors of the Christian and Chivalric systems of manners and religion, who created forms of opinion and action never before conceived; which, copied into the imaginations of men, became as generals to the bewildered armies of their thoughts. It is foreign to the present purpose to touch upon the evil produced by these systems: except that we protest, on the ground of the principles already established, that no portion of it can be imputed to the poetry they contain.

It is probable that the astonishing poetry of Moses, Job, David, Solomon, and Isaiah, had produced a great effect upon the mind of Jesus and his disciples. The scattered fragments preserved to us by the biographers of this extraordinary person, are all instinct with the most vivid poetry. But his doctrines seem to have been quickly distorted. At a certain period after the prevalence of doctrines founded upon those promulgated by him, the three forms into which Plato had distributed the faculties of mind underwent a sort of apotheosis, and became the object of the worship of Europe.[5] Here it is to be confessed that "Light seems to thicken," and

> "The crow makes wing to the rooky wood,
> Good things of day begin to droop and drowse,
> And night's black agents to their preys do rouse."[a]

But mark how beautiful an order has sprung from the dust and blood of this fierce chaos! how the World, as from a resurrection, balancing itself on the golden wings of knowledge and of hope, has reassumed its yet unwearied flight into the Heaven of time. Listen to the music, unheard by outward ears, which is as a ceaseless and invisible wind, nourishing its everlasting course with strength and swiftness.

The poetry in the doctrines of Jesus Christ, and the mythology and institutions of the Celtic conquerors of the Roman empire, outlived the darkness and the convulsions connected with their growth and victory, and blended themselves into a new fabric of manners and opinion. It is an error to impute the ignorance of the dark ages to the Christian doctrines or the predominance of the Celtic nations. Whatever of evil their agencies may have contained sprang from the extinction of the poetical principle, connected with the progress of despotism and superstition. Men, from causes too intricate to be here discussed, had become insensible and selfish: their own will had become feeble, and yet they were its slaves, and thence the slaves of

[a] *Macbeth*, III. ii. 51–53; answering Peacock's "the darkness thickened with the progress of the light"

the will of others: lust, fear, avarice, cruelty, and fraud, characterised a race amongst whom no one was to be found capable of *creating* in form, language, or institution. The moral anomalies of such a state of society are not justly to be charged upon any class of events immediately connected with them, and those events are most entitled to our approbation which could dissolve it most expeditiously. It is unfortunate for those who cannot distinguish words from thoughts, that many of these anomalies have been incorporated into our popular religion.

It was not until the eleventh century that the effects of the poetry of the Christian and Chivalric systems began to manifest themselves. The principle of equality had been discovered and applied by Plato in his Republic, as the theoretical rule of the mode in which the materials of pleasure and of power produced by the common skill and labour of human beings ought to be distributed among them. The limitations of this rule were asserted by him to be determined only by the sensibility of each, or the utility to result to all.[6] Plato, following the doctrines of Timæus and Pythagoras, taught also a moral and intellectual system of doctrine, comprehending at once the past, the present, and the future condition of man. Jesus Christ divulged the sacred and eternal truths contained in these views to mankind, and Christianity, in its abstract purity, became the exoteric expression of the esoteric doctrines of the poetry and wisdom of antiquity. The incorporation of the Celtic nations with the exhausted population of the south, impressed upon it the figure of the poetry existing in their mythology and institutions. The result was a sum of the action and reaction of all the causes included in it; for it may be assumed as a maxim that no nation or religion can supersede any other without incorporating into itself a portion of that which it supersedes. The abolition of personal and domestic slavery, and the emancipation of women from a great part of the degrading restraints of antiquity, were among the consequences of these events.

The abolition of personal slavery is the basis of the highest political hope that it can enter into the mind of man to conceive. The freedom of women produced the poetry of sexual love. Love became a religion, the idols of whose worship were ever present. It was as if the statues of Apollo and the Muses had been endowed with life and motion, and had walked forth among their worshippers; so that earth became peopled by the inhabitants of a diviner world. The familiar appearance and proceedings of life became wonderful and heavenly; and a paradise was created as out of the wrecks of Eden. And as this creation itself is poetry, so its creators were poets; and language was the instrument of their art: "Galetto fù il libro, e chi lo scrisse."[a] The Provençal Trouveurs,[b] or inventors, preceded Petrarch, whose verses are as spells, which unseal the inmost enchanted fountains of the delight which is in the grief of love. It is impossible to feel them without becoming a portion of that beauty which we contemplate: it were superfluous to explain how the gentleness and the elevation of mind connected with these sacred emotions can render men more amiable, and generous and wise, and lift them out of the dull vapours of the little world of self. Dante understood the secret things of love even more than Petrarch. His *Vita Nuova* is an inexhaustible fountain of purity of sentiment and language: it is the idealised history of that period, and those intervals of his life which were dedicated to love. His apotheosis of Beatrice in Paradise, and the gradations of his own love and her loveliness, by which as by steps he feigns himself to have ascended to the throne of the Supreme Cause, is the most glorious imagination of modern poetry. The acutest critics have justly reversed the judgment of the vulgar, and the order of the great acts of the "Divine Drama," in the measure of the admiration which they accord to the Hell, Purgatory, and Paradise. The latter is a perpetual hymn of everlasting Love. Love, which found a worthy poet in Plato alone of all the antients, has been celebrated by a chorus of the greatest writers of the renovated world; and the music has penetrated the caverns of society, and its echoes still drown the dissonance of arms and superstition. At successive intervals, Ariosto, Tasso, Shakspeare, Spenser, Calderon, Rousseau, and the great writers of our own age, have celebrated the dominion of love, planting as it were trophies in the human mind of that sublimest victory over sensuality and force. The true relation borne to each other by the sexes into which human kind is distributed, has become less misunderstood; and if the error which confounded diversity with inequality of the powers of the two sexes has become partially recognised in the opinions and institutions of modern Europe, we owe this great benefit to the worship of which Chivalry was the law, and poets the prophets.

The poetry of Dante may be considered as the bridge thrown over the stream of time, which unites the modern and antient World. The distorted notions of invisible things which Dante and his rival Milton have idealised, are merely the mask and the mantle in which these great poets walk through eternity enveloped and disguised. It is a difficult question to determine how far they were conscious of the

[a] "The book was the Galehaut, and he that wrote it," from Dante, *Inferno*, v, 137; Galehaut being the knight of King Arthur's court who first arranged a meeting between Lancelot and Guinevere
[b] troubadors

distinction which must have subsisted in their minds between their own creeds and that of the people. Dante at least appears to wish to mark the full extent of it by placing Riphæus, whom Virgil calls *justissimus unus*,[a] in Paradise, and observing a most heretical caprice in his distribution of rewards and punishments. And Milton's poem contains within itself a philosophical refutation of that system, of which, by a strange and natural antithesis, it has been a chief popular support. Nothing can exceed the energy and magnificence of the character of Satan as expressed in "Paradise Lost." It is a mistake to suppose that he could ever have been intended for the popular personification of evil. Implacable hate, patient cunning and a sleepless refinement of device to inflict the extremest anguish on the enemy, these things are evil; and, although venial in a slave, are not to be forgiven in a tyrant; although redeemed by much that ennobles his defeat in one subdued, are marked by all that dishonours his conquest in the victor. Milton's Devil as a moral being is as far superior to his God, as One who perseveres in some purpose which he has conceived to be excellent in spite of adversity and torture, is to One who in the cold security of undoubted triumph inflicts the most horrible revenge upon his enemy, not from any mistaken notion of inducing him to repent of a perseverance in enmity, but with the alleged design of exasperating him to deserve new torments. Milton has so far violated the popular creed (if this shall be judged to be a violation) as to have alleged no superiority of moral virtue to his God over his Devil. And this bold neglect of a direct moral purpose is the most decisive proof of the supremacy of Milton's genius.[7] He mingled as it were the elements of human nature as colours upon a single pallet, and arranged them in the composition of his great picture according to the laws of epic truth; that is, according to the laws of that principle by which a series of actions of the external universe and of intelligent and ethical beings is calculated to excite the sympathy of succeeding generations of mankind. The Divina Commedia and Paradise Lost have conferred upon modern mythology a systematic form; and when change and time shall have added one more superstition to the mass of those which have arisen and decayed upon the earth, commentators will be learnedly employed in elucidating the religion of ancestral Europe, only not utterly forgotten because it will have been stamped with the eternity of genius.

Homer was the first and Dante the second epic poet: that is, the second poet, the series of whose creations bore a defined and intelligible relation to the knowledge and sentiment and religion and

---

[a] most just one; *Aeneid*, II, 426

political conditions of the age in which he lived, and of the ages which followed it; developing itself in correspondence with their development. For Lucretius had limed the Wings of his swift spirit in the dregs of the sensible world; and Virgil, with a modesty which ill became his genius, had affected the fame of an imitator, even whilst he created anew all that he copied; and none among the flock of Mock-birds, though their notes were sweet, Apollonius Rhodius, Quintus Calaber Smyrnetheus, Nonnus, Lucan, Statius, or Claudian,[8] have sought even to fulfil a single condition of epic truth. Milton was the third epic poet. For if the title of epic in its highest sense be refused to the Æneid, still less can it be conceded to the Orlando Furioso, the Gerusalemme Liberata, the Lusiad, or the Fairy Queen.[9]

Dante and Milton were both deeply penetrated with the antient religion of the civilized world; and its spirit exists in their poetry probably in the same proportion as its forms survived in the unreformed worship of modern Europe. The one preceded and the other followed the Reformation at almost equal intervals. Dante was the first religious reformer, and Luther surpassed him rather in the rudeness and acrimony, than in the boldness of his censures of papal usurpation. Dante was the first awakener of entranced Europe; he created a language, in itself music and persuasion, out of a chaos of inharmonious barbarisms. He was the congregator of those great spirits who presided over the resurrection of learning; the Lucifer[a] of that starry flock which in the thirteenth century shone forth from republican Italy, as from a heaven, into the darkness of the benighted world. His very words are instinct with spirit; each is as a spark, a burning atom of inextinguishable thought; and many yet lie covered in the ashes of their birth, and pregnant with a lightning which has yet found no conductor. All high poetry is infinite; it is as the first acorn, which contained all oaks potentially. Veil after veil may be undrawn, and the inmost naked beauty of the meaning never exposed. A great poem is a fountain for ever overflowing with the waters of wisdom and delight; and after one person and one age has exhausted all its divine effluence which their peculiar relations enable them to share, another and yet another succeeds, and new relations are ever developed, the source of an unforeseen and an unconceived delight.

The age immediately succeeding to that of Dante, Petrarch, and Boccaccio, was characterized by a revival of painting, sculpture, music, and architecture. Chaucer caught the sacred inspiration, and

---

[a] the morning star; by name also suggesting a link between the defense of Dante here and of Milton two paragraphs earlier

the superstructure of English literature is based upon the materials of Italian invention.

But let us not be betrayed from a defence into a critical history of Poetry and its influence on Society. Be it enough to have pointed out the effects of poets, in the large and true sense of the word, upon their own and all succeeding times, and to revert to the partial instances cited as illustrations of an opinion the reverse of that attempted to be established by the Author of the Four Ages of Poetry.

But poets have been challenged to resign the civic crown to reasoners and mechanists on another plea. It is admitted that the exercise of the imagination is most delightful, but it is alleged, that that of reason is more useful. Let us examine as the grounds of this distinction, what is here meant by utility. Pleasure or good, in a general sense, is that which the consciousness of a sensitive and intelligent being seeks, and in which, when found, it acquiesces. There are two modes or degrees of pleasure, one durable, universal and permanent; the other transitory and particular. Utility may either express the means of producing the former or the latter. In the former sense, whatever strengthens and purifies the affections, enlarges the imagination, and adds spirit to sense, is useful. But the meaning in which the Author of the Four Ages of Poetry seems to have employed the word utility is the narrower one of banishing the importunity of the wants of our animal nature, the surrounding men with security of life, the dispersing the grosser delusions of superstition, and the conciliating such a degree of mutual forbearance among men as may consist with the motives of personal advantage.

Undoubtedly the promoters of utility, in this limited sense, have their appointed office in society. They follow the footsteps of poets, and copy the sketches of their creations into the book of common life. They make space, and give time. Their exertions are of the highest value, so long as they confine their administration of the concerns of the inferior powers of our nature within the limits due to the superior ones. But whilst the sceptic destroys gross superstitions, let him spare to deface, as some of the French writers have defaced, the eternal truths charactered upon the imaginations of men. Whilst the mechanist abridges, and the political economist combines, labour, let them beware that their speculations, for want of correspondence with those first principles which belong to the imagination, do not tend, as they have in modern England, to exasperate at once the extremes of luxury and want. They have exemplified the saying, "To him that hath, more shall be given; and from him that hath not, the little that he hath shall be taken away." The rich have become richer, and the poor have become poorer; and the vessel of the state is driven between the Scylla and Charybdis of anarchy and despotism. Such are the effects which must ever flow from an unmitigated exercise of the calculating faculty.[10]

It is difficult to define pleasure in its highest sense; the definition involving a number of apparent paradoxes. For, from an inexplicable defect of harmony in the constitution of human nature, the pain of the inferior is frequently connected with the pleasures of the superior portions of our being. Sorrow, terror, anguish, despair itself, are often the chosen expressions of an approximation to the highest good. Our sympathy in tragic fiction depends on this principle; tragedy delights by affording a shadow of the pleasure which exists in pain. This is the source also of the melancholy which is inseparable from the sweetest melody. The pleasure that is in sorrow is sweeter than the pleasure of pleasure itself. And hence the saying, "It is better to go to the house of mourning, than to the house of mirth." Not that this highest species of pleasure is necessarily linked with pain. The delight of love and friendship, the ecstasy of the admiration of nature, the joy of the perception and still more of the creation of poetry is often wholly unalloyed.

The production and assurance of pleasure in this highest sense is true utility. Those who produce and preserve this pleasure are Poets or poetical philosophers.

The exertions of Locke, Hume, Gibbon, Voltaire, Rousseau,[11] and their disciples, in favour of oppressed and deluded humanity, are entitled to the gratitude of mankind. Yet it is easy to calculate the degree of moral and intellectual improvement which the world would have exhibited, had they never lived. A little more nonsense would have been talked for a century or two; and perhaps a few more men, women, and children, burnt as heretics. We might not at this moment have been congratulating each other on the abolition of the Inquisition in Spain. But it exceeds all imagination to conceive what would have been the moral condition of the world if neither Dante, Petrarch, Boccaccio, Chaucer, Shakspeare, Calderon, Lord Bacon, nor Milton, had ever existed; if Raphael and Michael Angelo had never been born; if the Hebrew poetry had never been translated; if a revival of the study of Greek literature had never taken place; if no monuments of antient sculpture had been handed down to us; and if the poetry of the religion of the antient world had been extinguished together with its belief. The human mind could never, except by the intervention of these excitements, have been awakened to the invention of the grosser sciences, and that application of analytical reasoning to the aberrations of society, which it is now attempted to exalt over the direct expression of the inventive and creative faculty itself.

We have more moral, political and historical wisdom, than we know how to reduce into practice; we have more scientific and economical knowledge than can be accommodated to the just distribution of the produce which it multiplies. The poetry in these systems of thought, is concealed by the accumulation of facts and calculating processes. There is no want of knowledge respecting what is wisest and best in morals, government, and political economy, or at least, what is wiser and better than what men now practise and endure. But we let "*I dare not* wait upon *I would,* like the poor cat i' the adage."[a] We want the creative faculty to imagine that which we know; we want the generous impulse to act that which we imagine; we want the poetry of life: our calculations have outrun conception; we have eaten more than we can digest. The cultivation of those sciences which have enlarged the limits of the empire of man over the external world, has, for want of the poetical faculty, proportionally circumscribed those of the internal world; and man, having enslaved the elements, remains himself a slave. To what but a cultivation of the mechanical arts in a degree disproportioned to the presence of the creative faculty, which is the basis of all knowledge, is to be attributed the abuse of all invention for abridging and combining labour, to the exasperation of the inequality of mankind? From what other cause has it arisen that these inventions which should have lightened, have added a weight to the curse imposed on Adam? Thus Poetry, and the principle of Self, of which Money is the visible incarnation, are the God and Mammon of the world.

The functions of the poetical faculty are twofold; by one it creates new materials for knowledge, and power and pleasure; by the other it engenders in the mind a desire to reproduce and arrange them according to a certain rhythm and order which may be called the beautiful and the good. The cultivation of poetry is never more to be desired than at periods when, from an excess of the selfish and calculating principle, the accumulation of the materials of external life exceed the quantity of the power of assimilating them to the internal laws of human nature. The body has then become too unwieldy for that which animates it.

Poetry is indeed something divine. It is at once the centre and circumference of knowledge; it is that which comprehends all science, and that to which all science must be referred. It is at the same time the root and blossom of all other systems of thought; it is that

[a] *Macbeth,* I. vii. 44–45

from which all spring, and that which adorns all; and that which, if blighted, denies the fruit and the seed, and withholds from the barren world the nourishment and the succession of the scions of the tree of life. It is the perfect and consummate surface and bloom of things; it is as the odour and the colour of the rose to the texture of the elements which compose it, as the form and the splendour of unfaded beauty to the secrets of anatomy and corruption. What were Virtue, Love, Patriotism, Friendship – what were the scenery of this beautiful Universe which we inhabit; what were our consolations on this side of the grave, and what were our aspirations beyond it, if Poetry did not ascend to bring light and fire from those eternal regions where the owl-winged faculty of calculation dare not ever soar? Poetry is not like reasoning, a power to be exerted according to the determination of the will. A man cannot say, "I will compose poetry." The greatest poet even cannot say it: for the mind in creation is as a fading coal, which some invisible influence, like an inconstant wind, awakens to transitory brightness: this power arises from within, like the colour of a flower which fades and changes as it is developed, and the conscious portions of our natures are unprophetic either of its approach or its departure. Could this influence be durable in its original purity and force, it is impossible to predict the greatness of the results; but when composition begins, inspiration is already on the decline, and the most glorious poetry that has ever been communicated to the world is probably a feeble shadow of the original conception of the Poet. I appeal to the great poets of the present day, whether it be not an error to assert that the finest passages of poetry are produced by labour and study. The toil and the delay recommended by critics, can be justly interpreted to mean no more than a careful observation of the inspired moments, and an artificial connexion of the spaces between their suggestions by the intertexture of conventional expressions; a necessity only imposed by the limitedness of the poetical faculty itself. For Milton conceived the Paradise Lost as a whole before he executed it in portions. We have his own authority also for the Muse having "dictated" to him the "unpremeditated song,"[a] and let this be an answer to those who would allege the fifty-six various readings of the first line of the Orlando Furioso. Compositions so produced are to poetry what mosaic is to painting. This instinct and intuition of the poetical faculty is still more observable in the plastic and pictorial arts; a great statue or picture grows under the power of the artist as a child in the mother's womb; and the very mind which directs the hands in

[a] *Paradise Lost*, IX. 23–24

formation is incapable of accounting to itself for the origin, the gradations, or the media of the process.

Poetry is the record of the best and happiest moments of the happiest and best minds. We are aware of evanescent visitations of thought and feeling sometimes associated with place or person, sometimes regarding our own mind alone, and always arising unforeseen and departing unbidden, but elevating and delightful beyond all expression: so that even in the desire and the regret they leave, there cannot but be pleasure, participating as it does in the nature of its object. It is as it were the interpenetration of a diviner nature through our own; but its footsteps are like those of a wind over a sea, which the coming calm erases, and whose traces remain only, as on the wrinkled sand which paves it.[a] These and corresponding conditions of being are experienced principally by those of the most delicate sensibility and the most enlarged imagination; and the state of mind produced by them is at war with every base desire. The enthusiasm of virtue, love, patriotism, and friendship, is essentially linked with these emotions; and whilst they last, self appears as what it is, an atom to a Universe. Poets are not only subject to these experiences as spirits of the most refined organisation, but they can colour all that they combine with the evanescent hues of this ethereal world; a word, or a trait in the representation of a scene or a passion, will touch the enchanted chord, and reanimate, in those who have ever experienced these emotions, the sleeping, the cold, the buried image of the past. Poetry thus makes immortal all that is best and most beautiful in the world; it arrests the vanishing apparitions which haunt the interlunations of life, and veiling them, or in language or in form, sends them forth among mankind, bearing sweet news of kindred joy to those with whom their sisters abide – abide, because there is no portal of expression from the caverns of the spirit which they inhabit into the universe of things. Poetry redeems from decay the visitations of the divinity in Man.

Poetry turns all things to loveliness; it exalts the beauty of that which is most beautiful, and it adds beauty to that which is most deformed; it marries exultation and horror, grief and pleasure, eternity and change; it subdues to union under its light yoke, all irreconcilable things. It transmutes all that it touches, and every form moving within the radiance of its presence is changed by wondrous

[a] a strong echo of Locke, *Essay Concerning Human Understanding*, Book II, chapter 10.4: "*Ideas* in the Mind quickly fade, and often vanish quite out of the Understanding, leaving no more footsteps or remaining Characters of themselves, than Shadows do flying over Fields of Corn; and the Mind is as void of them, as if they never had been there."

sympathy to an incarnation of the spirit which it breathes; its secret alchemy turns to potable gold the poisonous waters which flow from death through life; it strips the veil of familiarity from the world, and lays bare the naked and sleeping beauty, which is the spirit of its forms.

All things exist as they are perceived; at least in relation to the percipient. "The mind is its own place, and of itself can make a Heaven of Hell, a Hell of Heaven."[a] But poetry defeats the curse which binds us to be subjected to the accident of surrounding impressions. And whether it spreads its own figured curtain, or withdraws life's dark veil from before the scene of things, it equally creates for us a being within our being. It makes us the inhabitants of a world to which the familiar world is a chaos. It reproduces the common Universe of which we are portions and percipients, and it purges from our inward sight the film of familiarity which obscures from us the wonder of our being. It compels us to feel that which we perceive, and to imagine that which we know. It creates anew the universe, after it has been annihilated in our minds by the recurrence of impressions blunted by reiteration. It justifies that bold and true word of Tasso: *Non merita nome di creatore, se non Iddio ed il Poeta.*[b]

A poet, as he is the author to others of the highest wisdom, pleasure, virtue and glory, so he ought personally to be the happiest, the best, the wisest, and the most illustrious of men. As to his glory, let Time be challenged to declare whether the fame of any other institutor of human life be comparable to that of a poet. That he is the wisest, the happiest, and the best, inasmuch as he is a poet, is equally incontrovertible: the greatest Poets have been men of the most spotless virtue, of the most consummate prudence, and, if we could look into the interior of their lives, the most fortunate of men: and the exceptions, as they regard those who possessed the imaginative faculty in a high yet inferior degree, will be found on consideration to confirm rather than destroy the rule.[12] Let us for a moment stoop to the arbitration of popular breath, and usurping and uniting in our own persons the incompatible characters of accuser, witness, judge and executioner, let us without trial, testimony, or form, determine that certain motives of those who are "there sitting where we dare not soar,"[c] are reprehensible. Let us assume that Homer was a drunkard, that Virgil was a flatterer, that Horace was a coward, that Tasso was a madman, that Lord Bacon was a peculator, that Raphael was a libertine, that Spenser was a poet laureate. It is inconsistent with this

---

[a] *Paradise Lost*, I. 254–55   [b] None merits the name of creator, except God and the poet
[c] *Paradise Lost*, IV. 829

division of our subject to cite living poets, but Posterity has done ample justice to the great names now referred to. Their errors have been weighed and found to have been dust in the balance; if their sins were as scarlet, they are now white as snow: they have been washed in the blood of the mediator and the redeemer, Time. Observe in what a ludicrous chaos the imputations of real or fictitious crime have been confused in the contemporary calumnies against poetry and poets; consider how little is, as it appears – or appears, as it is; look to your own motives, and judge not, lest ye be judged.

Poetry, as has been said, in this respect differs from logic, that it is not subject to the control of the active powers of the mind, and that its birth and recurrence has no necessary connexion with consciousness or will. It is presumptuous to determine that these are the necessary conditions of all mental causation, when mental effects are experienced insusceptible of being referred to them. The frequent recurrence of the poetical power, it is obvious to suppose, may produce in the mind an habit of order and harmony correlative with its own nature and with its effects upon other minds. But in the intervals of inspiration, and they may be frequent without being durable, a Poet becomes a man, and is abandoned to the sudden reflux of the influences under which others habitually live. But as he is more delicately organized than other men, and sensible to pain and pleasure, both his own and that of others, in a degree unknown to them, he will avoid the one and pursue the other with an ardour proportioned to this difference. And he renders himself obnoxious to calumny, when he neglects to observe the circumstances under which these objects of universal pursuit and flight have disguised themselves in one another's garments.

But there is nothing necessarily evil in this error, and thus cruelty, envy, revenge, avarice, and the passions purely evil, have never formed any portion of the popular imputations on the lives of poets.

I have thought it most favourable to the cause of truth to set down these remarks according to the order in which they were suggested to my mind, by a consideration of the subject itself, instead of following that of the treatise that excited me to make them public. Thus although devoid of the formality of a polemical reply; if the view they contain be just, they will be found to involve a refutation of the doctrines of the Four Ages of Poetry, so far at least as regards the first division of the subject. I can readily conjecture what should have moved the gall of the learned and intelligent author of that paper; I confess myself, like him, unwilling to be stunned by the Theseids of the hoarse Codri of the day. Bavius and Mævius undoubtedly are, as they ever were, insufferable persons. But it belongs to a philosophical critic to distinguish rather than confound.

The first part of these remarks has related to Poetry in its elements and principles; and it has been shewn, as well as the narrow limits assigned them would permit, that what is called poetry, in a restricted sense, has a common source with all other forms of order and of beauty, according to which the materials of human life are susceptible of being arranged, and which is Poetry in an universal sense.

The second part will have for its object an application of these principles to the present state of the cultivation of Poetry, and a defence of the attempt to idealize the modern forms of manners and opinions, and compel them into a subordination to the imaginative and creative faculty. For the literature of England, an energetic development of which has ever preceded or accompanied a great and free development of the national will, has arisen as it were from a new birth. In spite of the low-thoughted envy which would undervalue contemporary merit, our own will be a memorable age in intellectual achievements, and we live among such philosophers and poets as surpass beyond comparison any who have appeared since the last national struggle for civil and religious liberty. The most unfailing herald, companion, and follower of the awakening of a great people to work a beneficial change in opinion or institution, is Poetry. At such periods there is an accumulation of the power of communicating and receiving intense and impassioned conceptions respecting man and nature. The persons in whom this power resides, may often as far as regards many portions of their nature, have little apparent correspondence with that spirit of good of which they are the ministers. But even whilst they deny and abjure, they are yet compelled to serve, the Power which is seated upon the throne of their own soul. It is impossible to read the compositions of the most celebrated writers of the present day without being startled with the electric life which burns within their words. They measure the circumference and sound the depths of human nature with a comprehensive and all-penetrating spirit, and they are themselves perhaps the most sincerely astonished at its manifestations; for it is less their spirit than the spirit of the age. Poets are the hierophants of an unapprehended inspiration; the mirrors of the gigantic shadows which futurity casts upon the present; the words which express what they understand not; the trumpets which sing to battle, and feel not what they inspire; the influence which is moved not, but moves. Poets are the unacknowledged legislators of the world.

Notes

INTRODUCTORY ESSAY

1 Samuel Johnson, *The Rambler*, ed. W. J. Bate and Albrecht B. Strauss, in *Works* (Yale edition, 1969), vol. 3, p. 205; and Oliver Goldsmith, "A Comparison between Sentimental and Laughing Comedy," in *Works*, ed. Arthur Friedman (Oxford, 1966), vol. 3, pp. 212–13.

2 Two articles, by Alan Liu and Mary Jacobus, have inquired into Wordsworth's conscious effort, in *The Prelude*, to give certain memories a special power by providing them with a secure genre to inhabit. Both scholars conclude that the effort visibly falters. In this questioning of the genres, they have been anticipated by Wordsworth himself, in the preponderance of his critical writings up to 1815. See Alan Liu, "'Shapeless Eagerness': The Genre of Revolution in Books 9 and 10 of *The Prelude*," *Modern Language Quarterly*, 43 (1982), no. 1, pp. 3–28; and Mary Jacobus, "The Law of/and Gender: Genre Theory and *The Prelude*," *Diacritics*, 14 (1984), no. 4, pp. 47–57.

3 Hazlitt, *Works*, ed. P. P. Howe, 21 vols. (1930–34), vol. 16, p. 206.

4 Bacon, *Advancement of Learning* (1951), II. xiv. 9, p. 153.

5 An 1817 letter to a friend, from the twenty-three year old Whewell, expresses his satisfaction on a first reading of the *Biographia*: "I find it full of good sense and fair rational criticism, and containing a condemnation of all those parts of Wordsworth, both of his theory and his practice, to which I should object – denying his whole theory about poetical diction and the resemblance of poetry to real life, and low life, and blaming almost all those poems which he has written upon his theory, condemning his prosaic style, his puerilities, his mystical and inflated language, and wonderments about the most every-day things, his *matter-of-factness*, his attachment to pedlars, his deification of children." Thus, "almost everything, that other people have made a pretext for laughing at the whole, he takes out and laughs at by itself." Mrs. Stair Douglas, *The Life and Selections from the Correspondence of William Whewell* (1881), p. 28.

6 Hazlitt, *Works*, vol. 16, pp. 121–22.

7 Quoted in Philip Connisbee, *Painting in Eighteenth-Century France* (Oxford, 1981), p. 193.

8 Schiller, *Letters*, trans. Reginald Snell (New York, 1965), p. 101.

9 *Ibid.*, p. 137.

10 Johnson, *Preface to Shakespeare*, in *Works*, ed. Arthur Sherbo (Yale Edition, 1968), vol. 7, p. 64.

11 Schlegel, "On Incomprehensibility," in *German Aesthetic and Literary*

Criticism: The Romantic Ironists and Goethe, ed. Kathleen M. Wheeler (1984), p. 33.

12 This was roughly the path taken by Paul de Man, from his reading of Schlegel for "The Rhetoric of Temporality," in Charles Singleton, ed., *Interpretation* (Baltimore, 1969), to his essays on Rousseau in *Allegories of Reading* (1979).

13 Hazlitt, *Works*, vol. 17, p. 118.

14 Schlegel, "Critical Fragments," in Wheeler, ed., *German Aesthetic and Literary Criticism*, p. 41.

15 John Ashbery, "And *Ut Pictura Poesis* Is Her Name," in *Houseboat Days* (New York, 1977), p. 45.

16 Hunt, *Wit and Humor, Selected from the English Poets* (New York, 1846), p. 204.

17 Hazlitt, *Works*, vol. 5, pp. 161–62.

18 Schiller, *Letters*, p. 53.

19 A forceful polemic against the "teleological" fallacy of anachronistic usage, respecting the early nineteenth century particularly, may be found in J. C. D. Clark, *English Society 1688–1832* (1985). The contraction of explanatory scope, however, which follows from this and similar arguments, is so extreme as to prove the impracticability of thinking at all without a degree of anachronism.

20 Sidney, *Apologie for Poetry*, ed. J. Churton Collins (Oxford, 1907), p. 45.

21 Shelley, *Critical Prose*, ed. Bruce R. McElderry, Jr. (Lincoln, Nebraska, 1967), p. 64.

WILLIAM WORDSWORTH, "ESSAY, SUPPLEMENTARY TO THE PREFACE" [OF 1815]

1 Notwithstanding his strictures on Samuel Johnson elsewhere in the essay, Wordsworth here echoes Johnson's argument against devotional poetry in the *Life of Waller*: "The ideas of Christian theology are too simple for eloquence, too sacred for fiction, and too majestic for ornament; to recommend them by tropes and figures, is to magnify by a concave mirror the sidereal hemisphere."

2 Guillaume de Salluste Dubartas (1544–90), author of a two-part epic in French concerning the creation of the earth. Wordsworth alludes to the *Premiere Sepmaine*. Ludovico Ariosto (1474–1535), one of the great figures of the Italian Renaissance, wrote *Orlando Furioso* – an epic, with elements of self-mockery, which deals with Charlemagne's fight against the Saracens.

3 Elkanah Settle and Thomas Shadwell were Grub Street hacks familiar to Dryden's readers and among the favorite butts of his satire.

4 Voltaire, in fact, had wavered in his condescension to Shakespeare, but he once spoke of "this writer's monstrous Farces, to which the name of Tragedy is given."

5 Friedrich Melchior, Baron Grimm (1723–1807) made the observations on Shakespeare in his *Correspondence*, an edition of which had lately been published. Comparing Shakespeare with Racine, he likened the former to

a "colossal statue, of which the conception is imposing and terrific, but the execution by turns crude, indifferent, and the work of the most delicate tact." By contrast, Racine was praiseworthy for his nobleness and elegance throughout, with a regularity as finely proportioned as that of the Apollo Belvedere.

6 An Augustan annotator of Shakespeare's works, as well as a commentator on them, Steevens collaborated with Samuel Johnson in his edition of 1773.

7 Johann Heinrich Voss (1751–1826) attempted free adaptations into German of both "L'Allegro" and "Il Penseroso."

8 The relevant passage occurs in the Preface to the 1814 edition of *The Excursion*: "I sing: – 'fit audience let me find though few!' / So prayed, more gaining than he asked, the Bard – / In holiest mood." The context of this assertion, as well as its grammar and syntax, allows it to refer at once to Milton and to Wordsworth himself. That Wordsworth should have remembered it as simple praise of *Paradise Lost* suggests the extent of his own identification with Milton.

9 Wordsworth adds the following note: "This opinion seems actually to have been entertained by Adam Smith, the worst critic, David Hume not excepted, that Scotland, a soil to which this sort of weed seems natural, has produced." He probably has in mind the arguments of Smith's essay on "The Imitative Arts" and Hume's "Of the Standard of Taste," both of which give strong conventionalist accounts of critical judgement, though neither suggests that the principles of taste are unstable. The tenor of Wordsworth's comment does not betray more than a passing familiarity with these essays.

10 Anthony Ashley Cooper, Third Earl of Shaftesbury (1671–1713) was the author of *Characteristics*, a miscellaneous set of essays and observations on philosophical topics. Wordsworth, among his other reasons, may have wished to praise Shaftesbury as an early exponent of an aesthetic point of view, by which the beauty of art was associated with virtue in the widest possible sense.

11 The biographer whom Wordsworth quotes is Patrick Murdoch, from a 1762 edition of Thomson's *Works*.

12 In a note Wordsworth quotes as evidence the following lines, from Dryden's *Indian Emperor*.

> CORTES *alone in a nightgown*
> All things are hush'd as Nature's self lay dead;
> The mountains seem to nod their drowsy head.
> The little Birds in dreams their songs repeat,
> And sleeping Flowers beneath the Night-dew sweat:
> Even Lust and Envy sleep; yet Love denies
> Rest to my soul, and slumber to my eyes.

13 This paragraph summarizes and reasserts Wordsworth's aim, first announced in the Preface to *Lyrical Ballads*, "to look steadily at my subject" and to avoid "falsehood of description." His attack on poetic diction – a fault that the Preface associated with the age of sensibility – is now broadened to include Pope and Dryden, fifty and a hundred years before.

14 Joseph Warton (1722–1800) wrote an influential essay on Pope (Part I, 1756; Part II, 1782) which defended the claims of irregular genius against the decorum of reason and sense that still prevailed in the generation after Pope's ascendancy.

15 William Collins's "Ode Occasioned by the Death of Mr. Thomson" imagined a passer-by ignorant of the site of Thomson's grave, and petitioned: "With him, sweet bard, may Fancy die, / And Joy desert the blooming year."

16 Thomas Percy's *Reliques of Ancient English Poetry* (1765) collected versions of the old English ballads. These gave an impetus to the self-conscious antiquarianism of Walter Scott in his shorter poems, and the self-conscious primitivism of Wordsworth and Coleridge in their *Lyrical Ballads*.

17 Gottfried August Bürger (1747–94), whose versions of the ballads, themselves influenced by the example of Percy, had a reciprocal influence on English literature through the writings of Scott and others.

18 Friedrich Gottlieb Klopstock (1724–1803) offered the discriminating criticism that Wordsworth here recalls, in a conversation in Hamburg in 1798.

19 *The Poems of Ossian*, James Macpherson's forgery of a Highland Epic, enjoyed a wide vogue in the latter part of the eighteenth century. By many readers and critics, the work was credited not only as an instance of the sublimity of naive, or folk, genius, but also as a discovery which ought to have great anthropological interest. Wordsworth's mock-encomium is meant as a demonstration that anyone might detect the forgery from the unnaturalness of Macpherson's pretended primitivism.

20 Malcolm Laing (1767–1818), the historian of Scotland, published in 1802 his dissertation on Ossian, to expose the delusion of the poem's authenticity.

21 Apart from her novels, her criticism, and her exposition of the doctrines of the French Enlightenment, Madame de Staël (1766–1817) was important to the English literature of Wordsworth's time as an authority on modern German thought. Her book, *The Influence of Literature upon Society*, was translated in 1812; and the passage to which Wordsworth alludes may be found in chapter 11: "the English, as well as the Germans, have, without doubt, often imitated the ancients, and drawn very useful lessons from that fruitful study; but their original beauties carry a sort of resemblance, a certain poetic grandeur, of which Ossian is the most splendid example."

22 The brother of Napoleon, Lucien Bonaparte was an eloquent Jacobin orator, whose presidency of the Council of 500 assisted Napoleon in his *coup* of the eighteenth of Brumaire. In the notes to his epic, *Charlemagne* (1814), he had, in adjacent sentences, regretted Milton's borrowing of a Plutonian splendor for the scenes of hell in *Paradise Lost*, and paid a glowing tribute to Ossian, as "le barde par excellence." Wordsworth's ironic mention of Lucien's "Epic ambition" mixes an appraisal of the worldly and literary designs of the Bonapartes.

23 Thomas Chatterton (1752–70) presented some of his poems as the

recovered writings of a fifteenth-century monk, Thomas Rowley. Along with the poems of Ossian, these were among the most warmly esteemed forgeries of the period.

24 The inclusion or exclusion of certain authors in Johnson's *Lives of the English Poets* was not, in fact, determined by Johnson himself but by his booksellers, who contracted for the *Lives* as prefaces to a list of poets drawn up in advance.

25 A three-way distinction is here implied between: (1) the public, that is, readers of books in general, whom Wordsworth despises but feels he ought to treat with "as much deference as it is entitled to"; (2) the people, considered as the source and proper subject of all poetry, with whom Wordsworth had seemed to ally himself in the Preface to *Lyrical Ballads*; and (3) the people "philosophically characterised" (i.e. by Wordsworth and by Coleridge), to whom this essay entrusts the final judgement of Wordsworth's poems. The people, in the latter sense, are not to be identified either with a single class in society, or with the suffrage of Wordsworth's literate contemporaries. They come close to representing Johnson's idea of the "common reader."

CHARLES LAMB, "ON THE TRAGEDIES OF SHAKSPEARE, CONSIDERED WITH REFERENCE TO THEIR FITNESS FOR STAGE REPRESENTATION"

1 The monument to David Garrick (1717–79), the greatest of eighteenth-century Shakespearean actors, is inscribed with the lines that follow, by Samuel Jackson Pratt (1749–1814), a poet Lamb detested.

2 Lamb adds this note on the error of levelling the power of speech with the power of writing: "It is observable that we fall into this confusion only in *dramatic* recitations. We never dream that the gentleman who reads Lucretius in public with great applause, is therefore a great poet and philosopher; nor do we find that Tom Davies, the bookseller, who is recorded to have recited the Paradise Lost better than any man in England in his day (though I cannot help thinking there must be some mistake in this tradition), was therefore, by his intimate friends, set upon a level with Milton."

3 John Kemble (1757–1823) and Sarah Siddons (1755–1831), the most celebrated classical actors of their time, dominated the English stage until the advent of Kean. They were admired for a majestic self-command and poise, which would err, if at all, on the side of frigidity rather than melodramatic excess.

4 An anthology of elocutionary practice texts, published in 1774 by the Reverend William Enfield.

5 An outstanding Restoration performer of Shakespeare, Thomas Betterton (1635–1710) was greatly admired by Pope and Steele among others.

6 John Banks (author of *The Innocent Usurper*) and George Lillo (author of *The London Merchant*), cited here as adepts of bourgeois melodrama.

7 In *The London Merchant*, the susceptible Barnwell is incited to murder his uncle by Millwood, the mistress of a house of entertainment.

8   Lamb adds in a note: "If this note could hope to meet the eye of any of the Managers, I would intreat and beg of them, in the name of both the Galleries, that this insult upon the morality of the common people of London should cease to be eternally repeated in the holiday weeks. Why are the 'Prentices of this famous and well-governed city, instead of an amusement, to be treated over and over again with the nauseous sermon of George Barnwell? Why *at the end of their vistoes* are we to place the *gallows*? Were I an uncle, I should not much like a nephew of mine to have such an example placed before his eyes. It is really making uncle-murder too trivial to exhibit it as done upon such slight motives; – it is attributing too much to such characters as Millwood; – it is putting things into the heads of good young men, which they would never otherwise have dreamed of. Uncles that think any thing of their lives, should fairly petition the Chamberlain against it."

   Though his tone is partly facetious, there is no reason to doubt the earnestness of Lamb's objection to a play like *The London Merchant*, or his disdain for the realistic theatre in general. He believed that spectators who saw at the theatre nothing but the texture of everyday life, would make their own deductions about the poetic justice of life outside the theatre, and emulate in practice the characters they had learned to sympathize with on the stage. Lamb's remarks belong to the history of morals as much as the history of taste. They presume that art has an influence on life and that the lower the art the more calculable its effects. Edmund Burke's comments on the theatrical energy of the French Revolution are part of the same family of speculations, and the italicized phrase in this note alludes to a sentence from his *Reflections*: "In the groves of *their* academy, at the end of every visto, you see nothing but the gallows."

9   Mrs. Beverley is the heroine of James Shirley's *The Gamester*. From Belvidera to Euphrasia, the remaining names belong respectively to the heroines of *Venice Preserved* by Thomas Otway, *The Fair Penitent* by Nicholas Rowe, *Measure for Measure* by Shakespeare, and *The Grecian Daughter* by Arthur Murphy. Together with Aaron Hill and John Brown, Murphy is named as an instance of the ordinary, rather than the egregiously bad, imagination at work in an age of decline.

10   Revised versions of Shakespeare by Colley Cibber (1671–1757) were particularly chargeable with opportunism: his *Richard III* cut half the play, and interlarded it with scenes from the other histories; while, under his hand, *King John* became a piece of explicit anti-Catholic propaganda. Nahum Tate's *King Lear* with a happy ending first appeared in 1681.

11   George Cooke (1756–1811) was renowned as a player of Machiavellian villains, *plotters* of great cunning and mental energy on the pattern of Marlowe's Barabbas or Shakespeare's Edmund.

12   John Home's *Douglas* (1756), with the character of Glenalvon, originally caused a stir in Scotland, where it was felt to have rivalled Shakespeare. The play was still part of the familiar repertory in Lamb's youth.

13   Lamb alludes to the special imaginativeness of Desdemona's relation to Othello, evoked by the line "I saw Othello's visage in his mind." This may

be taken to mean: "in his *mind* and not merely in the colour of his skin." However, Lamb objects, a performance cannot help insisting on the character's actual, as distinct from his intellectual, physiognomy. The result is that one's response to such a line in the theatre is liable to be unimaginative.

14 Tom Brown (1663–1704), an epigrammatist, lampooner, and translator of the classics, made the remark in his "Observations on Virgil, Ovid, and Homer."

15 In keeping with neoclassical practice, Dryden and Davenant revised *The Tempest* to trim or balance its grotesque exuberances. Johnson's *Life of Dryden* describes the result as follows: "The effect produced by the conjunction of these two powerful minds was, that to Shakespeare's monster Caliban is added a sister-monster Sycorax; and a woman who, in the original play, had never seen a man, is in this brought acquainted with a man, that had never seen a woman."

16 Hazlitt recorded a similar complaint about the stage-props in *A Midsummer Night's Dream*: "Bottom's head in the play is a fantastic illusion, produced by magic spells: on the stage it is an ass's head, nothing more; certainly a very strange costume for a gentleman to appear in."

17 Lectures on astronomy were given in the winter at Theatre Royal, Haymarket. The curious apparatus that Lamb mentions – called an Orrery after Charles Boyle, Earl of Orrery, who commissioned the first to be built about 1700 – served to demonstrate by a clockwork mechanism the relative motions of the sun and planets.

CHARLES LAMB, "ON THE ACTING OF MUNDEN"

1 Joseph Munden (1758–1832), the comedian and caricaturist, performed steadily at Covent Garden from 1790 to 1811. Cockletop was the leading character in John O'Keefe's *Modern Antiques* (1792). Described, by Lamb's friend B. W. Procter, as a man "credulous beyond ordinary credulity," he displays this trait in several exchanges with his skeptical tormentors, who are able to persuade him that, for example, a phial of water really contains "Cleopatra's Tear." Says Cockletop (gratefully): "What a large tear!"

2 John Liston (1776–1846) played Ophelia in an admired *Hamlet Travestie*; Charles Farley (1771–1859) devised the Covent Garden pantomimes; Edward Knight (1774–1826) was a prominent rival comedian.

3 In his essay "On Some of the Old Actors" Lamb memorializes Dicky Suett as "the Robin Good-Fellow of the Stage," and says of his *O La!*: "He drolled upon the stock of these two syllables richer than the cuckoo."

4 Curry and Dornton figure respectively in George Colman the Younger's *Inkle and Yarico* (1787) and Thomas Holcroft's *The Road to Ruin* (1792).

5 Charles Johnson's *Cobbler of Preston* (1716) was based on *The Taming of the Shrew*.

CHARLES LAMB, "ON THE ARTIFICIAL COMEDY OF THE LAST CENTURY"

1 Alsatia was the name of a debtors' sanctuary in the precinct of Whitefriars, the subject of Thomas Shadwell's *Squire of Alsatia*.

2 Cato served as the Roman censor: Lamb imagines his powers dispersed among the public.

3 The theosophical system of Emanuel Swedenborg (1688–1772) allowed three separate spheres for bad and three for good spirits.

4 These characters are to be found in Congreve's *Way of the World*, Farquhar's *The Inconstant*, Etherege's *Man of Mode*, and Congreve's *Double Dealer*.

5 The allusion is to Congreve's *Love for Love*.

6 All of these characters are from William Wycherley's *Love in a Wood* (1672).

7 Lamb refers specifically to Francis Bacon's *New Atlantis* (1627), an unfinished account of utopian life on an island in the Atlantic, where people live in accord with moral laws.

8 John Palmer appeared as Joseph Surface in the opening performance of Richard Brinsley Sheridan's *The School for Scandal* (May 8, 1777). He was felt to be well matched to the part by affinity, and by the general knowledge of his addiction to pleasure.

9 Carrington Bowles, of 69 St. Paul's Churchyard, was a publisher of prints. Lamb describes this specimen of his work as an example of the "unrealising" effects by which a solemn thing may be rendered ludicrous, or vice versa, simply by the artifice of portrayal. With his favorite actors of Congreve such effects are voluntary; in the case of the print they appear to have been unintended.

10 Thomas King acted the part of Sir Peter Teazle in *The School for Scandal* from its opening to his retirement in 1802.

11 Crabtree, Sir Benjamin Backbite, and Mrs. Candour are the easily routed malefactors of the play.

12 Because Sheridan himself was manager of Drury Lane and because the production was ideally suited to the resources of his actors, Lamb speaks of it as a "manager's comedy."

WILLIAM HAZLITT, "WHY THE ARTS ARE NOT PROGRESSIVE?"

1 Hazlitt adds this note: "In speaking thus of Claude, we yield rather to common opinion than to our own. However inferior the style of his best landscapes may be, there is something in the execution that redeems all defects. In taste and grace nothing can ever go beyond them. He might be called, if not the perfect, the faultless painter. Sir Joshua Reynolds used to say, that there would be another Raphael, before there was another Claude." Hazlitt himself seems to have regarded Claude (like Milton) as something between a naive and a sentimental artist. The interest such figures hold for him is that they mingle the natural strength of the classic with the personal associations of the modern.

2 This is an ironic catalogue, including works of fashionable literature, academic painting, modern French and Scottish letters, none of them favorites with Hazlitt.

WILLIAM HAZLITT, "ON MR. KEAN'S IAGO"

1 Edmund Kean (1787–1833) broke free of the conventions of Shakespearean performance, as epitomized by John Kemble, in favor of a style of impulsive speech and gesture. Hazlitt was his first and best appreciator, and admired him especially in the roles of Shylock and Othello.

2 The contemporary critic is Hazlitt, in a review published six weeks earlier in a different paper.

3 Jacobinism here denotes any levelling tendency of the mind; but with the Jacobins of the French Revolution, Hazlitt professed a steady sympathy; the implied moral judgement of Iago is ambivalent.

4 La Rochefoucauld's maxims interpret manifestations of sympathy as expressions of self-interest. In this sentence, Hazlitt associates Iago's antipathy for the other characters with his indifference to his own fortunes; while no mere selfish motive will account for what he does, his conduct is consistent with La Rochefoucauld's insight: just as benevolence and selfishness go together, so do malevolence and selflessness.

5 Iago is described in the play as an ancient, that is, an ensign or flag-bearer.

6 An air-pump sucked oxygen out of a glass container, often for the sake of observing the effects on an animal. It was therefore a convenient symbol of an experimental scientific attitude of heartless detachment. Hazlitt would have known pictures like "An Experiment on a Bird in the Air Pump," by Joseph Wright of Derby (1734–97), who painted a good many similar academic or laboratory scenes by candlelight. A passage from Edmund Burke's "Letter to a Noble Lord" – Hazlitt's favorite of all his writings – concerns the hardened altruism with which the Jacobins pursued their experiments in political morality: "These philosophers consider men in their experiments, no more than they do mice in an air pump, or in a recipient of mephitic gas."

WILLIAM HAZLITT, "ON IMITATION"

1 Hazlitt's definition of the word goes beyond the "just and lively resemblance" of eighteenth-century criticism. Imitation, in his view, works by detecting new properties in an object, as much as by reproducing visible ones. It invites the spectator to compare the object with its representation, in order to savor the individual power of the artist's conception, and not only to judge its accuracy. Thus the discoveries of the spectator as he looks at a painting are like those of the artist as he creates it. The mind is supposed to take pleasure in such comparisons for their own sake, and the appeal of imitations is that they rouse the mind to activity.

2 Hazlitt adds this note: "In a fruit or flower-piece by Vanhuysum, the minutest details acquire a certain grace and beauty from the delicacy with

which they are finished. The eye dwells with a giddy delight on the liquid drops of dew, on the gauze wings of an insect, on the hair and feathers of a bird's nest, the streaked and speckled egg-shells, the fine legs of the little traveling caterpillar. Who will suppose that the painter had not the same pleasure in detecting these nice distinctions in nature, that the critic has in tracing them in the picture?"

3 Both Hazlitt and Lamb defended Hogarth against attacks on the immorality of his subjects.

4 Hazlitt adds this note: "We allude particularly to Turner, the ablest landscape painter now living, whose pictures are, however, too much abstractions of aerial perspective, and representations not so properly of objects of nature as of the medium through which they are seen. They are the triumph of the knowledge of the artist, and of the power of the pencil over the barrenness of the subject. They are pictures of the elements of air, earth, and water. The artist delights to go back to the first chaos of the world, or to that state of things when the waters were separated from the dry land, and light from darkness, but as yet no living thing nor tree bearing fruit was seen upon the face of the earth. All is 'without form and void.' Some one said of his landscapes that they were *pictures of nothing, and very like*."

5 The British Institution exhibited many paintings, including some by painters of the Royal Academy. Hazlitt's dismissal of the pretensions of both corporate bodies is in keeping with his general distrust of academic encouragement for the arts. Such encouragement, it seemed to him, had a false premise, namely that genius could be formed by instruction and with the help of rules. He believed that the Royal Academy in particular, by inducing painters to regard their calling as a profession, implicitly gave its sponsorship to a principle of universal suffrage in the arts (where that principle could never apply).

WILLIAM HAZLITT, "ON 'GUSTO'"

1 The word denotes taste, but taste understood in a special sense: as an active process of knowing and savoring, rather than a settled curriculum for receiving impressions. None of the definitions given in the *Oxford English Dictionary* captures Hazlitt's meaning; of the two with which it overlaps ("keen relish"; "artistic style"), the examples quoted from Congreve and Sterne may be considered as precursors. As a critical term of some precision, apart from the enthusiastic vagueness of "grand gusto," it seems to have been naturalized in English by Hazlitt in this essay.

2 Benjamin West (1738–1820), Reynolds's successor as president of the Royal Academy.

3 The description has acquired a special importance since the *St. Peter Martyr* was destroyed by fire in 1867.

4 Hazlitt adds this note: "Raphael not only could not paint a landscape; he could not paint people in a landscape. He could not have painted the heads or the figures, or even the dresses, of the St. Peter Martyr. His

figures have always an *in-door* look, that is, a set, determined, voluntary, dramatic character, arising from their own passions, or a watchfulness of those of others, and want that wild uncertainty of expression, which is connected with the accidents of nature and the changes of the elements. He has nothing *romantic* about him."

5 This is meant chiefly as an allusion to the Elgin Marbles, still in the first years of their display to a curious public. An instructive lesson was deduced from them by Hazlitt, Keats, and others, concerning the naturalism of the classics. Hazlitt for example praised the marbles because of, and not in spite of, their resemblance to simple casts of the human form.

WILLIAM HAZLITT, "CORIOLANUS"

1 Both terms are here construed broadly: "imagination" includes what other critics such as Coleridge would define more particularly as *fancy*; while "understanding" comes close to being a synonym for *judgement* in its common eighteenth-century sense.

2 The sentence offers a deliberately grotesque application of the Sermon on the Mount, from Matthew xxv. 29.

WILLIAM HAZLITT, "ON THE PERIODICAL ESSAYISTS"

1 The *Tatler* and *Spectator* (1709–12) were collaborative periodicals by Joseph Addison and Richard Steele. The *Rambler* (1750–52), a series of brief moral essays, was Johnson's production alone.

2 Boswell's *Life* prints several such letters, written by Johnson for his friends or associates in *their* persons, to assist them in the conduct of ordinary worldly business.

3 The preceding sentence has a structure to match the fault it describes, a merely habitual reliance on balance and antithesis. It echoes such celebrated Johnsonian elaborations as the weighing of Shakespeare's gifts for tragedy and comedy, in the *Preface to Shakespeare*: "In his tragick scenes there is always something wanting, but his comedy often surpasses expectation or desire. His comedy pleases by the thoughts and the language, and his tragedy for the greater part by incident and action. His tragedy seems to be skill, his comedy to be instinct."

4 A pamphlet by William Lauder had sought to expose *Paradise Lost* as a tissue of plagiarisms from modern Latin poets. Surprisingly, given his usual suspicion both of Scotchmen and crank pamphleteers, Johnson wrote a Preface and a Postscript endorsing the work (1750), which he disavowed a year later when it had been proved a forgery. Hazlitt regards the embarrassing episode as an instance of Johnson's hatred for all disestablishmentarian politics, including Milton's.

WILLIAM HAZLITT, "ON THE PICTURESQUE AND IDEAL: A FRAGMENT"

1 Sir Joshua Reynolds in his *Discourses* treated the ideal and the particular as incompatible values. Hazlitt in this essay wants to show that they are compatible, to the point of being identical with each other. So, where Reynolds argued for a subordination of the detail to the general form, Hazlitt restores the authority of the detail in works of art, by insisting on its naturalness *and* its ideality. Ideal, in his usage, implies "having the character of, or relation to, an idea."

2 James Northcote was Reynolds's biographer, himself still active as a painter, and Hazlitt liked to visit his studio and talk. The *Conversations of James Northcote* (1830) – a book of dialogues by Hazlitt, which he sometimes called "Boswell Redivivus" – gives a lively impression of the character and opinions of both men.

3 Alexander von Humboldt (1769–1859) would have been asked the question in his capacity as a man of science and not simply as an explorer.

4 Of the works discussed in the preceding two paragraphs, Veronese's *Marriage at Cana* is still in the Louvre; so is at least one Rubens landscape that Hazlitt knew (*Landscape with Rainbow*); Rembrandt's *Jacob's Dream* is in the British Museum.

WILLIAM HAZLITT, "MR. COLERIDGE"

1 For a period in the mid-1790s, Coleridge entered into sympathy with the Unitarians, and shared their belief in Jesus Christ as the type of all virtuous reformers. In 1798 he came close to joining the Unitarian ministry; even then, however, his emphasis on revelation placed him at odds with the rational emphasis of the sect; in later years, as a professed Trinitarian, he denounced his former allies as "*Psilanthropists*, or assertors or the *mere* humanity of Christ."

2 Particularly those of Kant and Schelling. *Transcendental* is Hazlitt's adjective for any theory of poetry that separates the value of a poem from the human will of a poet. Some such division is taken for granted in Coleridge's treatment of Imagination in the *Biographia Literaria*, as elsewhere in his use of an organic metaphor to suggest the unity and self-sufficiency of a poem.

3 Hazlitt adds this note: "Mr. Coleridge named his eldest son (the writer of some beautiful Sonnets) after Hartley, and the second after Berkeley. The third was called Derwent, after the river of that name. Nothing can be more characteristic of his mind than this circumstance. All his ideas are indeed like a river, flowing on for ever, and still murmuring as it flows, discharging its waters and still replenished –

'And so by many winding nooks it strays
With willing sport to the wild ocean!'"

4 To the foregoing catalogue all annotation is vain. It shows that Coleridge might with equal plausibility claim to be (a) an idealist metaphysician, (b) a poet, (c) an irresolute disciple of the French and German Enlighten-

ment, (d) a critic of poetry, and (e) an inveterate speculator, too infinite in scope to achieve anything of finite worth. Hazlitt writes partly as an admirer – he had met Coleridge when young, and always acknowledged a debt to him – so that the extravagant detail of the record is itself a kind of homage: he is showing Coleridge that he has not missed a step. The tone (unenthralled, but not quite ironic) accords with his judgement of Coleridge in the essay "On Consistency of Opinion": "I can hardly consider Mr. Coleridge as a deserter from the cause he first espoused, unless one could tell what cause he ever heartily espoused, or what party he ever belonged to, in downright earnest. He has not been inconsistent with himself at different times, but at all times."

5   By the *unclean side* Hazlitt means the side of the allied sovereigns against Napoleon.

6   William Godwin (1756–1836), the author of *Political Justice* and *Caleb Williams*, and the subject of the preceding sketch in *The Spirit of the Age*.

7   This is an allusion to (among other events) the treason trials of 1794, the imprisonment, in 1813, of Leigh and John Hunt for seditious libel, and the more recent attacks on the "Cockney School," which were widely supposed to have contributed to the fatal illness of Keats.

LEIGH HUNT, "POEMS BY JOHN KEATS"

1   By "cant" Hunt evidently means poetic diction: the sort of habitual refinement that would lead a poet to call birds "the feathered race" or fish "the finny tribe." It becomes *inverted* cant when it moves toward elegant regularity rather than elegant variation.

2   Balthasar Denner (1685–1749), a German painter admired by Frederick II for the finish of his portraits, later came into disrepute for the mere professionalism of his craftsmanship. An involuntary grotesqueness of effect, owing to a vivid rendering of inconsequent details, was among his conspicuous faults, as the line of verse below will attest. Peter Pindar was the pen-name of John Wolcot (1738–1819), a writer of squibs and occasional satires: the quotation is from his "Lyric Odes to the Royal Academicians for MDCCLXXXIII," Ode 8.

3   The suggestion is that Keats's treatment of mythology in "I stood tip-toe" may be traced back to Wordsworth's in *The Excursion*, IV, 847–57. Wordsworth looked on the classical deities as spontaneous projections of the mind, invented at moments of natural awe and pleasure, from an exuberance of animistic faith.

LEIGH HUNT, "ON THE REALITIES OF IMAGINATION"

1   In an 1887 selection of Hunt's essays, Arthur Symons remarked that parts of this one were "particularly fine," but added that it was disfigured as a whole by two digressions, which contained long extracts from Milton and Ben Jonson. The present editor has followed Symons's abridgement, indicating the omitted passages with suspension dots.

2   For cadence, in the amplification of particulars and in the cumulative

dignity of effect, this is an extraordinary passage. It looks forward to the prose of Ruskin and, more distantly, Pater, whose essay "Charles Lamb" ends with the following homage to a model that seems to be Hunt as much as Lamb: "He felt the genius of places; and I sometimes think he resembles the places he knew and liked best, and where his lot fell – London, sixty-five years ago, with Covent Garden and the old theatres, and the Temple gardens still unspoiled, Thames gliding down, and beyond to north and south the fields at Enfield or Hampton, to which, 'with their living trees,' the thoughts wander 'from the hard wood of the desk' – fields fresher, and coming nearer to town then, but in one of which the present writer remembers, on a brooding early summer's day, to have heard the cuckoo for the first time. Here, the surface of things is certainly humdrum, the streets dingy, the green places, where the child goes a-maying, tame enough. But nowhere are things more apt to respond to the brighter weather, nowhere is there so much difference between rain and sunshine, nowhere do the clouds roll together more grandly; those quaint suburban pastorals gathering a certain quality of grandeur from the background of the great city, with its weighty atmosphere, and portent of storm in the rapid light on dome and bleached stone steeples."

THOMAS DE QUINCEY, "ON THE KNOCKING AT THE GATE IN 'MACBETH'"

1   The implicit contrast throughout the foregoing paragraph is between understanding and imagination: the former storing up deductions from the laws of nature and human behavior; the latter affording glimpses of the possible modifications of those laws. De Quincey inherits the contrast from Coleridge, and uses both terms in a Coleridgean way. Understanding is assigned to a lower, customary, merely rational order of abstract thinking; imagination to a higher, originary, associative and poetic order of thinking and feeling. Critics who start with these senses of the words often go on to identify understanding with the literal dimension of meaning and imagination with the figurative. But here, De Quincey points to a curious ambiguity. The understanding may become so assured in its comprehension that it actually excludes certain perceptions as outside the reach of its usual procedure. His example comes from the rendering of perspective in paintings: ignoring what pictures show, the understanding sometimes overrules the evidence of sight, so that it fails to see why "a horizontal line should not *appear* a horizontal line." Thus it tends to obliterate the image, and proves an unreliable guide even to the literal seeing of objects. It would seem to follow that there is a close and unsuspected relation between "image" and imagination.

2   A full narrative of the Williams murders is given in De Quincey's essay "On Murder Considered as One of the Fine Arts." To judge by what he says there, his appreciation of Williams's "brilliant and undying reputation" is not intended ironically.

3   De Quincey here offers a perverse echo of Wordsworth's "Tintern

Abbey," where the contemplation of nature's forms is prized for the sake of "that serene and blessed mood" in which "Almost suspended, we are laid asleep / In body, and become a living soul." Wordsworth, however, described such sleep (the effect of a sublime vision) as a healing premonition of death; whereas De Quincey exhibits the scene's "awful parenthesis" (the effect of a murder) as a strange disruption of life. The Wordsworthian phrases also mingle with De Quincey's memory of another passage (*Macbeth*, II. ii. 35): "Methought I heard a voice cry 'Sleep no more! / Macbeth does murder sleep.'"

THOMAS DE QUINCEY, "ON WORDSWORTH'S POETRY"

1 After reading the *Lyrical Ballads*, De Quincey, then in his seventeenth year, wrote to Wordsworth in a strain of unlimited admiration, offering "to sacrifice even his life" for Wordsworth, and hoping to "advance some negative reasons why you may suffer me, if but at a distance, to buoy myself with the idea that I am not wholly disregarded in your sight." Six years later, in 1809, he became a tenant of Dove Cottage in Grasmere, which Wordsworth had recently vacated. His estrangement from Wordsworth seems to have been caused in part by his pecuniary incapacity, in part by the alienating effects of his addiction to opium, and in part by a clash between Wordsworth's proprietary regard for the cottage and the high-handed interventions of De Quincey's maidservant. These matters are discussed at length in his *Recollections of the Lakes and the Lake Poets*. By his own account there, his relationship with Wordsworth passed through consecutive stages of idolatry (as a reader); emulation (as an intimate disciple); dependence (as a neighbor); and resentment (as a thwarted dependent).

2 Broadly speaking, Wordsworth's theory was that eighteenth-century poetry had been corrupted by its gradual incorporation of "poetic diction": a trite, stereotyped, artificially poeticizing form of speech that relied heavily on stock epithets and personifications. In the Preface to *Lyrical Ballads*, he argued that poetry which complied with such norms was at war with sincere feeling and impassioned human speech. De Quincey objects not to Wordsworth's negative demonstration that an old idiom had become impracticable, but to his positive claim for the new idiom he invented, that it reproduced "the language really used by men" in speaking of "incidents and situations from common life." A similar criticism had already been advanced by Coleridge in the *Biographia Literaria*.

3 This character appears in three poems of 1799: "Matthew," "Two April Mornings," and "The Fountain."

4 James Frederick Ferrier (1808–64), a Scottish metaphysician who explored the function and vindicated the necessity of consciousness in all knowledge.

5 De Quincey adds the following note: "This, and another similar remedy, called Godfrey's Cordial, both owing their main agencies to opium, have through generations been the chief resource of poor mothers when

embarrassed in their daily labours by fretful infants. Fine ladies have no such difficulty to face, and are apt to forget that there is any such apology to plead."

6   De Quincey adds the following note: "The reader must not understand the writer as unconditionally approving of the French Revolution. It is his belief that the resistance to the Revolution was, in many high quarters, a sacred duty, and that this resistance it was which forced out, from the Revolution, the benefits which it has since diffused. The Revolution, and the resistance to the Revolution, were the two powers that quickened each other for ultimate good. To speak by the language of mechanics, the case was one which illustrated the composition of forces. Neither the revolution singly, nor the resistance to the Revolution singly, was calculated to regenerate social man. But the two forces in union, where the one modified, mitigated, or even neutralised, the other at times, and where, at times, each entered into a happy combination with the other, yielded for the world those benefits which, by its separate tendency, either of them had been fitted to stifle."

This note is given as an elaborate, but characteristic, example of De Quincey's idealizing dialectics. It is remarkable that he adduces no evidence. The main visible consequences of resistance to the Revolution were, in France, the Terror and the ascent of Napoleon and, in England, widespread economic distresses and the repression of political dissent. These would be pertinent to an account that supposed the Revolution was good or evil or both, and that the resistance to it was noble or cynical or both. But De Quincey's explanation takes place far enough above the battles to disdain any empirical weighing of "the composition of forces." The entire passage falls in with Coleridgean habits of thought – the phrases "modified, mitigated, or even neutralized" and "two forces in union" being noteworthy in this regard – and it is possible that we are reading something De Quincey heard him say.

7   De Quincey adds this note: "It was not, however, that all poets then lived in towns; neither had Pope himself generally lived in towns. But it is perfectly useless to be familiar with nature unless there is a public trained to love and value nature. It is not what the individual sees that will fix itself as beautiful in his recollections, but what he sees under a consciousness that others will sympathise with his feelings. Under any other circumstances familiarity does but realise the adage, and 'breeds contempt.' The great despisers of rural scenery, its fixed and permanent undervaluers, are rustics." Pope lived in Twickenham, where he designed his own grotto, and allowed nature to grow carefully wild.

THOMAS DE QUINCEY, "THE POETRY OF POPE"

1   De Quincey has in mind such authors as Congreve and Wycherley, and the larger tradition of characters which he sees as culminating in Pope's *Moral Essays*. A character in this sense was an artful abstract of personal qualities: the word refers to the finished literary performance, and not to the actual person on whom it was based. A similar idea survives in the

modern colloquial sense of "having character," that is, having sufficient moral substance to be worth writing a character of.

2 The distinction between understanding and "higher understanding or reason" (roughly translatable as intuition or insight) may be traced to Coleridge. The distinction between the literature of knowledge and the literature of power De Quincey borrows from the first published version of Hazlitt's "Why the Arts Are Not Progressive?"

3 From Bacon's essay "Of Friendship": "Heraclitus saith well in one of his enigmas, 'Dry light is ever the best.' And certain it is, that the light that a man receiveth by counsel from another, is drier and purer than that which comes from his own understanding and judgment; which is ever infused and drenched in his affections and customs."

4 Pierre Simon Laplace (1749–1827), the French mathematician and astronomer, established the invariability of planetary mean motions, and in doing so helped to demonstrate the stability of the solar system. His researches, and his great work, the *Méchanique Céleste*, appear to De Quincey secondary only in relation to Newton, on whose foundations they built.

5 This sentence plays on the Christian senses of "militant" and "triumphant," according to which the church, militant for a time, remains visible, but, triumphant forever, becomes invisible. In the same way the literature of knowledge is known by its finite visible effects on readers, and the literature of power is known by its measureless invisible effects.

6 De Quincey adds the following note: "The reason why the broad distinctions between the two literatures of power and knowledge so little fix the attention lies in the fact that a vast production of books, – history, biography, travels, miscellaneous essays, &c., – lying in the middle zone, confound these distinctions by interblending them. All that we call 'amusement' or 'entertainment' is a diluted form of the power belonging to passion, and also a mixed form; and, where threads of direct *instruction* intermingle in the texture of these threads of *power*, the absorption of the duality into one representative *nuance* neutralises the separate perception of either. Fused into a *tertium quid*, or neutral state, they disappear to the popular eye as the repelling forces which, in fact, they are."

7 The authors to whom De Quincey alludes are John Phillips (1676–1709) and John Dyer (1699–1757).

8 Gaius Marius and Quintus Sertorius were Roman generals of the late second and early first centuries B.C.

9 Marco Girolamo Vida, of Cremona (1490–1566), wrote a poem about the game of chess, and was singled out for praise in Pope's *Essay on Criticism* (lines 704–08).

10 William Warburton and Jean Pierre de Crousaz were commentators on the *Essay on Man*. De Quincey's conceit about didactic poetry and its interpretation depends on our knowing that Hebrew words are formed from consonant groups with points but no lettering to indicate vowel sounds. Thus, the original of the word Jehovah is pronounced in Hebrew "Yah-weh" but is spelled only by the letters YHWH. Pope's *Essay on Man*,

which De Quincey compares to such a word, was notoriously slippery in its theology, owing that quality in equal measure to philosophical innocence and rhetorical cunning. De Quincey's charge was anticipated by Johnson in the *Life of Pope*: "Having exalted himself into the chair of wisdom, he tells us much that every man knows, and much that he does not know himself. . . . Never were penury of knowledge and vulgarity of sentiment so happily disguised. The reader feels his mind full, though he learns nothing." But De Quincey's strictures on the *Essay* belong, as Johnson's did not, to a general argument against the very idea of didactic poetry. There is a difference of kind, he thinks, between a forced enigma and an unforced sublimity: between the blank spaces that sometimes appear in the puzzle-solving language of Pope, and the atmosphere of suggestiveness that is rightly associated with great poetry.

THOMAS LOVE PEACOCK, "AN ESSAY ON FASHIONABLE LITERATURE"

1 The Minerva Press in Leadenhall Street had become a byword for the trash novels which it turned out at a tremendous rate. Robert ("Romeo") Coates, an Amateur of Fashion as he called himself, was famous for dressing in a style of gaudy ostentation, the very reverse of Beau Brummell's fastidious and minimal dandyism. An actor of no talent, he arranged several performances before an unwilling public, to bear out his motto: "Whilst I live, I'll crow."

2 Matthew Gregory Lewis (1775–1818) took his nickname from the sensational gothic romance, *The Monk*, which he produced in ten weeks at the age of nineteen. He went on to write several works for the stage, but, in his last years, passed gradually into demi-celebrity and finally obscurity. August Friedrich von Kotzebue (1761–1819), the fashionable German dramatist, was well known in England for his *Menschenhass und Reue (Misanthropy and Repentence*, translated as *The Stranger).*

3 This class of readers depended implicitly on the opinions of the great reviews, which they quoted often and with much complacency. In chapter 5 of *Nightmare Abbey*, Peacock gives a parody table of contents for a typical issue of the *Quarterly*, as it is received, opened, and read aloud by a guest at the country seat of the hero's father. The narrator there observes that its editors were "persons in high favour at court, and enjoyed ample pensions for their services to church and state."

4 A typical "rotten borough," with its one voter at election time and one vote in parliament, Old Sarum was a familiar symbol of Old Corruption.

5 Drummond, the author of *Philosophical Sketches on the Principles of Society and Government*, commanded the interest of Shelley as well as Peacock, for his attack on literal-minded interpretations of the bible. His *Academical Questions* (1805) was addressed to readers outside the universities.

6 Wordsworth was of course still alive. His literary fortunes had improved as his political views crept closer to those of the ministerial establishment. So far as Peacock is concerned, the "independent and high thinking" part

of Wordsworth has died, and the *late* Mr. Wordsworth who lives on merely happens to share the same name.

7 Robert Forsyth (1766–1846) was a special enthusiasm of Peacock's. A speculative writer on politics, morals, and poetry, he believed in the survival of everything that has "a tendency to improve" mankind. Forsyth's evolutionary arguments for reform, which Peacock cites approvingly in the preceding sentence, also have points in common with Shelley's historical view of language in the "Defence of Poetry."

8 The review in question, which appeared in the *Edinburgh Review*, is everything that Peacock calls it. It is now commonly attributed to Thomas Moore.

9 This sentence, with the long quotation that follows, clearly forms the text that Peacock had before him, but his manuscript itself gives neither the quotation nor the reference. The passage was interpolated by his editors, H. B. F. Brett-Smith and C. E. Jones, and it is reprinted here without change.

10 The words "nothing can be more," between "and" and "true," are another editorial interpolation which the present editor accepts as plausible.

11 Swift describes the three coats in Section 11 of *A Tale of a Tub*. The chapter elaborates an allegory in which fashions of thought are interchangeable with fashions of dress: in this, as in its style of irony, it is among the few apparent sources for Peacock's essay.

12 At this point it seems likely that Peacock meant to add some observations on the naturalistic particularity of such ballads as "Sir Patrick Spence." The choice is apt, in view of Coleridge's use of the same ballad in his epigraph to "Dejection: an Ode."

13 "Christabel" belongs on the same side with Homer and Milton. That Chaucer should appear as their opposite is puzzling, if, as the preceding sentences imply, the larger comparison is between naive and sentimental poetry.

14 As will be seen, Peacock stopped after a single observation, which offers a general and intuitive defense of the poem, rather than a commentary on the sentence quoted.

THOMAS LOVE PEACOCK, "THE FOUR AGES OF POETRY"

1 "The Danish Boy" and "Lucy Gray" both derive from local superstitions, and both deal with the ghosts of children who are said to haunt a special place.

2 This attack on "ethical" poetry seems to be directed against Byron and, more particularly, Shelley. *Queen Mab* and *Alastor* fit the description. But even without any traceable allusion, Peacock's ridicule of poetry as a vehicle for social reform would have been better calculated than any other part of his essay to draw a response from Shelley.

PERCY BYSSHE SHELLEY, "A DEFENCE OF POETRY"

1 The Aeolian harp's sound was caused by the wind passing across the strings. Its melody therefore was wandering, and its music free of voluntary agency. As a romantic topic, its appeal has to do with the suggestion that the poet is inspired by uncontrollable powers and that the writing of poetry is distinct from common exertions of the will.

2 Since the poet "participates in" an indestructible order of things, which he looks at both from within his time and from beyond it, he is properly to be associated with Janus, the god of doorways, who looks before and after. In proposing that the moral sublimity of an utterance may be traced in such minute details as a loss of grammatical discreteness among "the moods of time, and the difference of persons, and the distinction of place," Shelley appears to follow the rhetorical teachings of Longinus.

3 Shelley's idea of an imitation that improves what it reflects is drawn from Renaissance defenses of poetry, with which it shares both Neoplatonic metaphors, such as that of the mirror, and a wish to correct the Platonic conception of the poet as a merely servile imitator. The contrast developed earlier in the paragraph, between a story and a poem, is partly derived from two sources: the description of poetry in Aristotle's *Poetics*, as superior to history on the ground that it deals with the universal and probable rather than the individual and actual; and the description of the poet in Sidney's *Apology for Poetry*, as superior to the historian on the ground that he selects his details artfully and so creates more striking examples of virtue.

4 At this point Shelley's idea of poetry cuts across boundaries that are usually taken to define literature as such. Poetry has become a name for what survives the corruption of society. Something that once seemed poetry, but that in retrospect looks like a token of passing manners, does not deserve the name after all. On this view poetry is simply a category of moral facts which we have preserved as a record of our nature. It incorporates everything we cannot help seeing as imperishable – everything we have not *allowed* to perish – whether in the form of writings, institutions, or beliefs. Shelley is careful to add that it can only have lasted in this way, and been chosen by a natural selection of the will, if it existed from the first as a cause of liberating change.

5 Harmonics, mathematics, and astronomy were replaced by magic, alchemy, and astrology, whose masters became objects of superstitious reverence – an instance of the process Shelley describes elsewhere in this essay, by which poetic imaginings are reduced to a practice.

6 Utility is not confined to that which is immediately usable: Plato, when he wrote of pleasure, referred to something beyond self-gratification; as, when he wrote of power, he referred to something beyond worldly sway. In employing this wider sense of "utility," as if everyone saw that it coincided with the good and the beautiful, Shelley refuses to give up the grounds of argument to utilitarians like Bentham. Their rule, "the greatest good for the greatest number," had issued in such judgements as "All other things being equal, push-pin is as good as poetry."

7 Shelley does not here intend to praise Milton's Satan, except by comparison with Milton's God. His suggestion, in alluding to the "bold neglect of a direct moral purpose," is that the poem's readers themselves are left to imagine the morality that guides its fable.

8 Late classical verse-makers, whose self-conscious extravagance does not compensate for their want of invention. Peacock may be responsible for Shelley's familiarity with some of these authors.

9 By Ariosto, Tasso, Camoëns, and Spenser, respectively. Among other considerations Shelley would have found the religious or national sentiments of these poems too explicit to qualify them as "epic in its highest sense."

10 This paragraph is a thinly concealed polemic against Thomas Malthus, the most influential of economic utilitarians. His *Essay on Population* (1798) taught that all schemes of social amelioration must fail, so long as the population continued to press against the limits of the means of subsistence; further, it argued that the population would continue to do so forever, because it increased geometrically while the supply of food increased arithmetically. For Malthus and his followers, the only conceivable checks on the growth of the population were misery and vice, which tended to limit the numbers of the poor in each generation. The theory served to justify a system which made the wealth of the rich appear to be inscribed in the nature of things.

11 All chosen as heroes of the Enlightenment, and all but Locke taken from Peacock's list. In the notes to *Queen Mab*, Shelley had already discussed Locke's arguments for a mild necessitarianism; in *The Triumph of Life*, he would imagine Rousseau's disappointment with the influence of his own teachings.

12 This repeats Sidney's argument from the virtuous character of poets to the virtue of their poems. As Shelley adapts it, the argument is circular, for the decisive evidence of "the interior of their lives" comes from the poems they wrote. Whatever one makes of his choice of tactics here, Shelley's defense as a whole applies to poetry and not poets. Its adequacy therefore does not rest on our crediting his general apology for the lives of poets.

Select booklist

PRIMARY SOURCES

The following periodicals first published a large share of the critical writings from which this anthology was selected. They are listed here with their dates of commencement.

Blackwood's Edinburgh Magazine (1817)
The Champion (1814)
The Edinburgh Magazine (1817)
The Edinburgh Review (1802)
The Examiner (1808)
The Liberal (1822)
The Literary Gazette (1817)
The Literary Journal (1803)
The London Magazine (1820)
The Monthly Magazine (1796)
The New Monthly Magazine (1814)
The Quarterly Review (1809)
The Westminster Review (1824)
The Yellow Dwarf (1818)

Such a list does not do justice to the career of Leigh Hunt, who conducted, while also contributing steadily to, a dozen separate periodicals in his lifetime, among them the *Reflector*, the *Tatler*, and *Leigh Hunt's London Journal*.

Of all the above journals, the highest ratio of genuine criticism to transient polemics is to be found in the *Examiner* under the editorship of John and Leigh Hunt, and in the *London Magazine* under the editorship of John Scott. But the most influential were certainly the *Edinburgh Review* and the *Quarterly Review*, the former edited by Francis Jeffrey and the latter by William Gifford, in keeping respectively with a Scottish Whig and an English Tory point of view.

The following editions and volumes are also useful.

De Quincey, Thomas, *Works*, ed. David Masson, 14 vols. (1889–90)
   Selected Essays on Rhetoric, ed. Frederick Burwick (1967)
Hazlitt, William, *Works*, ed. P. P. Howe, 21 vols. (1930–34)
Hunt, Leigh, *Autobiography* (1850)

The Companion (1828)
Dramatic Essays, ed. William Archer and Robert W. Lowe (1894)
Essays, ed. Arthur Symons (1887)
Imagination and Fancy (1844)
The Indicator (1819–21)
Literary Criticism, ed. Lawrence H. and Carolyn W. Houtchens (New York, 1956)
Lord Byron and Some of His Contemporaries (1828)
Men, Women, and Books (1846)
Wit and Humor (1846)
Lamb, Charles, *Works*, ed. Thomas Hutchinson (1908)
Lamb, Charles and Mary, *Letters*, ed. Edwin W. Marrs, Jr., 3 vols. (Ithaca, 1975)
Peacock, Thomas Love, *Works*, ed. H. B. F. Brett-Smith and C. E. Jones, 10 vols (1924–34)
Memoirs, Essays, and Reviews, ed. Howard Mills (1970)
Shelley, Percy Bysshe, *Complete Works*, ed. Roger Ingpen and Walter E. Peck, 7 vols. (New York, 1926–30)
Literary Criticism, ed. Bruce R. McElderry, Jr. (Lincoln, Nebraska, 1967)
Wordsworth, William, *Prose Works*, ed. W. J. B. Owen and Jane Worthington Smyser, 3 vols. (Oxford, 1974)

GENERAL HISTORICAL STUDIES

The political conditions of the early 1800s are vividly rendered in Elie Halévy's *England in 1815*, trans. E. I. Watkin and D. A. Barker (1949); E. P. Thompson's *The Making of the English Working Class* (1963), the most impressive study of the social history of these decades, affords a great many pertinent comments on the intersection of popular and literary cultures; the first three chapters of Raymond Williams's *Culture and Society* (1958) give an important, though limited and partly commonplace, sketch of the situation of the individual artist.

On the romantic idea of taste and judgement, and the several vocabularies it helped to make for criticism, the following works are noteworthy: M. H. Abrams, *The Mirror and the Lamp* (1953); W. J. Bate, *From Classic to Romantic* (1946); Patrick Parrinder, *Authors and Authority* (1977); René Wellek, *A History of Modern Criticism, 1750–1950* (London, 1955–   ), especially volumes II and III; W. K. Wimsatt, Jr. and Cleanth Brooks, *Criticism: A Short History* (New York, 1957).

Comprehensive literary histories of romanticism have long been available, beginning with Henry A. Beers's *A History of English Romanticism in the Eighteenth Century* (New York, 1899); a recent and frankly partial example, valuable for its independence and *aperçus*, is Marilyn Butler's *Romantics, Rebels, and Reactionaries* (1981). It is unlikely that many such histories will be tried in the next generation since the concepts of theme and periodization on which they depend no longer seem as clearly explanatory as they once did. Much of the more interesting recent work on romantic literature and criticism has come from a consideration of linguistic usage and the theory of language: Hans Aarsleff, *The Study of Language in England 1780–1860* (Princeton, 1967); Paul de Man, *The Rhetoric of Romanticism* (New York, 1984); and William Empson, *The Structure of Complex Words* (1951) variously exemplify this tendency. On the definition of romanticism, see the essays collected in *Romanticism and Consciousness*, ed. Harold Bloom (New York, 1970); *Romanticism and Language*, ed. Arden Reed (Ithaca, 1984) includes a fine essay by Mary Jacobus on the prose of De Quincey, Hazlitt, and Lamb; *Power and Consciousness*, ed. Conor Cruise O'Brien and William Dean Vanech (New York, 1969) has observant essays on Wordsworth (by E. P. Thompson), Coleridge (by David Erdman), and Burke (by Conor Cruise O'Brien).

An excellent survey of the nineteenth-century culture of "letters," which started with the *Edinburgh Review* and its rivals, is John Gross, *The Rise and Fall of the Man of Letters* (1969). John Clive's *Scotch Reviewers* (Cambridge, Mass., 1957) covers the founding, policy, principles and adjustments of the *Edinburgh Review* itself. *The Yearbook of English Studies*, 16 (1986), on periodicals, contains articles on related subjects by J. H. Alexander, David Bromwich, and Joanne Shattock.

Among many other personal memoirs or collective biographies by frontline witnesses, Thomas Carlyle's *Reminiscences*, ed. J. A. Froude (1881); Benjamin Robert Haydon's *Diaries*, ed. Willard B. Pope, 5 vols. (Cambridge, Mass., 1960–63); and Harriet Martineau's *Autobiography*, ed. Maria Weston Chapman (1887) are outstanding. The best single book on the period and its characters remains Hazlitt's *The Spirit of the Age*.

CRITICISM AND BIOGRAPHIES

Two works of general theory held the field in the critical writing of the time: Archibald Alison, *Essays on the Nature and Principles of Taste* (1790); and Richard Payne Knight, *Analytical Inquiry into the Principles of Taste* (1805). Both are still worth knowing: a competent summary of their precepts, with a cautious objection to the freedom of associations which the former implicitly and the latter explicitly had supposed, may be found in Francis Jeffrey's review of Alison for the *Edinburgh Review* (May 1811), reprinted as the first article of his four-volume *Contributions to the Edinburgh Review* (1844).

Much of the modern discussion of Wordsworth's criticism has been preoccupied with Coleridge's criticism. Exceptions to the rule, which are directly or obliquely suggestive concerning Wordsworth's prefaces, the "Essay, Supplementary," and "Essays upon Epitaphs," include Frederick A. Pottle, "The Eye and the Object in the Poetry of Wordsworth," in *Wordsworth: Centenary Studies*, ed. Gilbert T. Dunklin (Princeton, 1951); Martin Price, "The Picturesque Moment," in *From Sensibility to Romanticism*, ed. Frederick W. Hilles and Harold Bloom (1965); Geoffrey Hartman, "Wordsworth, Inscriptions, and Romantic Nature Poetry," also in *From Sensibility to Romanticism*; and Frances Ferguson, *Language as Counter-Spirit* (1977). Mary Moorman's *William Wordsworth: A Biography*, 2 vols. (Oxford, 1957) is definitive.

To a surprising extent, Lamb has remained till now the property of literary gossips, and the subject therefore of anecdote rather than criticism. Geoffrey

Tillotson, "The Historical Importance of Certain 'Essays of Elia'," in *Some British Romantics*, ed. James V. Logan, John E. Jordan, and Northrop Frye (Columbus, Ohio, 1966) gives reasons for the interest of his work, as distinct from his life. Among a plenitude of biographies, both scholarly and popular, E. V. Lucas's *Charles Lamb* (1905) is the most complete. Winifred Courtney's *Young Charles Lamb 1775–1802* (1982) supersedes Lucas in its treatment of these years, and is revelatory as well in its attention to Lamb's radicalism.

Of the principles of Hazlitt's criticism (which must be derived by the expositor, since he chose to state none), Elisabeth Schneider, *The Aesthetics of William Hazlitt* (1933) gives a fair view in a short space; Roy Park, *Hazlitt and the Spirit of the Age* (Oxford, 1971) adds to Schneider's emphasis on the particularity of his criticism; John Kinnaird, *William Hazlitt: Critic of Power* (New York, 1977) offers a broad and well-informed survey of Hazlitt's intellectual career, with some discussion of almost everything he wrote; David Bromwich, *Hazlitt: The Mind of a Critic* (New York, 1983) explores the idea of power as a matter of critical practice, by tracing Hazlitt's responses to Burke, Wordsworth, and Coleridge. W. P. Albrecht, *Hazlitt and the Creative Imagination* (Lawrence, Kansas, 1965) and John L. Mahoney, *The Logic of Passion* (New York, 1978) make a valuable conspectus of Hazlitt's doctrines though both presume his adherence to a general belief in creativity. An essay on Hazlitt in Michael Foot's *Debts of Honour* (1980) is exceptional among the many personal appreciations which his writing has continued to attract. Herschel Baker's *William Hazlitt* (Cambridge, Mass., 1962) is the most widely trusted biography; Ralph M. Wardle's *Hazlitt* (Lincoln, Nebraska, 1971) has more details, with a warmer view of its subject. As a whole Catherine Macdonald Maclean's *Born Under Saturn* (1943) exhibits a subtler understanding of Hazlitt's character than any of its successors.

Hunt is the most important figure of the age still to be neglected by modern criticism. Louis Landré's intellectual biography, *Leigh Hunt*, 2 vols. (Paris, 1935–36) has not yet been translated. Edmund Blunden's *Leigh Hunt: A Biography* (1930) and *Leigh Hunt's "Examiner" Examined* (1928) are smaller appreciative studies, the latter being useful partly for the reviews which it reprints. Carl Woodring's introduction to *Leigh Hunt's Political and Occasional Essays*, ed. Lawrence H. and Carolyn W. Houtchens (New York, 1962) is incisive throughout, and goes beyond the declared limits of its subject.

By contrast, De Quincey has received a lot of notice, little of it relevant to his criticism. A main topic of concern has been his debt to, and his understanding of, German ideas. Sigmund K. Procter, *Thomas De Quincey's Theory of Literature* (Ann Arbor, 1943) makes the best of the rather equivocal evidence; René Wellek, "De Quincey's Status in the History of Ideas," *Philological Quarterly*, 23 (July 1944) makes the worst and very plausibly. John E. Jordan, *Thomas De Quincey, Literary Critic: His Method and Achievement* (Berkeley, 1952) is a balanced appraisal of De Quincey's interest in the psychology of author and reader; Lawrence Stapleton, *The Elected Circle* (Princeton, 1973) includes intelligent estimates of his writing on style and rhetoric. Horace A. Eaton, *Thomas De Quincey* (New York, 1936) remains the standard biography.

The best discussion of Peacock's criticism may be found in Marilyn Butler's

Peacock Displayed (1979), chapter 8. Lively general accounts of his qualities as a writer are Humphry House, "The Works of Peacock," *Listener*, 42 (8 December 1949); and Edmund Wilson, "The Musical Glasses of Thomas Love Peacock," in the same author's *Classics and Commercials* (New York, 1951).

Of the political background of Shelley's historicism, Carl Woodring, *Politics in English Romantic Poetry* (1971), chapter 6, gives a brief but suggestive account. The argument of the "Defence" in particular is interpreted in keeping with a theme of dialogue, in Earl R. Wasserman, *Shelley: A Critical Reading* (Baltimore, 1971); and as part of a Longinian tradition in critical theory, in Paul Fry, *The Reach of Criticism* (1983). The most persuasive view of the essay in relation to Shelley's reading and thinking about language is William Keach, *Shelley's Style* (1984), chapter 1. Newman Ivey White's *Shelley*, 2 vols. (New York, 1940) and Richard Holmes's *Shelley: The Pursuit* (New York, 1975) are copious and readable biographies.